The Share of Top Wealth-Holders
in National Wealth
1922–56

NATIONAL BUREAU OF ECONOMIC RESEARCH
NUMBER 74, GENERAL SERIES

The Share of Top Wealth-Holders in National Wealth

1922–56

ROBERT J. LAMPMAN
UNIVERSITY OF WISCONSIN

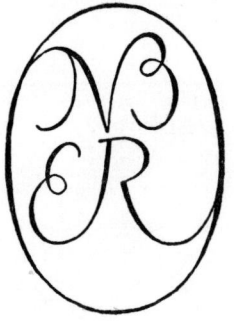

A STUDY BY THE
NATIONAL BUREAU OF ECONOMIC RESEARCH

PUBLISHED BY
PRINCETON UNIVERSITY PRESS
PRINCETON, NEW JERSEY
1962

Copyright © 1962 by National Bureau of Economic Research, Inc.

All Rights Reserved

L.C. Card No. 62-7413

LIBRARY
FLORIDA STATE UNIVERSITY
TALLAHASSEE, FLORIDA

PRINTED IN THE UNITED STATES OF AMERICA

NATIONAL BUREAU OF ECONOMIC RESEARCH
1961
OFFICERS

Harold M. Groves, *Chairman*
Arthur F. Burns, *President*
Albert J. Hettinger, Jr., *Vice President*
Murray Shields, *Treasurer*
Solomon Fabricant, *Director of Research*
Geoffrey H. Moore, *Associate Director of Research*
Hal B. Lary, *Associate Director of Research*
William J. Carson, *Executive Director*

DIRECTORS AT LARGE

Wallace J. Campbell, *Nationwide Insurance*
Erwin D. Canham, *Christian Science Monitor*
Solomon Fabricant, *New York University*
Marion B. Folsom, *Eastman Kodak Company*
Crawford H. Greenewalt, *E. I. du Pont de Nemours & Company*
Gabriel Hauge, *Manufacturers Hanover Trust Company*
A. J. Hayes, *International Association of Machinists*
Albert J. Hettinger, Jr., *Lazard Frères and Company*
H. W. Laidler, *League for Industrial Democracy*
George B. Roberts, *Larchmont, New York*
Harry Scherman, *Book-of-the-Month Club*
Boris Shishkin, *American Federation of Labor and Congress of Industrial Organizations*
George Soule, *South Kent, Connecticut*
Joseph H. Willits, *Armonk, New York*
Donald B. Woodward, *A. W. Jones and Company*
Theodore O. Yntema, *Ford Motor Company*

DIRECTORS BY UNIVERSITY APPOINTMENT

V. W. Bladen, *Toronto*
Arthur F. Burns, *Columbia*
Lester V. Chandler, *Princeton*
Melvin G. de Chazeau, *Cornell*
Frank W. Fetter, *Northwestern*
R. A. Gordon, *California*

Harold M. Groves, *Wisconsin*
Gottfried Haberler, *Harvard*
Walter W. Heller, *Minnesota*
Maurice W. Lee, *North Carolina*
Lloyd G. Reynolds, *Yale*
Theodore W. Schultz, *Chicago*

Willis J. Winn, *Pennsylvania*

DIRECTORS BY APPOINTMENT OF OTHER ORGANIZATIONS

Percival F. Brundage, *American Institute of Certified Public Accountants*
Harold G. Halcrow, *American Farm Economic Association*
Theodore V. Houser, *Committee for Economic Development*
S. H. Ruttenberg, *American Federation of Labor and Congress of Industrial Organizations*
Murray Shields, *American Management Association*
Willard L. Thorp, *American Economic Association*
W. Allen Wallis, *American Statistical Association*
Harold F. Williamson, *Economic History Association*

DIRECTORS EMERITI

Oswald W. Knauth, *Beaufort, South Carolina*
Shepard Morgan, *Norfolk, Connecticut*
N. I. Stone, *New York City*

RESEARCH STAFF

Moses Abramovitz
Gary S. Becker
William H. Brown, Jr.
Gerhard Bry
Arthur F. Burns
Phillip Cagan
Joseph W. Conard
Frank G. Dickinson
James S. Earley
Richard A. Easterlin
Solomon Fabricant
Milton Friedman

Raymond W. Goldsmith
Millard Hastay
Daniel M. Holland
Thor Hultgren
F. Thomas Juster
C. Harry Kahn
Simon Kuznets
Hal B. Lary
Robert E. Lipsey
Ruth P. Mack
Jacob Mincer

Ilse Mintz
Geoffrey H. Moore
Roger F. Murray
Ralph L. Nelson
G. Warren Nutter
Richard T. Selden
Lawrence H. Seltzer
Robert P. Shay
George J. Stigler
Norman B. Ture
Herbert B. Woolley

Relation of the Directors to the Work and Publications of the National Bureau of Economic Research

1. The object of the National Bureau of Economic Research is to ascertain and to present to the public important economic facts and their interpretation in a scientific and impartial manner. The Board of Directors is charged with the responsibility of ensuring that the work of the National Bureau is carried on in strict conformity with this object.

2. To this end the Board of Directors shall appoint one or more Directors of Research.

3. The Director or Directors of Research shall submit to the members of the Board, or to its Executive Committee, for their formal adoption, all specific proposals concerning researches to be instituted.

4. No report shall be published until the Director or Directors of Research shall have submitted to the Board a summary drawing attention to the character of the data and their utilization in the report, the nature and treatment of the problems involved, the main conclusions, and such other information as in their opinion would serve to determine the suitability of the report for publication in accordance with the principles of the National Bureau.

5. A copy of any manuscript proposed for publication shall also be submitted to each member of the Board. For each manuscript to be so submitted a special committee shall be appointed by the President, or at his designation by the executive Director, consisting of three Directors selected as nearly as may be one from each general division of the Board. The names of the special manuscript committee shall be stated to each Director when the summary and report described in paragraph (4) are sent to him. It shall be the duty of each member of the committee to read the manuscript. If each member of the special committee signifies his approval within thirty days, the manuscript may be published. If each member of the special committee has not signified his approval within thirty days of the transmittal of the report and manuscript, the Director of Research shall then notify each member of the Board, requesting approval or disapproval of publication, and thirty additional days shall be granted for this purpose. The manuscript shall then not be published unless at least a majority of the entire Board and a two-thirds majority of those members of the Board who shall have voted on the proposal within the time fixed for the receipt of votes on the publication proposed shall have approved.

6. No manuscript may be published, though approved by each member of the special committee, until forty-five days have elapsed from the transmittal of the summary and report. The interval is allowed for the receipt of any memorandum of dissent or reservation, together with a brief statement of his reasons, that any member may wish to express; and such memorandum of dissent or reservation shall be published with the manuscript if he so desires. Publication does not, however, imply that each member of the Board has read the manuscript, or that either members of the Board in general, or of the special committee, have passed upon its validity in every detail.

7. A copy of this resolution shall, unless otherwise determined by the Board, be printed in each copy of every National Bureau book.

(Resolution adopted October 25, 1926, as revised February 6, 1933, and February 24, 1941)

*To Harry Gordon Lampman
and Bernice Pierce Lampman*

CONTENTS

Acknowledgments	xxv
Preface	xxvii
1. Introduction and Summary	1
The Meaning of Wealth	1
The Limits of Personal Wealth as Studied Here	3
Wealth-Holding Decisions	5
Inequality of Wealth Distribution	6
Role of Government	8
Earlier Studies of Wealth Distribution	8
Sources of Data and Methods of Estimation Used in This Study	12
Summary	15
Characteristics of Top Wealth-Holders	17
Composition of Estate	21
Size Distribution	23
Determinants of Changes in Inequality	26
2. The Federal Estate Tax "Samples" and the Estate-Multiplier Method	27
The Basic Data	28
Number of Returns	28
Age of Decedents	31
Basic Tables on Decedents' "Estate Tax Wealth"	35
Sampling Limitations and Statistical Reliability of Estimates	36
The Estate-Multiplier Method	41
Selection of Appropriate Mortality Rates	42
Illustration of Estate-Multiplier Method	48
Two Adjustments to Basic Data	53
3. Adjustment of Basic Variant Estimates for 1953 to Approximate Aggregates of "Prime Wealth" and "Total Wealth"	57

CONTENTS

General Provisions of Estate Tax Law	58
Classification of Wealth Items and Tabulation by Type of Property	60
Adjustments to Basic Variant Estimates	62
Overcount Arising from Insurance Valuation	63
Underreporting	65
Gifts	67
Proceeds of Life Insurance	71
Last Medical Expenses	72
Personal Trust Funds, Annuities, and Pension Funds	72

4. Characteristics of Top Wealth-Holders in 1953   84
   Estate Size   84
   Age   87
      Distribution of Estate Tax Wealth Among Age Groups   89
      Relationship Between Age and Estate Size for Total Population   89
      Relationship Between Age and Estate Size for Top Wealth-Holders   91
   Sex   96
   Marital Status   99
   Families Among Top Wealth-Holders   100
   Community Property   102
   State and Region of Residence   105
   Income and Savings   107
   Occupation   108

5. Types of Property Held by Top Wealth-Holders   135
   Change over Time, 1922–53   135
   Composition of Estate by Age and Sex of Top Wealth-Holders, 1953   145
   Composition of Estate by Size   146
   Composition of Estate by Income Level   153
   Composition of Estate by Occupation   155

6. The Share of Top Wealth-Holders in Personal Wealth, 1922–56   191
   The Share of Top Wealth-Holders in 1953   191
   Comparison with Survey of Consumer Finances Findings for 1953   195
   Historical Changes in Inequality   197

CONTENTS

Changes in Share of Wealth Held by Top One Per Cent of Adults, by Type of Property	208
Comparison with Wealth Distribution in England and Wales	210
Comparison with Changes in Income Inequality	215
7. Determinants of Inequality of Wealth-Holding	**218**
List of Determining Factors	218
Price Change as a Determinant of Inequality	220
Changes in Share of Savings of Top Wealth-Holders	229
Digression on Relationships Between Wealth Inequality and Income Inequality	230
Estimate of Share of Saving of Top Wealth-Holders	234
The Process of Transfer of Wealth	237
Summary Statement on Causes of Changes in Wealth Inequality, 1922–53	244
Appendix A: Underlying Data and Estimates	**245**
Appendix B: Some Considerations of Price Change	**275**
Appendix C: Predicting Estate Tax Returns	**279**
Index	**283**

TABLES

1. Different Estimates of Top Wealth-Holders, 1953 — 16
2. Selected Characteristics of Top Wealth-Holders, 1953 — 17
3. Percentage of Top Wealth-Holders in Total Population and in Selected Groups, 1953 — 18
4. Median Age of Male Top Wealth-Holders in Non-Community Property States, by Gross Estate Size, 1953 — 18
5. Percentage of Gross Estate in Selected Assets and Liabilities for Three Gross Estate Sizes in Three Age Groups of Male Top Wealth-Holders, 1953 — 22
6. Share of Personal Sector Wealth (Equity) Held by Top Wealth-Holders, Selected Years, 1922–56 — 24
7. Number of Estate Tax Returns for 1916–54 Related to Total Deaths and Population — 29
8. Gross and Economic Estates, Aggregates and Average Per Return, 1922–54 — 30
9. Distribution of Decedents by Age Group, Estate Tax Returns and Total White Population, 1953 — 32
10. Distribution of Estate Tax Decedents by Age Group in Inferred Years of Death, Selected Years, 1922–53 — 32
11. Estate Tax Decedents and Total Population, by Age Group, Selected Years, 1922–53 — 33
12. Distribution of Estate Tax Decedents by Sex and Age Group, Selected Years, 1922–53 — 34
13. Estate Tax Returns Filed in 1954 for Male Decedents, by Age Group and Type of Property — 37
14. Estate Tax Returns Filed in 1954 for Female Decedents, by Age Group and Type of Property — 38
15. Estate Tax Returns Filed in 1954, by Type of Property and Gross Estate Size — 39
16. Top Fifth White Male Mortality as a Percentage of General White Male Mortality, Chicago, 1940 — 43

TABLES

17. Professional, Technical, Administrative, and Managerial Mortality as a Percentage of White Male Mortality, United States, 1950 — 44
18. Mortality of Ordinary Life and $5,000 Whole-Life Policyholders as a Percentage of White Male Mortality, United States, 1953 — 45
19. Adjusted Mortality Rates and Multipliers for Males, 1953 — 48
20. Adjusted Mortality Rates and Multipliers for Females, 1953 — 48
21. Mortality Rates and Multipliers for Total U.S. White Population, Male and Female, 1953 — 49
22. Estimated Estate Tax Wealth of Males, by Type of Property and Age Group, 1953 — 50
23. Estimated Estate Tax Wealth of Both Sexes, by Type of Property and Age Group, 1953 — 51
24. Estimated Estate Tax Wealth of Both Sexes, by Estate Size and Type of Property, 1953 — 52
25. Different Estimates of Number of Estate Tax Wealth-Holders and Aggregate Estate Tax Wealth in 1953 — 53
26. Estimation of Living Estate Tax Wealth-Holders and Aggregate Gross or Economic Estate from Estate Tax Returns Including Those Without Age Information, Selected Years, 1922–53 — 54
27. Data on Life Insurance Policy Reserves, 1944, 1953, and 1956 — 56
28. Estimate of Average Ratio of Equity to Face Value of Life Insurance by Age Group, 1953 — 56
29. Summary of Adjustments Made in Estimating Basic, Prime, and Total Wealth Variants of Estate Tax Wealth and Wealth-Holders, 1953 — 62
30. Adjustments to Number of Top Wealth-Holders and Aggregate of Gross Estate Due to Insurance Overcount — 64
31. Individual Income Tax Returns with Income Frequency Distribution from Estates and Trusts — 78
32. Individuals with Trusts in Active Investor Sample, by Income and Wealth Groups — 80
33. Value of Property Held in Trust as Percentage of

TABLES

Wealth Held by Individuals in Active Investor Sample, by Income and Wealth Groups ... 81
34. Percentage Distribution of Estate Tax Wealth-Holders and Basic Variant Aggregate Gross Estate by Gross Estate Size, 1953 ... 109
35. Estate Tax Wealth-Holders as a Percentage of Total Population, by Sex and Age Group, 1953 ... 110
36. Hypothetical Number of Top Wealth-Holders Within Age Cohorts of 100,000 Starting at Age 20, by Sex ... 111
37. Percentage Distribution of Estate Tax Wealth and Wealth-Holders by Age Group, 1944 and 1953 ... 112
38. Percentage Distribution of Estate Tax Wealth and Wealth-Holders by Sex and Age Group, 1953 ... 113
39. Distribution of Selected Balance Sheet Items by Age Group, 1950 ... 113
40. Distribution of Spending Units by Total Assets Within Age Group, 1950 ... 114
41. Selected Data on Life Cycle of Husband-Wife Families ... 114
42. Data on Income, Assets, and Net Worth: Positions of Spending Units at Different Stages of Life Cycle in 1953 ... 115
43. Selected Data on Sources of Receipts of Aged Economic Units, Classified by Source, 1951 ... 116
44. Percentage Distribution of Net Value of Total Assets of Aged Economic Units by Type of Unit and Amount of Asset Holdings, 1951 ... 117
45. Average Gross Estate of Top Wealth-Holders, by Sex and Age Group, 1953 ... 117
46. Median Age of Top Wealth-Holders, by Sex and Gross Estate Size, 1953 ... 118
47. Percentage Distribution of Male Top Wealth-Holders in Non-Community Property States by Gross Estate Size Within Age Groups, 1953 ... 119
48. Percentage Distribution of Male Top Wealth-Holders in Non-Community Property States by Age Group Within Gross Estate Sizes, 1953 ... 120
49. Percentage Distribution of Estate Tax Wealth by Sex and Gross Estate Size, 1953 ... 121
50. Number of Estate Tax Wealth-Holders, by Sex, Age Group, and Marital Status, 1953 ... 122

TABLES

51. Total Population and Estate Tax Wealth-Holders, by Sex, Age Group, and Marital Status, 1953 — 123
52. Population and Income Payments in 1953 and Estate Tax Returns for 1949, 1950, 1953, and 1954 Combined, Community Property States and U.S. — 124
53. Percentage Distribution of Estate Tax Wealth by Sex and Age Group in Community Property and Common Law States, 1953 — 125
54. Percentage Distribution of Estate Tax Wealth by Sex and Gross Estate Size in Community Property and Common Law States, 1953 — 126
55. Percentage Composition of All Estates for Men and Women in Community Property and Common Law States, 1953 — 127
56. Rank and Percentage of U.S. Total of Population and Income Payments for 1953 and Estate Tax Returns for 1949, 1950, 1953, and 1954 Combined, by Region — 128
57. Population and Income Payments in 1953 and Estate Tax Returns for 1949, 1950, 1953, and 1954 Combined, by State — 129
58. Distribution of Spending Units by Income Within Asset Groups, 1950 — 132
59. Average Annual Percentages of Various Types of Income in Total Income, Upper Income Groups and Total Population, 1919–38 — 132
60. Average Annual Shares of Upper Income Groups in U.S. Totals of Various Types of Income, 1919–38 — 133
61. Asset-Income Ratios, by Income of Spending Units, 1950 — 133
62. Distribution of Spending Units by Total Assets Within Occupational Groups, 1950 — 134
63. Percentage Distribution of Gross Estate by Type of Property for All Persons and for Top Wealth-Holders, 1953 — 157
64. Estate Composition, Living Top Wealth-Holders, 1944 and 1953 — 157
65. Composition of Gross Estate, by Type of Property, for All Estate Tax Returns, Current Values, 1922–54 — 158
66. Percentage Composition of Net Taxable Estates over

TABLES

$100,000 for Selected Years, 1922–54, in Current and Constant 1925 Dollars ... 160
67. Indexes of Asset Prices, 1919–57 ... 162
68. Bond and Stock Yields, 1926–56 ... 163
69. Composition of Net Worth Within Age Groups, 1953 ... 164
70. Distribution of Selected Balance Sheet Items by Age Group, 1950 ... 165
71. Percentage Distribution of Gross Estate by Type of Property and Age Group, Top Wealth-Holders of Both Sexes, 1953 ... 166
72. Percentage Distribution of Gross Estate by Type of Property and Age Group, Male Top Wealth-Holders, 1953 ... 167
73. Percentage Distribution of Gross Estate by Type of Property and Age Group, Female Top Wealth-Holders, 1953 ... 168
74. Percentage Distribution of Gross Estate by Type of Property and Sex, Top Wealth-Holders, Selected Estate Sizes, 1953 ... 169
75. Percentage Distribution of Gross Estate by Type of Property and Gross Estate Size, Top Wealth-Holders of Both Sexes, 1953 ... 170
76. Percentage Distribution of Gross Estate by Type of Property and Gross Estate Size, Male Top Wealth-Holders, 1953 ... 171
77. Percentage Distribution of Gross Estate by Type of Property and Gross Estate Size, Female Top Wealth-Holders, 1953 ... 172
78. Percentage Distribution of Type of Property by Gross Estate Size, Top Wealth-Holders of Both Sexes, 1953 ... 173
79. Percentage Distribution of Type of Property by Gross Estate Size, Male Top Wealth-Holders, 1953 ... 174
80. Percentage Distribution of Type of Property by Gross Estate Size, Female Top Wealth-Holders, 1953 ... 176
81. Distribution of Selected Balance Sheet Items by Owners' Net Worth, 1950 ... 178
82. Percentage Composition of Gross Estate by Estate Size and Sex for Selected Age Groups, 1953 ... 179
83. Percentage Composition of Gross Estate by Age and Sex for Selected Estate Sizes, 1953 ... 182

TABLES

84. Composition of Net Worth Within Income Groups, 1953 — 185
85. Distribution of Selected Balance Sheet Items by Income Group, 1950 — 186
86. Percentage Distribution of Asset Holdings of Individuals in Active Investor Sample, by Income and Wealth Groups — 187
87. Composition of Corporate Equity Asset Holdings for Income Groups of Wisconsin Individuals, 1949 — 188
88. Composition of Net Worth Within Occupational Groups, 1953 — 189
89. Distribution of Selected Balance Sheet Items by Occupational Group, 1950 — 190
90. Role of Top Wealth-Holders in National Balance Sheet Accounts, 1953 — 192
91. Proportion of Net Worth and Components Held Within Net Worth Groups, 1953 — 196
92. Selected Data Relating Top Wealth-Holders to Population and Estate Tax Wealth to National Balance Sheet Aggregates, for Selected Years, 1922–56 — 200
93. Share of Top Groups of Wealth-Holders in Total Population and in Total Equity, Personal Sector, Selected Years, 1922–56 — 202
94. Share of Top Groups of Wealth-Holders in Total Adult Population and in Total Equity, Personal Sector, Selected Years, 1922–56 — 204
95. Selected Data on Top Wealth-Holders, 1922 and 1953 — 206
96. Share of Total Equity, Personal Sector, Held by Top 0.47 Per Cent of Persons, 1922 and 1953 — 207
97. Share of Personal Sector Assets and Liabilities Held by Top One Per Cent of Adults, 1922, 1929, 1939, 1945, 1949, and 1953 — 209
98. Number of Persons Aged 25 and over in Each Capital Group, England and Wales, 1946 and 1947 — 211
99. Estimated Distribution of Total Adult Population by Gross Estate Size, United States, 1953 — 213
100. Distribution of Capital in England and Wales, 1911–13, 1924–30, 1936–38, and 1946–47 — 216
101. Personal Sector Wealth in 1922 Prices and in Current Prices, 1922–53 — 218

TABLES

102. Selected Data on Top One Per Cent of Adults, 1922–53 — 220
103. Percentage Changes in Money Value of Typical 1953 Estates of Selected Sizes, 1922–56 — 222
104. Changes in Money Value of Typical 1953 Estates of Selected Sizes from Application of Asset Prices of Selected Years — 223
105. Effects of Price Change upon 1922 Estates of Two Sizes, 1922–53 — 224
106. Calculation of Share of Wealth Held by Top One Per Cent of Adults with Each Asset Type Reduced to 1922 Prices — 225
107. Actual and Hypothetical Shares of Top Wealth-Holder Groups in Personal Sector Gross Estate, 1922–53 — 228
108. Hypothetical Distribution of Wealth Among Adult Males — 230
109. Comparison of Distribution of Money Income and Net Worth Among Spending Units, 1952–53 — 231
110. Distribution of Income Among All Persons, 1951 — 233
111. Calculation of Share of Saving of Top One Per Cent of Income Recipients, 1922–48 — 236
112. Composition of Total Adult Population, by Sex and Age Group, 1922 and 1953 — 240
113. Top Wealth-Holders as a Percentage of Total Adult Population, by Sex and Age Group, 1922 and 1953 — 241
114. Actual and Hypothetical (Assuming 1922 Frequency Rates) Number of Top Wealth-Holders, by Sex and Age Group, 1953 — 241
A-1. Estate Tax Returns Filed in 1954 for Male Decedents with Gross Estate Sizes of $60,000 to $70,000 in Non-Community Property States, by Age Group and Type of Property — 246
A-2. Estate Tax Returns Filed in 1954 for Female Decedents in Community Property States, by Age Group and Type of Property — 247
A-3. White and Adjusted Mortality Rates and Multipliers, for Both Sexes, by Age Group, 1922, 1924, 1944, 1946, and 1947 — 248
A-4. White Mortality Rates and White and Adjusted

TABLES

	Multipliers, by Sex and Age Group, 1922 and 1947–50	249
A-5.	Distribution of Economic Estate by Age Group, Based on Adjusted Mortality Rates, 1922, 1944, and 1946	250
A-6.	Distribution of Gross Estate by Age Group, Based on Adjusted Mortality Rates, 1947–50	251
A-7.	Distribution of Gross Estate by Estate Size, Based on Adjusted Mortality Rates, 1948–50	252
A-8.	Distribution of Economic Estate by Age Group, Based on White Rates, Before and After Corrections for Insurance and for Age Unspecified, 1922, 1944, and 1946	254
A-9.	Distribution of Gross Estate by Age Group, Based on White Mortality Rates, 1947–50 and 1953	255
A-10.	Distribution of Net or Economic Estate by Estate Size, Based on White Mortality Rates, 1922, 1944, and 1946	257
A-11.	Distribution of Gross Estate by Estate Size, Based on White Mortality Rates, 1948–50	258
A-12.	Number of Decedent Estate Tax Wealth-Holders by Sex, Age Group, and Marital Status, 1953	259
A-13.	Estate Tax Returns and Taxable Gross Estate for 1949, 1950, 1953, and 1954 Combined Related to Population and Income Payments in Non-Community Property States and Average of Community Property States, 1953	261
A-14.	Distribution of Spending Units by Total Assets Within Income Groups, 1950	262
A-15.	Distribution of Spending Units by Saving Within Asset Groups, 1950	262
A-16.	Distribution of Spending Units by Total Assets Within Saving Groups, 1950	263
A-17.	Role of Top Wealth-Holders in National Balance Sheet Accounts, 1949	264
A-18.	Role of Top Wealth-Holders in National Balance Sheet Accounts, 1945	266
A-19.	Role of Top Wealth-Holders in National Balance Sheet Accounts, 1939	268
A-20.	Role of Top Wealth-Holders in National Balance Sheet Accounts, 1929	270

TABLES

A-21. Role of Top Wealth-Holders in National Balance Sheet Accounts, 1922 — 272

A-22. Percentage Distribution of Estate Tax Wealth by Gross Estate Size, 1944 and 1953 — 274

B-1. Amount of Money Needed in 1929–52 to Have Construction Purchasing Power and Consumer Purchasing Power Comparable to $100,000 in 1953 — 275

B-2. Comparison of Estate Tax Wealth Distribution in 1944 and 1953, Taking Consumer Price Changes into Account — 277

CHARTS

1. Average Gross Estate of Top Wealth-Holders, by Sex and Age Group, 1953 — 19
2. Share of Personal Sector Equity Held by Top Wealth-Holders, 1953 — 23
3. Share of Personal Sector Wealth Held by Top Wealth-Holders, Selected Years, 1922–56 — 25
4. Number of Federal Estate Tax Returns and Amount of Gross Estate Reported, Current Values, 1922–54 — 31
5. Derivation of Adjusted Mortality Rates for Males, 1953 — 47
6. Persons with Gross Estates Greater Than Stated Amounts, by Sex, 1953 — 85
7. Top Wealth-Holders, by Sex and Gross Estate Size, 1953 — 86
8. Top Wealth-Holders, by Sex and Age Group, 1953 — 87
9. Hypothetical Number of Top Wealth-Holders Within Age Cohorts of 100,000 Starting at Age 20, by Sex — 88
10. Distribution of Top Wealth-Holders and Their Gross Estates, by Sex and Age Group, 1953 — 90
11. Median Age of Top Wealth-Holders, by Sex and Gross Estate Size, 1953 — 92
12. Distribution of Male Top Wealth-Holders by Gross Estate Size, Within Three Age Groups, Non-Community Property States, 1953 — 93
13. Distribution of Male Top Wealth-Holders by Age Group Within Four Gross Estate Sizes, Non-Community Property States, 1953 — 94
14. Lorenz Curves of Wealth Among Male Top Wealth-Holders in Three Age Groups, Non-Community Property States, 1953 — 95
15. Lorenz Curves of Wealth Among Female Top Wealth-Holders in Three Age Groups, Non-Community Property States, 1953 — 96

CHARTS

16. Lorenz Curves of Wealth Among Top Wealth-Holders, by Sex, 1953 — 97
17. Top Wealth-Holders, by Sex and Marital Status, 1953 — 99
18. Lorenz Curves of Wealth Among Male Top Wealth-Holders, Community Property and Common Law States, 1953 — 104
19. Lorenz Curves of Wealth Among Female Top Wealth-Holders, Community Property and Common Law States, 1953 — 105
20. Ranking of Regions by Number of Decedent Top Wealth-Holders, Four-Year Total of 1948, 1949, 1953, and 1954 — 106
21. Percentage Composition of Net Taxable Estates over $100,000 for Selected Years, 1922–54 — 138
22. Equities Expressed as Percentage in Current and Constant Dollars of Total Assets of Decedents with Net Taxable Estates over $100,000, 1922–54 — 141
23. Nonequities Expressed as Percentage in Current and Constant Dollars of Total Assets of Decedents with Net Taxable Estates over $100,000, 1922–54 — 142
24. Relationship Between Stock-Bond Yields and Stock-Bond Holdings of Decedents with Net Taxable Estates over $100,000, 1926–56 — 144
25. Lorenz Curves of Gross Estate, Real Estate, and Stock Among Top Wealth-Holders, 1953 — 148
26. Lorenz Curves of Cash, U.S. Bonds, and State and Local Bonds Among Top Wealth-Holders, 1953 — 149
27. Lorenz Curves of Insurance and Liabilities Among Top Wealth-Holders, 1953 — 150
28. Distribution of Selected Assets by Gross Estate Size Within Three Age Groups, Males, 1953 — 151
29. Distribution of Selected Assets by Age Group Within Three Estate Sizes, Males, 1953 — 152
30. Top Wealth-Holders and Adult Population, Selected Years, 1922–56 — 198
31. Upper Sections of Lorenz Curves of Personal Sector Equity (Basic Variant) Held by Upper Percentiles of Total Population, Selected Years, 1922–56 — 203
32. Upper Sections of Lorenz Curves of Personal Sector

CHARTS

	Equity (Basic Variant) Held by Upper Percentiles of Adult Population, Selected Years, 1922–56	205
33.	Persons with Gross Estates Greater Than Stated Amounts, England and Wales, 1946–47, and United States, 1953	210
34.	Lorenz Curves of Gross Estates Among Adults, England and Wales, 1946–47, and United States, 1953	212
35.	Upper Section of Lorenz Curves of Gross Estate Held by Top Percentiles of Adults, England and Wales and United States, Selected Years, 1911–53	214
36.	Share of Wealth Held by Top One Per Cent of Adults, in Current Dollars and in 1922 Dollars, 1922–56	224
37.	Lorenz Curves of Total Money Income and Net Worth Among Spending Units Ranked by Income and Net Worth	232

xxiii

Acknowledgments

THIS study was initiated and the greater part of it was done while I was a Research Associate at the National Bureau of Economic Research, and on leave from the University of Washington. I cannot imagine an environment more conducive to empirical research than that provided me by the Bureau during that year. I have also been aided by the research funds of the Department of Economics and the Graduate School of the University of Wisconsin.

Many people generously provided help and critical advice during the course of my work. I am particularly indebted to Raymond W. Goldsmith, who was instrumental in the undertaking and who maintained an unflagging interest in it to the end, reading every draft of each chapter. The manuscript has also benefited from careful reading by Thomas R. Atkinson, P. F. Brundage, Solomon Fabricant, George Garvy, Selma Goldsmith, Harold M. Groves, C. Harry Kahn, Simon Kuznets, Horst Mendershausen, Geoffrey H. Moore, Joseph A. Pechman, Victor Perlo, and Murray Shields. Helen K. DeMond was helpful in interpreting Internal Revenue Service data.

Others who made helpful suggestions include: Gary S. Becker, J. Keith Butters, Richard W. Effland, C. Lowell Harriss, A. James Heins, Daniel M. Holland, F. Thomas Juster, James B. MacDonald, Ruth Mack, Morris Mendelson, John R. Meyer, John G. Myers, Guy H. Orcutt, Neal Potter, H. B. Porterfield, Leo Raskind, Theodore Scher, Mortimer Spiegelman, P. O. Steiner, and Lawrence E. Thompson.

At various times I have had research assistance from four persons. Elaine Saleman and Irving Brown carried through the calculations and researches needed for the writing of a first draft. Robert Ross aided me through the detailed work of Chapter 7 and Richard Pollock was more nearly a collaborator than an assistant in work on Chapters 5 and 7.

The manuscript has been much improved by the editorial work of Mary Wing and Marie-Christine Culbert. The charts were drawn by

ACKNOWLEDGMENTS

H. Irving Forman who did much to improve the accuracy and clarity of the book. Secretarial and clerical work was done by Dorothy Chesterton and her associates at the Bureau and by Geraldine Hinkel and her associates at the University of Wisconsin.

To all these people and to others too numerous to list, I am grateful both for their concrete help and for their sharing in the joys and tribulations of scholarly effort.

Madison, Wisconsin   ROBERT J. LAMPMAN

Preface

RELATIVELY little inquiry has been made into the size distribution of wealth in the United States. Hence, this study becomes part of a scant literature on the subject of personal wealth-holding.[1]

It is based largely upon data derived from federal estate tax returns and is intended to be an exhaustive treatment of those data by use of what is known as the "estate-multiplier" method. This method has been applied to American data only once before, in the work of Mendershausen and Goldsmith. This study is unique in that for the first time estate tax wealth estimates are integrated with Goldsmith's national balance sheet estimates.

I hope that others will be able to work from the findings and speculations presented here to make further contributions to a full-fledged analysis of wealth distribution as related to income distribution. Further research is needed on many topics before the analytical and descriptive work in this field may be said to be complete. For instance, better data are needed on savings and transfers of wealth, better information is needed on the use of personal trust funds and on capital gains and losses. Study of the relation between income and wealth-holding in a given year and the gathering of life histories in order to account for changes over time are among the methods which hold the greatest promise for future research. It is also urged that federal estate tax data be tabulated in full detail at regular intervals, say every five years, to enable follow-up studies of American top wealth-holders.

[1] Chapter 6 appeared in an earlier version in *The Review of Economics and Statistics,* November 1959, and was reprinted as National Bureau Occasional Paper 71, 1960.

The Share of Top Wealth-Holders
in National Wealth
1922–56

CHAPTER 1

Introduction and Summary

THIS book is an inquiry into the facts concerning the wealth of persons. It offers new information on the numbers, characteristics, and behavior of wealth-holders. How many people accumulate or hold wealth in sizable amounts? How many people have "large" holdings of specific kinds of property? Are relatively wealthy persons young or old, men or women? What are their incomes, occupations, and places of residence? How does the marital status of persons in the wealthy group vary? How do differences in property law as it relates to marriage affect these people?

It is perhaps unnecessary to point out that answers, sometimes misinformed, to these and similar questions often underlie policy decisions in business and government.[1] They are helpful in analyzing such issues as the following: Who is hurt or helped most by inflation or deflation? What groups are most likely to purchase insurance or tax-exempt bonds or to make large philanthropic contributions? What groups will be most directly affected by a change in tax policy affecting dividends, inheritance, or home ownership? Who will be most benefited by a change in the rate of interest?

We also seek to measure the concentration of wealth-holding and to discover whether this concentration has been increasing or decreasing in recent years. Is it true, as Karl Marx asserted a hundred years ago, that the overriding tendency of capitalism is toward ever-increasing inequality? Or have fiscal policy and institutional change worked to reduce the importance of the relatively rich group in America?

THE MEANING OF WEALTH

In defining the subject of the inquiry, it will be useful here to consider four concepts: capital, assets, wealth, and property. Capital, as

[1] W. I. King, who pioneered in this field, referred to two groups in the 1920's who were particularly interested in wealth and income distribution information as "reformers" and "sales managers." The former, he believed, wanted facts in order to carry out their social programs better. The latter wanted such information to gauge correctly the demand for their products. (Cited by C. L. Merwin, Jr., "American Studies of the Distribution of Wealth and Income by Size," *Studies in Income and Wealth*, Volume Three, New York, National Bureau of Economic Research, 1939, p. 23.)

economists use the term, has two meanings. One is physical goods which are man-made and useful in further production, including such things as buildings, machinery, and improvements to land. Another meaning is a stock of money value resulting from saving or creation of new money. This stock may be held in liquid form (in currency or deposit credit) or converted into title to real or representative capital. A further distinction is sometimes made between producer and consumer capital, the latter being owner-occupied housing and durable consumer goods.

The assets of the individual producer unit, in conventional accounting terms, may include such tangible things as land, buildings, machinery, raw materials, goods in process, and animals, and such intangible things as franchises, patent rights, copyrights, and good will. On the consumer unit's balance sheet assets will include claims against or promises from business and government organizations, and may include consumer capital items. It is not customary to calculate the capital value of the earning power of individuals, nor of outlays made on health or education and designed to increase that earning power.

Wealth is a term which applies to all assets with market value, including both producer and consumer capital goods, intangible as well as tangible assets, and accounted for without regard to the "rights" that may be attached to the holding of the wealth. Net worth, or equity, is the difference between assets and liabilities.

A person's claim to wealth may indicate right to the use of, income from, or control over assets. The meaning of wealth ownership is the subject of property law. In the earliest statements of legal theory a property right was conceived of as absolute control over a tangible object such as land, a building, an animal, or a human being. This absolute control included the right to direct the use of the object, the right to receive any income produced by such use, and the right to sell or otherwise dispose of the object. In general, the assumption was that all these rights were to be held and exercised by the same person. Correlatively, the liability for loss and responsibility for damages resided with the person who held title.

In the course of centuries, the legal concept of property has undergone many changes. By common law, statute, and constitutional amendment, the meaning and content of the term "property" have been under constant revision. Thus, the right to hold certain things as personal property has been withdrawn, as in the case of ownership of a human person. Certain uses of objects owned are forbidden by law,

INTRODUCTION AND SUMMARY

as in the case of zoning laws which limit the uses to which property may be put. At the same time, the opportunity to claim new property rights has been expanded. Thus, the innovation of the business corporation was a startling change in property rights, a change which introduced limited liability and altered the balance between income rights and control of the use and disposition of property. Indeed, the corporation scattered among many persons the rights, duties, and responsibilities of property ownership. Under it, one group may exercise control through minority ownership, a second (e.g., nonvoting stockholders) may enjoy income with no voice in control, and a third (creditors) may share in losses because of the limited liability of the owners. The possibility of disjunction among the holders of property rights and duties is magnified by such devices as corporate holding companies which provide an additional lever for minority control.

The modern capitalist economy has a complicated network of arrangements which relate in diverse ways the functions of (1) supplying capital in both debt and equity forms (often through intermediaries between the supplier of capital and the business organization which makes the actual outlay for capital goods purchase) and (2) directing the use of the capital. The connection between those who perform the first function and those who perform the second is often quite remote. Similarly, there is, in some cases, a separation between the groups who are responsible for managing the capital funds and those who receive the income from the funds.

THE LIMITS OF PERSONAL WEALTH AS STUDIED HERE

Since there is a fractioning of the property rights attached to individual parcels of wealth, it is difficult to apportion or indicate the sharing of those rights by means of a wealth distribution. It is helpful to envision a distribution not only among individuals but also among sectors, including persons, financial intermediaries, business corporations, nonbusiness organizations, and governments. While it is possible to allocate the market value of assets held in full title to each sector and to allocate the market value of intersectoral promises, it is not possible thereby to indicate in all cases the power share of the persons in the several sectors. Power attaches to wealth in a complicated and shifting pattern and depends upon organizational position within one sector as much as or more than it does upon holding personal title to assets. Hence, the power or control aspects of wealth are not fully distributed in a personal wealth distribution. Some residual power stays with the nonpersonal sectors and attaches to persons only as they are active within the individual sectors. A changing relationship between persons and nonpersonal sectors can considerably confound comparisons of personal wealth distributions over time. Consider, for example, the introduction of nonfunded retirement pay plans for corporate executives. Such a plan would keep wealth in the corporate sector while showing increased lifetime income for the employees. In other ways, the organizational sectors may function as wealth-holders "on behalf of" individuals, thereby making a comparison of two personal wealth distributions quite unrealistic. While personally held wealth may not, in some cases, connote any intersectoral power, it is still true, of course, that such wealth is an important means to power within each sector.

An interesting example of the intersectoral problem is trusteed property which relates persons to financial intermediaries. With personal trust funds we are moving into the twilight zone where classical property rights are shadowed. Depending upon the terms of the trust agreement, a beneficiary may have only a contingent interest in only part of the income, he may have no power of direction over the use of the property at any time, and he may have no right to sell the property or even to dispose of it at the time of his death. The rights he does not have in the property are exercised by the trustee under the supervision of the court and subject to the limitations set forth by the creator of the trust. On the other hand, again depending upon the terms of the trust, a beneficiary may enjoy full right to all income of the property, and he may have power at some point to dispose of the principal or to assign his rights to its income.

We proceed still further into the shadows if we consider the assets of nonpersonal trust funds or foundations which have a charitable purpose. It should be recognized that these trust funds are sometimes used as devices for control and magnification of the control possible on other grounds. The founder of such a trust not only may direct the purposes for which income or principal may be spent, but he may also settle on the trustees he names, who in turn have the power to name their successors, the power to manage (that is to say, to vote the stock of) the property in trust. On the other hand, as in the case of the Ford family, the assignment of nonvoting stock to a foundation may make possible continuation of family control of the original corporation. But in some cases these control elements are of minor or no significance. A somewhat similar problem of intersectoral accounting arises about the assets of financial intermediaries. In the case of banks and insurance companies and trusteed pension funds, there is an element of control which attaches to the fiduciary responsibility of the officers who do not themselves own the property they are managing.

Quite arbitrarily, we have restricted the limits of inquiry in this study to what is defined as the personal sector of the economy, including households, farm and nonfarm unincorporated businesses, and personal trust funds.

WEALTH-HOLDING DECISIONS

In this study we are concerned with the behavior of wealth-holders in deciding how much and what kind of property they will hold. Each person makes decisions about borrowing, owning, and lending. More particularly, he decides whether to take direct title to consumer or producer capital goods or land; whether to hold representative capital, i.e., claims, in the form of cash or securities, upon the assets of other persons or corporations or governments; whether to participate in capital markets directly or through financial intermediaries such as banks, insurance companies, or trust funds. He must also make decisions about the ways in which he will transfer his assets or obligations to others. In making these decisions, people are guided by time preference, precautionary, speculative, and power motives to select investments which they believe best meet their needs.

The relative strength of these motives among various socio-economic groupings may be assessed by a cross-sectional analysis of their asset holdings and debts at a moment in time. In some cases, such an analysis makes it possible to predict how decisions of persons will change as their age, income, size of estate, or other characteristics change.

The decisions made by individuals about wealth accumulation and wealth-holding are important, not only for the individual and his family, but for the whole economy. In the aggregate, these decisions have an important influence on the rate of capital accumulation, the price of capital, and the distribution of income, economic welfare, and power among persons. Finally, they determine which institutional arrangements will flourish and which will wither away from disuse.

From the point of view of the individual, wealth accumulation is a substitute for wages or salary or an additional income; it is a way to bridge the gaps in the lifetime flow of labor income due to illness, old age, unemployment, or the premature death of the family breadwinner. It is, then, a way to security and independence. Wealth is also a means of achieving power and influence over the chances of others in business, in government affairs, and in the expression and communication of ideas. It is a way for one person to gain preferment for his heirs or otherwise to lengthen his shadow across generations to come. Interestingly, wealth can be highly specialized to fulfill specific aims. Thus, insurance and annuities will meet certain security aims, and corporate stock acts as a lever on the control of business affairs. Trust agreements may be used to accomplish many specific purposes.

From the point of view of the individual firm, equity in the form of working capital is a practical necessity. Although land and fixed capital could presumably be rented from others, again as a practical matter, money will not ordinarily be available for plant expansion except as it is "led" by equity. From a national point of view, capital accumulation is a necessity to raise living standards. If it is not done privately, it must be done socially.

INEQUALITY OF WEALTH DISTRIBUTION

Presumably, since wealth is a good thing to have, it would be good for all families to have some. Also, it would seem that the wider the distribution of wealth, the broader the political base for capitalism. There is doubtless a maximum degree of concentration of wealth which is tolerable in a democracy and compatible with an ideology of equality of economic opportunity. However, inequality due to differences in wealth-holding by age and family responsibilities may have quite a different political meaning from a similar degree of inequality within either the young or the old age group. Rigid class lines arise from great differences in inherited wealth as well as from different motivation, different opportunity for education, and different choice of occupation. To some extent, the difference between "democratic" and "oligarchic" systems of wealth-holding will be drawn as the body politic considers the individual, on the one hand, or the family of several generations, on the other, as the appropriate wealth-holding unit. To a considerable extent, American social policy has developed out of the belief that each generation of individuals should stand on its own with a minimum "handicapping" by previous generations.

In this connection, it should be emphasized that inequality of wealth-holding is not the only determinant of income inequality. Indeed, to the extent that wealth is held by low-ranking wage or salary

INTRODUCTION AND SUMMARY

earners, it tends to offset income inequality. While capital and land are basic factors in production, and while total wealth is over three times as large as total annual income, the owners of these factors do not receive in the form of property income the greater part of the product in this or any other country. Only about 25 per cent of all income may be characterized as property income.[2]

The size distribution of income is determined by "(a) the rates of pay received by various agents of production and the extent of their utilization, and (b) the distribution among persons of the ownership of these productive agents. Two classes of productive agents must be distinguished: physical property or non-human capital, and human capital representing the productive capacity of individuals. In turn, the latter is divided into 'natural' endowment or 'abilities,' and productive capacity acquired by investment in training."[3] Thinking in these terms, this study is confined to the distribution of nonhuman capital.

There is no particular degree of concentration of wealth which is required for the working of a capitalist system. However, there may be a minimum degree of inequality consistent with a particular set of capitalist institutions, a particular technology, and a particular level of production. Composition of estate data generally show that nonproprietors place consumer capital and security objectives ahead of high yield at high-risk objectives. Only after the first set of objectives is achieved by accumulating property do most nonproprietors move on to the second. This suggests that, particularly as the proportion of the population who are proprietors falls, the availability of equity capital (at existing yields) is a function of the inequality of wealth distribution. If the inequality of wealth-holding were to be sharply reduced, maintenance of the present flow of equity capital could be accomplished only by raising equity yields or by new institutional arrangements for transmuting security-motivated wealth-holding into high-yield-motivated holding.[4] This transmutation is accomplished by

---

[2] The precise percentage which one selects depends upon what part of "proprietors' income" one assigns to property and what part to service income, how one treats undistributed corporate profits, and whether he imputes an income to consumer capital.

[3] Jacob Mincer, "A Study of Personal Income Distribution," unpublished Ph.D. dissertation, Columbia University, 1957, p. 136. See also Mincer, "Investment in Human Capital and Personal Income Distribution," *Journal of Political Economy*, August 1958, pp. 281–302.

[4] It is worth noting here that there is an important distinction, as emphasized by Veblen, between the equity investor who seeks long-term profit out of self-

INTRODUCTION AND SUMMARY

insurance company or pension fund purchase of corporate stock. It could also be accomplished by mutualization or provision of capital by patrons, as is indeed done in some cases of corporations' internal financing.

ROLE OF GOVERNMENT

History suggests that public enterprise often follows where equity needs are not privately met. The American people have shown themselves to be pragmatic on the issue of public versus private ownership of capital. About 20 per cent of all wealth in the United States is publicly owned. A vital belief in the efficacy of private enterprise has not precluded a considerable role for government in property regulation, control, and ownership. Indeed, as we have emphasized above, property is a legal concept, and property rights exist only as defined and enforced by government. The meaning of private property increases as governments protect its owners against loss through thievery and embezzlement, as buyers of securities are protected against fraud or misinformation, as orderly markets for sale of assets are maintained, and as wealth-holders are assured against threats of inflation or financial panic and mass liquidation. Government has also affected property values and the security of property by regulation of financial intermediaries, by insuring and even making direct provision for the extension of credit to individuals. By sale of land, as in the Homestead Act, and by social insurance, as in the case of Old Age, Survivors, and Disability Insurance, the federal government has engineered the widespread ownership of property rights. By influencing the transfer of property through gift or bequest and by affecting the possibility for accumulation of large estates, government fiscal policy plays a part in determining the distribution of wealth among persons and among sectors of the economy.

EARLIER STUDIES OF WEALTH DISTRIBUTION

Interest in the facts of wealth distribution is not new, nor is concern with the questions which turn around those facts in any way novel. However, there has been surprisingly little systematic empirical in-

---

managed business and the speculator who holds or sells on the basis of anticipated profits with no hope or intention of constructively influencing the policy of the business. Certainly the great majority of stockholders in large corporations belong in the latter category of equity investors and view the highly regulated stock market as an escape route from anticipated falls in value due to poor management. Hence, a wide equity market removes some of the "risk" while diluting control.

INTRODUCTION AND SUMMARY

vestigation of this subject in the United States. Up to the close of World War II, only ten scholars are known to have attempted to estimate the nation-wide size distribution of personally held wealth. Apparently the first efforts along this line were made by G. K. Holmes[5] and C. B. Spahr,[6] both for the year 1890. Holmes worked from a census of tangible wealth, while Spahr started from probate data on estates in selected New York counties. W. R. Ingalls[7] was apparently the first investigator to use federal income tax data to make a wealth distribution by income classes. W. I. King[8] used income tax information, census data on farm wealth, estate data of several kinds, and income data of many kinds to contrive what was undoubtedly, up to that time, the most careful estimate of wealth distribution. His study was for the year 1921.

These early investigators showed great fortitude and imagination in the face of what must have looked like insurmountable obstacles, such as the paucity of data. One catches their spirit in these comments by Frederick R. Macaulay,[9] who was one of the researchers on the first National Bureau of Economic Research project on income estimates:

Construction of an income frequency distribution for all income recipients in the United States from the existing data . . . necessarily involves an extremely large amount of pure guessing. It is only because of the practical value of even the roughest kind of an estimate that any statistician would think of attacking the problem. . . .

Some hypothetical reasoning is inevitable in such a statistical study as the present one. The investigator must not lose heart. Sir Thomas Browne in his rolling periods sagely remarks that "what song the Syrens sang, or what name Achilles assumed when he hid himself among women, though puzzling questions, are not beyond all conjecture!"

Work on wealth distribution which was carried on in the 1930's and early 1940's included that of Lewis Corey, R. R. Doane, Maxine Yaple, Fritz Lehmann, Charles Stewart, and Mary S. Painter.[10] All of

[5] "The Concentration of Wealth," *Political Science Quarterly*, December 1893, pp. 589–600.

[6] *The Present Distribution of Wealth in the United States*, New York, 1896.

[7] *Current Economic Affairs*, York, Pa., 1924. *Wealth and Income of the American People*, 2nd ed., York, Pa., 1924.

[8] "Wealth Distribution in the Continental United States at the Close of 1921," *Journal of American Statistical Association*, June 1927, pp. 135–153. This article was based on an unpublished book-length manuscript at the National Bureau.

[9] *Income in the United States*, II, New York, National Bureau of Economic Research, 1922, pp. 424–425.

[10] The citations for the relevant works of these authors and the years to which their estimates apply are as follows: Corey, *The Decline of American Capitalism*,

INTRODUCTION AND SUMMARY

these authors worked with some combination of census, income tax, and estate tax statistics. Most of them produced estimates of wealth by income class in contrast to estimates by wealth class.

Several important steps in the study of wealth distribution taken since World War II were prerequisites for any advance in understanding which is contributed by the present study. One was the first demonstration in this country of the use of the estate-multiplier method. This pioneering work was done by Horst Mendershausen. While earlier investigators had used estate tax data, none of them had used this method to estimate the distribution of wealth among living persons. Mendershausen's study, "The Pattern of Estate Tax Wealth,"[11] is the platform from which this inquiry departs. A second step was the completion of a set of national balance sheet accounts for a limited number of benchmark years. These accounts, as published by Goldsmith,[12] show considerable detail by sectors of the economy and by type of property, and make possible the calculation of the shares of several types of wealth held by the top wealth-holding groups. The preliminary balance sheet for 1953 was prepared for use in this study by the National Bureau of Economic Research.

A third and highly significant postwar contribution to the study of wealth distribution was made by the Survey Research Center of the University of Michigan. In connection with the Survey of Consumer Finances carried out under the sponsorship of the Federal Reserve System's Board of Governors, the Survey Research Center conducted the first nation-wide sample study of assets and net worth held by spending units. This was done for 1950. A second interviewing survey was carried out for 1953.[13] These sample survey studies yield a broad picture of the distributions of the national total of most kinds of property, and it is to be hoped that they will be continued and pub-

---

New York, 1934; estimate for 1928. Doane, *The Measurement of American Wealth*, New York, 1938; estimates for 1929–32. Yaple, "The Burden of Direct Taxes as Paid by Income Classes," *American Economic Review*, December 1936; estimates for 1928–32. Lehmann (with Max Ascoli), *Political and Economic Democracy*, New York, 1937; estimate for 1930. Stewart, "Income Capitalization as a Method of Estimating the Distribution of Wealth by Size Groups," *Studies in Income and Wealth*, Volume Three; estimates for 1922–36. Painter, "Distribution of Wealth in Estates and Estate Tax Yield," unpublished ms., NBER, 1946. W. L. Crum's *The Distribution of Wealth* (Boston, 1935) was limited to a study of the estates of decedents filing estate tax returns in 1916–33.

[11] Part III of Raymond W. Goldsmith's *A Study of Saving in the United States*, III, Princeton, 1956, pp. 277–381.

[12] *Ibid.*, pp. 3–138.

[13] The findings of these studies are published in the *Federal Reserve Bulletin*.

INTRODUCTION AND SUMMARY

lished at frequent intervals as the basic source of information on wealth distribution.

From the point of view of this study, the Survey of Consumer Finances inquiries have a special usefulness. They provide an independently arrived at set of estimates against which our findings for 1953 can be checked for accuracy and from which additional information of explanatory and analytical value can be drawn.

The Survey studies and ours should be viewed as complementary in two ways. In the first place, the estate tax data make possible an extension of the wealth-holding series back to 1922. Hence, when the conjunction of the two sets of findings for 1953 is established, there is a basis for historical perspective which the Survey cannot provide. In the second place, the Survey, since it is based on a small sample of about 3,500 spending units, is limited in the amount of detail it can supply for the top wealth-holding groups. In general, the Survey's top group is "open-ended" for the "over $25,000 net worth" class, and information on this group is based on a sample of less than 200. In contrast to this, federal estate tax data provide no information at all on the wealth-holdings of persons with less than $60,000 of gross estate, but do provide a large sample of top wealth-holders. In 1953, for example, there were 36,699 estate tax returns. The decedents for whom these returns were filed all ranked within the upper 2 per cent of decedents as ranked by total asset holdings. When the distribution of decedent wealth-holders is converted to a distribution of living wealth-holders by the estate-multiplier method, we find that it describes the holdings of the upper 1.6 per cent of adults, who in turn represent approximately the upper 2.5 per cent of spending units. (It should be noted that a spending unit with two or more wealth-holders will often occupy a quite different rank from any of the individual wealth-holders within the spending unit.)

Thus, federal estate tax data provide an independent route to knowledge about upper wealth groups. In some important respects, this method should be superior to the survey method. In the first place, the tax returns are compulsory reports usually prepared and certified by disinterested parties with access to all records. To duplicate such reliable information by interview for a similar number of cases would be extraordinarily difficult and expensive.[14] Secondly, this

---

[14] J. K. Butters, L. E. Thompson, and L. L. Bollinger comment on this point as follows in *Effects of Taxation: Investment by Individuals* (Boston, 1953, p. 12):

"The reason that other investigators have never assembled more detailed and extensive information on the top income and wealth classes is not that there has

INTRODUCTION AND SUMMARY

method may be expected to give not only a broad coverage of property types, but also a relatively full valuation of those items which are reported.

In a somewhat different way the findings derived from estate tax data by the estate-multiplier method may be considered complementary to the findings of wealth studies based on the capitalization of income method. The latter type of study can yield results only for those types of property that yield income, and when the source of data is income tax returns, only for those types of property that yield income reported on tax returns. The most recent work to follow the income capitalization method, and one which is drawn upon in this study, is Thomas R. Atkinson's *The Pattern of Financial Asset Ownership: Wisconsin Individuals, 1949*.[15]

SOURCES OF DATA AND METHODS OF ESTIMATION USED IN THIS STUDY

The principal source of data for this study is tabulations of federal estate tax returns. The federal estate tax has been in existence since 1916 and some information on returns filed has been published for most years. The minimum filing requirement, which is currently $60,000, has varied from $40,000 to $100,000 over the period. However, the necessary information on age and sex of decedents, cross-classified by type of property, is presented in such a way that a detailed representation of the distribution of wealth among living persons can be derived for relatively few years. For 1953 the Internal Revenue Service made available to the National Bureau the most complete tabulation of estate tax returns that has ever been prepared. In this tabulation the variables of gross estate size, age, sex, and residence

---

been a general lack of interest in this subject, but rather that the cost and technical difficulties involved have been too great. The difficulties of sampling upper income and wealth classes are much greater than for the population as a whole. The tasks of designing a representative sample, of getting access to the individuals to be interviewed, and of obtaining frank and complete financial information from them, are all much more formidable in tapping the top income and wealth classes than for the general run of the population."

The study by Butters *et al.* was based on interviews with a sample of 746 "active investors" as drawn from the files of investment bankers and security dealers. Most of these were in the upper 5 per cent of income receivers and almost half were in the upper 1 per cent. Butters *et al.* state that "to our knowledge, the sample contains the largest body of financial information yet assembled by interviews with individuals in the upper income and wealth classes" (p. 15).

Also relevant here is L. R. Klein, K. H. Straw, and Peter Vandome, "Savings and Finances of the Upper Income Classes," *Bulletin of the Oxford Institute of Statistics*, November 1956, pp. 293–319.

[15] Princeton for National Bureau of Economic Research, 1956.

INTRODUCTION AND SUMMARY

(by community property state or non-community property state) of decedents were cross-classified by type of property. For 1944 a similar breakdown by gross estate size, age, and type of property had been prepared by the Internal Revenue Service, which formed the basis for the intensive study by Horst Mendershausen referred to above. For 1948, 1949, and 1950 there is information by age and gross estate size which makes it possible to estimate aggregate gross estate without a breakdown by type of property. Similar, but unpublished, data for 1941 and 1946 were made available to Mendershausen. There are published data on economic estate by net estate size and age for 1922, 1924, 1941, 1944, and 1946. Finally, data on the sex of decedents by age and size of estate are available only for the years 1922, 1923, 1948, 1949, 1950, and 1953.

The method which was followed in dealing with estate tax returns is known as the estate-multiplier method.[16] Bernard Mallett was apparently the first person to apply this method. By use of it in 1908, he developed British wealth estimates.[17] Corrado Gini[18] of Italy and G. H. Knibbs[19] of Australia were among the first to follow Mallett in using this method.

The estate-multiplier method has also been used in the Netherlands[20] and in New Zealand.[21] In the latter case, the method has been used regularly to prepare the official estimates of private wealth. In recent years many scholars have used this method with British data and have contributed to what is probably the most adequate historical series on changes in wealth concentration for any country. Kathleen Langley has correlated these studies and extended them to the postwar period.[22]

The estate-multiplier method, which is described in detail in Chapter 2, calls for multiplying the number and property of decedents in each age-sex group by the inverse of the mortality rate for that age-

[16] These two paragraphs are largely based upon Mendershausen's study (Goldsmith, *Saving in U.S.*, III, pp. 280–283).

[17] "A Method of Estimating Capital Wealth from the Estate Duty Statistics," *Journal of the Royal Statistical Society*, March 1908.

[18] *L'ammontare o la Composizione della Richezza delle Nazioni*, Torino and New York, 1914.

[19] *The Private Wealth of Australia and Its Growth as Ascertained by Various Methods, Together with a Report of the War Census of 1915*, Melbourne, 1918.

[20] J. B. Derksen, "Berekening van Let Nationale vermogen nit de aangiften voor de successie belasting," *De Nederlandiche Conjunctuur*, May 1939.

[21] *New Zealand Official Year-Book*, Wellington, various years.

[22] "The Distribution of Capital in Private Hands in 1936–38 and 1946–47," *Bulletin of the Oxford University Institute of Statistics*, December 1950 and February 1951. Other British studies are cited by Langley.

sex group. This process yields an estimate of the number of living persons and the amount of estate in each age-sex group and in each estate size. A simple hypothetical example will illustrate what is involved. Suppose that out of a population of 1,000 men aged 40 to 50, two men died in one year with estates of $100,000 or more. Suppose further that it is known that 5 per cent of all the 1,000 men aged 40 to 50 died in that year. Then it may be assumed that the two men who died with $100,000 were 5 per cent of all the living men in the group with $100,000. Hence, to estimate the number of living men with $100,000, we should multiply two by twenty (the inverse of 5 per cent) to get the answer of forty living men with $100,000 or more.

The main disadvantage of thus deriving wealth estimates from estate tax returns is that the "sampling" is done by death rather than by a random draw of living persons. This means that a connection between decedent wealth-holders and living wealth-holders can be made only by using a set of mortality rates which are assumed to apply to the upper wealth-holding groups. The selection of mortality rates presents an opportunity for considerable error in the estimation of the number of living persons in each estate size, and, similarly, in the aggregate of wealth held by such persons. Other problems arise in that decedents' reported estates may differ from the "actual" estates of nondecedents in the same age-sex groups.

The transformation of evidence on decedents in a given year into a distribution of wealth among persons who were alive in that year is like the work of an archaeologist who reconstructs the artifacts of an earlier civilization from buried or scattered ruins. It is also similar to the estimation of the plant and animal population of an earlier period from samples collected from volcano, flood, or glacier. The great naturalist Louis Agassiz spent a season in 1861 drawing specimens from a glacier. Of this experience he wrote, "While residing upon this glacier and tracing the connection of the features it now presents with the phenomena of an earlier period, of which it is but a miniature representation, I have often been impressed with the importance for the philosopher of magnifying or reducing the facts which may be within his reach to such an extent that they may become a living representation of another state of things."[23]

The procedure adopted in this study of magnifying the facts within our reach so that they may become "a living representation of another state of things" involves two separate steps. One is the multiplication

[23] On a plaque in the Museum of Comparative Zoology at Cambridge.

INTRODUCTION AND SUMMARY

of the basic data by inverse mortality rates, whereby the number of persons with basic variant estate tax wealth and the amounts of such wealth are estimated. These are best described as estimates of the number of living persons who would have been liable to report for federal estate tax purposes had they died in that year.

The second step is the adjusting of the basic variant estimates to yield, as nearly as possible, the estimates of top wealth-holders which would be found by an ideal census of the wealth of living persons. Here an effort is made to assess the peculiarities of the method of sampling by federal estate tax law and to make quantitative corrections in those instances in which, by law or practice, the coverage or evaluation of individual wealth items differs from an ideal definition of personal wealth. In the course of this inquiry two ideal definitions were improvised. "Prime wealth" is used to mean the wealth to which a person has full title and over which he has power of disposal. "Total wealth" is a broader concept; it includes prime wealth and also wealth in which a person may have an income interest but over which he may not have any present power of disposal. Examples of the latter are rights to personal trust funds or to equities in pension and retirement funds.

Summary

This study falls into two parts. One deals with sources of data and methods of estimation and the other with presentation and analysis of findings.

The first part, comprising Chapters 2 and 3, is concerned with the procedures, information, and concepts that are required to move from raw data on the estates of decedents, as reported for federal estate tax purposes, to estimates of the wealth held by a measurable fraction of the living population. In general, the multiplication process is discussed in Chapter 2 and all adjustments for deficiencies of the basic data are considered in Chapter 3. The nontechnical reader who is more interested in the results than in how they were derived may skip directly to Chapter 4.

After examining the number of returns by age-sex groups over the years, it is concluded that the estate tax series is usable for the purpose at hand. There are no erratic or unexplainable variations in the total numbers, nor in the age composition of the group. The over-all sample size is sufficiently large to make gross errors due to sampling variation quite unlikely for the over-all estimates. However, the individual cells for some age-sex groups are so small as to yield results with large sampling errors.

The greatest possibility of error in the over-all estimates is not in sampling variation, however, but in the selection of the set of mortality rates to use in multiplying.

The first substantive problem attacked in the book is the estimation of the number of top wealth-holders in 1953, that is, living persons with $60,000 or more. Starting with the number of decedents represented on estate tax returns (36,699), the estimate is made by "blowing up" that number by inverse mortality rates. Using adjusted mortality rates, which are selected to reflect the more favorable mortality

TABLE 1
DIFFERENT ESTIMATES OF TOP WEALTH-HOLDERS, 1953

Definition of Wealth and Mortality Rates	Number of Top Wealth-Holders	Aggregate Gross Estate (billion dollars)
Basic variant		
Adjusted mortality	1,659,000	309.2
White population mortality	1,417,000	257.2
Prime wealth variant		
Adjusted mortality	1,626,000	327.5
Total wealth variant		
Adjusted mortality	1,776,000	381.1

rate of upper economic groups, an estimate of 1,659,000 top wealth-holders is derived (Table 1). Using the mortality rate of the white population without adjustment for class differences yields the considerably lower estimate of 1,417,000. The true number of top wealth-holders for that year probably lies somewhere between these two estimates, but it is believed to be closer to the adjusted mortality estimate than to the white mortality estimate. Hence, throughout the book the greater part of the discussion is in terms of the adjusted mortality estimates.

By the same blowing up process, the 1,659,000 top wealth-holders are estimated to have held $309.2 billion of gross estate. This amount, which is the basic variant estimate, refines the estate tax data in only one respect, namely, in multiplying life insurance amounts by different multipliers from those used for all other assets, so that insurance amounts are reduced from face value to estimates of owner's equity. These basic variant estimates are then examined with some care to

INTRODUCTION AND SUMMARY

see how they compare with those which would be found by a census of living wealth-holders that used ideal definitions of personally held wealth. Our rough estimates lead to the conclusion that the basic variant aggregate estimates are not substantially different from an ideally arrived at estimate of "prime wealth," but are considerably lower than the aggregates of "total wealth." That is, we found that about 1.66 million persons had $309.2 billion of basic variant wealth, 1.63 million persons had $327.5 billion of prime wealth, and 1.78 million persons had $381.1 billion of total wealth.

The adjustments of the basic variant made in estimating the prime wealth variant include subtraction for persons originally counted in the group by virtue of the excess of insurance face value over equity, addition for underreporting by taxpayers, additions for gifts and life insurance proceeds "in float" during the year, and subtractions for trust property, annuities, and pensions originally included in the basic variant. The prime wealth variant is in turn modified to yield the total wealth variant estimates by making additions to the former for personal trust funds, annuities, and private and governmental pensions.

On the basis of the several estimates, it is concluded that for most purposes the basic variant estimates are close enough to prime wealth variant estimates to warrant their use in the discussion of top wealth-holder characteristics and the composition of their estates. However, the difference between the basic variant and total wealth variant estimates is so notable that this distinction is brought up frequently in the book.

CHARACTERISTICS OF TOP WEALTH-HOLDERS

The median age of the 1953 top living wealth-holders was 54 years (Table 2). Over half of the number were between 40 and 60 years of age. While top wealth-holders made up only 1.04 per cent of the total

TABLE 2
Selected Characteristics of Top Wealth-Holders, 1953

Characteristic	Both Sexes	Men	Women
Number of persons	1,659,000	1,144,000	514,000
Median gross estate size ($)	112,800	116,800	105,200
Average gross estate size ($)	182,000	162,400	220,500
Share of top wealth (per cent)	100	60	40
Median age (years)	54	52	57

INTRODUCTION AND SUMMARY

population and only 1.6 per cent of the adult population they accounted for 3.5 per cent of the men over 50.

Approximately 1.4 million of the 1.7 million top wealth-holders are heads of households, the 0.3 million being (according to our estimate) the number of married women and dependent children in the group. We find that a minimum of 2.28 per cent of households and 2.35 per cent of married couples have at least one member owning $60,000 of gross estate (Table 3). This compares closely with the

TABLE 3
PERCENTAGE OF TOP WEALTH-HOLDERS IN TOTAL POPULATION AND IN SELECTED GROUPS, 1953

	Top Wealth-Holders		
	Both Sexes	Men	Women
All persons	1.04	1.44	0.64
Adults (20 and over)	1.60	2.26	0.98
Persons (65 and over)	3.00	4.00	2.50
Married persons	1.40	2.30	0.70
Widowers and widows	2.69	3.10	2.60
Households with at least one top wealth-holder	2.28		

TABLE 4
MEDIAN AGE OF MALE TOP WEALTH-HOLDERS IN NON-COMMUNITY PROPERTY STATES, BY GROSS ESTATE SIZE, 1953

Gross Estate Size (thous. dollars)	Median Age (years)
60 to 100	54
100 to 200	53
200 to 500	53
500 to 2,000	56
2,000 and over	67

SOURCE: Table 48.

Survey of Consumer Finances finding that 3 per cent of spending units in 1950 had $60,000 or more of total assets.

The association of age and size of estate is quite clear for men; that is, average estate rises with age and median age rises with estate size (Chart 1). (The latter association is remarkably slight, however. See Table 4.) For women, on the other hand, this relationship is much more irregular.

Women top wealth-holders have gradually increased, both in numbers and in wealth, relative to men so that they comprised one-third of

INTRODUCTION AND SUMMARY

CHART 1
Average Gross Estate of Top Wealth-Holders, by Sex and Age Group, 1953

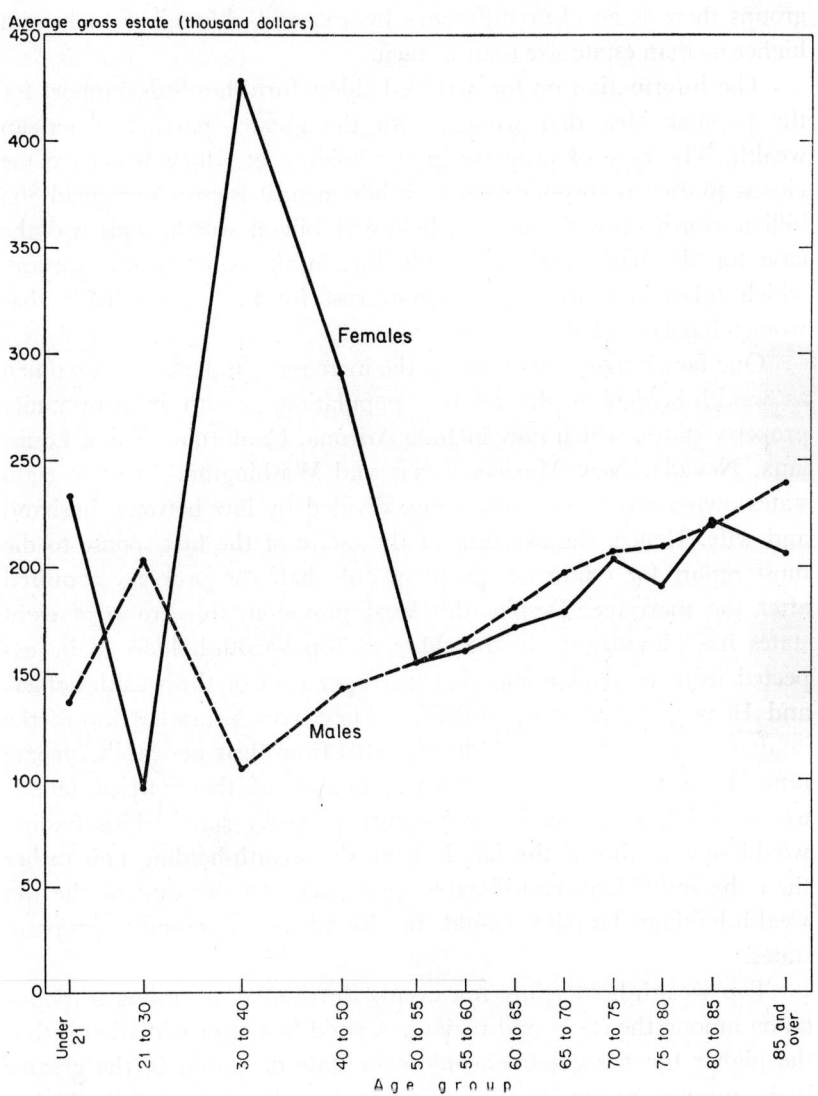

Source: Table 45.

all top wealth-holders in 1953 (while only one-fourth in 1922) and held 40 per cent of the wealth of the group (Table 2). Women have a larger average estate size than men, although within most age groups there is no clear difference by sex, and although men have a higher median estate size than women.

The information on top wealth-holders furnishes little support for the popular idea that women own the greater part of American wealth. The type of property in the holding of which women come closest to men is corporate stock. While men, it is estimated, held $63 billion worth of stock, women held $54 billion worth. This was the case for the basic variant wealth, but in the total wealth variant, which takes into account personal trust funds, it is probable that women have over half the corporate stock.

One factor that contributes to the increasing importance of women as wealth-holders is the relative population growth in community property states, which now include Arizona, California, Idaho, Louisiana, Nevada, New Mexico, Texas and Washington. In these eight states ownership is, in many cases, divided by law between husband and wife. Hence, the executor of the estate of the first spouse to die must report for estate tax purposes only half the property acquired after the marriage. Despite this legal provision, this group of eight states has almost exactly the share of top wealth-holders to be expected from its population, that is 18 per cent of the wealth-holders and 18 per cent of the population. They have somewhat less of the estate tax wealth than would be expected from their per capita income rank, however. A disproportionate number of the married female top wealth-holders are in community property states. This finding would suggest that if the family were the wealth-holding unit rather than the individual, considerably more than 18 per cent of the top wealth-holding families would be found in community property states.

Top wealth-holders are not evenly distributed according to population among the states and regions. A good first approximation is that the higher the per capita income of a state or region is, the greater is the number of wealth-holders per thousand people and the higher is the average estate per wealth-holder. A second approximation, using past income ranks, would explain the fact that some states with a declining income rank, like the New England states, Kansas, and Nebraska, have more estate tax wealth than their current income rank would predict. The reverse situation may explain the relatively low

INTRODUCTION AND SUMMARY

share of Utah and Washington. Quite unexplained by this hypothesis is the failure of some central states—notably Michigan, Ohio, and Indiana—to turn up their share of estate tax wealth.

As would be expected, there is considerable overlap between top wealth-holder status and high income rank. Certain occupational groups, particularly the self-employed, professional, and managerial groups, are overrepresented among the top wealth-holders.

COMPOSITION OF ESTATE

Among the top wealth-holders taken as a group, corporate stock is the single most preferred type of asset and accounted for 39 per cent of gross estate in 1953. Real estate, with 22 per cent, is second in importance, and cash (including deposits of all types in financial institutions) is third with 9 per cent. While there have been cyclical swings, there has been remarkably little noncyclical change over the decades in the pattern of top wealth-holders' holdings of the various broad types of assets. The general pattern of investment in current dollars for top estates is virtually the same in the 1920's as in the 1950's even though there have been important changes in prices, incomes, and the structure of the economy. Top wealth-holders have a lower ratio of debt to gross estate in the postwar years than in the 1920's and a far lower ratio than in the depression decade of the 1930's.

Whether there has been any important change in "preference" of top wealth-holders for the several types of assets is a matter of judgment. Reducing each type of asset to constant dollars and comparing changes in constant dollar composition with changes in relative yields furnishes plausible evidence that cyclical changes in such composition are guided by yield changes and hence that there are not cyclical changes in preference. Over the long term it seems more sensible to think in terms of current dollar composition. Changes in current dollar composition are compatible with changes in relative yields and it is, therefore, concluded that there have been no important changes in asset preferences.

The most important variable available to us in explaining differences in composition of estate is estate size, with larger estates having relatively more corporate stock and less real estate, more state and local bonds and less miscellaneous property (the largest component of which is unincorporated business). The percentage of estate held in stock tends to rise with age and the percentage held in

INTRODUCTION AND SUMMARY

miscellaneous property tends to fall. Liabilities decline gradually as a percentage of gross estate after age 40. Estates of women differ from men's estates of the same sizes principally in having a smaller share in insurance and in having smaller liabilities.

By first examining the estates of each sex by age groups within estate sizes and then looking at the estates by estate sizes within age groups (for a tabular version of the latter, in abridged form, see Table

TABLE 5
PERCENTAGE OF GROSS ESTATE IN SELECTED ASSETS AND LIABILITIES FOR THREE GROSS ESTATE SIZES IN THREE AGE GROUPS OF MALE TOP WEALTH-HOLDERS, 1953

Age Group	Gross Estate Size (thous. dollars)		
	70 to 80	150 to 200	2,000 to 3,000
	PERCENTAGE IN REAL ESTATE		
30 to 40	45	36	(10)[a]
55 to 60	35	29	16
75 to 80	37	28	4[b]
	PERCENTAGE IN STOCK		
30 to 40	9	17	(67)[a]
55 to 60	20	28	40
75 to 80	22	33	68
	PERCENTAGE IN CASH		
30 to 40	10	7	(3)[a]
55 to 60	13	11	2
75 to 80	17	12	6
	PERCENTAGE IN MISCELLANEOUS PROPERTY		
30 to 40	30	27	(1)[a]
55 to 60	14	14	(9)[c]
75 to 80	6	7	4
	PERCENTAGE IN DEBTS AND MORTGAGES (LIABILITIES)		
30 to 40	16	21	(1)[a]
55 to 60	6	10	28
75 to 80	3	5	3

SOURCE: Table 82.
[a] No cases, age 40–50 substituted.
[b] Adjacent age groups have percentages of 17 and 11.
[c] 60–65 age group substituted as more representative.

5), we are able to identify real estate as predominantly a smaller-estate asset; U.S. bonds as a smaller-estate, older-age asset; state, local, and "other" bonds as larger-estate assets; stock as a larger-estate, older-age asset; cash as a smaller-estate, older-age asset; mortgages and notes as smaller-estate, older-age assets; life insurance as a lower- and middle-estate, middle-age asset; miscellaneous property as a lower- and middle-estate, younger-age asset; and debts and mortgages as younger-age liabilities.

22

INTRODUCTION AND SUMMARY

From these and related facts of estate composition, this picture of changing preference emerges. As people get richer, they shift from purchase of consumer capital, including real estate and life insurance, to U.S. bonds and mortgages and notes. As they get still richer, they shift over to corporate stock and state, local, and "other" bonds. As people get older, they reduce their liabilities, "cash out" of miscellaneous property (which includes interest in unincorporated business) and life insurance, and convert to larger holdings of cash, U.S. bonds, corporate stock, and mortgages and notes. As wealth moves into the hands of women, liabilities are reduced, life insurance falls as a percentage of estate and, consequently, all other types of property rise in relative importance.

The differences in type of property held by the several estate sizes are associated with different degrees of inequality among top wealth-holders for each type of asset. The most unequally distributed type of property is state and local bonds and the least concentrated is real estate.

SIZE DISTRIBUTION

Over 30 per cent of the assets and equities of the personal sector of the economy in 1953 are assignable to the top wealth-holders who were 1.6 per cent of the total adult population that year (Chart 2). The top group owned at least 80 per cent of the corporate stock, virtually all of the state and local government bonds, and between 10 and 33 per cent of each other type of property in the personal sector

CHART 2
Share of Personal Sector Equity^a Held by Top Wealth-Holders, 1953

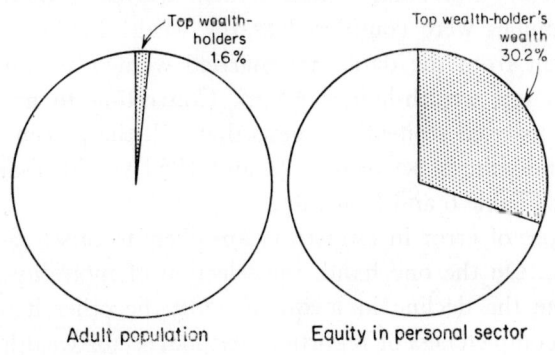

Source: Table 92, cols. 15 and 17.
^a Prime wealth variant.

in that year. These percentages are quite close to those found by the Survey of Consumer Finances for the same year.

The top wealth-holder group has varied in number and percentage of the total population over the years. Also, its share of total wealth has varied. It appears, however, that the degree of inequality increased from 1922 to 1929, fell to below the pre-1929 level in the 1930's, fell still more during the war and up to 1949, and increased from 1949 to 1956. However, the degree of inequality was considerably lower in 1953 than in either 1929 or 1922.

To make a comparison of degrees of wealth concentration, it is convenient to consider a constant percentage of the total adult population. The top 1 per cent of adults held 24 per cent of personal sector

TABLE 6
SHARE OF PERSONAL SECTOR WEALTH (EQUITY) HELD BY TOP WEALTH-HOLDERS, SELECTED YEARS, 1922–56

Year	Top 1 Per Cent of Adults	Top 0.5 Per Cent of All Persons	Top 2 Per Cent of Families[a]
1922	31.6	29.8	33.0
1929	36.3	32.4	
1933	28.3	25.2	
1939	30.6	28.0	
1945	23.3	20.9	
1949	20.8	19.3	
1953	24.2	22.7	28.5
1956	26.0	25.0	

[a] Families here defined as all adults less married females.

equity in 1953, 31 per cent in 1939, 36 per cent in 1929, and 32 per cent in 1922. It is probable that the decline thus indicated in inequality among individual wealth-holders is greater than would be found if families were considered as the wealth-holding units, since it is apparent from the data that married women are an increasing part of the top wealth-holder group. Converting to a measure of "adults less married women" suggests that half the percentage decline found for individuals between 1922 and 1953 would disappear on a family basis (Table 6 and Chart 3).

Two types of error in estimation are likely to offset each other in some degree. On the one hand, the selection of mortality rates tends to understate the decline in inequality. On the other hand, the differences in completeness of reporting personal sector wealth and estate tax wealth may tend to overstate the decline. It is difficult to imagine

INTRODUCTION AND SUMMARY

any combination of errors which would yield a result of increasing concentration over time.

Interestingly, the conclusions about changes in concentration of wealth over the years are not affected by selection of one or another variant of wealth.

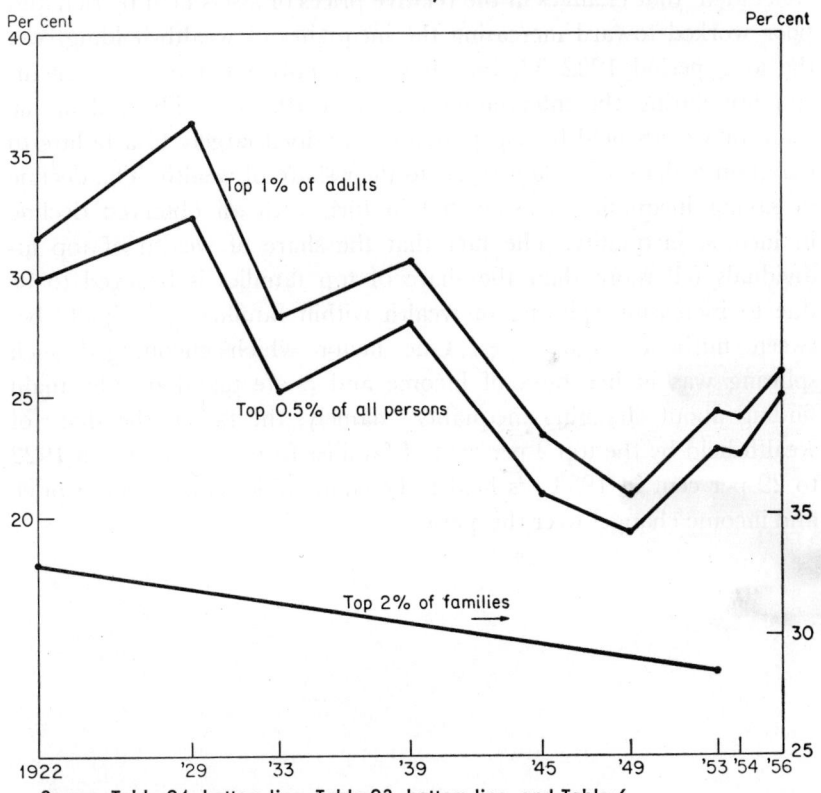

CHART 3
Share of Personal Sector Wealth[a] Held by Top Wealth-Holders, Selected Years, 1922–56

Source: Table 94, bottom line; Table 93, bottom line; and Table 6.
[a] Equity, basic variant.

The leading exception to the general picture of declining concentration is corporate stock. In the total wealth variant the top 1 per cent of adults' share of each type of property declined between the 1920's and the 1950's, except for stock and state and local bonds. For stock, their share ranged from 60 to over 70 per cent.

Inequality of wealth distribution is considerably greater in Great

INTRODUCTION AND SUMMARY

Britain than in the United States, but a pattern of similar decline in inequality is observable in the two countries.

DETERMINANTS OF CHANGES IN INEQUALITY

The final chapter of the book is devoted to inquiry into the causes for changes in the degree of inequality of wealth-holding. Three processes which may contribute to change are discussed. These are price change, accumulation of wealth out of income, and transfer of wealth. It is concluded that changes in the relative prices of assets held by rich and poor worked toward increasing the inequality of wealth-holding over the long period 1922–53, but that they contributed to lessening inequality during the intervening period of 1929–49. The fall in the share of wealth held by top families is ascribed largely to a failure to maintain a share of saving equal to their share of wealth. The decline of saving inequality is associated in turn with an observed decline in income inequality. The fact that the share of wealth of top individuals fell more than the share of top families is believed to be due to increasing splitting of wealth within families, principally between husbands and wives. One factor which encouraged such splitting was higher rates of income and estate taxation. The main finding about changing inequality—namely, the fall in the share of wealth held by the top 2 per cent of families from 33 per cent in 1922 to 29 per cent in 1953—is held to be compatible with observed price and income changes over this period.

CHAPTER 2

The Federal Estate Tax "Samples" and the Estate-Multiplier Method

THIS chapter describes the steps involved in producing from the raw data provided by federal estate tax returns estimates of the number of living persons with basic variant estate tax wealth. These steps include: (1) A presentation of the number of estate tax returns since 1916. (2) An appraisal of the stability over time of the numbers of returns by age group and amount of aggregate gross estate reported in them. (3) A presentation of the basic tables on the estate tax wealth of decedents. (4) An inquiry into the statistical reliability of samples of this size. (5) A statement of the estate-multiplier method of blowing up the sample of decedents to represent the number of living estate tax wealth-holders (referred to throughout the book as "top wealth-holders"). (6) The selection of appropriate mortality rates to use in deriving multipliers for each year and for each age-sex group of decedents. (7) An illustration, using 1953 data, of the actual procedure followed in the multiplier process to arrive at the tables used in all later discussions of the basic variant of estate tax wealth. This variant is best described as the number of persons and the amount of aggregate gross estate tax wealth which would be subject to the federal estate tax under the extraordinary assumption that all persons had died in the year. (8) Two adjustments to the basic data. One is a discussion of the accounting for those tax returns with no age information; the second involves the selection of special multipliers for use in blowing up the amount of life insurance held by each age group. Tables are presented showing mortality rates and multipliers and giving the results of multiplication for 1953. The 1953 tables here illustrate the methods followed. The tables for all the other years for which data are available are included in Appendix A so that another investigator may check the accuracy of the work done or enter his own assumptions in redoing any part of the work.

The Basic Data

NUMBER OF RETURNS

The federal estate tax law requires that a return be filed for each decedent who had a gross estate above a prescribed minimum. In 1953 there were 36,699 decedents whose estates were reported on the basis of a $60,000 minimum. These are all the returns which were filed in 1954, and they should represent the 1953 decedents since virtually all of them were for persons who died in the calendar year 1953. This number includes nontaxable as well as taxable returns and excludes only the returns for nonresident aliens. This group was 2.42 per cent of all persons who died in that year and 0.023 per cent of the total population[1] (Table 7). In the prewar years, only about 1 per cent of all decedents were represented by estate tax returns. The number of returns is determined in part by the level of the exemption which was $50,000 in 1922–26, $100,000 in 1926–32, $50,000 in 1932–35, $40,000 in 1935–42, and $60,000 after 1942.

The 1953 returns were larger in number and in aggregate gross estate ($7.4 billion) than in any previous year (Table 8 and Chart 4). In 1922, 13,013 returns were filed reporting $2.5 billion of aggregate gross estate. The first sharp break occurs in the series with the rise in the exemption from $50,000 to $100,000 in 1926. While the number of returns fell to 9,353 in 1926, the amount of aggregate gross estate did not fall substantially until 1931–32. The marked lowering of the exemption to $50,000 in 1932 was followed by a rise in the number of returns, but neither the number of returns nor the reported aggregate gross estate returned to the levels of the middle 1920's until 1936.

The number of returns and the aggregate gross estate varied very little from 1936 through 1944. There were about 15,000 returns and about $3 billion in gross estate all during the period. The 1942 change in the exemption from $40,000 to $60,000 was accompanied by the elimination of a $40,000 insurance exclusion from gross estate. However, the amount shown here for aggregate gross estate includes the amount of tax-exempt insurance assignable to returns filed from 1936

---

[1] It is not relevant, in appraising the size of the sample, to compare the decedents with the total number in the age-sex group of the living population. Rather, the decedents for whom estate tax returns are filed make up a sample of an unknown number of living persons with $60,000 or more of gross estate. See discussion of estate-multiplier method below.

TABLE 7
NUMBER OF ESTATE TAX RETURNS FOR 1916–54 RELATED TO
TOTAL DEATHS AND POPULATION

Inferred Year of Death	Total	Number of Returns Per 1,000 Deaths in U.S.	Per 100,000 Population in U.S.
1916–20[a]	42,230	—	—
1921[b]	12,203	—	—
1922	13,013	10.1	11.8
1923	12,403	9.2	11.1
1924	14,013	10.6	12.3
1925	13,142	9.7	11.3
1926	9,353	6.6	8.0
1927	8,079	6.0	6.8
1928	8,582	5.9	7.1
1929	8,798	6.1	7.2
1930	8,333	6.0	6.8
1931	7,113	5.2	5.7
1932	8,727	6.4	7.0
1933	10,353	7.7	8.2
1934	11,110	7.9	8.8
1935	11,605	8.3	9.1
1936	15,037	10.2	11.7
1937	15,932	11.0	12.4
1938	15,221	11.0	11.7
1939	15,435	11.1	11.8
1940	15,977	11.3	12.1
1941	16,215	11.6	12.2
1942	15,187	11.0	11.3
1943	14,303	9.8	10.7
1944	15,898	11.3	12.0
1945			
1946	20,899	15.0	14.8
1947	23,356	16.2	16.2
1948	24,552	17.0	16.7
1949	25,858	17.9	17.3
1950	27,958	19.2	18.4
1951			
1952			
1953	36,699	24.2	23.0
1954	36,595	24.7	22.5

SOURCE: Annual volumes of *Statistics of Income*. The estate tax data in all subsequent tables also are derived from this source unless otherwise indicated.
[a] Sept. 8, 1916, to Jan. 1921.
[b] Jan. 15, 1921, to Dec. 31, 1921.

TABLE 8
Gross and Economic Estates, Aggregates and Average Per Return, 1922–54

		Gross Estate		Economic Estate	
Year	Number of Returns	Aggregate ($ mill.)	Per Return ($ thous.)	Aggregate ($ mill.)	Per Return ($ thous.)
1922	13,013	2,495	192	2,200	169
1923	12,403	2,350	190	2,081	168
1924	14,013	2,958	211	2,642	189
1925	13,142	3,386	258	3,065	233
1926	9,353	3,146	336	2,836	303
1927	8,079	3,503	434	3,111	385
1928	8,582	3,844	448	3,493	407
1929	8,798	4,109	467	3,723	423
1930	8,333	4,042	485	3,622	435
1931	7,113	2,796	393	2,404	338
1932	8,727	2,027	232	1,686	193
1933	10,353	2,244	217	1,930	186
1934	11,110	2,435	210	1,918	173
1935	11,605	2,296	198	2,024	174
1936	15,037	2,853	190	2,442	162
1937	15,932	3,141	197	2,824	177
1938	15,221	2,837	186	2,558	168
1939	15,435	2,727	177	2,469	160
1940	15,977	2,877	180	2,607	163
1941	16,215	2,825	174	2,566	158
1942	15,187	2,712	179	2,447	161
1943	14,303	2,913	204	2,694	188
1944	15,898	3,438	216	3,227	203
1946	20,899	4,228	202	3,993	191
1947	23,356	4,775	204	4,501	193
1948	24,552	4,933	201	4,646	189
1949	25,858	4,918	190	4,622	179
1950	27,958	5,505	191	N.A.	N.A.
1953	36,699	7,412	202	7,011	191
1954	36,595	7,467	204	7,085	194

SOURCE: Beginning with 1936, the amounts shown here for gross estate exceed those in the original source by the amount of tax exempt insurance. For 1922–46, Mendershausen's study in Raymond Goldsmith, *A Study of Saving in the United States*, III, Princeton, 1956, Table E-14.

to 1942. The 1942 change in the exemption obscures the fact that there was some rise in number of estates over $60,000 from 1939 to 1944 (from 11,000 to 16,000).

After 1944 the number of returns and the total gross estate reported rise sharply so that by 1953 and 1954 there are about 36,600 returns and $7.4 billion of gross estate. Interestingly, there was no

CHART 4
Number of Federal Estate Tax Returns and Amount of Gross Estate Reported, Current Values, 1922–54

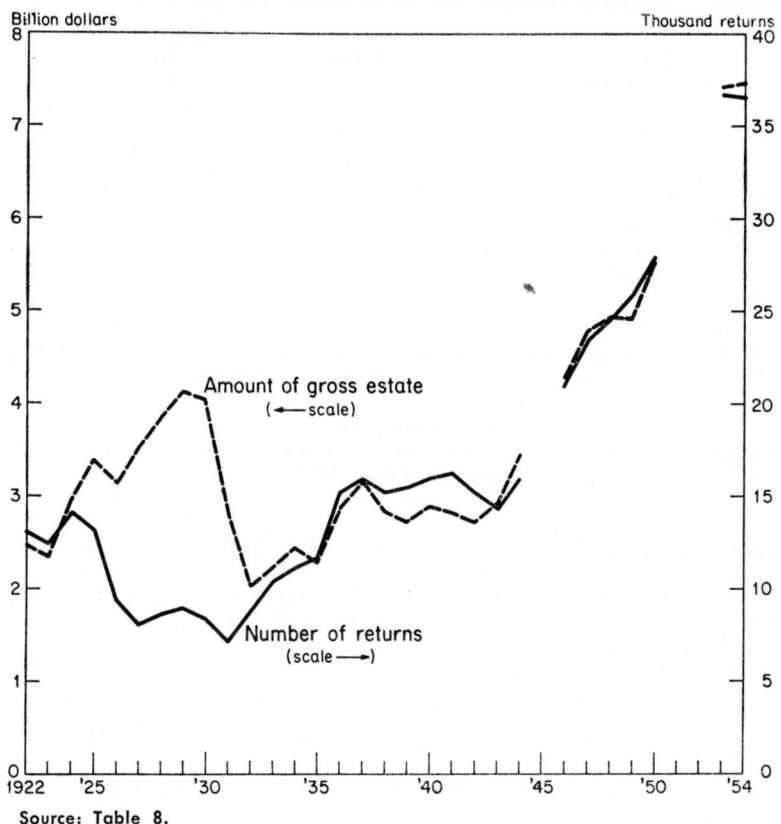

Source: Table 8.

striking change in the size of the average return, which stayed at around $200,000 from 1943 through 1954. This is due to the influx of relatively large numbers of small estates.

AGE OF DECEDENTS

Table 9 indicates that the decedents represented on estate tax returns, with a median age of 72, are older than decedents in the total white population, with a median age of 70. While only 35.9 per cent of all white decedents were over 75, 41.5 per cent of estate tax decedents were over 75 in 1953.

Because of the heavy reliance of the estate-multiplier method on age information, it is important to examine carefully the data we have

TABLE 9
DISTRIBUTION OF DECEDENTS BY AGE GROUP, ESTATE TAX RETURNS AND TOTAL WHITE POPULATION, 1953
(per cent)

	Decedents	
Age Group	Estate Tax Returns	Total White Population[a]
Under 55	10.3	18.6
55 to 65	19.5	18.5
65 to 75	28.7	27.0
75 to 85	28.5	25.6
85 and over	13.0	10.3
All age groups	100.0	100.0
Median age (in years)	72.0	70.0

[a] Excluding deaths in armed forces and of persons under 16.

TABLE 10
DISTRIBUTION OF ESTATE TAX DECEDENTS BY AGE GROUP IN INFERRED YEARS OF DEATH, SELECTED YEARS, 1922–53
(per cent)

Age Group	1922	1923	1924	1941	1944	1946	1947	1948	1949	1950	1953
20 to 30[a]	0.3	0.3	0.4	0.1	0.7	0.4	0.2	0.2	0.2	0.2	0.1
30 to 40	1.9	1.6	1.6	0.8	1.3	1.0	0.8	1.1	0.9	0.8	0.8
40 to 50	6.3	6.2	5.7	3.8	4.6	4.8	4.9	4.9	4.8	4.4	4.1
50 to 60	15.6	16.1	16.6	11.1	13.2	14.8	14.5	14.3	14.5	14.3	13.4
60 to 70	27.7	28.1	28.4	24.2	24.1	24.6	24.5	24.0	24.3	24.7	25.3
70 to 80	30.1	29.6	28.8	34.8	31.9	30.8	31.3	31.1	30.6	30.5	30.1
80 and over	18.1	18.1	18.5	25.2	24.2	23.7	23.8	24.4	24.7	25.1	26.2
All age groups	100.0	100.0	100.0	100.0	100.0	100.0	100.0	100.0	100.0	100.0	100.0
Number of returns covered	11,658	11,394	12,917	15,448	15,181	19,975	22,366	23,568	24,828	26,957	35,489

SOURCE: For 1922–46, Mendershausen in Goldsmith, *Saving in U.S.*, III, Table E-4.
[a] Combines groups "under 25" and "25 to 30" for 1922–24, and "under 21" and "21 to 30" for 1941, 1944, and 1946. The age of most of the decedents in this group is literally between 20 and 30, but in a few cases the decedent's age may have been under 20.

on age. Table 10 shows that of the 1953 estate tax decedents more than half (56.3 per cent) are to be found in the age groups of 70 and over. In each year over the last decade of the series, about 55 per cent of estate tax decedents have been in these age groups, but there has been a slight increase in the age group of 80 and over, which is true of decedents generally. Conversely, there is a trend toward smaller percentages in the younger ages. In every year since 1946 (which may include some World War II military deaths), less than 1.5 per cent of estate tax decedents have been under age 40. The year 1953, with only 0.9 per cent in these age groups, stands at the low end of the range for the postwar years, with 1946 at the high end of the range with 1.4 per cent. At first glance, it would seem that the 1953 decedents were an abnormally old group. A midpoint percentage of those under 40 for the postwar years would be 1.1.

Table 11 relates the ages of estate tax decedents to the ages of the total population. It serves to emphasize the peculiar age composition of our sample in 1953. While there are 3.43 estate tax returns per

TABLE 11
Estate Tax Decedents and Total Population, by Age Group, Selected Years, 1922–53

	Age Group						
	20 to 30	30 to 40	40 to 50	50 to 60	60 to 70	70 and over	All Age Groups Covered
				1922			
Number of returns	38	217	731	1,831	3,230	5,629	11,658
U.S. population (mill.)	18.9	16.3	12.7	8.9	5.3	3.0	65.2
Returns per 10,000 of population	0.02	0.13	0.57	2.03	6.04	19.14	1.79
				1941			
Number of returns	20	118	581	1,724	3,742	9,259	15,444
U.S. population (mill.)	23.0	20.1	17.2	13.5	8.7	5.4	87.9
Returns per 10,000 of population	0.01	0.06	0.34	1.28	4.30	17.15	1.76
				1944			
Number of returns	101	197	699	2,014	3,666	8,504	15,181
U.S. population (mill.)	23.6	20.9	17.7	14.4	9.2	5.9	91.7
Returns per 10,000 of population	0.04	0.09	0.39	1.40	4.00	14.51	1.66
				1946			
Number of returns	71	191	955	2,949	4,916	10,893	19,975
U.S. population (mill.)	23.7	21.4	18.2	14.9	9.6	6.2	94.1
Returns per 10,000 of population	0.03	0.09	0.52	2.00	5.12	17.51	2.12
				1950			
Number of returns	55	216	1,200	3,851	6,658	14,977	26,957
U.S. population (mill.)	23.9	22.8	19.3	15.5	11.1	7.3	100.0
Returns per 10,000 of population	0.02	0.09	0.62	2.48	6.02	20.61	2.70
				1953			
Number of returns	52	300	1,464	4,726	8,969	19,978	35,489
U.S. population (mill.)	23.1	23.6	20.6	16.2	11.7	8.1	103.4
Returns per 10,000 of population	0.02	0.13	0.71	2.91	7.73	24.53	3.43

Source: For 1922–46, Menderşhausen in Goldsmith, *Saving in U.S.*, III, Table E-6.

THE FEDERAL ESTATE TAX "SAMPLES"
TABLE 12
DISTRIBUTION OF ESTATE TAX DECEDENTS BY SEX AND AGE GROUP, SELECTED YEARS, 1922–53

Age Group	Men Number	Per Cent	Women Number	Per Cent	Men Number	Per Cent	Women Number	Per Cent
	1922				1923			
Under 25	10	.1	5	.2	8	.1	7	.2
25 to 30	20	.2	3	.1	14	.2	12	.4
30 to 40	166	1.9	51	1.8	135	1.6	48	1.6
40 to 50	572	6.5	159	5.5	547	6.6	151	5.0
50 to 60	1,467	16.7	346	11.9	1,464	17.6	367	12.1
60 to 70	2,532	28.9	698	24.1	2,471	29.6	734	24.1
70 to 80	2,599	29.6	915	31.6	2,382	28.5	988	32.5
80 to 90	1,244	14.2	626	21.6	1,164	14.0	637	21.0
90 and over	149	1.7	96	3.3	174	2.0	91	3.0
All age groups	8,759	100.0	2,899	100.0	8,359	100.0	3,035	100.0
No age given	961		394		722		287	
	1948				1949			
Under 21	3	}0.2	1	}0.2	6	}0.2	1	}0.2
21 to 30	30		13		30		13	
30 to 40	189	1.1	58	0.8	176	1.0	41	0.5
40 to 50	966	5.9	194	2.7	969	5.7	219	2.9
50 to 60	2,751	16.7	607	8.5	2,971	17.3	630	8.2
60 to 70	4,369	26.5	1,291	18.2	4,620	26.9	1,424	18.6
70 to 80	4,856	29.5	2,484	35.0	4,980	29.0	2,613	34.1
80 to 85	1,855	11.3	1,317	18.6	1,864	10.9	1,367	17.8
85 and over	1,450	8.8	1,134	16.0	1,543	9.0	1,361	17.7
All age groups	16,469	100.0	7,099	100.0	17,159	100.0	7,669	100.0
No age given	622		362		654		376	
	1950				1953			
Under 21	5	}0.2	2	}0.1	5	}0.2	2	}0.1
21 to 30	41		7		37		8	
30 to 40	180	1.0	36	0.4	243	1.0	57	0.5
40 to 50	987	5.3	213	2.6	1,213	5.0	251	2.2
50 to 60	3,146	16.9	705	8.4	3,847	15.9	879	7.8
60 to 70	5,082	27.4	1,576	18.8	6,885	28.5	2,084	18.4
70 to 80	5,409	29.1	2,804	33.4	6,932	28.7	3,754	33.2
80 to 85	2,090	11.3	1,524	18.2	2,630	10.9	2,060	18.2
85 and over	1,630	8.8	1,520	18.1	2,379	9.8	2,223	19.6
All age groups	18,570	100.0	8,387	100.0	24,171	100.0	11,318	100.0
No age given	638		363		751		459	

10,000 population over age 20, and 24.53 per 10,000 over age 70, there are only .02 returns per 10,000 between the ages of 20 and 30. This table also raises some doubts about the representativeness of the age distribution for 1953. While the total number of returns almost doubled from 1946 to 1953, the number in the 20 to 30 age bracket fell from 71 in 1946 to 55 in 1950 to 52 in 1953. Part of this drop may be explained by the drop in the absolute numbers in this age group in the total population, from 23.7 million in 1946 to 23.1 million in 1953.

Table 12 affords another check on the reasonableness or stability of the age composition of the postwar samples. It presents some of the same information shown in Table 11 but broken down by sex. Not only are women estate tax decedents older than the men, but they seem to be getting rapidly older. While the percentage of men over 80 only rose from 20.1 in 1948 to 20.7 in 1953, the percentage of women over 80 rose from 34.6 to 37.8 over the same period.

This table also suggests that one of the reasons for the unusually high rate of aging of estate tax decedents is the increasing proportion of women among them. In 1948 the ratio of men to women was 2.3; in 1949 and 1950 it was 2.2; and in 1953 it was 2.1.

In summary, the fact that estate tax decedents are older in 1953 than in preceding years may be due to several factors. First, all decedents in the population are older than in earlier years. Second, there are more women per 100 among estate tax decedents than in earlier years. Third, the age of women decedents is rising faster than that of men decedents. And fourth, in addition to the above, there may be a random element which yielded an older than "normal" group in that one year. However, we conclude that the 1953 decedents are not much, if at all, older than normal.

From this review of the data, we conclude that the federal estate tax returns provide a series of annual samples which do not fluctuate erratically, and in which the distribution among age groups does not vary unreasonably from year to year.

BASIC TABLES ON DECEDENTS' "ESTATE TAX WEALTH"

Aside from the data in *Statistics of Income* summarized above, we have had access to unpublished data for 1953. For that year we have more complete data on a larger number of decedents than for any other year. The estate tax returns for the full group of 36,699 decedents are, with some exceptions for age, tabulated by sex, age, size of gross estate, and community property versus common law state, and cross-classified by type of property. The basic tables derived from this set of tabulations are too numerous to reproduce here. There are four tables by type of property (one for males and one for females in each of the two groups of states) for each of sixteen estate size classes, which makes a total of sixty-four tables. Each of the sixty-four shows the number of decedents and total of each type of property for twelve different age groups. There is another group of tables by age and type of property, with one each for males and females in the two groups of states, which make a total of four tables. The estate-multiplier method has been applied to the sixty-eight tables of basic data and the results are presented below in this and the following chapters. A specimen table from each group of basic tables is included in Appendix A.

To indicate what the size of sample in various cells is like, three summary tables of raw data are set forth here. Two—one for males and one for females—show the classification of 1953 estate tax returns by type of property and by age of decedents (Tables 13 and 14). The other shows the same returns classified by type of property and size of gross estate (Table 15).

SAMPLING LIMITATIONS AND STATISTICAL RELIABILITY OF ESTIMATES

It is important to recognize that the estate tax returns provide a presumably random sample[2] stratified by age, not of the total population nor of all decedents, but of living persons with $60,000 or more of gross estate. The universe from which this stratified sample is drawn is, we find, on the order of 1.4 to 1.7 million persons. Hence a sample of 36,699 is about 2 per cent of the universe.[3] For some of the age groups, the sample is considerably more than 2 per cent of the living population with $60,000 or more of wealth, and for others it is considerably less than 2 per cent.

The statistical reliability of estimates based upon sample data does not depend upon the percentage of the universe drawn in the sample. One does not always materially improve one's results by increasing the size of the sample. Rather, reliability is related to the nature of the

[2] The possibility that the way death draws from various economic groups is not random is discussed in the section on the selection of appropriate mortality rates, the inverses of which are used to multiply the data from the tax returns. Here we are considering only those errors which may arise from random forces and which would be manifest in sampling variation.

[3] In appraising the size of the sample, it is relevant to note that the Survey of Consumer Finances uses a sample size of 3,500 to yield results applicable to all the nation's spending units.

AND THE ESTATE-MULTIPLIER METHOD

TABLE 13
Estate Tax Returns Filed in 1954 for Male Decedents, by Age Group and Type of Property
(thousand dollars)

Age Group	Number of Returns	Real Estate	U.S. Govt. Bonds	State and Local Bonds	Other Bonds	Stock	Cash	Mortgages and Notes	Life Insurance	Miscellaneous Property	Gross Estate	Debts and Mortgages	Economic Estate
Age unknown	751	37,222	6,994	1,071	748	30,466	13,937	6,112	7,750	10,985	115,283	10,288	104,995
Under 21	5	141	109	—	29	340	30	1	95	31	776	8	768
21 to 30	37	574	261	241	125	3,740	744	173	1,121	1,623	8,602	466	8,136
30 to 40	243	8,389	655	186	225	6,813	1,793	877	9,058	5,810	33,807	5,252	28,555
40 to 50	1,213	49,680	6,930	1,300	1,097	52,577	13,142	5,661	41,303	35,195	206,886	27,810	179,076
50 to 55	1,477	59,237	11,093	1,618	1,085	75,582	22,244	9,617	39,580	36,827	256,880	29,773	227,107
55 to 60	2,370	99,320	21,857	6,169	2,807	132,562	36,983	16,505	59,423	54,435	430,059	45,788	384,271
60 to 65	3,200	142,223	31,090	11,391	6,147	204,565	57,763	21,735	77,561	69,475	621,952	57,158	564,794
65 to 70	3,683	162,333	38,818	15,626	5,952	287,845	75,551	31,867	74,896	67,334	760,222	48,072	712,250
70 to 75	3,563	154,627	47,280	20,550	9,325	311,167	75,753	28,386	58,829	55,786	761,703	37,086	724,617
75 to 80	3,369	144,382	49,366	15,780	8,614	314,317	75,595	28,166	42,294	42,652	721,165	26,494	694,671
80 to 85	2,630	126,898	46,508	19,472	8,554	242,717	63,674	20,388	25,399	31,187	584,797	18,151	566,646
85 and over	2,378	109,820	52,589	24,003	9,348	264,999	58,012	16,789	14,368	22,962	572,890	23,129	549,761
All age groups	24,922	1,094,846	313,550	117,407	54,056	1,927,690	495,221	186,277	451,677	434,302	5,075,022	329,375	4,745,647

TABLE 14
Estate Tax Returns Filed in 1954 for Female Decedents, by Age Group and Type of Property
(thousand dollars)

Age Group	Number of Returns	Real Estate	U.S. Govt. Bonds	State and Local Bonds	Other Bonds	Stock	Cash	Mortgages and Notes	Life Insurance	Miscellaneous Property	Gross Estate	Debts and Mortgages	Economic Estate
Age unknown	459	17,997	5,900	781	1,157	23,310	9,124	3,213	687	4,581	66,748	2,994	63,754
Under 21	2	30	7	29	—	30	9	—	5	361	470	4	466
21 to 30	8	158	14	—	8	436	26	43	40	81	807	30	777
30 to 40	57	2,639	676	1,380	228	15,415	2,213	237	430	1,664	24,882	1,892	22,990
40 to 50	251	12,128	6,206	9,059	346	29,242	4,947	2,695	1,095	8,267	73,987	3,671	70,316
50 to 55	342	14,768	3,290	1,079	444	18,015	4,759	1,853	1,329	8,424	53,958	3,859	50,099
55 to 60	537	23,085	6,061	1,506	1,202	33,328	8,965	3,211	2,176	7,878	87,412	4,307	83,105
60 to 65	820	35,363	8,789	5,025	1,405	53,927	16,960	4,925	3,407	12,949	142,730	5,698	137,032
65 to 70	1,264	45,906	15,087	9,438	3,312	96,418	26,236	9,382	2,712	19,149	227,640	8,272	219,368
70 to 75	1,686	66,805	24,363	24,582	5,425	151,637	36,525	8,935	3,997	22,111	344,381	11,224	333,157
75 to 80	2,068	77,738	29,023	16,122	5,743	183,965	47,020	11,648	3,662	22,912	397,832	10,367	387,465
80 to 85	2,060	74,574	33,830	25,189	8,994	233,566	46,240	10,631	2,803	21,453	457,280	8,717	448,563
85 and over	2,223	85,659	43,993	27,723	8,928	215,644	46,791	10,251	2,130	17,468	458,587	10,374	448,213
All age groups	11,777	456,850	177,239	121,913	37,192	1,054,933	249,815	67,024	24,473	147,298	2,336,714	71,409	2,265,305

TABLE 15
ESTATE TAX RETURNS FILED IN 1954, BY TYPE OF PROPERTY AND GROSS ESTATE SIZE
(million dollars)

Type of Property	Total	Under 60	60 to 70	70 to 80	80 to 90	90 to 100	100 to 120	120 to 150	150 to 200	200 to 300	300 to 500	500 to 1,000	1,000 to 2,000	2,000 to 3,000	3,000 to 5,000	5,000 and over
No. of returns	36,632	1,317	5,205	3,951	3,381	4,010	5,694	4,841	3,691	2,401	1,396	500	111	77	40	17
Real estate	$1,549	$30	$126	$110	$104	$135	$204	$216	$210	$164	$130	$68	$24	$12	$9	$4
U.S. government bonds	491	8	29	23	23	32	52	55	59	63	61	34	15	12	11	15
State and local bonds	239	—	—	—	—	1	3	3	6	15	33	42	24	29	37	48
Other bonds	91	1	2	3	3	4	7	8	11	13	16	10	3	5	4	1
Corporate stock	2,981	20	79	69	69	103	200	239	313	388	476	372	140	185	165	163
Cash	744	15	57	44	40	56	87	86	89	83	75	49	19	18	11	13
Mortgages and notes	253	4	16	14	13	19	32	35	37	34	26	12	6	3	1	3
Insurance	475	3	20	24	24	33	69	81	75	61	45	23	7	4	4	2
Misc. property	581	111	28	26	27	37	64	73	79	74	70	47	20	15	12	5
Gross estate	7,394	87	358	315	303	419	715	795	877	895	934	656	258	284	253	253
Debts and mortgages	400	1	13	15	18	19	34	46	55	57	55	37	14	13	13	10
Economic estate	6,994	86	345	300	285	400	681	749	822	838	879	619	244	271	240	243

NOTE: 67 returns are missing because only those filing under acts of 1948 or later are included.

data and the absolute size of the sample. The distribution of wealth is highly skewed, with values in the sample ranging from $60,000 to over $10 million. Mean averages in such a distribution are subject to large sampling errors because the mean is highly sensitive to the presence or absence of a few high-valued cases.

The 36,699 sample is broken down into a large number of age groups within sex. For some of the tables there is the further division into community property and non-community property states. Means are then computed for gross estate size (and for other quantities as well) for each of these cells. The sampling error for some of these means is, as would be expected, quite large, depending upon the absolute number of cases in the cell and the range of gross estate sizes in the cell. An example of a large error is found in the cell for females aged 30 to 40 in community property states. The sample size is nineteen and the mean gross estate for the sample is $271,809. The standard error of that sample mean is $81,514. That is to say, 68 per cent of the samples drawn from the universe of women who reside in community property states, are 30 to 40 years of age, and hold at least $60,000 in gross estate would have a mean gross estate of $271,809 ± $81,514. Several other examples of standard errors of sample means are as follows: females, non-community property, age 55 to 60, sample size of 407 cases, mean gross estate of $161,663 ± $8,716; males, non-community property, age 30 to 40, sample size of 208 cases, mean gross estate of $140,178 ± $6,415; males, non-community property, age 80 to 85, sample size of 2,256 cases, mean gross estate of $227,137 ± $11,578. For the total sample of 36,699, the standard error of the mean of a stratified sample is $203,600 ± $4,515, or about 2 per cent.

These few examples are enough to indicate the need for caution in interpreting the tables on estimated means. Generally speaking, the largest errors attach to the younger age groups and the breakdowns by community property versus non-community states within age-sex groups. No great weight should be assigned to any one cell's mean, especially when it seems out of line with adjacent cells' means. On the other hand, differences in means have to be quite large to be statistically significant and the user should be cautious in imputing meaning to differences among means of a few thousand dollars. Where possible, tentative conclusions based upon means should be checked against estimates of medians or percentages of totals.

The statistical reliability of estimates of percentages is considerably higher than that of estimates of absolute total amounts or of means. For example, the estimate that women under age 50 owned 46.6 per cent of women's aggregate gross estate will be found to be true within 1.96 percentage points ninety-five times out of a hundred. Other examples of percentage error at the 5 per cent level are these: 2.6 ± 0.3 per cent of community property females have $1 million or more of gross estate; 10.9 ± 0.3 per cent of all top wealth-holders have between $60,000 and $70,000 of gross estate.

The Estate-Multiplier Method

The federal estate tax returns provide us with a "sample" of the rich. To be in this sample, a person must have died in the year and have had $60,000 or more of gross estate at the time of death. Hence we have a 100 per cent sample of decedent estate tax wealth-holders, which can at the same time be considered as a small sample of top wealth-holders who were alive in the previous year. Our problem is to estimate the total number of living top wealth-holders.

From this reporting for tax purposes, we estimate that in 1953 2.42 per cent of all decedents had $60,000 or more of gross estate and hence that 97.58 per cent had less. If the same relationship obtained among the living adult population as among the decedents, 2.42 per cent of the 103.4 million persons over 20 years of age in 1953, or 2.48 million living persons, would hold $60,000 or more of gross estate. This may be considered a very rough first approximation. It assumes that death occurs randomly among the rich and the nonrich. However, since there is a positive association between age and frequency of death, and since we know there is a nonrandom association between age and size of estate, there is reason to believe that the ratio of decedent estate tax wealth-holders to all decedents is higher than the ratio of living estate tax wealth-holders to the total living population.

It is best to think of the estate tax filings as a series of samples for age and sex groups. If death drew randomly from each age and sex group, one could derive the number of living estate tax wealth-holders in each group by multiplying the number of decedent wealth-holders with specified age-sex characteristics by the inverse of the frequency with which death drew from that age-sex group. Thus, if there were two decedent wealth-holders in a particular age-sex group, and if we knew that 5 per cent of that age-sex group had died in 1953, then we would estimate that twenty (the inverse of 5 per cent) times two, or forty, living persons in that age-sex group were estate tax wealth-holders. Since we are dealing with a series of age-sex group samples, we need a series of age-sex multipliers.

Besides age-sex differentials, which are very important in mortality statistics, race and class differences should also be taken into account. There is some reason to believe that the mortality rate for top wealth-holders is more favorable, particularly at younger ages, than that for the total population. In the first place, the presumption that the non-white population is underrepresented in the upper few percentiles of wealth-holders argues for using the white population's mortality rates.[4] In the second place, within the white population there seem to be significant differences among economic groups, the higher status groups having more favorable mortality rates.

SELECTION OF APPROPRIATE MORTALITY RATES

Unfortunately, however, there is no sure guide to selecting the set of mortality rates appropriate to the upper few percentiles of wealth-holders. Surprisingly little is known about the ways in which mortality differs by income or wealth class. Apparently no study has ever been made of these particular relationships. The several types of study relevant to the problem at hand are those measuring differential mortality by census tract, occupation, education, and size of insurance policy.

A study, which ranked Chicago census tracts by average house rental and then compared the 1940 mortality by groups of identical age, sex, and racial characteristics, found that the mortality rate of white males in the top fifth of the census tracts was only 76 per cent of that of all white males in the 20 to 30 age group, 87 per cent in the 55 to 65 age group, and 99 per cent in the 75 and over age group (Table 16). Similar results were found for Buffalo in 1939–41 by Yeracaris.[5]

Occupational differences in mortality have been studied in Great Britain and in the United States. In both countries, the higher status occupations are found to have relatively more favorable mortality rates, although the differences seem to be narrowing over time. Using 1930 data, Jessamine Whitney found the death rate of men in the lowest social-economic group was almost double that of men in the

---

[4] By choosing the mortality experience of the white population we do not, of course, confine the results to white wealth-holders, nor do we destroy the meaningfulness of a comparison of top wealth-holders with the total population.

[5] Constantine A. Yeracaris, "Differential Mortality, General and Cause-Specific in Buffalo, 1939–41," *Journal of the American Statistical Association,* December 1955, pp. 1235–1247.

highest.[6] A similar finding for Britain in 1930–32 was reported in a study of the Registrar-General.[7] A leading finding of this study was that even greater differentials were observable for the wives of men classified by occupation. Sir Percy Stock concluded from this finding that " . . . the contribution made by the actual work done to the

TABLE 16
Top Fifth White Male Mortality as a Percentage of General White Male Mortality, Chicago, 1940

Age Group	Per Cent
20 to 30	76
30 to 40	66
40 to 55	77
55 to 65	87
65 to 75	88
75 and over	99

Source: Albert J. Mayer, "Differentials in Length of Life, City of Chicago: 1880–1940," unpublished Ph.D. dissertation, University of Chicago. Cited by Mendershausen in Goldsmith, *Saving in the U.S.*, III, p. 303. Also, see Albert J. Mayer and Philip M. Hauser, "Class Differentials in Expectation of Life at Birth," *Revue de l'Institut International de Statistique*, No. 314, 1950, pp. 197–200. Reprinted in *Class, Status, and Power*, R. Bendix and S. Lipset (eds.), Glencoe, 1953, pp. 281–284.

men's social mortality gradient from all causes must be very small compared with the contribution made by the accompanying environmental, economic, or selective factors."[8] A follow-up study of British experience showed an important narrowing of occupational differences over time, and particularly in 1921–31.[9]

[6] *Death Rates by Occupation Based on Data of the United States Census Bureau, 1930*, New York, 1934.
[7] Cited by Louis I. Dublin, Alfred J. Lotka, and Mortimer Spiegelman, *Length of Life*, rev. ed., New York, 1949, p. 214.
[8] *Ibid.*, p. 215.
[9] *Registrar-General's Decennial Supplement, England and Wales*, 1951, Part I, London, 1954. For further analysis of these findings and comment on the issues, see W. P. D. Logan, "Social Class Variation in Mortality," *Public Health Reports*, December 1954, pp. 1217–1223; Ian Sutherland, *British Journal of Social Medicine*, April 1947, pp. 126–134; and J. Daric, *Mortality by Occupation and Socio-Economic Status*, Vital Statistics-Special Report, Vol. 33, No. 10, Washington, 1951. A critical review of the Registrar-General's report appears in the *Journal of the Institute of Actuaries*, June 1955, pp. 85–87. Also relevant are Mortimer Spiegelman, "Recent Trends and Determinants of Mortality in Highly Developed Countries," *Trends and Differentials in Mortality*, New York, 1956, pp. 51–60; Harold F. Dorn, "Some Problems for Research in Mortality and Morbidity," *Public Health Reports*, January 1956; C. Horace Hamilton, "Ecological and Social Factors in Mortality," *Eugenics Quarterly*, December 1955; Leon Tabah, "Mortality According to Social Class," *Le Concours Medical*, July 1955; and Jena Redei, "Differential Mortality in Capitalist Countries," *Statisztikai Szemle*, January 1956.

The leading work on occupational differences in mortality in the United States is that of I. M. Moriyama and L. Guralnick,[10] which is for 1950. They found that the standardized mortality ratio (which is an age-adjusted rate shown as a ratio to the average death rate for all men 20 to 65) ranges, for five broad occupation levels, from 84 for the professions to 165 for laborers. However, the ratios for the first four groups are relatively close together. These groups are professional workers; technical, administrative, and managerial workers; proprietors, clerical, sales, and skilled workers; and semiskilled workers. Their respective ratios are 84, 87, 96, and 100. The clearest pattern of high occupational status associated with low mortality is found at the

TABLE 17
Professional, Technical, Administrative, and Managerial Mortality as a Percentage of White Male Mortality, United States, 1950

Age Group	Per Cent
20 to 25	78.1
25 to 30	66.9
30 to 35	70.1
35 to 45	91.5
45 to 55	95.1
55 to 60	102.1
60 to 65	100.5
65 and over	n.a.

Source: Derived from Moriyama and Guralnick in *Trends and Differentials in Mortality*, Figure 1, p. 67.

younger ages, under 45. For ages 55 to 65, the curves for the first four groups overlap considerably.[11]

Presumably the experience of the top two occupational classes, which include 13 per cent of the labor force, is most nearly applicable to the top wealth-holder group. The combined experience of those two classes is expressed as a percentage of white male mortality in Table 17, which shows a clear class advantage at younger ages but no advantage at all after 55. A similar age pattern was found independently for physicians compared to the white male population.[12]

[10] "Occupational and Social Class Differences in Mortality," *Trends and Differentials in Mortality*, pp. 61–73.
[11] *Ibid.*, pp. 66–68.
[12] Frank Dickinson and L. W. Martin, "Physician Mortality, 1949–51," *Journal of American Medical Association*, December 15, 1956, pp. 1462–1468. For further discussion of the occupational difference and fragmentary evidence of mortality differences by educational level, see Dublin, *et al.*, *Length of Life*, Chap. 11.

Insurance companies have, of course, an economic interest in knowing how mortality differs among various groups. They have not, however, made any systematic study of the variation in mortality by income or wealth classes. Mortality by type and size of insurance policy bears on the problem at hand, but it is difficult to know how much weight to attach to the findings because of possible differences in medical selection. The Metropolitan Life Insurance Company has published serially the mortality of persons insured under industrial premium-paying policies[13] and it is significantly higher than that for all categories of buyers of ordinary life insurance. In turn, the mortality of all buyers of ordinary life insurance is higher than that of those

TABLE 18
Mortality of Ordinary Life and $5,000 Whole-Life Policyholders as a Percentage of White Male Mortality, United States, 1953

Age Group	Per Cent
20 to 25	55.5
25 to 30	68.4
30 to 35	68.5
35 to 45	56.8
45 to 55	70.2
55 to 60	88.9
60 to 65	79.5
65 to 70	85.5
70 to 75	93.4
75 to 80	84.5
80 to 85	89.2
85 and over	86.2

buying relatively large life insurance policies. The records of one large insurance company, which were made available to us, reveal an extraordinarily low mortality for men holding whole-life policies of $5,000 or more and under age 50, and an experience similar to that of all ordinary life policy-holders after age 50. This particular series shows instability over the years, and is not altogether convincing as evidence of the more favorable mortality rate of the top income and wealth classes within the top occupational groups. However, it does provide some basis for believing that the occupational data should be corrected for a lower mortality.

Table 18 shows the relationship between the mortality of white males and that of a synthetic group of nonindustrial life insurance policyholders in 1953. The finding is synthesized from the records of

[13] See issues of that company's *Statistical Bulletin*.

all ordinary life insurance and of $5,000 and over whole-life policies. In both cases, the effect of medical selection has been minimized by recording only the deaths which occurred more than five years after the policy was issued. Equal weight was accorded to the two groups' experiences.

In deciding how much weight to give to the occupational and insurance data on differential mortality, we have been aided by the counsel of actuaries and others in the insurance industry, as well as specialists in demography.[14] This counsel is, however, divided and inconclusive. There is general agreement that mortality differences have narrowed over time, but there is also considerable uncertainty about the dimensions of socio-economic differences and the reasons for those differences.[15] While the size of life insurance policy information cited above suggests there is a positive correlation between economic status and favorable mortality rates, one careful observer of group life insurance and pension plans concludes that experience provides us with no evidence that "the executive dies sooner or later than the clerk."

In view of the uncertainty that surrounds this matter, it would seem desirable to use two sets of mortality rates which bracket the possible range. At one end of the range is the mortality for all whites. At the other end is a composite of the mortality reported for the upper occupational groups and the holders of large insurance policies. The procedure used to select the latter set of rates, which are hereafter referred to as "adjusted mortality rates," is portrayed graphically in Chart 5. In that figure three sets of mortality rates are plotted for 1953. The top line is for white males. The line for the upper two occupational classes combined lies well below the line for white males at younger ages, but touches it at age 55 (cf. Table 17). The line representing those holding large insurance policies (cf. Table 18) stays well below the line for white males across all the age brackets. The adjusted mortality rate is derived by drawing a line which splits the difference between the occupational and insurance data up to age

---

[14] Those who have been helpful on this issue include Mortimer Spiegelman, Ray M. Peterson, Morris Pitler, Mrs. Eleanor Daniel, Irving Rosenthal, Lillian Guralnick, and Ansley Coale.

[15] For a good reflection of the uncertainty, see William K. White, "Actuarial Bases: Mortality Levels," *Proceedings of New York University Tenth Annual Conference on Labor,* Emmanuel Stein (ed.), New York, 1957, pp. 103–119. This author, who is actuary of Aetna Life Insurance Company, points out that in pension planning practice " . . . any number of differing mortality bases are being used" (p. 118).

AND THE ESTATE-MULTIPLIER METHOD

CHART 5
Derivation of Adjusted Mortality Rates for Males, 1953

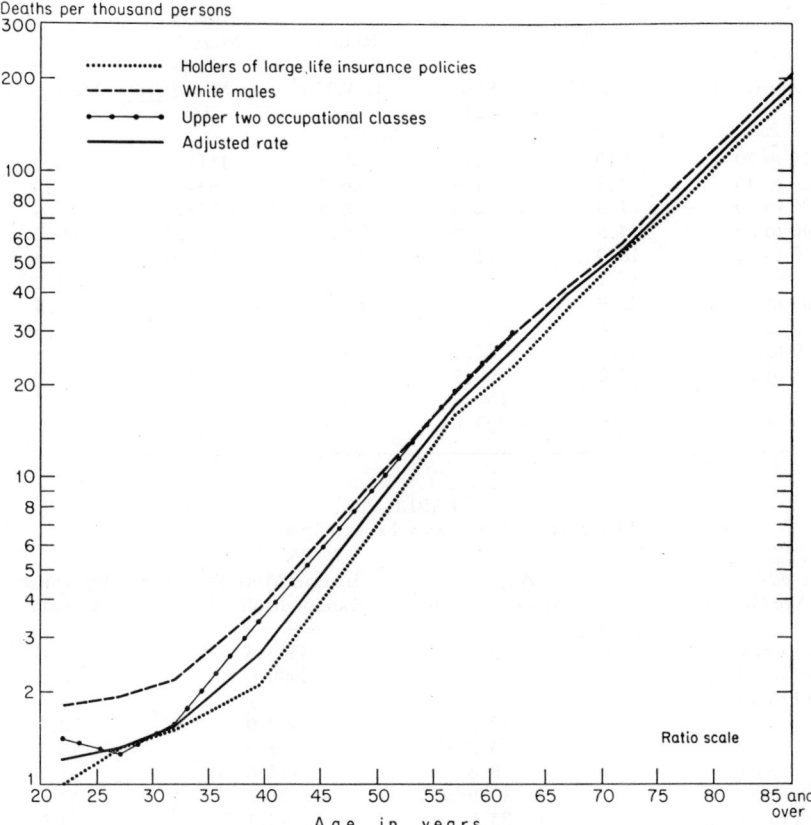

Source: Tables 17, 18, and 19. The adjusted rate is derived by inspection (see text).

65 and then continues midway between the lines for white males and for insurance holders. The rates were then read off the adjusted mortality line and are shown in Table 19.[16] The relationship these rates bear to white male rates for the same year, which may be observed in column 3 of Table 19, is the basis for the calculation of a set of adjusted mortality rates for females (Table 20). Table 21 gives the white rates and multipliers for both males and females. A full set of white and adjusted rates for every year for which the estate tax data have age information is reproduced in Appendix A.

[16] Mendershausen used for his selected risk rates the experience of holders of large life insurance policies. This line would make an erratic pattern across but generally below the insurance line shown in Chart 5. Several British studies referred to in Chapter 6 have used mortality rates for selected occupational classes.

TABLE 19
Adjusted Mortality Rates and Multipliers for Males, 1953

Age Group	Mortality Rate		Ratio of Adjusted to White	Inverse Mortality Rate or Multiplier	Insurance Multiplier
	Adjusted (1)	White (2)	(3)	(4)	(5)
15 to 20	0.9	1.3	69.2	1111.1	50.0
20 to 30	1.2	1.8	66.7	833.3	37.5
30 to 40	1.8	2.3	78.3	555.6	45.6
40 to 50	4.5	5.9	76.3	222.2	40.2
50 to 55	10.0	11.9	84.0	100.0	30.3
55 to 60	17.1	18.5	92.4	58.5	22.2
60 to 65	25.9	28.2	91.8	38.6	17.5
65 to 70	39.1	41.5	94.2	25.6	13.3
70 to 75	54.9	57.8	95.0	18.2	10.5
75 to 80	83.0	90.5	91.7	12.0	7.7
80 to 85	125.0	134.6	92.9	8.0	5.7
85 and over	189.0	203.1	93.1	5.3	4.1

TABLE 20
Adjusted Mortality Rates and Multipliers for Females, 1953

Age Group	Adjusted Mortality Rate	Inverse Mortality Rate or Multiplier	Insurance Multiplier
15 to 20	0.3	3333.3	150.0
20 to 30	0.5	2000.0	90.0
30 to 40	1.1	909.1	74.5
40 to 50	2.5	400.0	72.4
50 to 55	5.2	192.3	58.3
55 to 60	8.8	113.6	43.2
60 to 65	13.9	71.9	32.6
65 to 70	23.6	42.4	22.0
70 to 75	37.1	27.0	15.6
75 to 80	62.2	16.1	10.3
80 to 85	104.4	9.6	6.8
85 and over	174.4	5.7	4.5

ILLUSTRATION OF ESTATE-MULTIPLIER METHOD

The inverse of the appropriate year's mortality rate for a given age-sex group is used as the "estate-multiplier" for that group. The reader may follow the multiplier process through by reference to Tables 13, 19, and 22. For example, consider the age-sex group of males aged 40 to 50. The 1953 sample in that group was 1,213 (col. 1, Table 13). The adjusted multiplier for that year and for that age-sex group is 222.2 (col. 4, Table 19). Hence, 1,213 multiplied by 222.2 is 269,-529, which is then the estimated number of living men aged 40 to 50 with $60,000 or more of estate tax wealth in 1953 (Table 22).

TABLE 21
Mortality Rates and Multipliers for Total U.S. White Population, Male and Female, 1953

	DEATHS PER 1,000 POPULATION					
	Mortality Rates			Inverse Mortality Rates		
AGE GROUP	Both Sexes	Male	Female	Both Sexes	Male	Female
15 to 20	0.9	1.3	0.5	1111.1	769.2	2000.0
20 to 30	1.2	1.8	0.8	833.3	555.6	1250.0
30 to 40	1.8	2.3	1.4	555.6	434.8	714.3
40 to 50	4.6	5.9	3.3	217.4	169.5	303.0
50 to 55	9.0	11.9	6.2	111.1	84.0	161.3
55 to 60	13.9	18.5	9.5	71.9	54.1	105.3
60 to 65	21.6	28.2	15.1	46.3	35.5	66.2
65 to 70	33.0	41.5	25.0	30.3	24.1	40.0
70 to 75	47.8	57.8	39.1	20.9	17.3	25.6
75 to 80	78.2	90.5	67.8	12.8	11.0	14.7
80 to 85	122.2	134.6	112.4	8.2	7.4	8.9
85 and over	193.8	203.1	187.3	5.2	4.9	5.3

Similarly, the amount of each type of asset (except for insurance) held by the age-sex sample group is multiplied by 222.2. For example, the group held $49,680,000 worth of real estate (col. 2, Table 13), which is raised to $11,038,896,000 (Table 22). Table 23 gives the estate tax wealth thus estimated for both sexes.

A full set of tables showing the estimated number of living persons by age group or by age-sex groups for all years other than 1953 for which age data are given in estate tax data is included in Appendix A. Estimates are made using both white and adjusted mortality rates. One age table for 1953 on the basis of white mortality rates is included.

Construction of similar tables by estate size (for example, Table 24) rather than by age is based on the same procedure as that detailed above for Table 22. However, more steps are involved since the amount of property in each age-sex group must be computed separately and then all property in the several age-sex groups within each estate size must be totaled to get the aggregate of wealth in each estate size. Hence, the value of real estate in estates of $60,000 to $70,000, found to be $3.8 million in Table 24 (col. 3, row 2), is the result of summing the estimates for real estate for all age-sex groups.[17]

---

[17] The multiplying process in this case begins with tables of which Appendix Table A-1 is a specimen. The totals at the bottom of that table, after multiplication across each age row by the appropriate multipliers for the age-sex group, and after totaling down each column, will represent the number of persons and the amount of each type of property in the group of males in non-community property states with between $60,000 and $70,000 of gross estate.

TABLE 22

ESTIMATED ESTATE TAX WEALTH[a] OF MALES, BY TYPE OF PROPERTY AND AGE GROUP, 1953
(million dollars)

Type of Property	Total	Under 21	21 to 30	30 to 40	40 to 50	50 to 55	55 to 60	60 to 65	65 to 70	70 to 75	75 to 80	80 to 85	85 and over
No. of wealth-holders	1,084,065	5,555	30,832	135,011	269,529	147,700	138,645	123,559	94,310	64,847	40,428	21,040	12,609
Average gross estate	$162,372	$136,969	$203,554	$104,902	$142,667	$155,240	$165,912	$181,063	$196,600	$206,820	$209,558	$219,581	$239,482
Real estate	43,859	157	478	4,661	11,039	5,924	5,810	5,490	4,156	2,814	1,733	1,015	582
U.S. govt. bonds	8,927	121	217	364	1,540	1,109	1,279	1,200	994	860	592	372	279
State and local bonds	2,802	—	201	103	289	162	361	440	400	374	189	156	127
Other bonds	1,558	32	104	125	244	109	164	237	152	170	103	68	50
Stock	62,322	378	3,117	3,785	11,683	7,558	7,755	7,896	7,369	5,663	3,772	1,942	1,404
Cash	16,223	33	620	996	2,920	2,224	2,164	2,230	1,934	1,379	907	509	307
Mortgages and notes	6,580	1	144	487	1,258	962	966	839	816	517	338	163	89
Life insurance	8,147	5	42	413	1,661	1,199	1,321	1,359	997	620	326	145	59
Misc. property	25,605	34	1,352	3,228	7,820	3,683	3,184	2,682	1,724	1,015	512	249	122
Gross estate	176,022	761	6,276	14,163	38,453	22,929	23,003	22,372	18,542	13,412	8,472	4,620	3,019
Debts and mortgages	19,848	9	388	2,918	6,179	2,977	2,679	2,206	1,231	675	318	145	123
Economic estate	156,179	752	5,888	11,245	32,274	19,952	20,325	20,165	17,314	12,737	8,154	4,475	2,897

[a] Adjusted mortality rates have been used, insurance amounts have been reduced to estimated equities, and no correction has been made for returns with age unspecified.

TABLE 23

Estimated Estate Tax Wealth[a] of Both Sexes, by Type of Property and Age Group, 1953
(million dollars)

Type of Property	Total	Under 21	21 to 30	30 to 40	40 to 50	50 to 55	55 to 60	60 to 65	65 to 70	70 to 75	75 to 80	80 to 85	85 and over
No. of wealth-holders	1,609,538	12,223	46,832	186,830	369,929	213,467	199,648	182,517	147,904	110,369	73,723	40,816	25,280
Average gross estate	$182,002	$189,397	$166,809	$232,257	$182,975	$155,185	$164,188	$178,071	$190,245	$205,356	$201,520	$220,550	$222,705
Real estate	65,736	257	794	7,060	15,860	8,764	8,432	8,033	6,102	4,618	2,985	1,731	1,070
U.S. govt. bonds	16,370	144	245	979	4,022	1,742	1,968	1,832	1,634	1,518	1,059	697	530
State and local bonds	10,241	97	201	1,358	3,913	369	532	801	500	1,038	449	398	285
Other bonds	2,757	32	120	332	382	194	301	338	292	316	195	154	101
Stock	114,747	478	3,989	17,799	23,380	11,022	11,541	11,773	11,457	9,757	6,734	4,184	2,633
Cash	27,014	63	672	3,008	4,899	3,139	3,182	3,449	3,046	2,365	1,664	953	574
Mortgages and notes	10,021	1	230	702	2,336	1,318	1,331	1,193	1,214	758	526	265	147
Life insurance	8,735	6	46	445	1,740	1,277	1,415	1,470	1,057	683	364	164	68
Misc. property	37,320	1,237	1,514	4,741	11,127	5,303	4,079	3,613	2,536	1,612	881	455	222
Gross estate	292,940	2,315	7,812	36,425	67,688	33,127	32,780	32,501	28,138	22,665	14,857	9,002	5,630
Debts and mortgages	25,714	22	448	4,638	7,647	3,719	3,168	2,616	1,582	978	485	229	182
Economic estate	267,231	2,293	7,354	31,787	60,041	29,408	29,613	29,884	26,559	21,687	14,372	8,773	5,449

[a] Adjusted mortality rates have been used, insurance amounts have been reduced to estimated equities, and no correction has been made for returns with age unspecified.

TABLE 24

Estimated Estate Tax Wealth[a] of Both Sexes, by Estate Size and Type of Property, 1953
(million dollars)

Type of Property	Total	Under 60	60 to 70	70 to 80	80 to 90	90 to 100	100 to 120	120 to 150	150 to 200	200 to 300	300 to 500	500 to 1,000	1,000 to 2,000	2,000 to 3,000	3,000 to 5,000	5,000 to 10,000	10,000 and over
No. of wealth-holders	1,609,530	1,492	175,562	171,238	168,705	146,874	217,732	210,067	180,721	162,904	98,173	49,386	18,449	3,922	2,191	1,522	591
Real estate	$65,623	$14	$3,809	$4,310	$4,848	$4,440	$7,246	$7,572	$8,235	$9,329	$6,762	$4,608	$2,453	$1,214	$358	$293	$132
U.S. govt. bonds	16,359	3	732	778	760	771	1,291	1,480	1,656	1,678	1,794	2,033	697	333	488	109	1,756
State and local bonds	10,242	0	16	8	11	25	31	73	69	229	578	1,060	1,686	1,174	914	616	3,752
Other bonds	2,848	0	147	62	80	103	125	255	199	405	504	422	246	58	124	86	32
Stock	114,750	49	2,106	2,376	2,820	2,930	5,445	6,805	8,364	12,211	14,546	16,141	14,329	4,265	4,571	10,339	7,453
Cash	27,019	7	1,559	1,610	1,414	1,489	2,399	2,772	2,676	3,218	2,706	2,347	1,676	1,253	625	735	533
Mortgages and notes	10,105	0	470	501	522	516	749	1,107	1,187	1,614	1,171	975	525	134	56	55	523
Life insurance	8,634	1	335	437	504	493	880	1,024	1,293	1,388	1,026	702	330	95	54	50	22
Misc. property	37,232	5	1,370	1,614	1,757	1,767	3,054	3,885	4,093	5,233	5,437	4,023	2,383	1,187	925	292	207
Gross estate	292,803	79	10,545	11,696	12,716	12,531	21,218	24,972	27,771	35,308	34,520	32,311	24,324	9,712	8,115	12,575	14,410
Debts and mortgages	25,647	3	750	847	1,274	1,127	1,969	2,389	2,938	4,431	3,688	2,577	1,421	1,175	639	313	106
Economic estate	267,158	76	9,795	10,850	11,441	11,404	19,249	22,583	24,831	30,878	30,833	29,734	22,902	8,537	7,477	12,262	14,305

[a] Adjusted mortality rates have been used, insurance amounts have been reduced to estimated equities, and no correction has been made for returns with age unspecified.

AND THE ESTATE-MULTIPLIER METHOD

The detailed tabulation necessary for tables on estate size by type of property is available only for 1944 and 1953. However, it is possible to make a simple breakdown by gross estate size for 1948, 1949, and 1950. Also, size distributions of net or economic estate are possible to estimate for 1922, 1944, and 1946. All these estimates are included in Appendix A.

The importance of the set of mortality rates selected to serve as the basis for multiplying is highlighted in Table 25, which shows estimates of 1953 aggregates based on the white and adjusted multipliers. The estimate of number of estate tax wealth-holders based on adjusted rates is 1.6 million, which is 17 per cent higher than that based upon

TABLE 25
DIFFERENT ESTIMATES OF NUMBER OF ESTATE TAX WEALTH-HOLDERS AND AGGREGATE ESTATE TAX WEALTH IN 1953[a]

| | MORTALITY RATES | | | | | |
| | White | | | Adjusted | | |
	Total	Male	Female	Total	Male	Female
No. of estate tax wealth-holders	1,371,187	920,186	451,001	1,609,538	1,084,066	525,472
Gross estate with insurance correction ($ mill.)	249,884	150,270	98,619	292,940	176,022	116,918
Economic estate with insurance correction ($ mill.)	228,415	133,665	93,755	267,231	156,179	111,052

[a] For returns with age specified.

white mortality rates. Also, the adjusted rates give a somewhat younger group of wealth-holders (with a median age of 55 compared to a median of 56 for the white rates) and a slightly higher ratio of females (2.06 males per female using the adjusted rates, and 2.04 using the white rates). There are no important differences in composition of estate by type of property which follow from the shift in mortality rates.

TWO ADJUSTMENTS TO BASIC DATA

In every year for which the tabulation of estate tax returns includes age data, there are some returns on which age is unknown or unspecified. Rather than throw these returns away, we have elected to blow them up by the average multiplier used in the estate-multiplier process for the sex group. This average multiplier, or "devolution rate," is computed by dividing the number of persons (or wealth) in

TABLE 26

ESTIMATION OF LIVING ESTATE TAX WEALTH-HOLDERS AND AGGREGATE GROSS OR ECONOMIC ESTATE FROM ESTATE TAX RETURNS INCLUDING THOSE WITHOUT AGE INFORMATION, SELECTED YEARS, 1922–53[a]

Year	No. of Decedents on Returns (1)	Personal Devolution Rate (2)	Estimated Number of Living Wealth-Holders (3)	Amount of Estate on Returns[b] ($ bill.)		Economic or Gross Estate Devolution Rate (6)	Estimated Amount of Estate of Living Wealth-Holders[b] ($ bill.)	
				Economic (4)	Gross (5)		Economic (7)	Gross (8)
			USING WHITE MORTALITY RATES					
1922[c]	13,013	34.9	454,154	2.2		33.8	74.4	—
1924[c]	14,013	35.3	494,659	2.6		31.2	81.1	—
1941[c]	16,215	32.6	528,609	2.6		27.8	72.3	—
1944[c]	15,898	41.5	659,767	3.2		36.8	117.8	—
1946[c]	20,899	41.1	858,949	4.0		36.4	145.6	—
1947	23,356	41.4	966,938		4.8	—	—	167.1
1948	24,552	38.2	937,886		4.9	34.1	—	177.9
1949	25,858	38.8	1,003,290		4.9	36.3	—	192.5
1950	27,958	38.6	1,079,179		5.5	35.0	—	
1953	36,699	38.6	1,416,581		7.4		235.2[d]	257.2[d]
			USING ADJUSTED MORTALITY RATES					
1922	13,013	39.8	517,370	2.2		37.0	81.3[d]	—
1924	14,013		—	2.6		33.3	86.6[d]	—
1941	16,215		—	2.6				
1944	15,898	49.3	782,173	3.2		39.0	124.7[d]	—
1946	20,899	50.0	1,044,950	4.0		38.3	153.2[d]	—
1947	23,356	43.4	1,013,650		4.8		—	196.0
1948	24,552	45.1	1,107,295		4.9	40.0	—	209.2
1949	25,858	45.9	1,186,882		4.9	42.7	—	236.2
1950	27,958	45.4	1,268,909		5.5	42.7	—	
1953	36,699	45.4	1,658,795		7.4	41.8	281.5[d]	309.3[d]

[a] Before insurance adjustment. For more detail, see tables in Appendix A.
[b] No age information by economic estate available for 1947, 1948, 1949, and 1950. No age information by gross estate available for 1922, 1924, 1941, 1944, and 1946.
[c] These estimates are by Mendershausen in Goldsmith, *Saving in U.S.*, III, Table E-37.
[d] Adjusted to include only equity value of insurance.

the part of the sample with age specified into the result of the multiplier process for persons (or wealth). In 1953 the adjusted mortality devolution rate was 45.4 for both sexes combined (Table 26). Use of this devolution rate against the number of 1953 decedent estate tax wealth-holders for whom no age was specified (751 males and 459 females in Tables 13 and 14) results in raising the estimate of living estate tax wealth-holders from 1,609,530 to 1,658,795. Similar changes follow for aggregate gross or economic estate (Table 26). This adjustment is, of course, based upon the assumption that the age distribution within the age unknown group is the same as among those for whom age was specified.

One more adjustment may conveniently be handled in the multiplying process: the reduction of life insurance to equity or cash surrender value to place this asset on the same footing as other assets. Life insurance, quite unlike other assets, changes in value by the fact of death. In order to know the value of the insurance prior to death, an estimate must be made of the relationship which exists on the average between face value of insurance[18] and equity in insurance by age group. An estimate for 1944 was made by a sample study of one insurance company's ordinary life insurance policyholders. That study, as reported by Mendershausen,[19] concluded that equity ranged from 7 per cent of face value for the 20 to 30 age group to 81 per cent for the 85 and over age group. After consideration of the several issues involved, we decided to revise these ratios downward. The main fact supporting this decision is that the reserve ratio for all life insurance outstanding fell between 1944 and 1956 from 24.3 to 19.3 per cent. At the same time ordinary insurance has fallen in importance among all types of insurance (Table 27).

Our estimates of the 1953 relationships are shown in Table 28. The multipliers for insurance then are computed as a fraction of the general multipliers for each age-sex group. Thus, for the 20 to 30 age group of males the insurance multiplier is 4.5 per cent of 1,111.1, or 50. The full set of insurance multipliers for 1953 is shown in Tables 19 and 20.

Table 26 presents a summary of the data on estate tax returns

[18] Estate tax law calls for the reporting, not of face value, but of actual proceeds of insurance on the life of the decedent. Proceeds may differ from face value by virtue of policy loans outstanding, double-indemnity provisions, benefit options for beneficiaries, and for other reasons. These complications are ignored here. For a more complete discussion of the legal issues, see Chapter 3.

[19] In Goldsmith, *Saving in U.S.*, III, pp. 304–306.

TABLE 27
DATA ON LIFE INSURANCE POLICY RESERVES, 1944, 1953, AND 1956

Year	Policy Reserves (1)	Life Insurance in Force in U.S. (million dollars) (2)	Reserve Ratio (per cent) (3)	Percentage Ordinary Insurance Was of Total (per cent) (4)
1944	35,577	145,771	24.3	65.0
1953	66,683	304,259	21.9	60.8
1956	79,738	412,630	19.3	57.6

SOURCE: Cols. 1, 2, and 4: *Life Insurance Fact Book*, New York, 1957, pp. 57 and 8; col. 3: col. 1 ÷ col. 2.

TABLE 28
ESTIMATE OF AVERAGE RATIO OF EQUITY TO FACE VALUE OF LIFE INSURANCE BY AGE GROUP, 1953

Age	Percentage Equity Is of Face Value
20 to 30	4.5
30 to 40	8.2
40 to 50	18.1
50 to 55	30.3
55 to 60	38.0
60 to 65	45.4
65 to 70	52.0
70 to 75	57.9
75 to 80	64.2
80 to 85	71.2
85 and over	78.1
All age groups	23.9

and of estimates of total numbers of living estate tax wealth-holders and the aggregates of their wealth for selected years from 1922 through 1953. Separate estimates on the basis of white and adjusted mortality rates are shown and include a correction for those returns with age unspecified and, where possible, the reduction of life insurance to equity value. The only years for which gross estate by age information is available before 1953 are 1948, 1946, 1944, and 1941. For 1922 and 1924 the best data are for economic estate within net estate classes by age. In estimating the aggregate of economic estate from this data, it is assumed that the average amounts of net and economic estate per return do not vary with age. Mendershausen found that this assumption seemed to be justified by a test made with the 1944 data.[20]

[20] *Ibid.*, p. 294. Also compare his Tables E-53 and E-35.

CHAPTER 3

Adjustment of Basic Variant Estimates for 1953 to Approximate Aggregates of "Prime Wealth" and "Total Wealth"

ALTHOUGH the multiplying process described in Chapter 2 may be the most important "adjustment," at least in quantitative terms, of the basic data on top wealth-holders, the fragment of a wealth distribution thus derived differs in some important respects from the fragment that would be derived by an ideal census of the wealth of living persons. This chapter considers the deficiencies of the basic variant estimates as measured against ideal definitions and methods of valuation of wealth. Two such definitions are introduced. Prime wealth is defined as the wealth owned outright and over which the owner has full power of disposal. Total wealth includes prime wealth and also wealth to which a person does not necessarily have actual title but in which he has an income interest.

The deficiencies of the basic variant estimates spring from the fact that estate tax data record only the parts of estates that must be reported for tax purposes by statute, court decisions, and administrative regulation. Estate tax laws, as well as inheritance tax, gift tax, and income tax laws, provide incentives to avoid tax liability by such devices as division of property within the family through gift or bequest, personal trust funds, and life insurance. Evasion by nonreporting or underreporting may also contribute to the incompleteness of the data as wealth estimates.

Every student of wealth distribution who has worked with these data has been aware of deficiencies in them. Crum,[1] for example, wrote that "The estate tax data do not, obviously, constitute a satisfactory sample of the wealth holdings of living individuals. Not only do the observations apply to a date when many individuals have made property arrangements in anticipation of death or in recognition that active life is over; but they record the facts in terms of the

[1] W. L. Crum, *The Distribution of Wealth*, Boston, 1935, p. 20.

special definitions of the tax law, and exclude from the record a very large number of estates too small to be taxed." He continues as follows: "And yet these data reflect highly important facts concerning the distribution of wealth for this peculiarly defined sample, and they reveal such striking relationships that the analyst becomes the more eager to have equally precise data for a more inclusive sample of the entire population."

Similarly, the literature on taxes alerts us to possible difficulties in the data. Thus Harold M. Groves and Wallace I. Edwards assert that in the case of the estate tax " . . . as nowhere else in the tax system, opportunity is afforded to divide oneself like an amoeba in the face of progressive rates (and exemptions), thus defeating progression and creating a capricious relative tax burden."[2]

General Provisions of Estate Tax Law

It should be emphasized at the outset that our interest in estate tax law is here confined to its usefulness as a source of information about the wealth of persons. Hence, those provisions of the law which enable a person to minimize tax liability without altering his reporting of gross estate are generally of no concern in this chapter.

Before discussing in detail the particular ways in which estate tax data are deficient for wealth estimation, it will be useful to consider the nature and general provisions of the federal estate tax law. Technically, the estate tax is an excise imposed upon the transfer of wealth. Unlike inheritance taxes, which are based upon the receipt of transfers, the estate tax looks to the whole estate of the decedent transferor.[3]

An estate tax return is required for the estate of every citizen or resident of the United States whose gross estate value at death exceeds $60,000.[4] The return is due fifteen months after the decedent's

---

[2] "A New Model for an Integrated Transfer Tax," *National Tax Journal*, December 1953, pp. 353–360. For another discussion of the loopholes in the law, see C. Lowell Harriss, "Sources of Injustice in Death Taxation," *National Tax Journal*, December 1954, pp. 289–308. Also by the same author is "Erosion of the Federal Estate and Gift Tax Bases," *Proceedings of the Forty-Eighth Annual Conference on Taxation*, National Tax Association, 1955, pp. 350–358.

[3] Many interesting controversies arise out of the distinctions among wealth transferred, wealth held before death, and wealth received. Some property interests, of course, are of very different value to the transferor and transferee. For example, consider life insurance and interest in personal trust funds. The marital deduction makes the estate tax somewhat like an inheritance tax in that tax liability is determined by disposition of estate.

[4] *Statistics of Income for 1953*, Washington, 1956, pp. 63–69.

ADJUSTMENT OF BASIC VARIANT ESTIMATES

death, although an extension of time for filing may be granted upon request. Valuation of gross estate by the standard of "fair market value," defined as "the price at which the property would change hands between a willing buyer and a willing seller, neither being under any compulsion to buy or to sell and both having reasonable knowledge of relevant facts," may be declared either as of the date of the decedent's death or under the optional valuation, whichever the executor may elect. The optional valuation is determined as of the date one year after the decedent's death, except that property distributed, sold, exchanged, or otherwise disposed of within the year is valued as of the date of disposition. This provision for optional valuation does not affect the minimum value of gross estate for which a return must be filed.

In computing the tax base, deductions from gross estate are allowed for liabilities and indebtedness of the decedent at the time of death, administrative expenses, losses during administration, property previously taxed, transfers for public, charitable, and religious uses, bequests to surviving spouse, and specific exemption. Progressive tax rates run up to a maximum of 77 per cent of the portion of the net estate over $10,000,000. Tax credits are allowed in whole or in part for state inheritance taxes, gift taxes, and foreign death duties.

The various classes of property interests[5] which make up the gross estate are described in detail in the statute. Among the includable interests are the dower or curtesy interests of the surviving spouse, property held in certain forms of joint ownership with right of survivorship, interests subject to the decedent's general power of appointment, proceeds of insurance on the life of the decedent,[6] interest in a joint and survivor annuity, and in some cases, property transferred by the decedent during his lifetime. The Internal Revenue Code requires, with stated exceptions, the inclusion of all types of property without regard to its location, with the exception of real property situated outside the United States. In general, the code requires inclusion of property to the extent of any interest therein.[7] The includable interest may be held as a partner, as a tenant in common, under community prop-

[5] The following several paragraphs are based upon James B. Lewis, *The Estate Tax*, New York, 1957, pp. 2–16 and pp. 95–112.

[6] Such life insurance could be excluded in 1953 if the decedent did not pay the premiums and did not possess any of the incidents of ownership at the time of his death. In 1954 the incidents of ownership test was eliminated. Insurance upon the life of another person is includable.

[7] The property law of the particular state generally controls the extent of an individual's interest.

erty laws, or as an interest in trust income or trust corpus or in the estate of a prior decedent.

The gross estate also includes any property deemed to have been transferred in contemplation of death. Only property transferred less than three years before death is ever considered as such and the executor may undertake to rebut the presumption. Certain incomplete lifetime transfers, where the deceased had retained a "string" or right of some kind, are includable in his gross estate. As to transfer of trust property, only that property transferred by a general power of appointment is within reach of the statute.

Where property was held in joint ownership with a surviving spouse or other person, only that part of the property economically attributable to him is includable in the decedent's gross estate. The statute looks to the origin of the property as well as to the form of title in such determinations.

The valuation of items included in gross estate is, of course, the subject of much controversy and litigation involving taxpayers and the government. Such controversies are most likely to arise where there is no established market for the property or where each property is unique. Evidence called for in setting a valuation may include market quotations, sales prices, original cost, and expert appraisals. One authority observes that "the Commissioners and the Courts both tend to view the fixing of value as a compromise process."[8] Insurance on the life of the decedent is valued on the basis of the amount receivable upon his death. This amount may differ from the face value of the insurance by virtue of double-indemnity provisions, loans against the policy, or benefit options of beneficiaries. Life estates, annuities, remainders, and reversions are valued on the basis of the present worth of the promised income using stated mortality tables and a stated interest rate.[9]

Classification of Wealth Items and Tabulation by Type of Property

In making adjustments to the basic variant estimates, it is important to know how the various wealth items have been classified and tabulated. *Statistics of Income* shows, for recent years, nine types of property.

[8] Lewis, *Estate Tax*, p. 99.
[9] After 1953 the value of an annuity arising out of employer contributions to qualified pension, profit-sharing and stock bonus plans is exempt from inclusion in gross estate. Survivor benefits under Old Age and Survivors Insurance have never been includable.

ADJUSTMENT OF BASIC VARIANT ESTIMATES

Information for that breakdown was assembled from the various taxpayer schedules in which they were reported.

Real estate in this tabulation includes "all real property situated in the United States, regardless of the schedule in which it is reported and embraces contracts to buy land, real estate jointly owned, as well as transfers of real estate made during life (by trust or otherwise) other than bonafide sales, and real estate with respect to which decedent possessed a general power of appointment."[10]

Bonds are tabulated in three categories: federal, state and local, and other bonds. The two categories of government bonds include all such bonds whether the interest thereon is taxable, tax-exempt, or partly tax-exempt. Any interest accrued on "other bonds" at time of death is reported with the value of the bonds.

Corporate stock includes common and preferred shares and debenture stock of domestic and foreign corporations, building and loan or savings and loan shares or certificates, Federal Land Bank stock, and similar holdings in corporate enterprises evidenced by certificates of ownership. Dividends accrued at time of death on such holdings are reported with the value of the stock.

Cash includes currency on hand or in safety deposit, bank notes, checks, bank deposits, postal savings accounts, cash in brokers' accounts, building and loan accounts, savings and loan accounts and the like.

Mortgages and notes include promissory notes, loans, mortgages, trust deeds, and contracts to sell land.

Taxable insurance is life insurance carried on the life of the decedent. Most life insurance is included in gross estate whether receivable by the estate or by other beneficiaries.

Miscellaneous property is the value of all other property in the gross estate not elsewhere tabulated, such as judgments, leaseholds, mineral and patent rights, pensions, royalties, tax sale certificates, debts due decedent, interest in unincorporated business, household goods and personal effects, farm products and growing crops, livestock, farm machinery, automobiles, shares in copartnerships or trust funds, remainderman interest, and annuities unless reported as insurance.[11]

For purposes of this study a special tabulation was made of economic estate, defined as gross estate less debts and mortgages. Debts and mortgages, in turn, are defined as " . . . all valid debts of the decedent existing at time of death whether or not then matured. In-

---
[10] *Statistics of Income for 1953*, p. 67.
[11] *Ibid.*

cluded are obligations secured by mortgages, notes secured by collateral, promissory notes, debts, claims against the decedent at date of death or other unsecured liens, and bonafide pledges or subscriptions of the decedent to make a contribution or gift for the use of religious, public, or charitable organizations."[12]

Adjustments to Basic Variant Estimates

As discussed above, the estate tax returns provide a "peculiar" sample for estimating the distribution of wealth among living persons. Correction is made for the main peculiarity—the nonrepresentative age

TABLE 29

SUMMARY OF ADJUSTMENTS MADE IN ESTIMATING BASIC, PRIME, AND TOTAL WEALTH VARIANTS OF ESTATE TAX WEALTH AND WEALTH-HOLDERS, 1953

	Persons	Wealth
Unadjusted basic variant	1,609,530	$292,803,000,000
Account for those returns with age unspecified	+49,265	+16,400,000,000
Basic variant	1,658,795	309,203,000,000
Those originally included with less than $60,000 gross estate	−1,492	−79,000,000
Wealth-holder overcount after reduction from face value of life insurance to equity	−111,704	−7,976,404,000
Underreporting by taxpayers	+75,000	+33,800,000,000
Gifts in "float"	+500	+60,000,000
Proceeds of life insurance in "float"	+4,513	+451,280,000
Trust property included		−6,000,000,000
Annuities and pensions included		−2,000,000,000
Total adjustments	−33,183	+18,255,876,000
Prime wealth variant	1,625,612	327,458,876,000
Personal trust funds	+50,000	+44,000,000,000
Annuities	+100,000	+5,300,000,000
Pensions, private		+1,900,000,000
Pensions, government		+2,400,000,000
Total adjustments	+150,000	+53,600,000,000
Total wealth variant	1,775,612	381,058,876,000

distribution—in the estate-multiplier process by the use of age-sex specific inverse mortality rates. A second peculiarity was also compensated for by using different multipliers for insurance to reduce the amounts reported for that asset to estimated equity. Both these corrections are discussed in Chapter 2.

[12] *Ibid.*

ADJUSTMENT OF BASIC VARIANT ESTIMATES

A list of further adjustments and the quantitative corrections arising from them for moving from basic variant to prime wealth and total wealth aggregates are summarized in Table 29. All these estimates are made on the basis of 1953 data. The items listed are discussed in order below. Several of the adjustments are necessarily crude and some turn upon quite arbitrary assumptions. Hence, the reader is cautioned against accepting them as facts. Our rough estimates lead to the conclusion that the basic variant aggregate estimates are not substantially different from a hypothetical and ideally arrived at estimate of prime wealth, but are considerably lower than the aggregates of total wealth. That is, we found that about 1.7 million persons had $309.2 billion of basic variant wealth; 1.6 million persons had $327.5 billion of prime wealth; and 1.8 million persons had $381.1 billion of total wealth.

There are two corrections which need to be made for overcounting of wealth-holders and aggregate gross estate. One is necessary because some decedents with less than $60,000 filed estate tax returns. The small correction called for is the subtraction of 1,492 wealth-holders and of $79 million of gross estate.[13]

OVERCOUNT ARISING FROM INSURANCE VALUATION

The second overcount arises from the fact that while the original returns include the face value of life insurance, we have, in the estate-multiplier process, reduced life insurance amounts to equities. Hence, some persons are included in the basic variant count even though they do not in fact have $60,000 when their insurance is thus reduced. In the basic variant estimates, the average size of gross estate in the $60,000 to $70,000 estate size group is only $60,051, which would

---

[13] Since legal peculiarities rather than economic realities govern the filing of returns with under $60,000 of gross estate, the information on decedents is of more interest than estimates of living persons in this class. These decedents were distributed among the age-sex groups as follows:

Age	Total	Non-Community Property		Community Property	
		Male	Female	Male	Female
Under 40	3	1	2	0	0
40 to 65	3	1	1	1	0
65 and over	17	9	5	2	1
Total	23	11	8	3	1

The sample size is only twenty-three, but it is otherwise notable only in that there is an overrepresentation of non-community property females. Composition of estate by type of property is not markedly different for this group than for the $60,000 to $70,000 gross estate class.

ADJUSTMENT OF BASIC VARIANT ESTIMATES

TABLE 30

ADJUSTMENTS TO NUMBER OF TOP WEALTH-HOLDERS AND AGGREGATE OF GROSS ESTATE DUE TO INSURANCE OVERCOUNT

Gross Estate Size (thous. dollars)	Numbers of Wealth-Holders Removed from Group					Estimated Average Gross Estate of Those Removed from Group (dollars)	Total Gross Estate Removed (dollars)
	Males, NCP States[a]	Males, CP States[b]	Females, NCP States[a]	Females CP States[b]	Total		
60 to 70	40,323	7,911	8,000	432	56,666	63,000	3,569,958,000
70 to 80	17,307	4,473			21,780	73,000	1,589,940,000
80 to 90	17,634	100			17,734	83,000	1,472,022,000
90 to 100	11,483				11,483	93,000	1,067,949,000
100 to 120	2,375				2,375	107,000	254,125,000
120 to 150	1,666				1,666	135,000	22,410,000
150 to 200							
Total	90,788	12,484	8,000	432	111,704		7,976,404,000

[a] NCP = Non-Community Property.
[b] CP = Community Property.

indicate that a considerable number in this class are not properly located in the ranking (Table 24). How much should the basic variant estimates be revised to take account of this revaluation of insurance?

Going back to the original tabulations and computing the face value of life insurance for living wealth-holders, we can obtain the average amount of face value minus equity per person in each age-sex group within each gross estate class. From these data we can, making certain assumptions, estimate the numbers in each age-sex group who should properly be ranked in a gross estate class of below $60,000. The necessary assumptions, which admittedly are very rough, are: (1) that in each age-sex group 60 per cent have $62,500 of gross estate and 40 per cent have $67,500; and (2) that within each age group of men 20 per cent have no insurance, 40 per cent have one-half the average face value minus equity found for the group, 20 per cent have one and a half times the average, and 20 per cent have twice the average; for women, that 30 per cent have no insurance, 25 per cent have one-half, 25 per cent have one and a half times, and 20 per cent have twice the average face value minus the equity.[14]

Following these assumptions, a total of 111,704 persons are reclassified as falling below the $60,000 gross estate class and $8 billion is removed from the aggregate gross estate. A summary of these calculations is shown in Table 30.

Most of the persons thus reclassified are men under 50. Few of the women, all of whom were in the $60,000 to $70,000 gross estate class, were found to be subjects for this reclassification. These findings are consistent with the knowledge that more men than women have insurance, that equity in insurance rises with age, and that the share of insurance in gross estate does not rise as estate size increases.

UNDERREPORTING

The first reason to suspect that estate tax data fail to indicate the full amount of "estate tax wealth" is the possibility of evasion by taxpayers. Not only may some of those who should file a return fail to do so, but there may also be underreporting of the full list of properties and undervaluation of some of the properties. It may be presumed that the number of persons who fail to file returns is quite small and

[14] These assumptions, which are critical in this calculation, are based upon data on insurance holdings of upper occupational and higher income groups as shown in *The Life Insurance Public*, New York, n.d., pp. 20–21.

ADJUSTMENT OF BASIC VARIANT ESTIMATES

that those who do so are mostly at the lower end of the estate size range.[15]

There is probably some underreporting, most commonly with tangible personalty (such as jewelry) and unregistered intangible property (such as cash). Undervaluation, especially according to a full market value standard, is also possible. The law provides for optional valuation dates which allow the executor of the estate some leeway in selecting a time most favorable to the taxpayer's interest.

It should also be pointed out that many extraordinarily difficult problems of valuation arise in administration of the estate tax. It is in regard to valuation that the greatest amount of death tax litigation arises. Among the most controversial subjects are the valuation of shares in closed corporations, interest in unincorporated business, and fractional and contingent interests in property through trust agreements. While we cannot venture far into this troubled territory of valuation and underreporting, it should be carefully noted that all the tabulated estate tax data are preaudit figures. C. Lowell Harriss made a special study of the effect of auditing on a sample of returns closed in 1941. He estimated the amount and distribution of additions to "net estate before specific exemption" resulting from audit and summarized his findings as follows:

On the average the increase was about one-tenth. It was somewhat greater for large than for small estates. The method of estimating, unfortunately, could not eliminate certain biases, and the data themselves are no better than the auditing process, which is by no means perfect. Some wealth which should be reported and taxed escapes the auditors; some, probably very much less, may be included improperly. On balance, the adjustment described in this article may fail by more than nominal amounts to account for all original underreporting. Unfortunately, there is no visible prospect of getting data which will offset the specific deficiencies which seem most serious, those resulting from poor taxpayer compliance. This poor compliance results in part from ignorance and in part from strong financial motives to reduce tax liability by minimizing

---

[15] The frequency distribution of wealth-holders, while highly skewed, does not rise as sharply with fall in estate size at the lower end of the range near $60,000 as one might expect a priori. The number in the $90,000 to $100,000 class was 147,000; in the $80,000 to $90,000 class, 169,000; in the $70,000 to $80,000 class, 171,000; in the $60,000 to $70,000 class, 176,000 (see Table 24). A possible explanation of this virtual flattening out of the frequency curve between $90,000 and $60,000 is that nonreporting is relatively more important near the minimum required for filing. The fact that the penalty for not reporting is not as large when no tax is due as when tax *is* due is, of course, a contributing factor. These facts have been borne in mind in estimating how many persons to add to the top wealth-holder group aside from those reporting $60,000 or more of gross estate.

ADJUSTMENT OF BASIC VARIANT ESTIMATES

the amount of wealth reported. The value of the adjustment may be questioned on other grounds. The basic data are . . . [for 1941]. The economy is obviously very different today from 1941. The writer suspects that the results of audit of estate tax returns have changed much less.[16]

Although Harriss' finding of a 10 per cent average increase due to auditing applies to net estate before specific exemption, it seems plausible to apply it without adjustment to our aggregates of gross and economic estate. It may tend to slightly overstate the case, since the auditing sometimes disallows deductions which reduce net estate before specific exemption but do not alter gross estate. On the other hand, this overstatement is undoubtedly offset by the tendency of audits to be on the low side of actual market value.

Harriss is unable to supply us with an estimate of the number of wealth-holders who should be added because of underreporting. Using data supplied in Harriss' article, we can make a rough estimate of the number of persons and the amount of wealth which should be transferred to the above $60,000 class from the group we have recorded as falling below that line. Since few of the smaller estates were adjusted upward by audit by more than 10 per cent, we may confine our attention to the $55,000 to $60,000 interval. In projecting the frequency of wealth-holders back below $60,000, it appears that a maximum of 150,000 persons would be in this class. Harriss found that about half of all returns were closed with no auditing change.[17] A maximum adjustment, therefore, would seem to be that half of those in the $55,000 to $60,000 class—75,000 persons—would have up to a 10 per cent adjustment which would be sufficient to move them up to $60,000 or more of gross estate. (See footnote 15 above.) 75,000 times $60,000 —$4.5 billion—should therefore be added to aggregate gross estate.

Thus it is concluded that underreporting and undervaluation should be corrected for by adding about 10 per cent to the aggregate of previously accounted for "estate tax wealth" and admitting another 75,000 to the group of "estate tax wealth-holders" along with their gross estates of $60,000 each. This correction as entered on Table 29 is $33.8 billion.

GIFTS

It is well known that by "estate planning" a person may seek to minimize his estate tax. The estate tax and the differential tax rates which

---

[16] C. Lowell Harriss, "Wealth Estimates as Affected by Audit of Estate Tax Returns," *National Tax Journal*, December 1949, p. 333.
[17] *Ibid.*, p. 321.

apply to gifts, as well as inheritance tax savings and income tax savings which follow from making gifts, provide an incentive to distribute property before death and undoubtedly equalize wealth-holding much more than would otherwise be the case.

Gifts and bequests are, of course, important determinants of the current distribution of wealth and one cannot look into all these transfers to find out what the distribution would be like without them. We are, however, interested in knowing how much wealth is actually in the possession of persons with at least $60,000 of gross estate but which we have not counted by the peculiar method of sampling that we have used.

One should not be so carried away by the emphasis on estate planning as to believe that tax minimization is the sole or even a major influence in wealth-holding decisions for all persons.[18] Neither should it be forgotten that planning to die with a certain estate is difficult. As Ecclesiastes (9:11) assures us " . . . time and chance happen to them all, for man does not know his time. Like fish which are taken in an evil net, and like birds which are caught in a snare, so the sons of men are snared at an evil time, when it suddenly falls upon them."

As far as outright gifts from one person to another are concerned, one should not leap to the conclusion that all such gifts are planned in preparation for death, nor that all gifts are excluded from the basic variant estate tax wealth estimate. Gifts determined to be "in contemplation of death" are properly to be counted in gross estate for tax purposes. Further, some of the wealth given away as *inter vivos* gifts by older persons (and hence not counted in their gross estates at time of death) is caught in the estimate of the gross estates of younger persons who received the gifts. Therefore, unless it can be demonstrated that either donors or donees have different mortality expectations from others in their age-sex groups,[19] the estate-multiplier method

---

[18] On this point W. L. Crum (*Distribution of Wealth,* p. 2) concluded that "The measurements of wealth afforded by the estate tax are impaired to an unknown degree by property arrangements made in anticipation of death. Some such arrangements are prompted merely by the desire of the property owner to carry into effect, under his living supervision, plans for the future distribution of his estate. Other arrangements are occasioned by the tax, and reflect the attempt of the property owner to organize his estate so that the tax will be minimized."

[19] It might seem reasonable to assume that persons, particularly at older ages, with shorter than average life expectancy for their age group, would be more likely to be donors than those with longer expectancies. To the extent that their gifts are not found to be "in contemplation of death," there is, then, an understatement of the total amount of estate tax wealth and of the size of the estates of old persons relative to those of younger persons. We have no evidence to support

ADJUSTMENT OF BASIC VARIANT ESTIMATES

may be assumed to give a generally accurate accounting of the "after-gifts" distribution of wealth.

It is useful to conceive of the problem this way. Consider three groups, each of which includes donors and donees.

A Non-Estate-Tax Wealth-Holders	B Estate Tax Wealth-Holders	C Nonpersonal Wealth-Holders
Donors	Donors	Donors
Donees	Donees	Donees

Now, every year a certain amount of wealth passes back and forth among and within these groups. Some of it passes at the time of death and some before. By making gifts before death, some persons transfer themselves from group B into group A. On the other hand, some persons, by virtue of being donees, move from group A into group B. In the case of a gift by a donor in group B to a donee in group C, the wealth moves outside the sphere of personally held wealth. We shall return to this case in the discussion of trust funds which follows.

In the case of a gift by a donor in group B to a donee in either group A or B in an earlier year (before 1953), we may assume that the donees share the same probability of dying in 1953 as all others of their age-sex group and hence are properly represented in the draw by death and subsequently in the multiplier process by which we derived the estimate of living "estate tax wealth-holders."[20] These probabilities are quite upset, however, in the case of gifts in 1953 by donors in group B who died in 1953. Their gross estates are reduced by the amount of the gifts, and it is highly unlikely that we picked up the donees in group B in the draw by death since many of the 1953 donors here considered died in the last half of 1953 and would have been unlikely to have made gifts to persons who died in the first half of 1953. Hence, we can refer to this amount as "float," or wealth which is not counted in the estate tax wealth estimate. This is undoubtedly a relatively small amount since no multiplication process is involved.

In 1953 there were 44,695 gift tax returns which reported a total

---

these assumptions, but this line of argument has been presented most persuasively to the author in conversation by Harold M. Groves.

[20] The "net deduction for property previously taxed" on 1953 estate tax returns was $30 million. This deduction applies to property taxed to another estate within the past five years either for gift tax or estate tax purposes.

A special problem exists in the case of a gift of life insurance on the life of the donor. This is discussed below in the section on proceeds of life insurance.

ADJUSTMENT OF BASIC VARIANT ESTIMATES

of $1,012,054,000 in gifts. All but $128,021,000 were noncharitable gifts, or gifts made to persons. There is no separate record of the share of these gifts made by persons who died in 1953. A very liberal estimate would be $200 million. Some of this amount, moreover, should be subtracted to compensate for some double-counting on both gift tax and estate tax returns of gifts determined to be "in contemplation of death." The 1953 estate tax returns claimed credit for gift tax paid of $2,093,000, which reflects a gift total of about $8 million. Perhaps one half of the latter was actually transferred in 1953. This indicates that perhaps as much as $4 million of gifts were determined to be in contemplation of death and included in the gross estate of decedents of that year. When submitted to the estate-multiplier process, this $4 million was translated into $160 million of estate tax wealth. Hence, our estimate of estate tax wealth already may include as much as $160 million of "float." $200 million minus $160 million equals $40 million, which is our estimate of gifts not previously counted.

It is, of course, possible that some of the donees of this $40 million are, through the receipt of gifts, raised into the $60,000 and over wealth class. We have no clues to what this number would be. To illustrate the problem, however, let us assume that the $40 million was given in equal parcels of $20,000 each to 2,000 donees. Suppose further that 1,000 of them were in the under $60,000 class and that 500 of them were thus moved into the over $60,000 class, bringing with them $40,000 of wealth apiece, totaling 500 times $40,000, or $20 million. Lacking any better evidence on this question, we estimate the full adjustment necessary for gifts "in float" to be an addition of 500 individuals to the wealth-holder total and an addition of $60 million ($40 million in float in 1953 plus $20 million of estate added by elevating the 500 persons into the $60,000 and over class) to the aggregate gross estate.[21]

---

[21] This conclusion that virtually nothing should be added to the "estate tax wealth" total because of *inter vivos* gifts is in sharp contrast to Mendershausen's conclusion that about 10 per cent of net estate should be added. He reasoned that since gifts in each year have averaged about 10 per cent of net estate and since gifts are encouraged by the estate tax, the estates of decedents filing estate tax returns were smaller by the amount of the gift total of one year. Following this line, he added 10 per cent to the inflated gross estate figure (this would mean an adjustment of $29 billion in 1953) to approximate the corrected wealth estimate. This procedure is wrong on three counts. First, it quite overlooks the fact that while estates of some decedents are smaller because of *inter vivos* gifts, others are larger. Second, it multiplies the gifts by the inverse mortality rates, when the gifts are, unlike the estates in the sample, an actual and full count of the transfers (with the exception of unreported gifts) during the year and hence do not need to be

ADJUSTMENT OF BASIC VARIANT ESTIMATES

PROCEEDS OF LIFE INSURANCE

The same problem of "float" appears with regard to the proceeds of life insurance on the lives of 1953 decedents. Here again we have a problem of transfer during the year of the sampling by death and less than random chance of drawing the insurance beneficiaries. It will be recalled that the estimating of estate tax wealth above involved multiplying the equity in life insurance owned by decedents. But what about the face value of the life insurance on the lives of the decedents of 1953? It should be noted that the life insurance proceeds following from deaths of earlier years are fully exposed to the "sampling-by-death" process.

The face value minus the policy holders' equity in insurance on the lives of 1953 estate tax wealth-holder decedents was $361 million. Some part of this amount undoubtedly goes to living persons with less than $60,000 of gross estate. Following the same assumptions as those made above for gifts to persons with less than $60,000, if the insurance proceeds were divided into $20,000 parcels and if half went to persons with less than $60,000, half of whom were thereby raised into the over $60,000 class, there would be 4,513 additional wealth-holders[22] who would bring an additional $270,780,000 of gross estate into the count. There would also be 9,025 beneficiaries who were already in the group of estate tax wealth-holders and who would have $180,500,000 which should be added to gross estate. The final estimate of the necessary correction for the effect of life insurance proceeds is: addition of 4,513 beneficiaries and addition of $451,280,000 to aggregate gross estate.

There is another matter having to do with life insurance which should be mentioned here. It is possible to make a gift of life insurance on one's life. By having the policy fully paid up and by having no incidents of ownership in the policy, the insured is legally entitled to exclude the full amount of the policy from his estate tax return. A 1954 amendment to the law widened this avenue of tax avoidance. Presumably the named beneficiary of such an insurance policy would

---

multiplied. Third, if one really wanted to know the pattern of estates before the effects of the estate tax were felt, he should include all gifts which could plausibly be interpreted as being made "in preparation" for death and not merely the arbitrary sum of one year's gifts. The latter sum may, indeed, include some gifts not properly assignable to the tax effect. There are, of course, many motives for making gifts other than minimizing estate tax.

[22] Method: 18,050 beneficiaries, 9,025 under $60,000, 4,513 raised to over $60,000. 4,513 times $60,000 equals $270,780,000 of additional gross estate.

value the policy on his estate tax return, if he predeceased the insured, by reckoning the face value discounted over the remaining life expectancy of the insured. To the extent that this is done, no correction of the basic variant estimate is needed.

LAST MEDICAL EXPENSES

Somewhat like the problem of gifts in preparation for death is the problem of "last medical expenses." The two problems are similar because they both suggest that the method of sampling by death may present a distorted picture of the wealth distribution among living persons. It may be that some estate tax decedents have, just prior to their deaths, consumed considerable portions of their estates in a period of illness with loss of income, high expenditure on medical and hospital care, and other expenses associated with serious illness. While this is true in some cases, it is not true in all; and not all long and expensive illnesses are closely followed by death. While it must be admitted that a sample of living persons would be superior to the sample of decedents, we are not sure what, if any, adjustments should be made on this particular count. It should be noted that the medical and hospital bills which are unpaid at time of death will be entered as debt on the estate tax return and will reduce economic estate but not gross estate.

PERSONAL TRUST FUNDS, ANNUITIES, AND PENSION FUNDS

The next subject to claim our attention is personal trust funds. The above discussion was about outright gifts. With a trust fund, a transfer of property is made from the creator of a trust agreement to an impersonal entity with a person or group of persons named to enjoy the income of the property settled in the trust. In some cases a creator may name himself as a beneficiary. Furthermore, the creator may retain during his lifetime the right to change the terms of the trust agreement. Trusts with such revocable clauses are sometimes referred to as "living trusts," as opposed to "irrevocable" and "testamentary" trusts. The trust agreement may specify that the beneficiaries are to receive either the income or the principal of the trust only in the event of certain contingencies. The trust agreement may also specify who will be (or the method of naming) the successor to the original beneficiaries of the trust.[23] Hence, property placed in trust is not of the same

[23] It should not be overlooked that there are often important strategic advantages to being a trustee with power to administer the property in trust.

character, particularly from the viewpoint of the beneficiary, as property owned outright and over which one has the power of disposal both during his life and at death. The only similarity in some cases, indeed, is the right to income. However, property in personal trust funds is personally owned wealth. At least it is not government-owned or corporate-owned property. Neither is it held in title by nonprofit organizations. As such, it is important to relate such property to the estate tax wealth distribution. The distinction between wealth owned outright and wealth in trust is made in this study in the definitions of the prime and total wealth variants.

The problems in estimating and allocating the amounts of wealth in trust are complex. Difficult conceptual issues are complicated by insufficient data. The general purpose of the following sections on personal trust funds, annuities, and pension funds is: (1) to estimate the amount of trust items included in the basic variant estimates; (2) to subtract that amount from the basic variant total to "purify" the prime wealth estimate; (3) to derive total wealth from prime wealth by adding to the latter an estimate of the full amount of trust items which are allocable to those with estate sizes of more than $60,000.

Personal Trust Funds

The basic variant wealth estimate of $309.2 billion includes some part of wealth in personal trust funds. Decedents must report their connection with personal trusts under certain circumstances if they are creators of trusts and under certain other circumstances if they are beneficiaries. Some persons who are either creators or beneficiaries do not have to report their connections at all. A creator must report if he had transferred property to a trust fund in contemplation of death or if he had placed property in trust but retained a "string" to it during his life, in other words, never completed the transfer during his life. In these cases the property is classified in the tabulations of estate tax returns according to its original form and not as interest in trust property. (See discussion of tabulation on pp. 60 ff.) Some property in personal trust funds is included in the gross estates of decedents who were not creators of trusts. In broad terms, the law reaches only those who have general, as opposed to special or no, powers of appointment. (For example, a beneficiary with full power of appointment over a $100,000 trust fund should report the full $100,000.) The gross estate of a person with an includable interest in property now in trust should report the present value of that future interest. For example, suppose a man dies at 40 while his mother, aged 70, is alive. Suppose further that the mother has an income interest in a $100,000 trust fund, the principal of which is to go to the son at the time of her death. The 40-year-old decedent would have as part of his estate $100,000 discounted over the years of life expectancy of his mother. For a slightly more complicated case, assume that the 40-year-old son, like his mother, has only an income interest in the property and that his son, aged 15, is the remainderman. If the latter dies at 15, his estate tax return would include the $100,000 discounted over the years of life expectancy of his 40-year-old father. It is apparent, therefore, that the fraction of all beneficiaries' interest in trust funds which is subject to the estate-multiplier process is dependent on the ages of all those who precede the remainderman in the line of succession to property in trust. In those instances where the remainderman is not a person, but an institution, for instance, we would not get any such reporting, of course.

It is known that the top wealth-holder group makes extensive use of personal trust funds. Evidence of this is provided by a study which matched gift tax returns with estate tax returns of 1945.[24] This study suggests that about 25 per cent of net estate, and hence about 20 per cent of gross estate, of decedent wealth-holders moves into trust funds. The relevant findings of that study, which was made by the Treasury staff, are summarized here. In 1945 there were 13,869 estate tax returns with $2.7 billion of net estate; 753 returns with over $500,000 of net estate were examined and matched with gift tax returns. These returns represented $1 billion of net estate and $0.3 billion of gifts. Of this $1.3 billion, 30 per cent was used to pay federal estate and gift taxes, 8 per cent went to charitable causes, and 63 per cent appeared in noncharitable transfers. Of the noncharitable transfers, 45 per cent was placed in trust. One-half of this, in turn, was set up to escape estate tax until the death of grandchildren and virtually all of it to pass the spouse without payment of tax. Hence, out of $2.7 billion of net estate (or $3 billion including gifts), at least 45 per cent of 63 per cent, or $0.8 billion, went into trust funds. This amount, which is 28 per cent of the total net estate, would, of course, be greater if this practice were followed by those with less than $500,000 net estate.

Knowledge of how much wealth moves into trust funds does not solve the problem of how much basic variant wealth held by living

---

[24] *Revenue Revision of 1950,* Hearings before the Committee on Ways and Means, 81st Congress, 2nd Session, Washington, 1950, Vol. I, pp. 75–89.

ADJUSTMENT OF BASIC VARIANT ESTIMATES

persons is simultaneously in trust. This estimate can be broken down into two parts: (1) How much creators' interest in trust funds is included in the basic variant aggregate? (2) How much beneficiaries' interest is included in that same aggregate?

Looking first at the creator's interest, it is clear that testamentary trusts are not involved in the double-counting, since the wealth in these cases does not move into trust until after the estate tax base has been accounted for. Further, irrevocable trusts established as outright gifts are not involved in the double-counting, since such wealth is not ordinarily reported as estate tax wealth. Except for gifts in contemplation of death, the double-counting which occurs involves revocable trusts, since such property is in trust but is also part of the creator's estate tax wealth.

Therefore the problem is to find out how much of all trust fund wealth is in revocable trusts. It is worth noting that the definition of "revocable" differs for income tax and estate tax purposes and has also differed over time. To put it another way, at a given time, how much of all wealth in trust was placed there by persons who are now living and who hold a string to the wealth? Undoubtedly a great part of the wealth now in trust was placed there by persons now deceased and some by persons long since deceased. However, it is probable that a sizable part of trust fund wealth is held under revocable clauses. Some such trust arrangements, known as short-term trusts and reverter trusts, are formulated as part of a lifetime strategy for minimizing income taxes rather than as ways of transferring property. More commonly a revocable trust is used as a will substitute. One authority summarizes the advantages of using it for this purpose as follows:

The revocable trust, as a will substitute, is and always has been an extremely useful estate planning tool. For any one of a variety of reasons, it may be adopted as the vehicle for the transmission of part or substantially all of an estate at death.

1. It assures a continuity of investment management and flow of income.
2. It avoids the publicity attendant on probate.
3. It eliminates, in most cases, court supervision.
4. It reduces the likelihood of attacks on the ground of fraud and undue influence by dissatisfied heirs.
5. It may in many cases be a less expensive means of transmitting the estate.
6. It offers a choice of law, where the law of the domicile prohibits the accomplishment of particular objectives.

7. In many states it offers immunity from the claims of creditors of the estate.
8. It may be used to avoid statutory restrictions on charitable gifts.
9. In some jurisdictions it permits avoidance of the widow's "forced share"; a result the testator may desire in order to protect rather than to deprive his spouse.
10. It offers opportunities for the creation of additional income tax entities.

In most cases the selection of a revocable trust as the medium for transmitting property at death will be dictated by one or two of the above reasons. In all cases, where the nature of the estate owner's assets does not make a living revocable trust undesirable, it will be worth considering.[25]

Lacking any good evidence on the point, we estimate that 10 per cent, or $6 billion, of the total wealth in trust was in revocable trusts. Another clue to how much creators' interest in trust property is included in the basic variant estimate is found in estate tax tabulations for recent years before 1953, which show that transfers during a decedent's life amount to about 4 per cent of gross estate. Some part of these transfers was undoubtedly done via trust funds, half of it, we might guess. The same source indicates that only 0.5 per cent of gross estate was in the form of powers of appointment and hence gives a clue to the amount of beneficiary interest in trust property. On this basis, and making some adjustment for differing blow-up factors for creators and beneficiaries, we estimate that 2 per cent of aggregate gross estate is simultaneously in trust and included in our estimate of the basic variant estate tax wealth of living persons; 2 per cent of $309 billion is $6 billion. Hence, to get an estimate of prime wealth "purified" of trust property, we subtract $6 billion from the basic variant aggregate. This amount is entered in Table 29.

How much wealth is in personal trust funds is difficult to estimate. Capitalizing at 5 per cent the amount of total income of personal trust funds reported on fiduciary income tax returns, namely $2.8 billion, yields the estimate of $56 billion in 1952. (The year 1952 is used because tabulations of these returns are published only for alternate years.) The 5 per cent yield rate is arbitrarily selected and subject to dispute, but the composition of income reported shows heavy emphasis upon equity investment. Dividend income is 59 per cent of total

[25] William J. Bowe, *Estate Planning and Taxation*, Buffalo, 1957, pp. 183–184.

ADJUSTMENT OF BASIC VARIANT ESTIMATES

income, while interest income is only 11 per cent. Capitalizing at 4 per cent would produce the larger estimate of $70 billion.[26]

Taking $56 billion as a conservative estimate of the total amount in personal trust funds, the next question is how much of that total is allocable to persons with estates of $60,000 or over.

In 1952, 422,663 taxable and nontaxable fiduciary income tax returns were filed, reporting a total income of $2,788,160,000. Of these returns 301,507 with $2,250,683,000 of the income were classified as "trusts" returns, and 121,156 with $537,477,000 of the income were classified as "estates" returns.

The total money income of fiduciaries is reduced to "balance income" by allowable deductions. The "balance income" of $2,551,-246,000 (the fiduciaries with "balance deficits" of $38,531,000 are tabulated separately) is then assignable for tax purposes either to beneficiaries or to fiduciaries. The "amount distributable to beneficiaries" was $1,942,771,000 and the net income taxable to fiduciaries was $636,054,000. In the case of returns for "estates," over half the total income was net income taxable to the fiduciaries, while in the case of "trusts" only about a fifth was taxable to the fiduciaries. In these cases where income is taxable to the fiduciaries, it may be presumed that income is not flowing out to beneficiaries until some condition is fulfilled or a legal determination is made. For example, income and principal may be held in trust until a child attains a stated age or in an estate until a contest over the validity of a will is resolved. Hence, an aggregate of $12.7 billion (the result of capitalizing $636 million) might be classified as "contingent assets." While marking them out as such, it would seem plausible to include them, along with annuities, as part of the trust fund variant of wealth.

In the same year, 1952, 425,669 individual income tax returns reported $1,711,235,000 of income from estates and trusts. This amount differs from the $1.9 billion "distributable to beneficiaries" because (aside from possible evasion and underreporting) some of the beneficiaries have less than $600 adjusted income and hence do not file an income tax return, some of the income is tax-exempt interest, and some of the beneficiaries are not persons.

---

[26] For a more extensive discussion of estimation of personal trust funds, see Raymond W. Goldsmith, *Financial Intermediaries in the American Economy Since 1900*, Princeton for National Bureau of Economic Research, 1958, pp. 174–176 and 295–296. Also see the paper by Raymond W. Goldsmith and Eli Shapiro entitled "An Estimate of Bank-Administered Personal Trust Funds," in *Journal of Finance*, March 1959, pp. 11–17.

ADJUSTMENT OF BASIC VARIANT ESTIMATES

TABLE

INDIVIDUAL INCOME TAX RETURNS WITH INCOME

Adjusted Gross Income Size	Number of Returns	Size of Specific Source					
		Under $100	$100 to $200	$200 to $300	$300 to $400	$400 to $500	$500 to $1,000
	(number of returns with income from estates and trusts)						
	(1)	(2)	(3)	(4)	(5)	(6)	(7)
Taxable and nontaxable returns							
No adjusted gross income	3,236	a	a	a	a	—	a
Under $600	5,945	a	a	a	a	—	a
$600 to $1,000	14,178	a	2,287	a	a	a	8,231
$1,000 to $1,500	28,356	2,287	2,287	a	3,202	a	6,861
$1,500 to $2,000	20,582	a	a	a	2,287	a	6,860
$2,000 to $2,500	24,242	a	a	a	2,287	a	3,202
$2,500 to $3,000	21,494	2,287	2,741	a	2,287	a	2,287
$3,000 to $4,000	40,276	2,287	5,950	5,489	2,744	a	4,574
$4,000 to $5,000[b]	32,688	4,578	2,329	2,308	2,287	3,222	5,489
$5,000 to $8,000	76,145	5,966	10,083	3,659	7,358	3,202	12,845
$8,000 to $10,000	29,023	4,575	2,287	a	2,287	a	4,141
$10,000 to $30,000	90,804	4,699	4,416	3,526	3,463	1,978	9,073
$30,000 to $50,000	19,918	610	561	410	362	377	1,499
$50,000 to $100,000	12,909	376	302	255	185	175	727
$100,000 to $500,000	5,568	128	68	61	43	51	171
$500,000 to $1,000,000	222	1	—	2	1	2	6
$1,000,000 and over	83	4	—	—	—	—	4
Total	425,669	32,373	36,974	22,569	30,164	17,262	68,259

There is considerable evidence to support a conclusion that most of the amount in trusts and estates should be allocated to persons with estates of over $60,000.

Of the 425,669 individual tax returns with income from estates and trusts, 106,244 show more than $3,000 income from estates and trusts alone (Table 31). Each of these 106,244 returns may be considered to represent a $60,000 principal. Their aggregate income is estimated to be $1.5 billion, which is 79 per cent of the total distributed income. Capitalized at 5 per cent, this is $30 billion.

Data gathered from a small sample of "active investors" by Butters, Thompson, and Bollinger suggests that the percentage of persons who have beneficial interest in trust funds rises with income and with total wealth (Table 32). Further, they found that while trust property made up only about 3 per cent of estates under $100,000, it made up between 8 and 22 per cent of larger estates (Table 33). For all those

ADJUSTMENT OF BASIC VARIANT ESTIMATES

31
FREQUENCY DISTRIBUTION FROM ESTATES AND TRUSTS

				Size of Specific Source						
$1,000 to $1,500	$1,500 to $2,000	$2,000 to $2,500	$2,500 to $3,000	$3,000 to $4,000	$4,000 to $5,000	$5,000 to $10,000	$10,000 to $25,000	$25,000 to $50,000	$50,000 to $100,000	$100,000 and over
				(number of returns with income from estates and trusts)						
(8)	(9)	(10)	(11)	(12)	(13)	(14)	(15)	(16)	(17)	(18)
a	—	a	a	a	—	a	a	a	a	—
a	—	—	a	—	—	a	—	—	—	—
—	—	—	—	—	—	—	—	—	a	—
9,603	a	—	a	—	—	—	—	—	—	—
a	5,489	—	—	—	—	—	—	—	—	—
a	5,031	6,403	—	a	a	—	a	—	—	—
3,202	a	a	3,202	a	—	—	—	—	—	—
5,489	4,117	a	2,287	4,594	—	—	—	—	—	—
2,785	a	2,288	a	a	2,745	a	a	a	a	a
5,966	5,031	3,679	2,287	4,137	2,744	9,188	—	—	—	—
2,804	a	1,850	a	a	a	5,091	a	—	—	—
7,820	4,961	4,312	3,372	5,664	5,649	14,945	16,263	652	a	—
1,045	909	719	665	1,160	836	2,996	4,663	3,073	32	a
522	495	433	338	551	496	1,766	2,582	2,170	1,508	28
184	118	113	85	153	182	535	968	833	988	887
2	2	2	4	21	3	13	12	20	24	107
1	1	—	—	1	1	5	8	5	8	45
43,084	29,813	23,919	15,008	20,858	14,485	35,468	24,990	6,771	2,599	1,073

SOURCE: *Statistics of Income for 1952*, Washington, 1956, p. 30, Table 5.
a Number of returns is subject to sampling variation of more than 100 per cent; therefore, data are not shown separately. However, they are included in totals.
b Includes nontaxable returns with adjusted gross income exceeding the class limit.

spending units who had trust property, such property averaged between a third and a half of total wealth for the several estate size groups (Table 33). While these findings apply to spending units rather than individuals, they seem to indicate that the greater part of property in the title of personal trust funds is attributable to those with total wealth holdings of $60,000 or more.

To decide how much to allocate to the top estate holders, we turn back to the income tax data. It was found that 79 per cent of fiduciary income distributable to beneficiaries was clearly allocable to persons with $60,000 estates since it was from parcels of trusteed wealth of at least $60,000 in value. Applying this 79 per cent to the total amount of $56 billion estimated to be in trust yields $44 billion as allo-

TABLE 32
Individuals with Trusts in Active Investor Sample, by Income and Wealth Groups
(per cent)

Item	Number of Cases	Individuals Who Are Beneficial Owners of Trusts	Individuals Who Have Established Living Trusts	Individuals Who Have Established Testamentary Trusts or Plan to Create Trusts	Nonduplicating Total
Income group					
Under $7,500	201	7%	2%	17%	23%
$7,500 to $12,500	182	11	6	29	38
$12,500 to $25,000	160	13	3	34	41
$25,000 to $50,000	121	27	19	36	55
$50,000 to $100,000	46	32	29	42	65
$100,000 and over	26	47	50	29	69
Not ascertained	10				
Wealth group					
Under $25,000	147	3	3	18	18
$25,000 to $50,000	121	8	2	29	36
$50,000 to $100,000	131	11	3	25	32
$100,000 to $250,000	158	20	9	35	49
$250,000 to $500,000	77	27	14	34	52
$500,000 to $1,000,000	41	39	31	37	70
$1,000,000 and over	41	48	40	35	73
Not ascertained	30				

SOURCE: J. K. Butters, L. E. Thompson, and L. L. Bollinger, *Effects of Taxation: Investment by Individuals*, Boston, 1953, Table XV-5, p. 362.

ADJUSTMENT OF BASIC VARIANT ESTIMATES

cable to the top group. It assumes that the capital sums yielding nondistributable income have the same size distribution as those yielding distributable income. Further, it assumes that no person will have less than $60,000 of trust property but at the same time a combination of trusteed and full-title property worth $60,000 or more. We do not

TABLE 33
VALUE OF PROPERTY HELD IN TRUST AS PERCENTAGE OF WEALTH HELD BY INDIVIDUALS IN ACTIVE INVESTOR SAMPLE, BY INCOME AND WEALTH GROUPS

		Value of Trust Property as Percentage of Wealth of	
Item	Number of Cases	Spending Units with Trust Property	All Spending Units in Sample
Income group			
Under $7,500	193	49%[a]	8%
$7,500 to $12,500	173	40	6
$12,500 to $25,000	156	50	9
$25,000 to $50,000	120	36	11
$50,000 to $100,000	42	37	7
$100,000 and over	24	38	24
Not ascertained	38		
Wealth group			
Under $25,000	146	38	1
$25,000 to $50,000	120	39	3
$50,000 to $100,000	130	32	3
$100,000 to $250,000	156	47	8
$250,000 to $500,000	76	29	9
$500,000 to $1,000,000	40	44	15
$1,000,000 and over	41	47	22
Not ascertained	37		

SOURCE: Butters et al., *Effects of Taxation*, Table XV-6, p. 363.
[a] In computing the relative importance of trust property held by this income group, one atypical case was omitted. This person was the beneficiary of a $4 million trust; all income received by the trust was retained within the trust for later distribution to him and so was not included in his income as reported to us. The inclusion of this trust would have raised the respective percentages for this income group to 85 and 39 per cent.

have the necessary information to estimate with any reasonable degree of accuracy the number of wealth-holders who should be raised to the above $60,000 class as a result of including trust fund wealth, but it is probably quite small—around 50,000.

Thus it is concluded that $44 billion of wealth and 50,000 persons should be added to the prime wealth variant estimates to represent the share of top wealth-holders in personal trust funds.

Annuities and Pensions

An estate tax return should include the present value of an annuity. The value of a pure annuity on one life is, of course, zero at time of death. The value of an annuity on two lives at the time of death of one beneficiary is its discounted benefits over the life expectancy of the surviving beneficiary.

Our basic variant estimate of estate tax wealth includes some amount for annuities and pensions in the "miscellaneous property" category. It includes some further amount to the extent that annuities were included in the "insurance" category. Examination of these two categories suggests that $2 billion is a reasonable estimate of what is included. Hence, that amount is subtracted from the basic variant as the final step in estimating the prime wealth variant aggregates (Table 29).

How much of annuity reserves should be added in moving on to total wealth variant estimates? The annuity reserves of U.S. life insurance companies in 1956 were $16.3 billion. But since some annuities are held by persons with less than $60,000 of gross estate, the amount we should add is considerably less than that. It would seem reasonable to believe that annuity reserves are more concentrated than life insurance reserves, about 14 per cent of which were held by the estate tax wealth-holder group. If we assume that the upper wealth group had 20 per cent of annuity reserves, we should add $5.3 billion to the previous total of the prime wealth variant. As in the case of personal trust funds, it is difficult to know how many persons to add to the estate tax wealth-holder group because the inclusion would raise their gross estate from less to more than $60,000. Again, a quite arbitrary figure must be selected. We put the number at 100,000 persons.

By the same line of reasoning, the estate-multiplier method underestimates the wealth held in the form of equity in pension and retirement funds, both insured and noninsured and both private and governmental. Pension fund reserves of life companies totaled $8.6 billion in 1953. The assets of noninsured private plans were about $10 billion in that year ($11.8 billion in 1954). Assuming that 10 per cent of the total is allocable to our top wealth-holders (since pension rights are somewhat more widely distributed than life insurance rights) leads to the conclusion that $1.9 billion should be added to their aggregate gross estate.

ADJUSTMENT OF BASIC VARIANT ESTIMATES

Government pension and retirement funds totaled $47.9 billion in 1952. Assuming that 5 per cent of this total may be allocated to the top wealth-holders means that $2.4 billion should be added to their aggregate gross estate.[27]

[27] No account is taken of the fact that reserves bear quite different relationships to future benefits in the several different types of pension plans in effect.

CHAPTER 4
Characteristics of Top Wealth-Holders in 1953

IN 1953 there were, it is estimated by the estate-multiplier method using adjusted mortality rates, 1.6 million persons with $60,000 or more of gross estate (unadjusted basic variant). This group, which comprised only 1 per cent of the total population and 1.6 per cent of the adult population, held over a quarter of all personally owned wealth and over half of the personally owned business assets in the nation. Ownership of such significant shares of wealth lends special interest to the personal characteristics of the top wealth-holders and the ways in which they differ from the rest of the population.

Only a limited range of basic socio-economic characteristics and some relationships among them can be derived from the data available. These characteristics are estate size, age, sex, marital status, family status, community property, state of residence, income, and occupation. The discussion throughout this chapter is in terms of basic variant estimates with no adjustment made for those returns with age unspecified.

Estate Size

The personally owned wealth of the total population in 1953 amounted to about $1 trillion. This means that the average gross estate for all 103 million adults was slightly less than $10,000. The median would, of course, be considerably lower. In contrast, the top wealth-holder group had an average gross estate of $182,000. The majority of this top group was clustered in estate sizes below that average. Of the 1.6 million top wealth-holders, over half had less than $125,000 of gross estate and less than 2 per cent (27,000 persons) had more than $1 million (Chart 6 and Table 34). (Tables 34 through 62 will be found at the end of this chapter.)

Men outnumbered women about two to one in the whole group, but there were more women than men with over $1.5 million of gross estate. This is indicated by the crossing of the lines for males and females in Chart 6. The number of men and women in each broad

TOP WEALTH-HOLDERS IN 1953

CHART 6
Persons with Gross Estates Greater Than Stated Amounts, by Sex, 1953

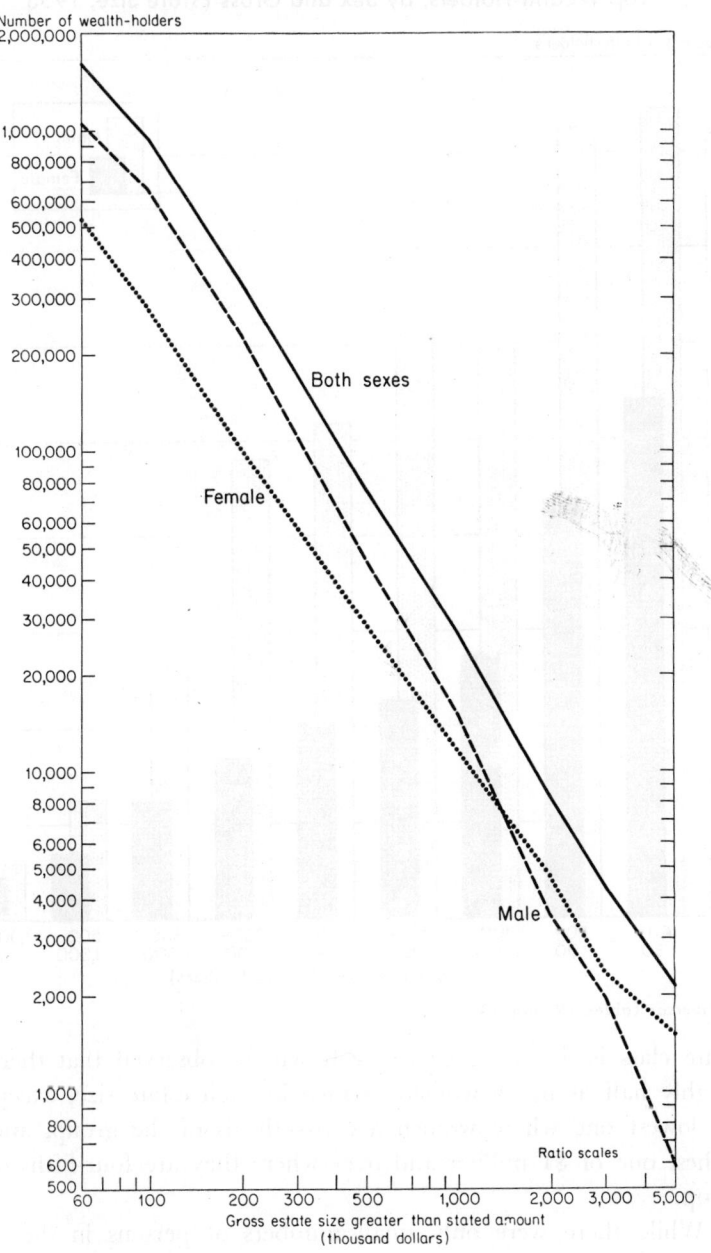

Source: Tables 24, 79, and 80.

CHART 7
Top Wealth-Holders, by Sex and Gross Estate Size, 1953

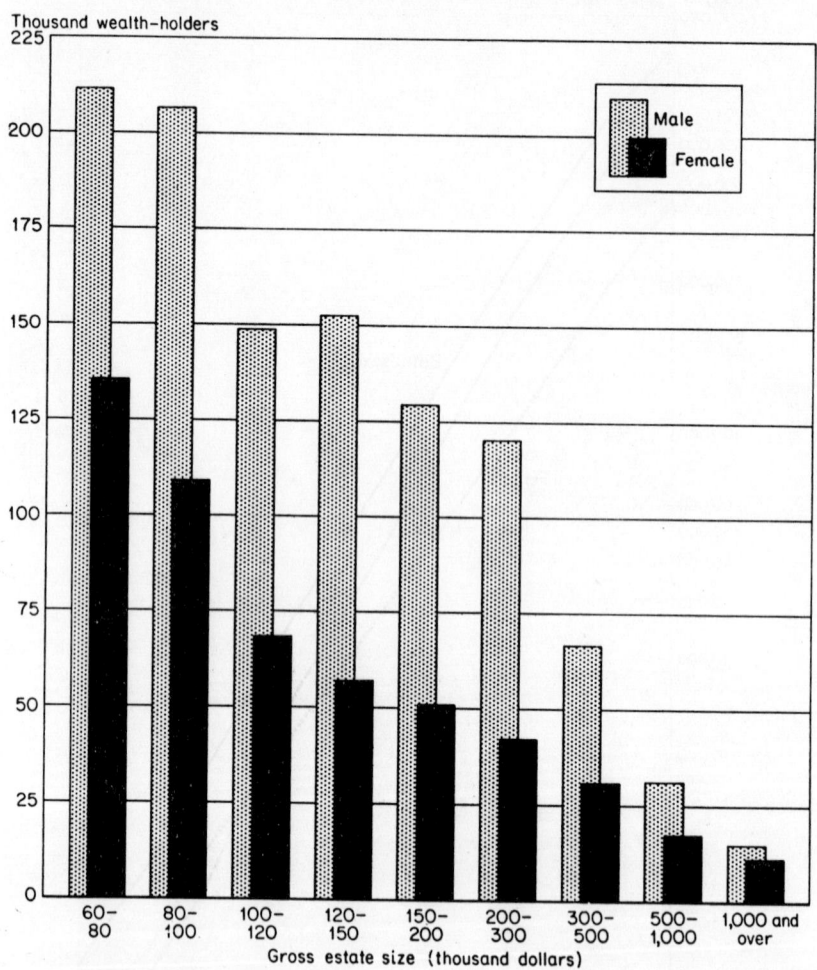

Source: Tables 79 and 80.

estate class is shown in Chart 7. It will be observed that there are roughly half as many women as men in each estate size, except for the lowest one where women are two-thirds of the group, and the highest one of $1 million and over where they are four-fifths of the group.

While there were only small numbers of persons in the larger estate sizes, wealth was highly concentrated in those classes. The top 11 per cent of persons held about 45 per cent of the wealth of the group, while the lower 50 per cent held only about 22 per cent (Table 34).[1]

Age

A leading characteristic of the top wealth-holders is that they are older than the rest of the adult population. Their median age in 1953 was 54 years, 52 for men and 57 for women. The median age of the total adult population in that year was 44 for men and 43 for women.

CHART 8
Top Wealth-Holders, by Sex and Age Group, 1953

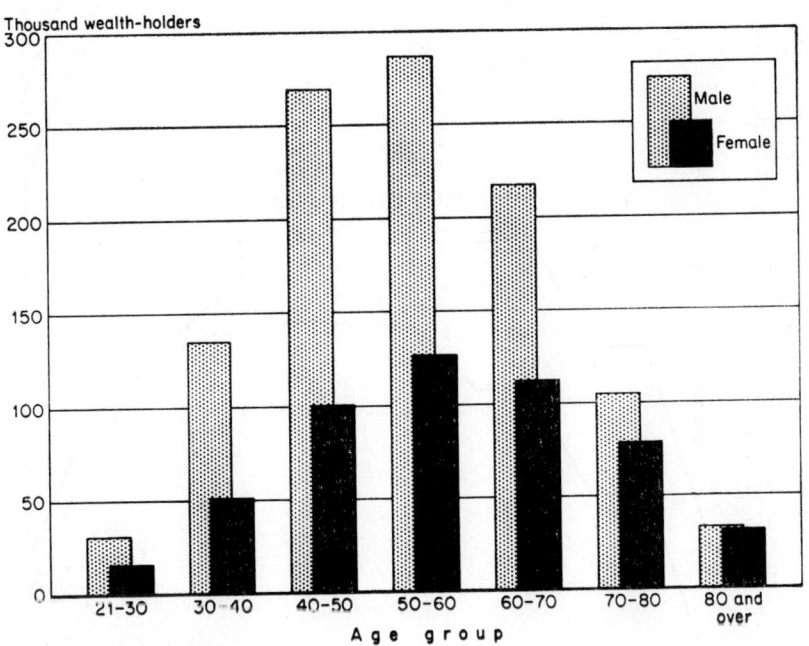

Source: Tables 72 and 73.

Within the top wealth-holder group, the 50 to 60 age bracket includes the largest number of both men and women (Chart 8 and Table 35). The numbers rise sharply from the under 30 bracket, which includes only 60,000 people, to the 40 to 50 group, with 383,000. After age 60 the numbers fall off rapidly so that the 80 and over age group includes only 67,000 people. Women do not exceed

[1] A more extensive discussion of inequality among wealth-holders and changes in inequality over time is included at the end of Chapter 6.

CHART 9

Hypothetical Number of Top Wealth-Holders Within Age Cohorts of 100,000 Starting at Age 20, by Sex

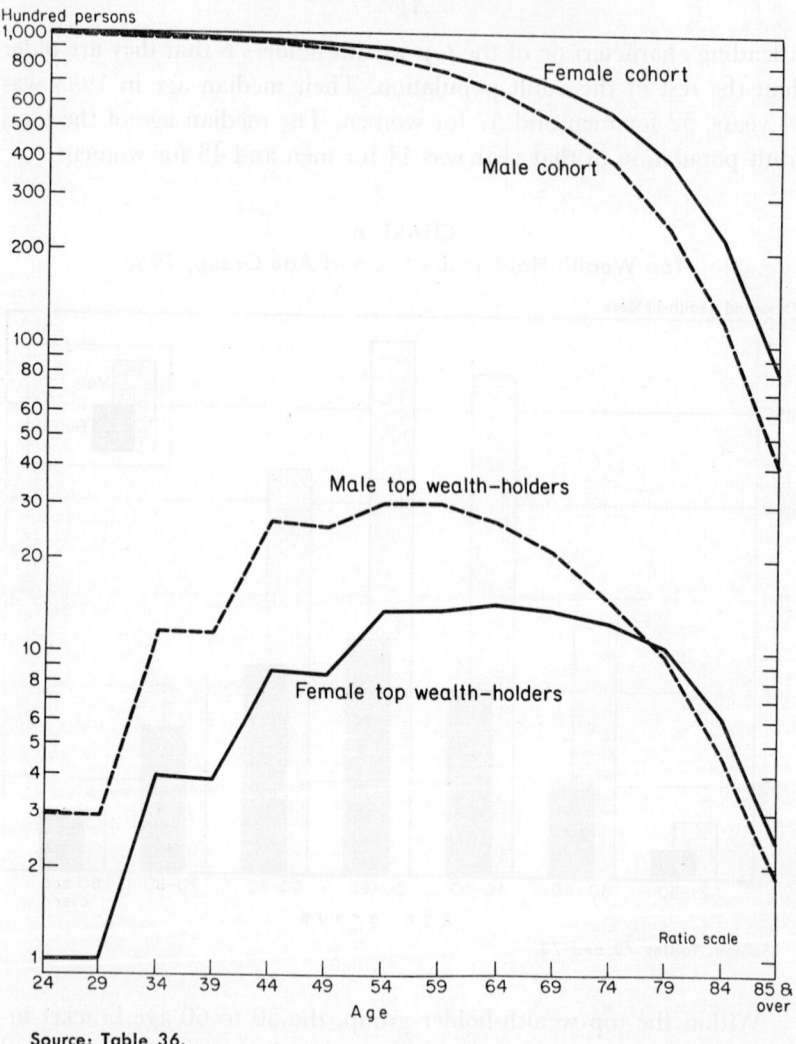

Source: Table 36.

men in number in any age bracket over 21, but almost equal them in the 80 and over bracket.

While top wealth-holders over 21 were only 1.6 per cent of the total adult population, about 3.5 per cent of men over 50 were top wealth-holders (Table 35). Interestingly, while the groups of men under age 60 show a rising trend in this percentage, there is no clear trend across the age brackets beyond that age. That is, about 4 per cent of every age group of men above 55 are top wealth-holders. Among women, on the other hand, there is a constant rise in the percentage of the age group who are estate tax wealth-holders, from 0.9 per cent in the 40 to 50 bracket to 3.0 per cent in the 85 and over bracket.

The way in which age and mortality are interrelated with the number of top wealth-holders is illustrated by a hypothetical example in Table 36 and Chart 9. The example is based on 1953 mortality rates and 1953 numbers of wealth-holders. According to this table, if we start with 100,000 males aged 20 in 1953, the expected number of wealth-holders reaches an absolute peak of 3,038 at age 59. In that year the number of persons remaining in the cohort is 75,943. From that age onward, the number of survivors and number of living top wealth-holders fall at approximately the same rate, so that at age 84 there are 467 wealth-holders and 11,978 persons left in the cohort. The number of female wealth-holders reaches a peak of 1,421 at age 64, and exceeds the number of male wealth-holders from age 79 on.

DISTRIBUTION OF ESTATE TAX WEALTH AMONG AGE GROUPS

Over half the number of top wealth-holders are found to be between 40 and 60 years of age. The age group 50 to 60 supplies the largest number of wealth-holders and the greatest share of aggregate gross estate in the ten-year interval age groups (Chart 10 and Table 37).[2] The aggregate of gross estate is differently distributed among the age groups for men and women. There is a relatively high concentration of wealth in the 50 to 70 age brackets for men, and in the over 75 and 30 to 50 age brackets for women (Table 38).[3]

RELATIONSHIP BETWEEN AGE AND ESTATE SIZE FOR TOTAL POPULATION

The Survey of Consumer Finances supplies us with information on the relationship between the age of spending unit heads and the wealth-holdings of spending units for the total population. Age of head is

---

[2] Table 37 summarizes the relationships between percentages of wealth-holders and percentages of aggregate gross estate among the age groups of living wealth-holders in 1944 and 1953. These relationships can be observed for 1948, 1949, and 1950, but without the insurance correction, in the tables in Appendix A.

The only notable difference between the distribution of 1944 and 1953 is the relatively greater weight of the 30 to 40 age bracket in 1944. This can be ascribed, at least in large part, to the different mortality rates used in the two studies.

[3] Substantially the same relationship was observed in net estate data by Mendershausen (R. W. Goldsmith, *A Study of Saving in the United States*, III,

positively associated with median size of asset holdings from age 18 to 65 (Table 39). The age group 65 and over shows a sharp drop in median assets held and, correlatively, a rise in the number with less than $1,000 in assets (Table 40). This suggests that the typical spending unit accumulates assets until the head is about 65 and then consumes assets, or at least drops in the asset ranking after 65. Studies of

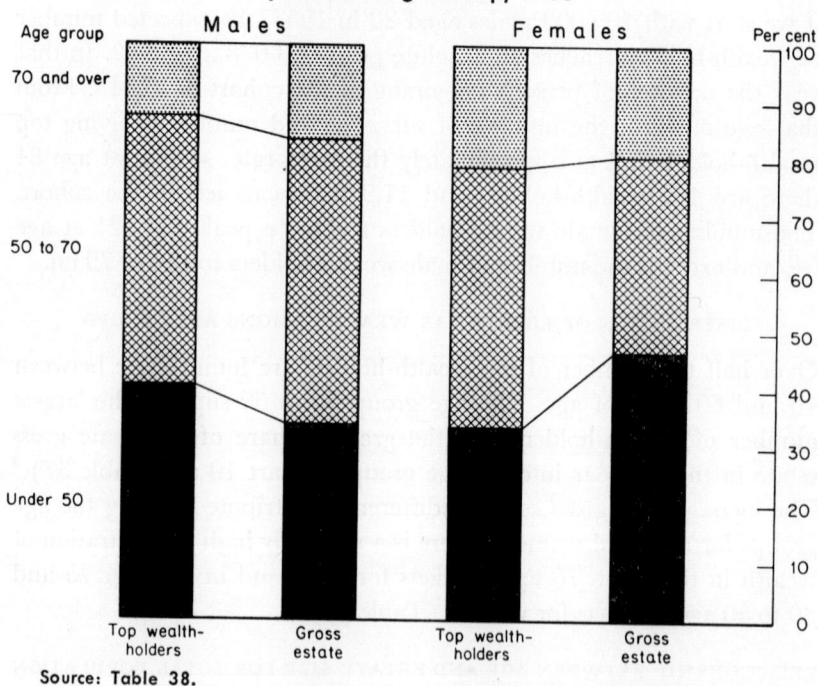

CHART 10
Distribution of Top Wealth-Holders and Their Gross Estates, by Sex and Age Group, 1953

Source: Table 38.

the financial positions of spending units and of husband-wife families at different stages of the "life cycle" in general show that median net worth and home ownership tend to increase with age through the life cycle, but that family income and size tend to peak when the head of the family is around 45 (Tables 41 and 42).

Because of the high median age of the top wealth-holders, and

---

Princeton, 1956, p. 351). The only other years for which tables by age and sex are available are 1948, 1949, and 1950 (see Appendix Tables A-6 and A-9).

also because of the relatively greater need of older people for asset income due to the loss of present and future earning power,[4] it is of interest to compare the economic position of top wealth-holders to that of the total aged population. Steiner and Dorfman found that income from assets accounted for 13 per cent of the total receipts of all persons over 65 in 1951; over half of total receipts was from earnings, 8 per cent from dissaving, 18 per cent from pensions, and 9 per cent from assistance.[5] While more than 60 per cent of the aged couples and more than 30 per cent of the aged unrelated individuals in their survey owned their own homes free and clear in 1951, only 25 per cent of the aged couples received any income from assets.[6] Less than 25 per cent of unrelated individuals received any income from assets. Steiner and Dorfman observe that "Asset income appears to have played two roles rather than one. For unrelated females, asset income was an important sole source of receipts and was, in total amount, the leading source. For couples, although asset income was frequently received, the amounts were often smaller, and it was important only as a second source of receipts."[7]

For more detail on the sources of receipts of the aged, see Table 43. A more direct comparison with the findings on the top wealth-holder group is afforded by Table 44, which shows asset holdings of "aged economic units." While 78 per cent of such units had some assets (excluding owner-occupied houses and life insurance), only 42 per cent held assets of $3,000 or more in value.

RELATIONSHIP BETWEEN AGE AND ESTATE SIZE FOR TOP WEALTH-HOLDERS

Within the group of top wealth-holders the average size of gross estate increases with age, but the progression is not regular (Table 45 and Chart 1).[8] For both sexes combined, there is a clear rise in average estate after age 50, but not before. For men alone, however, there is a much clearer association with age than for both sexes combined. Here

---

[4] This loss of earning power may be considered as a loss of asset value. Dublin et al. calculate, using a 2.5 per cent interest rate, the present value of the annual earnings of a man 35 years old at $63,000; at age 55 the present value will have fallen to $28,500 (Louis I. Dublin, Alfred J. Lotka, and Mortimer Spiegelman, *Length of Life*, rev. ed., New York, 1949, Table 67, p. 276).

[5] Peter O. Steiner and Robert Dorfman, *The Economic Status of the Aged*, Berkeley and Los Angeles, 1957, Table 8.3, p. 96.

[6] *Ibid.*, pp. 68 and 96.

[7] *Ibid.*, p. 114.

[8] To observe this relationship for other years, see Appendix Tables A-5 and A-6.

the progression is very regular from age 30 onward. The greater irregularity is found for women.

A similar, rather limited association between age and estate size is found by computing the median age for each estate size. Among men the median age rises only for the gross estate sizes of $300,000 and over, but there is, nonetheless, an over-all positive association. Women's median ages, however, show no such association (Table 46 and Chart

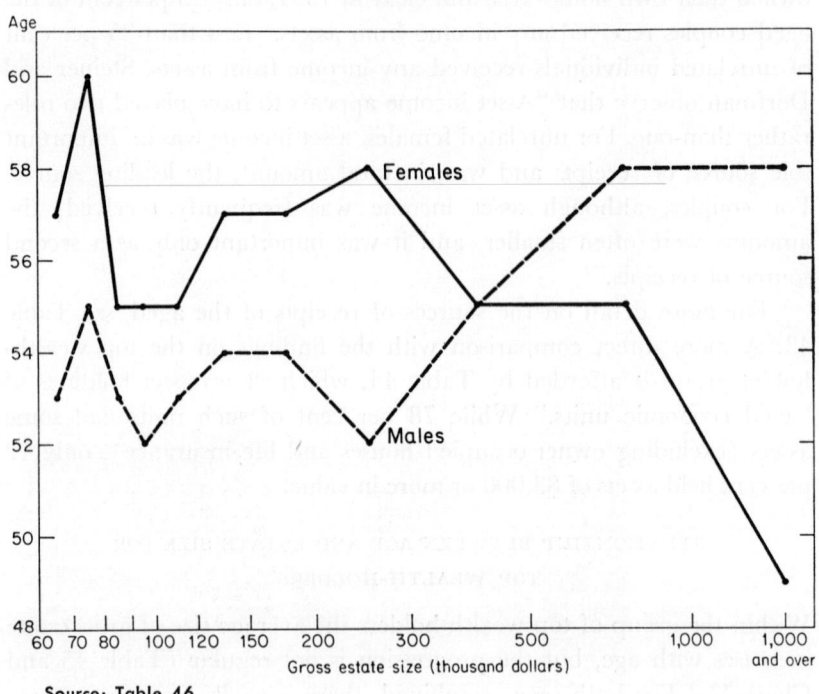

CHART 11
Median Age of Top Wealth-Holders, by Sex and Gross Estate Size, 1953

Source: Table 46.

11). Nor does any association appear when the women in the community property states are considered separately from those in non-community property states, as shown in the same table.

In order to get more insight into the relationship between age and estate size, it is useful to look into the distribution of persons by estate size within age groups and the distribution of persons by age within estate size groups. Further, to limit the number of variables at work, it is reasonable to consider only men in non-community property states. We would expect there to be a clearer positive relationship between age and estate size for men than for women, since inheritance is doubtless less important for men than for women.

Looking first at the distribution by estate size within age groups, we find no rise in median estate size across the age groups (Table 47, bottom line). The median is, of course, less sensitive to changes in the higher estate sizes than the mean average, but it is also less given to

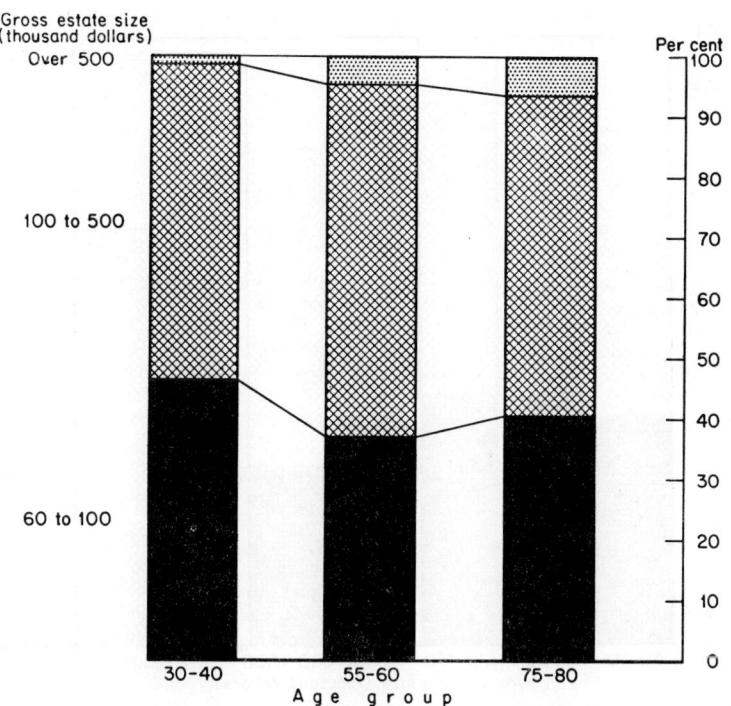

CHART 12

Distribution of Male Top Wealth-Holders by Gross Estate Size, Within Three Age Groups, Non-Community Property States, 1953

Source: Table 47.

large sampling errors. In Table 45 the range of difference in mean gross estate by age should be interpreted with caution since the standard error of the mean of each age-sex group is quite large. However, the general nature of the association between advanced age and size of estate is apparent in the general diagonal that runs from the top left to the bottom right of Table 47. Only in the highest age groups do persons with the largest estate sizes appear. This slant is interpreted in Chart 12. A similar kind of slant appears when the same data are turned around to represent a distribution by age within gross estate classes (Table 48 and Chart 13). Here the most striking point is that no younger persons appear in some of the larger estate sizes. The reader is cautioned against interpreting a finding of this kind in too literal a fashion, since all the data are derived from the sampling-by-death process and a range of error attaches to each number of each

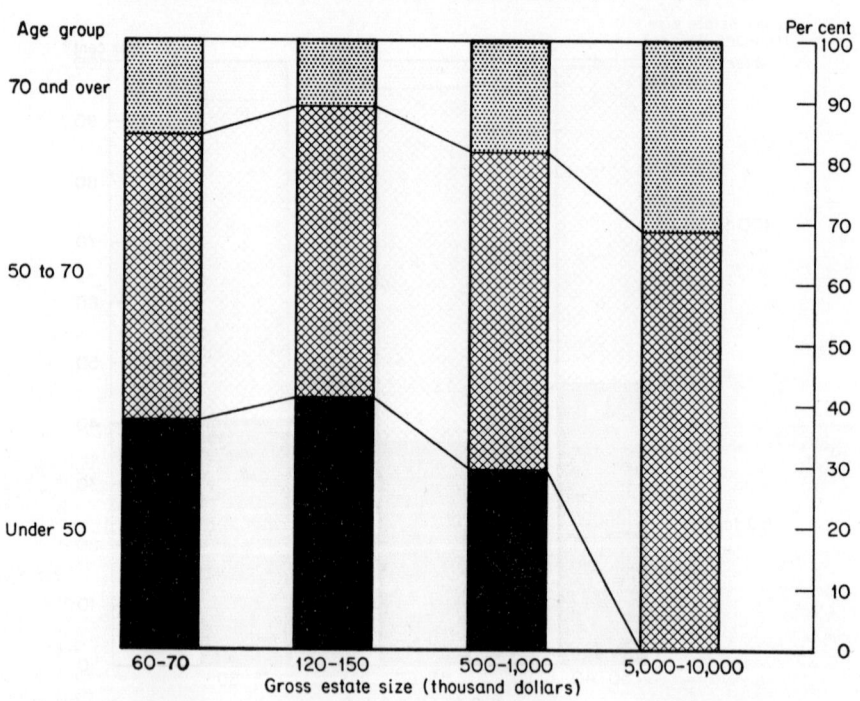

CHART 13

Distribution of Male Top Wealth-Holders by Age Group Within Four Gross Estate Sizes, Non-Community Property States, 1953

Source: Table 48.

cell, even if that number is zero. Equally important as the absence of younger persons in the higher estate classes is the fact that about the same percentage of all age groups are found in the smaller estate sizes. This suggests that people enter the top wealth-holder group at all ages and also that they may enter the group—presumably by inheritance, gift, or other sudden increase in assets—at a relatively high estate class. The fact that the top wealth-holder group is open at the bottom and at the "sides" explains the finding that while the median estate rises with age up to 65 years for all spending units, it does not so rise within the top wealth-holder group. This means that the top wealth-holder data cannot shed any new light on the process of accumulation of wealth up to a certain age, nor on the process of consumption or division of assets after a certain age.

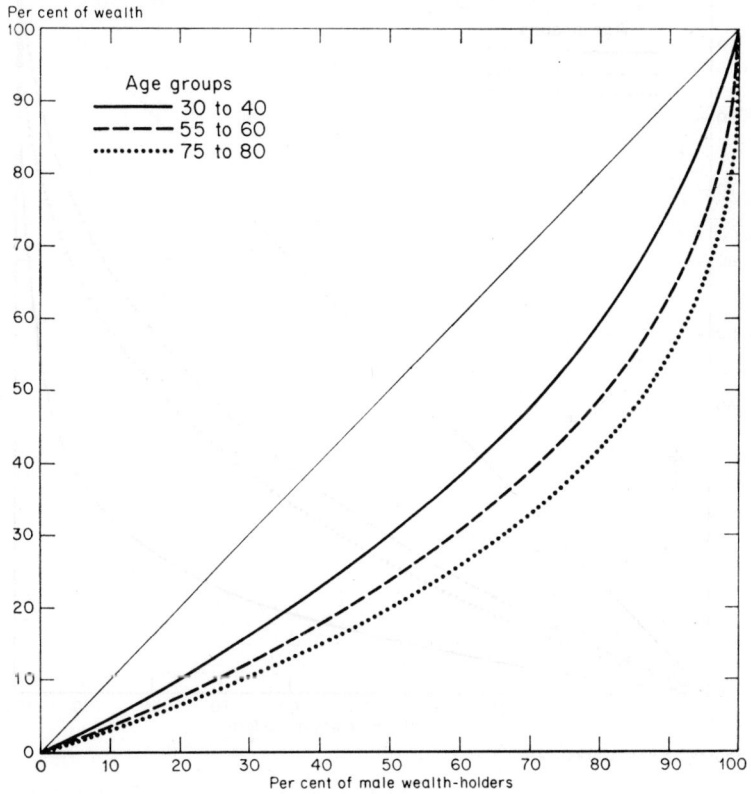

CHART 14

Lorenz Curves of Wealth Among Male Top Wealth-Holders in Three Age Groups, Non-Community Property States, 1953

Source: Tables 47 and 48 and NBER worksheets.

We can, however, add some information on how median age changes by estate size. According to the Survey of Consumer Finances, the median age of the heads of spending units rises from 33 at the lowest positive net worth group to 53 for the $25,000 and over group. In the top wealth-holder group, the median age of men holds constant at 52 to 53 for gross estate sizes ranging from $60,000 up to $300,000.

After $300,000, the median age rises to age 73 for the largest estate sizes (Chart 11). Hence, it seems to be generally true that the representative richer person is older than the representative person with less wealth.

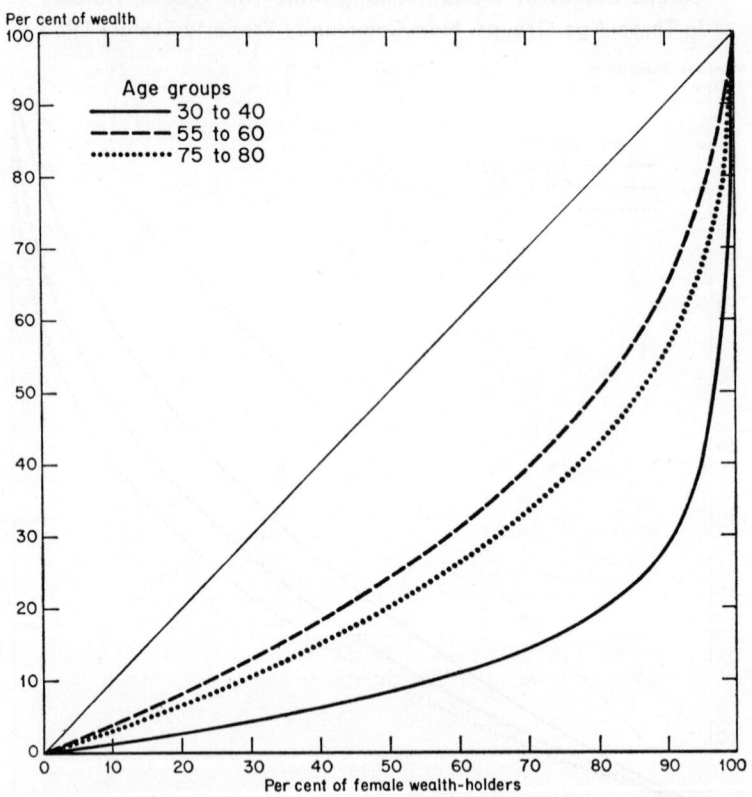

CHART 15

Lorenz Curves of Wealth Among Female Top Wealth-Holders in Three Age Groups, Non-Community Property States, 1953

Source: NBER worksheets.

Among the top wealth-holders wealth is distributed in such a way that there is in general less inequality among younger age groups than among older age groups (Charts 14 and 15). This is true both for men and women, with the exception of the younger women who appear to have the most unequal distribution of all.

Sex

Women comprised one-third of all top wealth-holders and held about 40 per cent of the gross estate of the group in 1953 (Table 38). They held a slightly higher share (41.8 per cent) of economic estate, or gross estate less liabilities.[9] The median age of women top wealth-holders is 56 compared to 52 years for men. Also, 12 per cent of the females in this group are over 75 years of age compared to only 7 per cent of the males (Table 38). Wealth is distributed more unequally among women top wealth-holders than among men (Chart 16).

CHART 16

Lorenz Curves of Wealth Among Top Wealth-Holders, by Sex, 1953

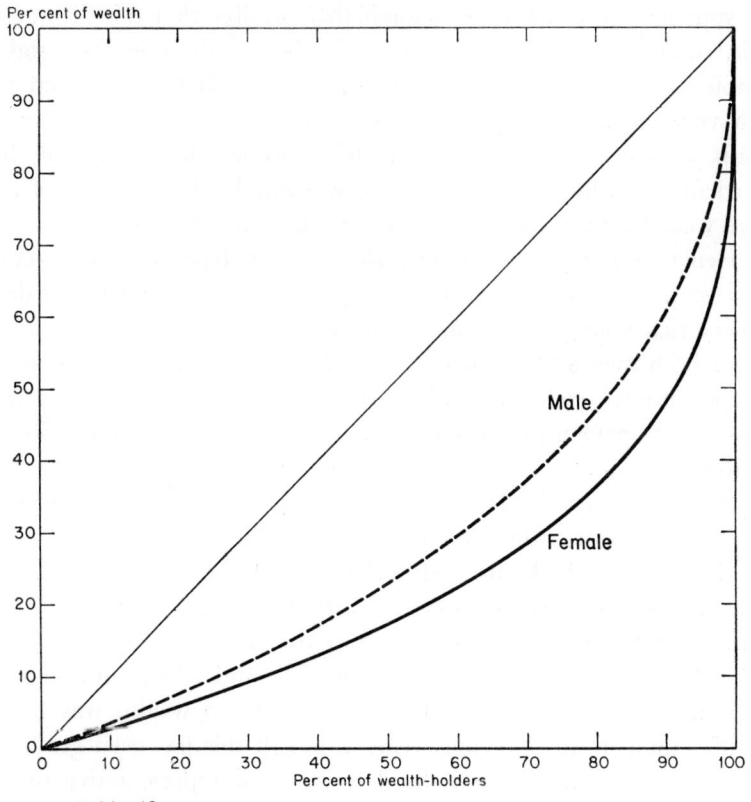

Source: Table 49.

Women top wealth-holders had a higher average estate than men, the respective averages being $220,500 and $162,372 (Table 49). On the other hand, however, men had a higher median gross estate

[9] Woman's share in the total wealth variant would probably be higher. If we arbitrarily assign to women three-fourths of the property in personal trust funds and 20 per cent of the pension, retirement, and annuity funds, their share would then be 42 per cent of the total wealth variant of top gross estate. Women have $54 billion of corporate stock in the basic variant; men, $63 billion. Women would probably have slightly more corporate stock than men in the total wealth variant.

and there are only a few age groups in which women had higher average estates than men (Table 38). Out of twelve age groups, women have higher averages in only four. Three of the four cases are in age groups under 50. This suggests that women must have an over-all average gross estate larger than that of men because they are more concentrated in a few age groups with relatively high average gross estate. Thinking along this line, one is struck (in Table 38) by the extraordinary and erratic divergence of the average gross estate and percentage of aggregate gross estate between the sexes in the younger age brackets. It is altogether possible that this divergence is in some part a "sampling error." The numbers in the original sample in the age groups under 50 are so small that one unusual case of a very large estate size would seriously affect the average for the group. In the 30 to 40 age group, for example, there were only 300 decedents, of whom fifty-seven were women. Under 30 years of age, there were only fifty-two decedents, of whom ten were women.

Hence, a part of the finding that women have a larger average gross estate than men may arise from a peculiar or unrepresentative draw of very rich younger women. Considering only the age groups above 50 for both men and women (that is, leaving out the four lowest age groups entirely) yields the entirely different result of a higher average gross estate for men than for women, $175,000 for men and $156,000 for women.

It appears that the 1953 sample of women decedents is somewhat atypical. The only other recent years for which age, sex, and estate size data are available are 1948, 1949, and 1950 (Appendix A). In each of those years the men top wealth-holders had a higher median estate than the women. This was also true in 1922. Women had a higher average estate size than men in 1922 and 1950, but about the same in 1948 and 1949. Women's share of top wealth was higher in 1953 than in any previous year, although this has been gradually increasing over time, so it is hard to say how representative the 40 per cent figure for that year is. As for the association of age and estate size, the 1948, 1949, and 1950 data seem to confirm the presence of an extraordinarily rich group of younger women. In 1948, women have a higher average estate in three out of four age groups under 50; in 1949, in two age groups; and in 1950, in all four age groups (Appendix Table A-6).

It is concluded that the 1953 results comparing men and women are not altogether representative and that the representative differences in average estate size (and particularly the differences by age groups) are probably not as great as shown in Chart 1 and Table 45. This leaves quite unexplained the intriguing puzzle of where the rich younger women come from and what happens to their wealth as they approach middle age.

Marital Status

Of the 1953 top wealth-holders 72 per cent were married, 16 per cent were widowers or widows, 3 per cent were divorced or separated, and 9 per cent were unmarried (Table 50 and Chart 17). (The

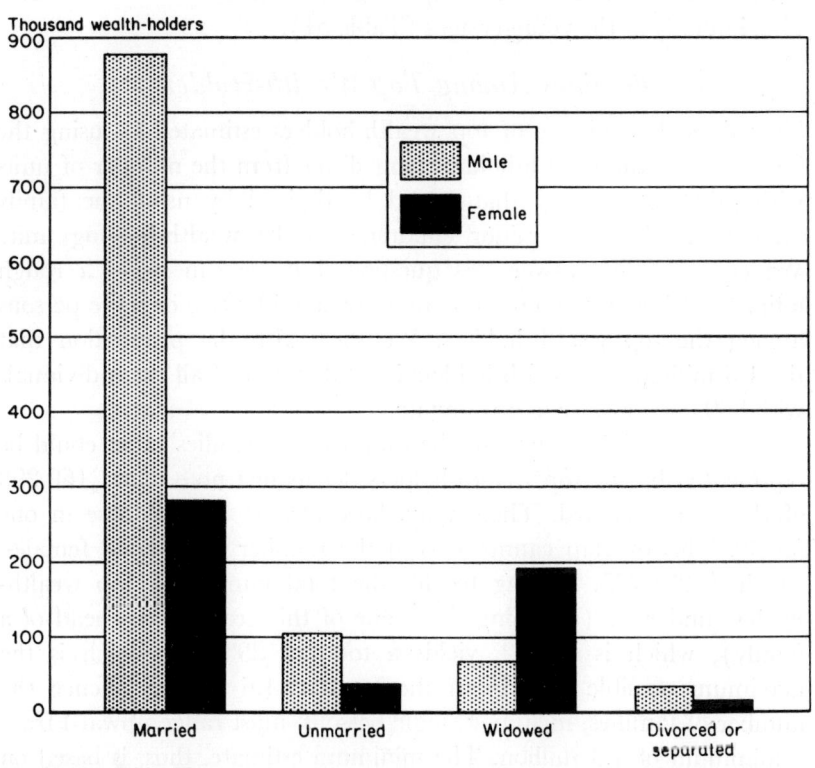

CHART 17
Top Wealth-Holders, by Sex and Marital Status, 1953

Source: Table 50.

derivation of these estimates is explained in Appendix Table A-12.) As would be expected, the distribution by marital status is not the same for men and women. About 85 per cent of the men in the group are married, while only about half of the women are married. (It is shown below that a disproportionate number of these married women are from community property states.) While an insignificant number of the men are widowers, over a third of the women are widows. Also as would be expected, most of the married top wealth-holders are found in the younger and middle age groups, and the widowers and widows are concentrated in the older age groups (Table 51).

Comparing this distribution with that for the total population yields the interesting result that the wealth-holders form a larger part of the widow and widower population than of any other marital status group (3.1 per cent for males and 2.6 per cent for females). They are also a relatively large part (2.3 per cent) of the married male group. Divorced and separated persons are considerably underrepresented in the wealth-holder group. Single persons are underrepresented also, but only at the younger ages (Table 51).

Families Among Top Wealth-Holders

How does the number of top wealth-holders estimated by using the individual as the wealth-holding unit differ from the number of units with $60,000 or more that would be derived by using the family (husband, wife, and minor children) as the wealth-holding unit? We cannot fully answer this question, but we can make a rough estimate of how many families are represented by two or more persons among the top wealth-holders. We start with the proposition that the 1.6 million top wealth-holders is a full count of all the individuals with $60,000 or more of gross estate.

To set a minium limit to the number of "families" that could be represented by the top wealth-holders, let us first note that 1,160,298 of them are married. There may, however, be two of these in one family. This overlap cannot exceed the number of married females, which is 281,735. Adding to this the total number of top wealth-holders under 21 (assuming that none of this group is the head of a family), which is 12,222, yields a total of 293,957, which is the maximum possible overlap in the total of 1.6 million. Hence the number of families, including single persons, must range upward from a minimum of 1.3 million. The minimum estimate, thus, is based on the assumption that the husband of every female top wealth-holder is also a top wealth-holder and that every minor wealth-holder has one, but not more than one, parent or minor sibling who is also a top wealth-holder.

Some unknown number of families who have one wealth-holder

with $60,000 or more have a second person with less than $60,000 of gross estate. Further, some unknown number who have two or more persons holding less than $60,000 each will have combined holdings of $60,000 or more.

The total number of "married couples, other family groups, and persons living alone" in 1953 was 57,090,000. Our minimum estimate of the number of such units with $60,000 or more of gross estate was 1.3 million, which is 2.3 per cent of the national total. The national total of married couples was 37.1 million, while our minimum estimate of married couples with $60,000 and over, which is the same as the number of married males, is 876,646. The latter is 2.4 per cent of the national total.

The Survey of Consumer Finances uses the "spending unit" as the income-receiving and wealth-holding unit. The spending unit, which is defined as a group of persons living alone and pooling their incomes, is not in all cases the same as a family by the Census definition. In 1953, the Survey found 3 per cent of spending units had $60,000 or more of total assets. This compares closely with our minimum estimate of 2.3 per cent of families and other households.

Community Property

The community property states are eight in number: Arizona, California, Idaho, Louisiana, Nevada, New Mexico, Texas, and Washington. In 1953 these states contained 17.9 per cent of the total national population and received 18.1 per cent of the personal income payments. They were represented on 6,160 (or 16.7 per cent) of the estate tax returns of that year out of a total of 36,699. The amount of gross estate reported on those returns came to $1.2 billion (or 16.2 per cent) out of the national total of $7.4 billion. When the data on these returns are blown up to represent the living population, we find that the community property states have 18.7 per cent of the top wealth-holders and 18.5 per cent of the estate tax wealth. Therefore, it would seem that these states are not underrepresented in either the number of wealth-holders or the amount of estate tax wealth.

However, the community property states, considered as a group, have a per capita income rank somewhat above the middle of all states (eighteenth among the forty non-community property states), so it would perhaps be reasonable to predict that they would have more than 18 per cent of the top wealth-holders. In relating the share of estate tax returns for four years to the share of total personal income payments, we find that the ratio for community property states (0.95) is somewhat below the national ratio of 1.00 (Table 52). This does not appear to be strong enough evidence, however, to change our first conclusion that community property states are not underrepresented in the top wealth-holder group.[10]

This finding is rather puzzling since community law provides for the "compulsory splitting" of property between spouses. (More precisely, this division applies only to property acquired after marriage.) Hence, we would expect that relatively more estates would be split out of the $60,000 and over group and the average size of estate would be smaller than in the common law states where such splitting is not automatic but can be accomplished only by actually making a gift.

The importance of this consideration can be seen in the fact that 51.4 per cent of the male top wealth-holders in non-community property states have estates under $120,000 (Table 54). Appendix Table A-12 suggests that 85 per cent of male top wealth-holders in these states are married. This means that 401,426 out of the 918,805 male top wealth-holders in non-community property states would not be top wealth-holders if those states had the institution of community property. By the same token, about 20 per cent of the wealth would not be counted.

The unexpectedly large number of top wealth-holders in community states is related to the striking difference in the proportion of women found in the two groups. It will be recalled that men outnumber women in the estimated total of top wealth-holders by about two to one. However, there are considerably fewer men (about one and a half) per woman among the top wealth-holders in the community property states. More specifically, women make up 41 per cent of the top wealth-holders in community property states and only 29 per cent in non-community property states (Table 53). Also a disproportionate number of the married females are from community property states (see Appendix Table A-12).

The higher frequency of women wealth-holders in community property states may be explained by two considerations. First, under community property law, a woman who predeceases her husband has to file the amount of one-half the marital estate, which is not normally the case in a common law state. Secondly, in community property states, a husband who predeceases his wife cannot place his

---

[10] The reader who wishes to pursue this question further is referred to Appendix Table A-13.

wife's share of the community property in a life estate and thereby avoid filing an estate tax at time of the wife's subsequent death, as is often the case with property transferred to wives at time of death in common law states.[11]

It is also possible that there is a radically different ratio of wealth to income before taxes in the two groups of states and that a husband-wife wealth distribution would show many more top wealth-holding units in community property than in non-community property states. This possibility is enhanced by the favorable treatment before 1948 of community property states under personal income tax law and the continued favorable treatment of mineral resources under the depletion provisions. The latter has special significance here since the community property states include several states that lead in oil production and mining.

Tables 53 and 54 present comparative data for the two groups of states. The women top wealth-holders in community property states are younger, with a median age of 54, than those in common law states. The men in the former states, however, are slightly older, with median ages of 54 and 52, respectively.

While the average gross estate is larger for women than for men in both groups of states, the difference by sex is more marked in the common law states, as would be expected from the greater age difference in these states. In the common law states the average is $161,000 for men and $231,000 for women; in the community property states it is $167,000 for men and $196,000 for women. A comparison of the distributions of wealth by size shows little difference in inequality for men in the two groups of states (Table 54 and Charts 18 and 19). For women, however, there is a clear difference, with greater inequality in the common law states. This occurs, in large part, because while 25 per cent of the aggregate gross estate of women is in gross estate sizes of over $5 million in the common law states, there is no wealth in those estate sizes for women in the community property states. The possibility that sampling error causes this result is, of course, to be borne in mind in interpreting the charts.

---

[11] It should be noted that the marital deduction introduced in 1948 lessened the tax incentive for husbands to make gifts before death to their wives and similarly reduced the tax advantage of using the life estate. The 1954 law, however, allowed a life estate to be counted in the marital deduction and hence restored the tax incentive for its use. Another possible explanation of why community states are not underrepresented may be that there is more voluntary splitting of estates via gifts to persons other than spouses in common law states than in community property states.

The composition of estates held by women is much more like that of men's estates in the community property states than in the common law states (Table 55).

What we find, then, is that in community property states, as opposed to common law states, women top wealth-holders are nearer

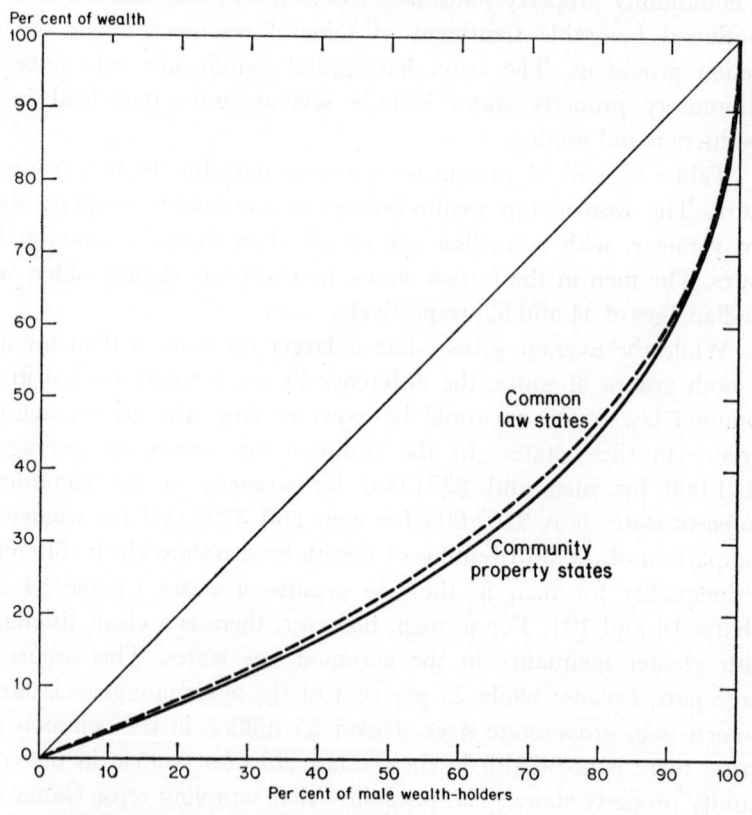

CHART 18
Lorenz Curves of Wealth Among Male Top Wealth-Holders, Community Property and Common Law States, 1953

Source: Table 54.

in age to men wealth-holders; the average size of their estates is closer to that of men's, and the composition of their estates is more similar to that of men's. All this is consistent with the idea that property is split without actual gift in the community property states and that there is consequently less splitting in common law states.

CHART 19
Lorenz Curves of Wealth Among Female Top Wealth-Holders,
Community Property and Common Law States, 1953

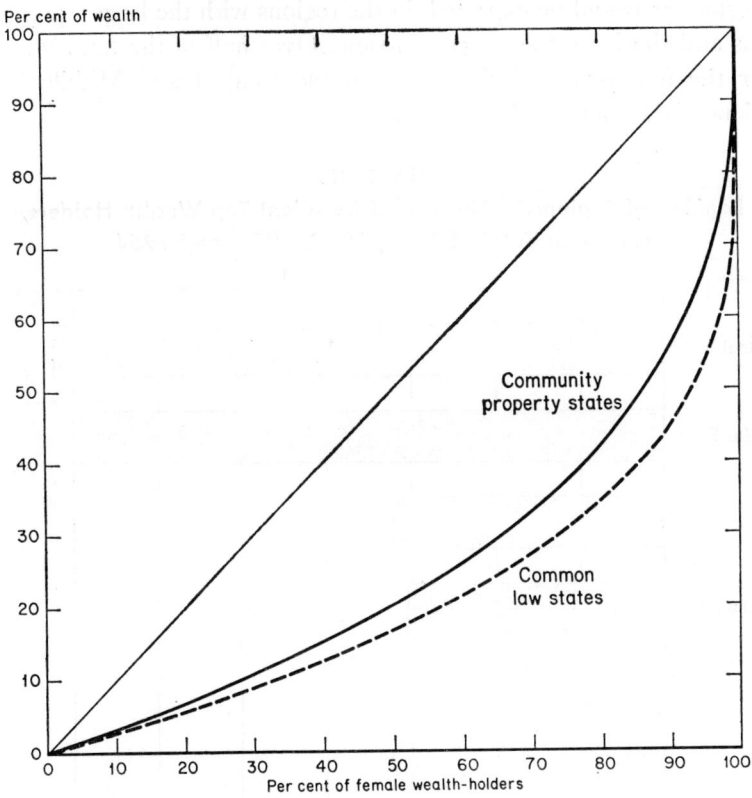

Source: Table 54.

State and Region of Residence

Unfortunately we do not have age and sex information for estate tax returns by state so the estate-multiplier method cannot be applied. It is probable that somewhat different results would follow from the multiplying process since mortality does differ by state and since the sex composition of decedent wealth-holders also differs by state. Further, only gross estate on taxable returns is classified by state. Hence the following findings should be treated with caution. In order to limit the error, the estate tax returns by state were combined for the last four years for which they were available: 1949, 1950, 1953, and 1954. Hence, in the following tables, meaning attaches only to the position of one state relative to another and not to the absolute sums shown, except where they are averaged.

The largest numbers of decedent estate tax wealth-holders are reported, as would be expected, in the regions with the largest populations and the largest aggregate income. Over half of the total returns over the four-year period were from the Central and Middle East regions of the country (Chart 20).

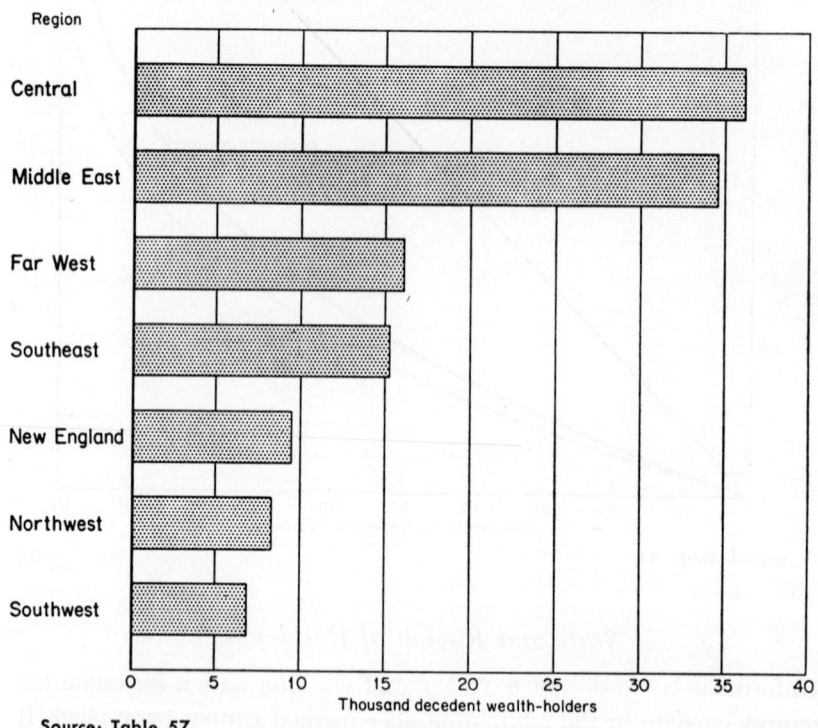

CHART 20
Ranking of Regions by Number of Decedent Top Wealth-Holders, Four-Year Total of 1948, 1949, 1953, and 1954

Source: Table 57.

It is also quite clear that there is some association between per capita income rank and number of returns per thousand of the population. The low per capita income regions, the Southeast and the Southwest, are considerably underrepresented in the number of returns and gross estate (see Table 56, cols. 10 and 11).

Among the higher per capita income regions, the Northwest and New England appear to be overrepresented, but the Central region is lower than its per capita income rank would lead us to expect. The relationship between the share of gross estate and the share of total income payments is exceptionally high for New England and relatively low for the Central and Far West regions.

Table 57 is set up to show the relationship of each state's population and income payments to the number of its estate tax returns and the total gross estate on them. Column 9 shows the ratio, by state, of the share of estate tax returns to the share of population. Iowa is the leading state in this measure, with 2.17 times as many returns as its share of the nation's population would predict. Mississippi and South Carolina are the lowest, with ratios of 0.36.

Column 10 shows the ratio of the share of gross estate on taxable returns to the share of income payments for each state. Delaware has twice as much gross estate as its share of income payments would predict, while Utah has only one-quarter as much as predicted by its share of income payments.

Many of these variations can be explained by per capita income rank, with the estate tax data magnifying the differences. The strong position of all the New England states, however, seems to be due to more than high income rank. A plausible explanation is the past high income rank of the region and the maintenance of an entrenched wealth position by some New England families. This region has the second highest per capita property income rank (Table 56, col. 5). The failure of some of the Central states, notably Michigan, Ohio, and Indiana, to turn up their share of gross estate is hard to explain in view of their high per capita income rank and high per capita property income rank. In the Northwest, Kansas and Nebraska have more than their share of gross estate. In the Far West, Washington—a high per capita income state—shows considerably less gross estate than its share of income payments and per capita income rank would predict. Some of these variations may be explained by differences in the industrial and occupational composition of the work force in these states. Some industries have a higher capital to income ratio than others. The fact that Iowa has more wealth-holders than predicted may be due to the high capital to income ratio in agriculture.

Income and Savings

The Survey of Consumer Finances provides evidence of a strong association between level of income and size of asset holding. Of particular interest to this study is their finding that 62 per cent of those spending units with assets of $60,000 or more have annual incomes of $7,500 and over (Table 58). At the same time, however, only 33 per cent of those with incomes of $7,500 or more have total assets of $60,000 or more (Appendix Table A-14). The median size of asset holdings for this top income group is $43,800. Of the group with assets over $60,000, 66 per cent saved at least $1,000 in 1949. On the other hand, 20 per cent of them dissaved during the year. Of those who saved at least $2,000, 89 per cent were in the top three asset classes (Appendix Tables A-15 and A-16).

The association of high income and larger wealth-holding is also indicated by the concentration of property income in the higher income groups. The relatively great importance of property income for the top percentiles of persons when ranked by per capita income is shown in the two tables reproduced here from Kuznets' work. Table 59 shows that while "property income" (in this case rent, interest, and dividends) is 15.8 per cent of the income of the total population, it is 48.7 per cent of the income of the top 1 per cent. Table 60 shows that this top 1 per cent received 40 per cent of the national total of property income.

Kuznets calculated that eliminating all property income would reduce the top percentile's share of total income from 13.1 to 8.1 per cent, and the top 5 per cent's share from 24.7 to 19.2. Redistributing property income equally would yield shares of 7.0 and 16.9 per cent for the top 1 per cent and the top 5 per cent, respectively.[12]

Income receipt and wealth-holding are, of course, causally interrelated in that wealth accumulation arises out of income and wealth yields income. One way to express the relationship at a given moment in time is by the wealth-income ratio. In the United States the wealth of all persons in recent years has been about three and a half times the income of all persons. However, this ratio varies by income level, with the highest ratios in the lowest and highest income groups. For the top income groups of $7,500 or more, the ratio was 5.5 in 1949 (Table 61). These ratios are, of course, primarily determined by the share of property income in total income.

Occupation

All studies of income status emphasize the importance of occupation as a leading determinant of income. It is true, of course, that occupa-

---

[12] Simon Kuznets, *Shares of Upper Income Groups in Income and Savings,* New York, National Bureau of Economic Research, 1953, pp. 28–29.

tion is interrelated with other variables such as age, sex, race, education, and place of residence, so that it cannot be considered the most fundamental determinant. However, a Census study for 1952 came up with a typical result. Of the upper 2 per cent of income recipients, almost three-fourths were either independent professionals, businessmen, or managerial workers. About one-tenth were farmers.[13]

Survey of Consumer Finances data reveal a similar relationship between occupation and size of total assets. The occupational groups which are overrepresented in the highest asset classes are the self-employed, the retired, farm operators, the professional and semiprofessional, and the managerial groups. The self-employed group shows the highest average and median, with 73 per cent of the group having assets over $10,000 (Table 62).

TABLE 34
PERCENTAGE DISTRIBUTION OF ESTATE TAX WEALTH-HOLDERS AND BASIC VARIANT AGGREGATE GROSS ESTATE BY GROSS ESTATE SIZE, 1953

Gross Estate Size (thous. dollars)	Wealth-Holders	Aggregate Gross Estate
60 to 70	10.90	3.6
70 to 80	10.63	4.0
80 to 90	10.47	4.4
90 to 100	9.12	4.3
100 to 120	13.52	7.3
120 to 150	13.02	8.5
150 to 200	11.20	9.5
200 to 300	10.10	12.1
300 to 500	6.09	11.8
500 to 1,000	3.07	11.0
1,000 to 2,000	1.17	8.3
2,000 to 3,000	0.24	3.3
3.000 to 5,000	0.14	2.8
5,000 to 10,000	0.09	4.3
10,000 and over	0.04	4.9
All sizes	100.00	100.0

[13] *Current Population Reports: Consumer Income,* P-60, No. 11, Washington, 1953, Table 1. For a discussion of occupation as a determinant of income, see Kuznets, *Shares of Upper Income Groups,* Part II, Chapter 5; Herman P. Miller, *Income of the American People,* New York, 1955, pp. 29 ff; and Jacob Mincer, "A Study of Personal Income Distribution," unpublished Ph.D. dissertation, Columbia University, New York, 1957.

TABLE 35

ESTATE TAX WEALTH-HOLDERS[a] AS A PERCENTAGE OF TOTAL POPULATION, BY SEX AND AGE GROUP, 1953

Age Group	Total Population			Top Wealth-Holders			Top Wealth-Holders as a Percentage of Total Population		
	Both Sexes	Male	Female	Both Sexes	Male	Female	Both Sexes	Male	Female
Under 21[b]	56,242,000	28,633,000	27,609,000	12,410	5,582	6,828	—	—	—
21 to 30[b]	23,169,000	11,513,000	11,658,000	47,476	31,258	16,218	0.2	0.3	0.1
30 to 40	23,641,000	11,599,000	12,042,000	193,973	139,546	54,427	0.8	1.2	0.4
40 to 50	20,594,000	10,185,000	10,409,000	383,200	277,976	105,224	1.9	2.7	0.9
50 to 55	8,696,000	4,306,000	4,390,000	219,936	151,826	68,110	2.5	3.5	1.5
55 to 60	7,506,000	3,703,000	3,803,000	206,152	142,895	63,257	2.7	4.0	1.7
60 to 65	6,457,000	3,181,000	3,275,000	188,074	127,266	60,808	2.9	4.0	1.8
65 to 70	5,181,000	2,516,000	2,665,000	152,033	97,124	54,909	2.9	3.9	2.0
70 to 75	3,851,000	1,801,000	2,050,000	113,419	66,982	46,437	2.9	3.7	2.2
75 to 80	2,334,000	1,071,000	1,263,000	74,752	41,306	33,446	3.2	3.9	2.6
80 to 85	1,247,000	554,000	693,000	41,293	21,211	20,082	3.3	3.8	2.8
85 and over	711,000	294,000	417,000	26,080	13,396	12,684	3.6	4.6	3.0
20 and over	103,387,000	50,721,000	52,665,000	1,658,795[c]	1,116,369[c]	542,426[c]	1.60	2.20	1.02
All ages	159,629,000	79,354,000	80,274,000	1,658,795	1,116,369	542,426[c]	1.04	1.41	0.67

[a] Adjusted to account for returns with age unspecified.
[b] For the total population, the age groups are "under 20" and "20 to 30".
[c] The entire under 21 age group has been added in here for lack of a detailed breakdown.

TABLE 36
HYPOTHETICAL NUMBER OF TOP WEALTH-HOLDERS WITHIN
AGE COHORTS OF 100,000 STARTING AT AGE 20, BY SEX

Age	Numbers of Persons Remaining in Cohort Starting with 100,000 Males at Age 20 (1)	Top Wealth-Holders Within Male Cohort (2)	Number of Persons Remaining in Cohort Starting with 100,000 Females at Age 20 (3)	Top Wealth-Holders Within Female Cohort (4)
24	98,953	297	99,600	100
29	98,016	294	99,103	100
34	96,942	1,163	98,441	394
39	95,447	1,145	97,382	390
44	93,085	2,606	95,882	863
49	89,375	2,502	93,650	843
54	83,757	3,015	90,280	1,354
59	75,943	3,038	85,639	1,370
64	65,483	2,685	78,923	1,421
69	52,673	2,107	69,076	1,382
74	39,028	1,483	56,411	1,241
79	24,381	975	39,711	1,032
84	11,978	467	22,088	618
85 and over	4,029	189	8,196	246

SOURCE: Cols. 1 and 3 based on 1953 mortality experience; cols. 2 and 4 estimated from Table 35.

TABLE 37
Percentage Distribution of Estate Tax Wealth and Wealth-Holders by Age Group, 1944 and 1953

Age Group	Number of Wealth-Holders	Total Gross Estate	Average Gross Estate (dollars)
	1944		
Total	876,442	$149.6 bill.	172,000
Under 30	3.2%	2.6%	
21 to 30			140,000
30 to 40	16.2	13.5	143,000
40 to 50	24.4	20.8	147,000
50 to 55	13.8	13.0	162,000
55 to 60	11.5	11.4	171,000
60 to 65	9.8	11.0	194,000
65 to 70	8.5	11.2	228,000
70 to 75	6.2	7.6	214,000
75 to 80	3.8	5.3	239,000
80 to 85	1.7	2.3	225,000
85 and over	0.9	1.3	242,000
	1953		
Total	1,609,538	$292.8 bill.	182,002
Under 21	.8%	.8%	189,397
21 to 30	2.91	2.7	166,809
30 to 40	9.7	12.4	232,257
40 to 50	23.0	23.1	182,975
50 to 55	13.3	11.3	155,185
55 to 60	12.4	11.2	164,188
60 to 65	11.3	11.1	178,071
65 to 70	9.2	9.6	190,245
70 to 75	6.9	7.7	205,356
75 to 80	4.6	5.1	201,520
80 to 85	2.5	3.1	220,550
85 and over	1.6	1.9	222,705

SOURCE: For 1944, Mendershausen in R. W. Goldsmith, *A Study of Saving in the United States*, III, Princeton, 1956, Tables E-58 and E-59.

TABLE 38
Percentage Distribution of Estate Tax Wealth and Wealth-Holders by Sex and Age Group, 1953

Age Group	Number of Wealth-Holders	Total Gross Estate	Average Gross Estate (dollars)	Median Age (years)
MALES				
Total	1,084,065	$176.0 bill.	162,372	52
Under 21	.5%	.4%	136,969	
21 to 30	2.8	3.6	203,554	
30 to 40	12.5	8.1	104,902	
40 to 50	24.9	21.8	142,667	
50 to 55	13.6	13.0	155,240	
55 to 60	12.8	13.1	165,912	
60 to 65	11.4	12.7	181,063	
65 to 70	8.7	10.5	196,600	
70 to 75	6.0	7.6	206,820	
75 to 80	3.7	4.8	209,558	
80 to 85	1.9	2.6	219,581	
85 and over	1.2	1.7	239,482	
FEMALES				
Total	525,472	$116.9 bill.	220,500	56
Under 21	1.3%	1.3%	233,080	
21 to 30	3.0	1.3	96,000	
30 to 40	9.9	19.0	429,610	
40 to 50	19.1	25.0	291,185	
50 to 55	12.5	8.7	155,060	
55 to 60	11.6	8.4	160,270	
60 to 65	11.2	8.7	171,800	
65 to 70	10.2	8.2	179,049	
70 to 75	8.7	7.9	203,264	
75 to 80	6.3	5.5	191,770	
80 to 85	3.8	3.7	221,581	
85 and over	2.4	2.2	206,061	

TABLE 39
Distribution of Selected Balance Sheet Items by Age Group, 1950

Age Group	Median Total Assets (dollars)	Per Cent of Total Item		
		Total Assets	Net Worth	1949 Income
18 to 25	550	2	1	7
25 to 35	2,500	11	9	23
35 to 45	5,500	21	20	26
45 to 55	6,500	25	26	22
55 to 65	9,800	24	25	15
65 and over	6,200	16	18	7
Not ascertained		1	1	—
All ages		100	100	100

Source: Goldsmith, *Saving in U.S.*, III, Tables W-52 and W-61.

TABLE 40
DISTRIBUTION OF SPENDING UNITS BY TOTAL ASSETS WITHIN AGE GROUPS, 1950
(per cent)

Age Group of Head of Spending Unit	All Cases (1)	Total Assets (dollars)								
		Zero (2)	100 to 500 (3)	500 to 1,000 (4)	1,000 to 2,000 (5)	2,000 to 5,000 (6)	5,000 to 10,000 (7)	10,000 to 25,000 (8)	25,000 to 60,000 (9)	60,000 and over (10)
18 to 25	100	19	28	17	16	11	5	3	1	a
25 to 35	100	7	15	11	13	19	16	16	2	1
35 to 45	100	4	8	7	10	18	19	23	10	1
45 to 55	100	4	3	4	7	16	20	31	11	4
55 to 65	100	6	4	4	6	13	18	32	12	5
65 and over	100	11	6	5	5	11	19	26	11	6
All spending units	100	7	10	8	10	15	17	22	8	3

SOURCE: Goldsmith, *Saving in U.S.*, III, Table W-61.
[a] No cases reported or less than 0.5 per cent.

TABLE 41
SELECTED DATA ON LIFE CYCLE OF HUSBAND-WIFE FAMILIES

PART A

Median Age of Husband	Mean Size of Family, 1953[a]	Median Family Income, 1950 (dollars)[b]	Percentage of Home-Owners in Husband-Wife Families, 1950[c]
Under 30	3.07		38.6
30	3.89	3,099	
40	4.21	3,545	56.0
50	3.63		63.8
55		3,506	
60	2.97		69.8
Over 60	2.67	1,721	72.5

PART B

Stage of Life Cycle of Family, 1950	Median Age of Husband[d]
First marriage	23
Birth of last child	29
Marriage of last child	50
Death of one spouse	64
Death of other spouse	72

[a] Paul C. Glick, *American Families*, New York, 1957, Table 33, p. 54.
[b] *Ibid.*, Table 64, p. 98.
[c] *Ibid.*, Table 65, p. 99.
[d] *Ibid.*, Table 33, p. 54.

TABLE 42

DATA ON INCOME, ASSETS, AND NET WORTH: POSITIONS OF SPENDING UNITS AT DIFFERENT STAGES OF LIFE CYCLE IN 1953

	All Spending Units	Young Single	Young Married, Childless	Young Married, Youngest Child Under 6	Young Married, Youngest Child 6 or over	Older Married, (over 45) with Children	Older Married, (over 45), No Children Under 18	Older Single	Others
Median Income, 1953 ($)	3,800	2,600	4,800	4,300	5,000	4,300	3,900	1,700	2,700
Percentage of units with income over $4,000 in 1953	47	18	65	60	72	60	49	21	23
Percentage of families where wife had wage or salary income	21	—	63	23	38	24	23	—	—
Percentage receiving transfer payments	22	13	16	18	—	14	24	38	50
Percentage receiving interest, dividends, trust funds, or royalties of $100 or more	7	2	4	4	—	8	15	11	2
Median liquid assets ($)	350	190	400	180	410	590	1,020	760	—
Median face value of life insurance ($)	—	1,800	4,700	4,600	4,600	4,600	1,700	1,300	—
Median net worth ($)	4,100	700	3,100	3,100	5,200	7,800	10,900	5,400	—
Percentage with net worth over $5,000	46	15	40	39	51	64	69	52	—

SOURCE: J. B. Lansing and J. N. Morgan, "Consumer Finances over the Life Cycle," *Consumer Behavior*, II, L. Clarke, ed., New York, 1955, Tables 4, 6, 8, 12, and 13.

TABLE 43
Selected Data on Sources of Receipts of Aged Economic Units, Classified by Source, 1951

Source of Receipts	Percentage of Units with Source		Percentage of Aggregate Receipts of Group	Size of Source (dollars)		Percentage of Units with Source		Mean Amount of Total Receipts for Those with Indicated Principal Source (dollars)
	At All	As Principal Source		Median Size of Receipts from Source	Mean Size of Receipts from Source	Less Than $200	$2,500 or More	
Earnings								
Couples	56.7	42.1	63.9	1,820	2,514	7.1	37.5	3,225
Unrelated males	34.3	22.8	52.0	1,323	1,885	10.8	24.4	2,082
Unrelated females	12.6	7.8	18.0	471	995	23.2	8.2	1,593
Assets								
Couples	25.4	8.6	9.4	517	822	23.0	5.9	2,265
Unrelated males[a]	16.5	6.2	9.2	385	673	27.5	6.2	1,543
Unrelated females	20.4	12.6	26.5	508	851	15.7	8.7	1,236
Dissaving								
Couples	16.0	4.4	5.6	531	782	20.1	6.0	1,894
Unrelated males[a]	14.2	5.8	6.6	399	578	25.0	—	1,157
Unrelated females	15.2	7.0	14.9	471	681	20.4	4.8	1,176
Pensions								
Couples	35.3	22.6	16.0	842	1,001	7.0	4.2	1,532
Unrelated males	33.7	25.8	21.0	653	780	5.5	1.8	909
Unrelated females	20.9	14.6	19.6	483	634	8.0	0.8	724
Assistance								
Couples	16.6	12.0	4.9	602	668	7.1		926
Unrelated males	25.4	19.3	10.8	468	512	8.9		538
Unrelated females	24.9	23.4	19.5	488	528	7.8		561

Source: Steiner and Dorfman, *Economic Status of Aged*, Table 8.13, p. 112.
[a] Sample dangerously small.

TABLE 44
PERCENTAGE DISTRIBUTION OF NET VALUE OF TOTAL ASSETS OF AGED ECONOMIC UNITS BY TYPE OF UNIT AND AMOUNT OF ASSET HOLDINGS, 1951

Net Value of Total Assets[a]	All Units	Couples	Unrelated Males	Unrelated Females
Total units	100.0	100.0	100.0	100.0
Units with no assets	22.0	12.4	33.5	25.9
Units with assets	78.0	87.6	66.5	74.1
$ 1 to $ 500	9.5	5.3	6.4	14.9
$ 500 to $1,000	6.9	3.3	9.9	9.0
$1,000 to $3,000	8.1	7.4	9.0	8.3
$3,000 and over	53.5	71.6	41.2	41.9

SOURCE: Steiner and Dorfman, *Economic Status of Aged*, Table 107, p. 234.
[a] Excludes owner-occupied houses and life insurance.

TABLE 45
AVERAGE GROSS ESTATE OF TOP WEALTH-HOLDERS, BY SEX AND AGE GROUP, 1953
(dollars)

Age Group	Both Sexes	Men	Women
Under 21	189,397	136,969	233,080
21 to 30	166,809	203,554	96,000
30 to 40	232,257	104,902	429,000[a]
40 to 50	182,975	142,667	291,185
50 to 55	155,185	155,240	155,060
55 to 60	164,188	165,912	160,270
60 to 65	178,071	181,063	171,800
65 to 70	190,245	196,600	179,049
70 to 75	205,356	206,820	203,264
75 to 80	201,520	209,558	191,770
80 to 85	220,550	219,581	221,581
85 and over	222,705	239,482	206,061
All ages[b]	182,002	162,372	220,500

[a] The average for common law states was $506,000 and for community property states, $267,000.
[b] The average economic estate for all ages was $166,029 for both sexes, $144,067 for men, and $211,330 for women.

TABLE 46
Median Age of Top Wealth-Holders, by Sex and Gross Estate Size, 1953

Gross Estate Size (thous. dollars)	Males, All States	Females, All States	Females, Non-Community Property States	Females, Community Property States
60 to 70	53	57	58	56
70 to 80	55	60	61	56
80 to 90	53	55	60	52
90 to 100	52	55	55	55
100 to 120	53	55	57	52
120 to 150	54	57	59	55
150 to 200	54	57	58	53
200 to 300	52	58	60	57
300 to 500	55	55	60	38
500 to 1,000	58	55	56	48
1,000 to 2,000	55	50	58	44
2,000 to 3,000	60	46	46	45
3,000 to 5,000	64	63	67	57
5,000 to 10,000	68	36	36	—
10,000 and over	73	46	46	—
1,000 and over	58	49		
All estate sizes	52	56	58	54

TABLE 47

Percentage Distribution of Male Top Wealth-Holders in Non-Community Property States by Gross Estate Size Within Age Groups, 1953

Gross Estate Size (thous. dollars)	Under 21	21 to 30	30 to 40	40 to 50	50 to 55	55 to 60	60 to 65	65 to 70	70 to 75	75 to 80	80 to 85	85 and over
Under 60	33.3	—	—	—	—	—	—	—	0.1	—	—	—
60 to 70	—	10.0	7.2	7.9	9.6	8.8	7.5	9.0	10.0	10.9	11.2	12.0
70 to 80	—	13.3	9.6	7.7	10.3	10.3	10.9	10.3	11.6	11.6	10.7	11.1
80 to 90	—	3.3	15.9	9.1	9.2	10.0	9.6	10.5	9.6	9.7	9.3	9.9
90 to 100	—	3.3	13.0	9.2	9.7	7.9	8.3	8.5	8.9	8.2	8.7	7.7
100 to 120	—	16.7	14.4	14.8	11.4	14.2	13.6	13.0	12.4	12.1	11.6	11.5
120 to 150	66.7	13.3	10.1	16.4	15.4	13.7	15.1	14.3	12.5	12.3	11.9	11.4
150 to 200	—	3.3	10.1	14.4	13.0	13.4	12.4	12.0	11.8	11.0	11.3	11.6
200 to 300	—	20.0	13.0	11.5	11.3	10.0	11.4	9.7	9.6	10.6	9.9	10.1
300 to 500	—	6.7	4.8	5.9	6.0	6.9	6.4	6.5	7.0	6.9	7.5	7.0
500 to 1,000	—	6.7	1.4	2.1	2.7	3.7	3.2	4.0	3.9	4.2	5.1	5.1
1,000 to 2,000	—	3.3	—	1.1	1.3	0.9	1.0	1.2	1.7	1.6	1.9	1.6
2,000 to 3,000	—	—	—	—	—	0.1	0.2	0.3	0.2	0.5	0.4	0.4
3,000 to 5,000	—	—	—	—	0.1	0.1	0.3	0.2	0.4	0.2	0.2	0.2
5,000 to 10,000	—	—	—	—	—	—	—	0.2	0.1	—	0.1	0.3
10,000 and over	—	—	—	—	—	—	—	—	—	—	0.1	0.2
Total	100	100	100	100	100	100	100	100	100	100	100	100
Median estate size (thous. $)	130	130	105	122	120	120	120	120	118	118	120	120

TABLE 48

PERCENTAGE DISTRIBUTION OF MALE TOP WEALTH-HOLDERS IN NON-COMMUNITY PROPERTY STATES BY AGE GROUP WITHIN GROSS ESTATE SIZES, 1953

Age Group	Gross Estate Size (thous. dollars)															
	Under 60	60 to 70	70 to 80	80 to 90	90 to 100	100 to 120	120 to 150	150 to 200	200 to 300	300 to 500	500 to 1,000	1,000 to 2,000	2,000 to 3,000	3,000 to 5,000	5,000 to 10,000	10,000 and over
Under 21	—	1.4	—	—	—	—	1.7	—	—	—	—	—	—	—	—	—
21 to 30	—	3.1	3.7	0.9	1.0	3.3	2.5	0.7	4.8	2.9	6.1	8.4	—	—	—	—
30 to 40	73.9	10.4	12.3	19.6	17.9	13.4	8.8	10.3	14.5	9.8	6.1	—	—	—	—	—
40 to 50	—	22.2	19.2	22.1	24.9	26.9	28.1	28.7	25.1	23.5	17.0	24.7	—	—	—	—
50 to 55	—	14.9	14.2	12.2	14.4	11.4	14.6	14.2	13.6	13.2	12.0	16.2	—	9.0	—	—
55 to 60	—	13.2	13.7	12.9	11.3	13.7	12.5	14.1	11.6	14.6	16.2	10.6	17.4	15.9	12.8	—
60 to 65	5.2	9.9	12.7	10.9	10.5	11.6	12.1	11.5	11.6	12.0	12.3	10.1	23.0	27.9	16.7	—
65 to 70	6.8	9.0	9.2	9.0	8.2	8.4	8.7	8.5	7.5	9.3	11.8	9.8	22.8	16.2	38.8	28.1
70 to 75	9.7	6.8	7.0	5.6	5.8	5.4	5.2	5.6	5.1	6.7	7.8	9.6	10.8	18.1	15.8	19.4
75 to 80	3.2	4.7	4.4	3.6	3.4	3.3	3.2	3.3	3.5	4.2	5.3	5.7	15.5	7.6	5.2	13.0
80 to 85	1.1	2.5	2.1	1.8	1.9	1.7	1.6	1.8	1.7	2.4	3.4	3.4	6.3	2.9	3.5	17.3
85 and over	—	1.6	1.3	1.2	1.0	1.0	0.9	1.1	1.1	1.3	2.0	1.7	4.2	2.4	6.9	22.7
Total	100	100	100	100	100	100	100	100	100	100	100	100	100	100	100	100
Median age (years)	37	54	56	53	52	53	53	53	52	55	57	55	67	64	67	75

TOP WEALTH-HOLDERS IN 1953

TABLE 49
PERCENTAGE DISTRIBUTION OF ESTATE TAX WEALTH BY SEX AND GROSS ESTATE SIZE, 1953

Gross Estate Size (thous. dollars)	Number of Wealth-Holders	Gross Estate	Average Gross Estate (dollars)	Median Gross Estate (dollars)
		MALES		
Total	100.00%	100.00%	$162,372	$116,800
Under 60	0.08	0.03		
60 to 70	9.18	3.25		
70 to 80	10.27	4.16		
80 to 90	10.00	4.43		
90 to 100	9.00	4.51		
100 to 120	13.70	7.88		
120 to 150	14.06	9.88		
150 to 200	11.86	10.81		
200 to 300	11.09	14.24		
300 to 500	6.16	12.96		
500 to 1,000	2.90	11.58		
1,000 to 2,000	1.07	8.63		
2,000 to 3,000	0.15	2.14		
3,000 to 5,000	0.13	2.88		
5,000 to 10,000	0.04	1.65		
10,000 and over	0.01	0.97		
		FEMALES		
Total	100.00%	100.00%	$220,500	$105,200
Under 60	0.13	0.03		
60 to 70	14.42	4.13		
70 to 80	11.34	3.75		
80 to 90	11.40	4.22		
90 to 100	9.32	3.94		
100 to 120	13.08	6.30		
120 to 150	10.89	6.49		
150 to 200	9.73	7.48		
200 to 300	8.06	8.76		
300 to 500	5.93	10.02		
500 to 1,000	3.40	10.20		
1,000 to 2,000	1.30	7.83		
2,000 to 3,000	0.44	5.09		
3,000 to 5,000	0.16	2.61		
5,000 to 10,000	0.20	8.28		
10,000 and over	0.09	10.87		

TABLE 50
NUMBER OF ESTATE TAX WEALTH-HOLDERS, BY SEX,
AGE GROUP, AND MARITAL STATUS, 1953[a]

Age Group	Married	Widowed	Divorced or Separated	Unmarried	Total
		MALES			
Under 21	—	—	—	5,556	5,556
21 to 30	14,999	833	—	14,999	30,831
30 to 40	111,676	1,667	7,223	14,446	135,012
40 to 50	241,309	5,555	7,555	15,110	269,529
50 to 55	130,500	4,000	3,700	9,500	147,700
55 to 60	119,048	5,206	4,388	10,004	138,646
60 to 65	103,911	7,257	3,513	8,839	123,520
65 to 70	73,037	9,472	2,688	9,114	94,311
70 to 75	45,245	10,556	1,929	7,116	64,846
75 to 80	23,736	10,188	768	5,736	40,428
80 to 85	9,592	7,696	528	3,224	21,040
85 and over	3,593	6,662	249	2,104	12,608
Age unknown	1,917	744	161	542	3,364
All ages	878,563	69,836	32,702	106,290	1,087,391
		FEMALES			
Under 21	—	3,333	—	3,333	6,666
21 to 30	6,000	2,000	2,000	6,000	16,000
30 to 40	37,273	5,455	4,546	4,546	51,820
40 to 50	75,200	16,800	2,800	5,600	100,400
50 to 55	43,844	15,769	1,538	4,615	65,766
55 to 60	38,056	19,539	1,136	2,272	61,003
60 to 65	29,982	25,165	1,007	2,732	58,886
65 to 70	22,260	27,645	763	2,926	53,594
70 to 75	15,120	27,297	702	2,430	45,549
75 to 80	8,388	22,653	306	1,932	33,279
80 to 85	3,533	14,851	154	1,238	19,776
85 and over	1,579	10,043	131	923	12,676
Age unknown	500	1,360	49	138	2,047
All ages	281,735	191,910	15,132	38,685	527,462

[a] Derived by using adjusted mortality rates.

TABLE 51
TOTAL POPULATION AND ESTATE TAX WEALTH-HOLDERS,[a] BY SEX, AGE GROUP, AND MARITAL STATUS, 1953

	Age Group								
	14 to 20	20 to 30	30 to 40[b]	40 to 50[b]	50 to 55[b]	55 to 65	65 to 75	75 and over[b]	Total
					MALES				
1. Married in population	164,000	6,498,000	9,958,000	8,408,000	3,734,000	5,534,000	3,216,000	1,110,000	38,612,000[d]
2. Married wealth-holders	—	14,999	111,676	241,309	130,500	222,959	118,282	36,921	876,646
3. Line 2 as % of line 1		0.2	1.1	2.9	3.5	4.0	3.7	3.4	2.3
4. Single in population	6,014,000	3,060,000	1,478,000	980,000	312,000	672,000	350,000	134,000	13,000,000
5. Single wealth-holders	5,556	14,999	14,446	15,110	9,500	18,843	16,230	11,064	105,748
6. Line 5 as % of line 4	0.09	0.5	0.1	1.5	3.0	2.8	4.6	8.2	0.8
7. Divorced or separated in population[c]	4,000	338,000	558,000	510,000	256,000	442,000	272,000	70,000	2,450,000
8. Divorced or separated wealth-holders	—	—	7,223	7,555	3,700	7,901	4,617	1,545	32,541
9. Line 8 as % of line 7			1.3	1.5	1.4	1.8	1.7	2.2	1.3
10. Widowed in population	—	8,000	106,000	158,000	100,000	512,000	678,000	666,000	2,228,000
11. Widowed wealth-holders	—	833	1,667	5,555	4,000	12,463	20,028	24,546	69,092
12. Line 11 as % of line 10		10.4	1.6	3.5	4.0	2.4	3.0	3.7	3.1
					FEMALES				
1. Married in population	884,000	9,072,000	10,432,000	8,376,000	3,440,000	4,520,000	2,220,000	480,000	39,426,000
2. Married wealth-holders	—	6,000	37,273	75,200	43,844	68,038	37,380	13,500	281,235
3. Line 2 as % of line 1		0.07	0.4	0.9	1.3	1.5	1.7	2.8	0.7
4. Single in population	5,526,000	2,304,000	856,000	730,000	328,000	558,000	338,000	154,000	10,774,000
5. Single wealth-holders	3,333	6,000	4,546	5,600	4,615	5,004	5,356	4,093	38,547
6. Line 5 as % of line 4	0.06	0.26	0.5	0.8	1.4	0.9	1.6	2.6	0.4
7. Divorced or separated in population[c]	44,000	576,000	868,000	770,000	348,000	344,000	162,000	48,000	3,160,000
8. Divorced or separated wealth-holders	—	2,000	4,546	2,800	1,538	2,143	1,465	591	15,083
9. Line 8 as % of line 7		0.3	0.5	0.4	0.4	0.6	0.9	1.2	0.5
10. Widowed in population	4,000	108,000	365,000	711,000	490,000	1,860,000	2,120,000	1,746,000	7,404,000
11. Widowed wealth-holders	3,333	2,000	5,455	16,800	15,769	44,704	54,942	47,547	190,550
12. Line 11 as % of line 10	83.3	1.8	1.5	2.4	3.2	2.4	2.6	2.7	2.6

SOURCE: Population data from *Current Population Reports: Population Characteristics*, P-20, No. 50, Washington, 1953.

[a] Excludes 5,411 estate tax wealth-holders with age unknown.
[b] Includes divorced, separated, and husband (wife) absent for other reasons, but excludes husband absent in Armed Forces.
[c] Total population in age group estimated from data on broader age group.
[d] Married males number less than married females because of exclusion of most men in Armed Forces.

TABLE 52

POPULATION AND INCOME PAYMENTS IN 1953 AND ESTATE TAX RETURNS FOR 1949, 1950, 1953, AND 1954 COMBINED, COMMUNITY PROPERTY STATES AND U.S.

State	1953 Population		1953 Income Payments		Total Returns in Four Years		Aggregate Gross Estate on Taxable Returns in Four Years		Col. 6 ÷ Col. 2	Col. 8 ÷ Col. 4
	Thousands (1)	Per Cent of U.S. Total (2)	Million Dollars (3)	Per Cent of U.S. Total (4)	No. (5)	Per Cent of U.S. Total (6)	Million Dollars (7)	Per Cent of U.S. Total (8)	(9)	(10)
Arizona	930	0.6	1,370	0.5	431	0.3	65,461	0.3	0.50	0.60
California	12,190	7.7	24,856	9.2	13,002	10.2	2,131,184	10.0	1.32	1.08
Idaho	603	0.4	851	0.3	288	0.2	38,100	0.2	0.50	0.66
Louisiana	2,884	1.8	3,602	1.3	1,018	0.8	193,495	0.9	0.44	0.69
Nevada	206	0.1	448	0.2	169	0.1	44,754	0.2	1.00	1.00
New Mexico	758	0.5	1,021	0.4	257	0.2	40,483	0.2	0.40	0.50
Texas	8,298	5.2	12,279	4.5	4,638	3.7	918,207	4.3	0.71	0.95
Washington	2,478	1.6	4,663	1.7	1,732	1.4	238,490	1.1	0.87	0.65
All community property states	28,347	17.9	49,090	18.1	21,535	17.0	3,670,174	17.1	0.95	0.94
Total U.S.	158,307	100.0	270,577	100.0	126,878	100.0	21,420,633	100.0	1.00	1.00
12 non-community property states with income ranks of 12 to 23									1.17	0.96
Median of 40 non-community property states									1.00	

SOURCE: Table 57.

TABLE 53
PERCENTAGE DISTRIBUTION OF ESTATE TAX WEALTH BY SEX AND AGE GROUP IN COMMUNITY PROPERTY AND COMMON LAW STATES, 1953[a]

Age Group	Community Property States			Common Law States		
	No. of Wealth-Holders	Aggregate Gross Estate	Average Gross Estate	No. of Wealth-Holders	Aggregate Gross Estate	Average Gross Estate
MALES						
All ages	165,260	$27.6 bill.	$167,000	918,805	$148.5 bill.	$161,000
Under 21	0.1%	1.8%		0.4%	0.2%	
21 to 30	3.5	2.9		2.7	3.7	
30 to 40	11.8	8.0		12.6	8.1	
40 to 50	26.1	25.5		24.6	21.2	
50 to 55	14.1	14.5		13.6	12.7	
55 to 60	11.2	10.1		13.1	13.6	
60 to 65	10.8	12.3		11.5	12.8	
65 to 70	8.3	8.9		8.7	10.8	
70 to 75	6.3	7.9		5.9	7.6	
75 to 80	3.6	4.7		3.7	4.8	
80 to 85	1.8	2.1		2.0	2.7	
85 and over	1.1	1.3		1.2	1.8	
FEMALES						
All ages	135,325	$26.4 bill.	$196,000	390,146	$ 90.3 bill.	$231,000
Under 21	2.5%	5.0%		0.9%	0.2%	
21 to 30	3.0	1.3		3.1	1.3	
30 to 40	12.8	17.1		8.9	19.6	
40 to 50	22.8	23.9		17.9	25.3	
50 to 55	12.4	10.9		12.6	8.1	
55 to 60	10.9	9.1		11.9	8.1	
60 to 65	10.1	9.7		11.6	8.4	
65 to 70	9.1	7.7		10.6	8.4	
70 to 75	7.0	6.5		9.3	8.3	
75 to 80	4.9	4.4		6.9	5.8	
80 to 85	2.9	2.6		4.1	4.1	
85 and over	1.8	1.8		2.6	2.4	

[a] Adjusted mortality rates have been used and insurance amounts have been reduced to equity.

TABLE 54
PERCENTAGE DISTRIBUTION OF ESTATE TAX WEALTH BY SEX AND GROSS ESTATE SIZE IN COMMUNITY PROPERTY AND COMMON LAW STATES, 1953

Gross Estate Size (thous. dollars)	Community Property States		Common Law States	
	No. of Wealth-Holders	Aggregate Gross Estate	No. of Wealth-Holders	Aggregate Gross Estate
MALES				
Total	165,260	$27.6 bill.	918,805	$148.5 bill.
Under 60	0.0%	0.0%	0.1%	0.0%
60 to 70	12.0	4.3	8.7	3.1
70 to 80	13.0	5.1	9.8	4.0
80 to 90	9.3	4.0	10.1	4.5
90 to 100	8.3	4.4	9.1	4.5
100 to 120	14.7	8.5	13.6	7.8
120 to 150	12.7	9.4	14.3	10.0
150 to 200	9.6	9.2	12.4	11.1
200 to 300	10.1	13.4	11.3	14.4
300 to 500	6.2	13.1	6.2	12.9
500 to 1,000	2.5	10.6	3.0	11.8
1,000 to 2,000	1.0	7.9	1.1	8.8
2,000 to 3,000	0.4	5.1	0.1	1.5
3,000 to 5,000	0.2	3.4	0.1	2.8
5,000 to 10,000	0.0	0.2	0.1	1.9
10,000 and over	0.0	1.4	0.0	0.9
FEMALES				
Total	135,325	$26.6 bill.	390,146	$ 90.3 bill.
Under 60	0.0%	0.0%	0.2%	0.0%
60 to 70	12.5	4.1	15.1	4.2
70 to 80	11.9	4.4	11.2	3.6
80 to 90	11.9	4.9	11.3	4.0
90 to 100	8.2	4.0	9.7	4.0
100 to 120	13.5	7.3	13.0	6.0
120 to 150	11.5	7.7	10.7	6.2
150 to 200	10.1	9.1	9.6	7.1
200 to 300	7.2	8.9	8.4	8.8
300 to 500	8.2	15.6	5.2	8.4
500 to 1,000	2.9	9.8	3.6	10.4
1,000 to 2,000	1.8	12.0	1.1	6.6
2,000 to 3,000	0.4	5.4	0.4	5.0
3,000 to 5,000	0.4	6.8	0.1	1.4
5,000 to 10,000	0.0	0.0	0.3	10.1
10,000 and over	0.0	0.0	0.1	14.2

[a] Adjusted mortality rates have been used and insurance amounts have been reduced to equity.

TABLE 55
Percentage Composition of All Estates for Men and Women in Community Property and Common Law States, 1953

Type of Property	Community Property States		Common Law States	
	Men	Women	Men	Women
Real estate	30.5	27.2	23.9	16.2
U.S. govt. bonds	4.0	6.0	5.3	6.5
State and local bonds	1.1	2.0	1.7	7.6
Other bonds	0.5	0.6	1.0	1.2
Corporate stock	30.9	31.2	36.2	48.8
Cash	9.4	8.5	9.2	9.4
Mortgage and notes	5.0	4.0	3.5	2.6
Life insurance equity	2.6	0.4	5.0	0.5
Miscellaneous property	16.0	20.0	14.3	7.1
Gross estate	100.0	100.0	100.0	100.0
Debts and mortgages	11.3	7.9	11.3	4.2
Economic estate	88.7	92.1	88.7	95.8

TABLE 56

RANK AND PERCENTAGE OF U.S. TOTAL OF POPULATION AND INCOME PAYMENTS FOR 1953 AND ESTATE TAX RETURNS FOR 1949, 1950, 1953, AND 1954 COMBINED, BY REGION

Region (ranked by per capita income)	Rank of Region					Region's Percentage of U.S. Total					
	Population (1)	Income Payments (2)	Number of Returns (3)	Gross Estate on Taxable Returns (4)	Per Capita Property Income (5)	Population (6)	Income Payments (7)	Number of Returns (8)	Gross Estate on Taxable Returns (9)	Col. 8 ÷ Col. 6 (10)	Col. 9 ÷ Col. 7 (11)
Far West	4	4	3	3	4	10.4	12.1	12.7	12.2	1.22	1.00
Middle East	2	2	2	1	3	23.2	27.1	27.3	32.0	1.17	1.18
Central	1	1	1	2	1	26.3	29.0	28.0	24.9	1.06	0.85
New England	6	5	5	5	2	6.1	6.6	7.5	9.1	1.23	1.39
Northwest	7	7	6	7	6	5.2	4.7	6.5	4.4	1.25	0.94
Southwest	5	6	7	6	7	7.7	6.5	5.4	5.8	0.70	0.89
Southeast	3	3	4	4	8	21.0	14.1	12.0	11.7	0.57	0.83

SOURCE: Table 57.

TOP WEALTH-HOLDERS IN 1953

TABLE 57
POPULATION AND INCOME PAYMENTS IN 1953 AND ESTATE TAX RETURNS FOR 1949, 1950, 1953, AND 1954 COMBINED, BY STATE

State	Population, 1953		Income Payments, 1953		Total Returns in Four Years		Aggregate Gross Estate on Taxable Returns in Four Years		Col. 6 ÷ Col. 2	Col. 8 ÷ Col. 4
	Thousands (1)	Per Cent of U.S. Total (2)	Million Dollars (3)	Per Cent of U.S. Total (4)	Number (5)	Per Cent of U.S. Total (6)	Million Dollars (7)	Per Cent of U.S. Total (8)	(9)	(10)
New England	9,697	6.1	17,686	6.6	9,473	7.5	1,943,588	9.1	1.23	1.39
Connecticut	2,162	1.4	4,744	1.8	2,452	1.9	617,271	2.9	1.36	1.61
Maine	914	0.6	1,287	0.5	765	0.6	127,023	0.6	1.00	1.20
Massachusetts	4,900	3.1	8,880	3.3	4,690	3.7	875,672	4.1	1.09	1.24
New Hampshire	527	0.3	818	0.3	499	0.4	88,217	0.4	1.33	1.33
Rhode Island	817	0.5	1,429	0.5	761	0.6	183,437	0.9	1.20	1.80
Vermont	377	0.2	528	0.2	306	0.2	51,968	0.2	1.00	1.00
Middle East	36,707	23.2	73,230	27.1	34,613	27.3	6,844,326	32.0	1.17	1.18
Delaware	358	0.2	825	0.3	411	0.3	132,875	0.6	1.50	2.00
D.C.	841	0.5	2,507	0.9	1,092	0.9	195,796	0.9	1.80	1.00
Maryland	2,541	1.6	4,402	1.6	1,936	1.5	358,530	1.7	0.93	1.06
New Jersey	5,141	3.2	10,153	3.8	5,203	4.1	893,971	4.2	1.28	1.11
New York	15,233	9.6	33,489	12.4	17,225	13.6	3,589,143	16.8	1.41	1.35
Pennsylvania	10,656	6.7	19,419	7.2	8,095	6.4	1,587,475	7.4	0.95	1.02
West Virginia	1,937	1.2	2,435	0.9	651	0.5	86,536	0.4	0.41	0.44
Southeast	33,257	21.0	38,118	14.1	15,282	12.0	2,507,682	11.7	0.57	0.83
Alabama	3,114	2.0	3,248	1.2	995	0.8	146,697	0.7	0.40	0.58
Arkansas	1,909	1.2	1,793	0.6	701	0.6	97,312	0.5	0.50	0.83
Florida	3,353	2.1	4,586	1.7	3,280	2.6	555,075	2.6	1.23	1.53
Georgia	3,585	2.3	4,245	1.6	1,338	1.0	224,368	1.0	0.43	0.62

(continued)

TOP WEALTH-HOLDERS IN 1953

TABLE 57 (concluded)

State	Population, 1953		Income Payments, 1953		Total Returns in Four Years		Aggregate Gross Estate on Taxable Returns in Four Years		Col. 6 ÷ Col. 2	Col. 8 ÷ Col. 4
	Thousands (1)	Per Cent of U.S. Total (2)	Million Dollars (3)	Per Cent of U.S. Total (4)	Number (5)	Per Cent of U.S. Total (6)	Million Dollars (7)	Per Cent of U.S. Total (8)	(9)	(10)
Kentucky	2,965	1.9	3,460	1.3	1,593	1.3	211,745	1.0	0.68	0.77
Louisiana	2,884	1.8	3,602	1.3	1,018	0.8	193,495	0.9	0.44	0.69
Mississippi	2,183	1.4	1,821	0.7	669	0.5	94,251	0.4	0.36	0.57
North Carolina	4,193	2.6	4,599	1.7	1,661	1.3	297,761	1.4	0.50	0.82
South Carolina	2,195	1.4	2,403	0.9	685	0.5	124,368	0.6	0.36	0.66
Tennessee	3,329	2.1	3,948	1.5	1,285	1.0	225,094	1.1	0.47	0.73
Virginia	3,547	2.2	4,413	1.6	2,057	1.6	337,516	1.6	0.72	1.00
Southwest	12,237	7.7	17,656	6.5	6,857	5.4	1,250,444	5.8	0.70	0.89
Arizona	930	0.6	1,370	0.5	431	0.3	65,461	0.3	0.50	0.60
New Mexico	758	0.5	1,021	0.4	257	0.2	40,483	0.2	0.40	0.50
Oklahoma	2,251	1.4	2,986	1.1	1,531	1.2	226,296	1.1	0.86	1.00
Texas	8,298	5.2	12,279	4.5	4,638	3.7	918,207	4.3	0.71	0.95
Central	41,632	26.3	78,416	29.0	36,202	28.0	5,323,322	24.9	1.06	0.85
Illinois	9,003	5.7	18,800	7.0	10,134	8.0	1,629,793	7.6	1.40	1.08
Indiana	4,136	2.6	7,584	2.8	3,188	2.5	395,201	1.8	0.96	0.64
Iowa	2,605	1.6	3,954	1.5	4,495	3.5	364,630	1.7	2.17	1.13
Michigan	6,852	4.3	13,723	5.1	3,334	2.6	682,570	3.2	0.60	0.62
Minnesota	3,053	1.9	4,724	1.7	2,613	2.0	325,043	1.5	1.05	0.88
Missouri	4,096	2.6	6,768	2.5	2,832	2.2	493,852	2.3	0.84	0.92
Ohio	8,369	5.3	16,840	6.2	6,490	5.0	1,034,826	4.8	0.94	0.77
Wisconsin	3,518	2.2	6,023	2.2	3,116	2.5	397,407	1.9	1.13	0.86

TOP WEALTH-HOLDERS IN 1953

Northwest	8,301	5.2	12,742	4.7	8,316	6.5	945,668	4.4	1.25	0.94
Colorado	1,413	0.9	2,367	0.9	1,360	1.1	177,381	0.8	1.22	0.88
Idaho	603	0.4	851	0.3	288	0.2	38,100	0.2	0.50	0.66
Kansas	2,006	1.3	3,110	1.2	2,569	2.0	296,745	1.4	1.53	1.16
Montana	614	0.4	1,037	0.4	615	0.5	67,601	0.3	1.25	0.75
Nebraska	1,347	0.9	2,065	0.7	2,004	1.6	210,597	1.0	1.77	1.43
North Dakota	621	0.4	804	0.3	411	0.3	37,224	0.2	0.75	0.66
South Dakota	657	0.4	895	0.3	547	0.4	54,084	0.2	1.00	0.66
Utah	734	0.5	1,108	0.4	296	0.2	29,743	0.1	0.40	0.25
Wyoming	306	0.2	505	0.2	226	0.2	34,193	0.2	1.00	1.00
Far West	16,476	10.4	32,729	12.1	16,135	12.7	2,605,603	12.2	1.22	1.00
California	12,190	7.7	24,856	9.2	13,002	10.2	2,131,184	10.0	1.32	1.08
Nevada	206	0.1	448	0.2	169	0.1	44,754	0.2	1.00	1.00
Oregon	1,602	1.0	2,762	1.0	1,232	1.0	191,175	0.9	1.00	0.90
Washington	2,478	1.6	4,663	1.7	1,732	1.4	238,490	1.1	0.87	0.65
Total	158,307	100.0	270,577	100.0	126,878	100.0	21,420,633	100.0	1.00	1.00

SOURCE: Col. 1: *Statistical Abstract of the United States: 1955*, Washington, 1955, Table 10, p. 14; cols. 3 and 4: *Survey of Current Business*, August 1954, Table 1, p. 10 and Table 4, p. 15; cols. 5 and 7: *Statistics of Income for 1953*, Washington, 1956.

TABLE 58
DISTRIBUTION OF SPENDING UNITS BY INCOME WITHIN ASSET GROUPS, 1950
(per cent)

Money Income Group Before Taxes, 1949	Total Assets (dollars)							
	Under 400[a] (1)	500 to 1,000 (2)	1,000 to 2,000 (3)	2,000 to 5,000 (4)	5,000 to 10,000 (5)	10,000 to 25,000 (6)	25,000 to 60,000 (7)	60,000 and over (8)
Under $1,000	32	16	13	11	14	7	6	3
$1,000 to $2,000	40	26	19	16	14	12	6	2
$2,000 to $3,000	18	32	33	26	22	15	12	5
$3,000 to $4,000	7	18	22	25	23	22	12	4
$4 000 to $5 000	2	5	9	12	12	18	12	6
$5,000 to $7,500	1	3	4	7	12	20	21	17
$7 500 and over	[b]	[b]	[b]	1	2	5	24	62
Not ascertained	1	[b]	[b]	2	1	1	4	1
All cases	100	100	100	100	100	100	100	100

SOURCE: Goldsmith, *Saving in U.S.*, III, Table W-54.
[a] Includes zero assets.
[b] Includes negative and zero net worth.

TABLE 59
AVERAGE ANNUAL PERCENTAGES OF VARIOUS TYPES OF INCOME IN TOTAL INCOME, UPPER INCOME GROUPS AND TOTAL POPULATION, 1919–38

	Total Population (1)	Top 1 Per Cent (2)	2nd and 3rd Percentage Band (3)	4th and 5th Percentage Band (4)	Top 5 Per Cent (5)	Lower 95 Per Cent (6)
1. Employee comp.	66.0	33.0	56.3	63.8	45.4	72.8
2. Entrep. income	18.2	19.0	22.5	19.1	19.9	17.6
3. Rent	3.0	3.9	5.2	5.3	4.5	2.5
4. Interest	6.5	13.2	8.2	7.1	10.6	5.1
5. Dividends	6.3	30.9	7.8	4.6	19.5	2.0
6. Total (1–5)	100.0	100.0	100.0	100.0	100.0	100.0
7. Entrep. income and rent	21.2	22.9	27.7	24.4	24.5	20.1
8. Dividends and interest	12.8	44.1	16.0	11.8	30.1	7.1
9. Service incomes	84.2	51.9	78.8	83.0	65.3	90.4
10. Property incomes	15.8	48.1	21.2	17.0	34.7	9.6
11. Total (9 + 10)	100.0	100.0	100.0	100.0	100.0	100.0

SOURCE: Simon Kuznets, *Shares of Upper Income Groups in Income and Savings*, New York, National Bureau of Economic Research, 1953, p. 26, Table 7.

TOP WEALTH-HOLDERS IN 1953

TABLE 60
AVERAGE ANNUAL SHARES OF UPPER INCOME GROUPS IN U.S.
TOTALS OF VARIOUS TYPES OF INCOME, 1919–38

	Percentage of Income Received by Given Percentage Band			
	Top 1	2nd and 3rd	4th and 5th	Top 5
1. Total income	13.1	6.6	4.9	24.7
2. Employee comp.	6.5	5.6	4.8	16.9
3. Entrep. income	13.7	8.1	5.2	26.9
4. Rent	17.9	11.4	8.9	38.3
5. Interest	27.5	8.5	5.5	41.5
6. Dividends	64.7	8.2	3.6	76.6
7. Entrep. income and rent	14.2	8.5	5.6	28.3
8. Dividends and interest	46.1	8.4	4.5	58.9
9. Service incomes	8.1	6.2	4.9	19.1
10. Property incomes	40.1	8.8	5.3	54.2

SOURCE: Kuznets, *Shares of Upper Income Groups*, p. 18, Table 3.

TABLE 61
ASSET-INCOME RATIOS, BY INCOME OF SPENDING UNITS, 1950

Money Income (1949) Before Taxes	Total Income		Total Assets		Assets-Income Ratio
	Per Cent	Billion Dollars	Per Cent	Billion Dollars	
Under $1,000	2	3.4	6	36.8	10.8
$1,000 to $2,000	9	15.7	8	49.0	3.1
$2,000 to $3,000	16	27.2	12	73.6	2.7
$3,000 to $4,000	19	32.3	14	85.8	2.7
$4,000 to $5,000	15	25.5	11	67.4	2.6
$5,000 to $7,500	19	32.3	17	104.2	3.2
$7,500 and over	20	34.0	31	190.0	5.5
Not ascertained	a	—	1	6.1	
All cases	100	170.0	100	613.0	3.6

SOURCE: Derived from Goldsmith, *Saving in U.S.*, III, Table W-50, p. 126.
a No cases reported or less than 0.5 per cent.

TABLE 62

DISTRIBUTION OF SPENDING UNITS BY TOTAL ASSETS WITHIN OCCUPATIONAL GROUPS, 1950
(per cent)

Occupational Group	All Cases (1)	Zero (2)	100 to 500 (3)	500 to 1,000 (4)	Total Assets (dollars)					
					1,000 to 2,000 (5)	2,000 to 5,000 (6)	5,000 to 10,000 (7)	10,000 to 25,000 (8)	25,000 to 60,000 (9)	60,000 and over (10)
Professional and semiprofessional	100	1	4	4	11	21	17	24	13	5
Managerial	100	a	4	1	3	14	19	36	19	4
Self-employed	100	1	a	1	3	9	13	38	24	11
Clerical and sales	100	7	16	8	9	18	17	19	6	a
Skilled and semiskilled	100	5	10	10	12	19	20	22	2	a
Unskilled and service	100	13	18	11	14	18	13	13	a	a
Farm operator	100	1	4	4	6	14	19	26	18	8
Retired	100	16	5	4	2	7	14	31	13	8
All other	100	16	15	9	11	12	19	15	3	a
All spending units	100	7	10	8	10	15	17	22	8	3

SOURCE: Goldsmith, *Saving in U.S.*, III, Table W-60.
[a] No case reported or less than 0.5 per cent.

CHAPTER 5

Types of Property Held by Top Wealth-Holders

THE pattern of investment of top wealth-holders is very different from that of the total population. The most striking differences are the top group's greater share of corporate stock and smaller share of real estate in gross estate.[1] While corporate stock accounts for only 15 per cent of the wealth of all persons, it is 39 per cent of the wealth of top wealth-holders. The corresponding shares of real estate are 39 and 22 per cent, respectively (Table 63). (Tables 63 through 89 will be found at the end of this chapter.) The top group shows relatively great interest in state and local government bonds, and relatively little interest in cash and life insurance. At the same time liabilities are a higher percentage of gross estate for all persons than they are for the top wealth-holders.

Why do these differences appear between the patterns of wealth of the top wealth-holders and the total population? Has there been a similar preference pattern among top wealth-holders in all recent years? What significant differences in investment preferences are to be observed within the top group? How are these differences associated with age, sex, estate size, income, and occupation? These questions are the subject of the present chapter.

Change over Time, 1922–53

Estate tax data for most years do not lend themselves to a blow-up of gross estate by type of property by the estate-multiplier method. The only year other than 1953 for which a breakdown of gross estate by type of property can be constructed for living top wealth-holders is 1944. Table 64, which makes this comparison for the two years, shows an increase in the percentage of gross estate held in real estate and a

---

[1] The following differences are based on the basic or prime wealth variants. The emphasis of top wealth-holders upon corporate stock and tax-exempt bonds would be heightened by the inclusion of personal trust funds. In 1952 about three-fifths of personal trust holdings were in stock, about one-fifth in bonds, and the remaining one-fifth in real estate and miscellaneous property.

decline in the percentage held in bonds of all types between 1944 and 1953. It is hard to know just how much this reported change represents a real change in preference for one type of asset over another because not only are quite different persons included in the samples, but varying proportions of the population are included in the top wealth-holder group in the two years, and there were important differential price shifts over the period. In 1944, only 782,000 persons are estimated to have had $60,000 or more of gross estate, compared to 1.6 million persons in 1953. This means that the 1953 percentage composition shown in Table 64 reflects in part the preferences of persons considerably farther down in the wealth ranking than in 1944, which explains part of the rise in the share of gross estate held in real estate. Also, the price of real estate rose over the period, while that of bonds did not, and this too would tend to produce the shift shown.

For further insight into the shifts in investment patterns of top wealth-holders, we are forced to turn to data on gross estate of decedent top wealth-holders as set forth in Table 65.[2] In interpreting this table, we should recall that the part of the total population included varies over the period due to changing price and income levels and changing exemptions. What the table shows is that corporate stock has been the most favored type of property among estate tax decedents since 1922. However, the percentage it has constituted of total gross estate has varied from 31.3 per cent in 1922 to 48.4 per cent in 1928. The high proportion in 1928 was due in large part to the fact that the exemption was $100,000 from 1926 to 1932. In 1953 stock accounted for 40.2 per cent of gross estate. Real estate has varied from a low of 13.4 per cent in 1930 to a high of 24.7 per cent in 1922. In recent years real estate has regained some of its earlier importance, with a rise from 15.1 per cent in 1943 to 20.9 per cent in 1953 and 1954.

Some other types of property show a strong cyclical swing, such as state and local bonds. This cyclical movement is most clearly apparent in the case of debts, which averaged about 10 per cent of gross estate in the 1920's and around 15 per cent in the early 1930's and fell to about 6 per cent in the postwar period, standing at 5.4 per cent in

[2] The careful reader will want to see how Tables 64 and 65 compare. This may be done for 1944 and 1953. In general, the gross estate of decedents as reported in Table 65 shows less emphasis upon real estate and miscellaneous property and a lower share of liabilities than for living persons as shown in Table 64. The difference for insurance is spurious since the insurance adjustment has been made for the living top wealth-holders but not for the decedents.

1953. This long-term decline in the debt-asset ratio is doubtless the most dramatic change shown in these data. Cash, which is reported separately only after 1940, shows remarkable stability at around 10 per cent.

To eliminate the effect of the changes in estate tax exemptions over the period, we may shift to the net estate data from decedents' estate tax returns. Isolating the returns for those with $100,000 or more of net estate facilitates a comparison over the years which gets more nearly at changes in preferences.[3] (The introduction of the marital deduction in 1948 drastically altered the relationship between gross and net estate. To compensate for that change, it has seemed best to show the data for 1948–54 for those with net estates over $60,000 as most nearly comparable to the pre-1948 group with net estates over $100,000.) These changes over time are set forth in Chart 21. Even after this correction for the changing exemptions, stock shows a sharp swing upward to 1929, reflecting the stock market boom of the late 1920's, and never regains its peak share of that year although it does rise from 1948 to 1954.[4] A similar but stronger narrowing and widening of the real estate share is observable. Lent suggests that "The relative decline of real estate [between 1922 and 1931] might be ascribed in part to the collapse in land values after the boom of the early 1920's and possibly in part to increased incorporation of such holdings. It may also reflect the breakup of large estates upon which so many early fortunes were founded."[5] It is necessary to add to this that real estate prices rose more than 100 per cent from the late 1930's to 1954, apparently reversing the long-term shift downward of real estate's share. It is also relevant to note that comparing the holdings of estate sizes of the same current dollar amounts during a period of rising asset prices incurs a bias toward the lower estate sizes in the later years.

While the cyclical swing in investment in tax-exempt bonds is quite clear, several observers have concluded that there is little evidence that the highly graduated tax structure has diverted venture capital to tax-free investments. Lent points out that "Despite greatly increased holdings of wholly tax-exempt investments, the relative

---

[3] Here we are following the procedure of George E. Lent as set out in his study, *The Ownership of Tax-Exempt Securities, 1913–1953*, Occasional Paper 47, New York, National Bureau of Economic Research, 1955, pp. 109 ff.

[4] Standard and Poor's composite stock price index rose from 124.4 in 1948 (1935–39 = 100) to 189.0 in 1953 and 226.9 in 1954.

[5] Lent, *Tax-Exempt Securities*, pp. 110–113.

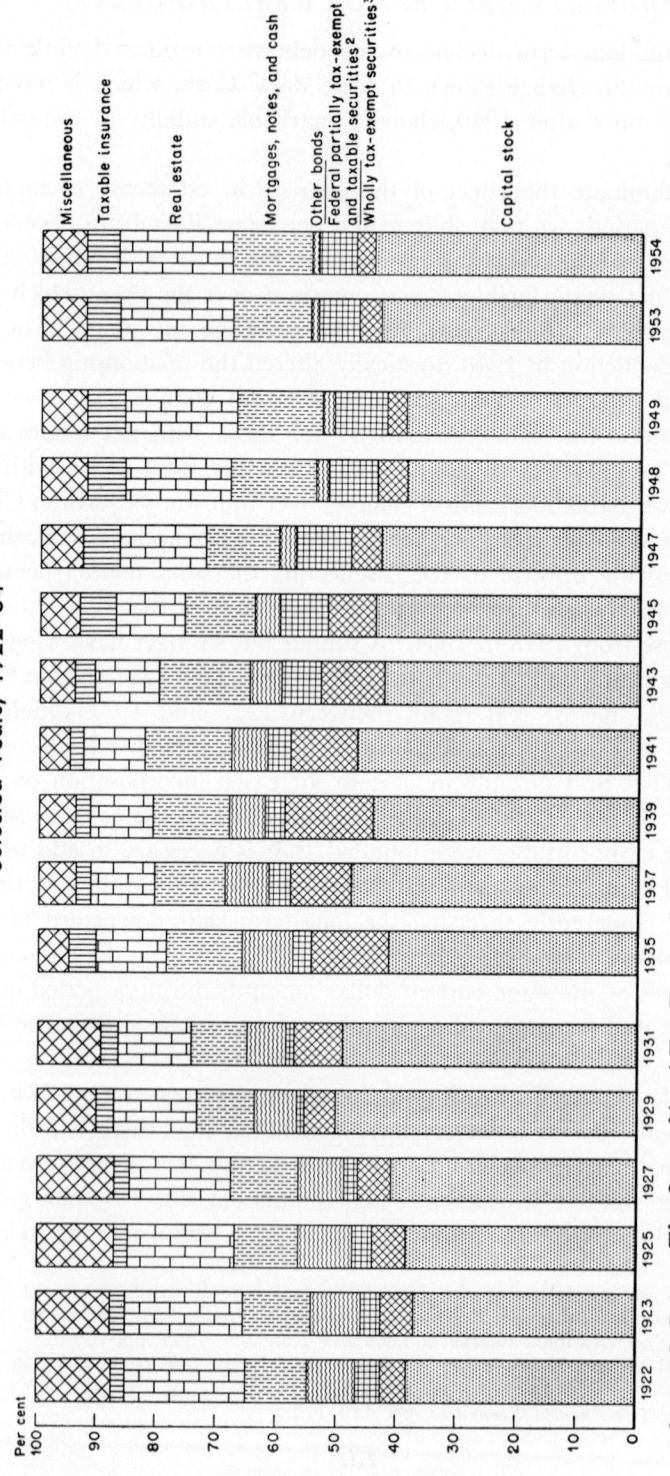

CHART 21

Percentage Composition of Net Taxable Estates over $100,000[1] for Selected Years, 1922–54

Source: G. E. Lent, *The Ownership of Tax-Exempt Securities, 1913–1953*, NBER, 1955, Table 10, p. 108. *Statistics of Income*, 1948–54.
[1] Net taxable estates over $60,000 from 1948.
[2] Includes only state and local bonds from 1953.
[3] Includes the grand total of all federal bonds from 1953.

amount of capital stock held by taxable estates has not suffered any decline below the period of the 1920's, when surtax rates were at a much lower level. The general rise in income tax rates has, however, been accompanied by an apparent redistribution of investments in capital stock and tax-free securities among investors in different wealth size classes."[6] That is, tax-exempt securities are now more heavily concentrated in the highest estate size classes than they were in the 1920's.[7]

We conclude that there was very little noncyclical change in the investment patterns of top wealth-holders for the various broad types of assets over the period 1922–54. The general pattern of investment for top estates is virtually the same in the 1950's as in the 1920's, even though there have been important changes in prices, incomes, and in the structure of the economy and its institutional arrangements.

The fact that the pattern of asset holding in current dollars does not seem to have changed over the long term does not, in itself, establish that "preferences" for the several types of assets have not changed. It may be thought that preferences are better measured in constant dollars, which makes it possible to distinguish changes in composition due solely to price change from those due to active adjustment of holdings. Suppose we make the hypothesis that a group experiencing no change in preferences would exhibit no changes in percentage composition when assets are valued in constant dollars. This hypothesis assumes that no other conditions, such as changing yields, relative availability of assets, or appreciation possibilities, would influence the result. The concept of preference involved here is based upon the idea that persons may seek a balance among types of assets to achieve a balance of purposes (i.e., yield, liquidity, certainty), without reference to current price changes. We shall return to an important modification of this concept of preference in the following section.

Defining preference as a pattern of percentage composition of asset holdings, each asset being valued in terms of its own base-period values, Table 66 makes it possible to test the proposition that there was no change in preference. (This table uses the indexes of asset

---

[6] *Ibid.*, p. 115.
[7] For a discussion of the shifting tax advantages by income brackets over time, see *ibid.*, pp. 92–94, and Butters *et al., Effects of Taxation: Investment by Individuals* (Boston, 1953), Chapter XI. The price of bonds has not moved up with equity investments, and hence if persons had merely held the same portfolio of investments from 1948 to 1954, the proportion in bonds (and life insurance and cash) would have fallen quite considerably.

prices shown in Table 67.) Column 4 of Table 66 shows that the percentage held in equities fell from a range of 67–74 per cent in the 1920's to a range of 50–61 per cent in the period after World War II, and thus offers a dramatic negation of the above proposition of unchanging preferences. Column 8 shows that there has, conversely, been a rising "preference" for nonequities over the same period, from about 30 per cent in the 1920's to 40–50 per cent in the postwar period. Therefore, by measuring preference in constant dollars, it is clear that there has been a change of preference by the group of top wealth-holders over the long term.

Charts 22 and 23 show the nature of the change for each type of asset. The chart on stock holdings (Chart 22) shows that in the period 1922–29 the top wealth-holders were not increasing the percentage of their assets (in real terms) held in stock. It suggests that this group converted to a higher share in stock after the stock market break of 1929. The long slide downward from 1941 to 1954 confirms the earlier pattern of a falling share of real assets in stock during a period of rising stock prices. Real estate and miscellaneous property shows a different cyclical pattern from that of stock, with the share going with the cycle, that is, rising in booms and falling in depression. The general cyclical pattern of nonequities (Chart 23) is that the top wealth-holders seek a rising share of such assets during booms, which are in turn associated with falling bond prices. Thus if preference is defined simply in terms of desire to hold fixed proportions of the several types of "real" assets, it appears that preference does shift both cyclically and over the long term.

Turning from this definition of preference to a more sophisticated definition involves consideration of investor motivations. Presumably, a rational investor will adopt a pattern of asset holding which best satisfies a complex of goals, including high yield, low risk, liquidity, and capital growth. His preferences or ordering of these motives may remain constant while he changes his investment pattern, this change being in response to the shifting characteristics of the assets. For example, the fact that an investor buys more of an asset when it has a higher yield does not necessarily mean his preference schedules have shifted, but may merely mean that he has moved to a different point on his preference schedule. Likewise, a person who holds more cash and fewer bonds when the rate of interest falls may not have shifted his liquidity preference schedule, but may only have moved to a new point on his schedule.

PROPERTY HELD BY TOP WEALTH-HOLDERS

CHART 22

Equities Expressed as Percentage in Current and Constant Dollars of Total Assets of Decedents with Net Taxable Estates over $100,000, 1922–54

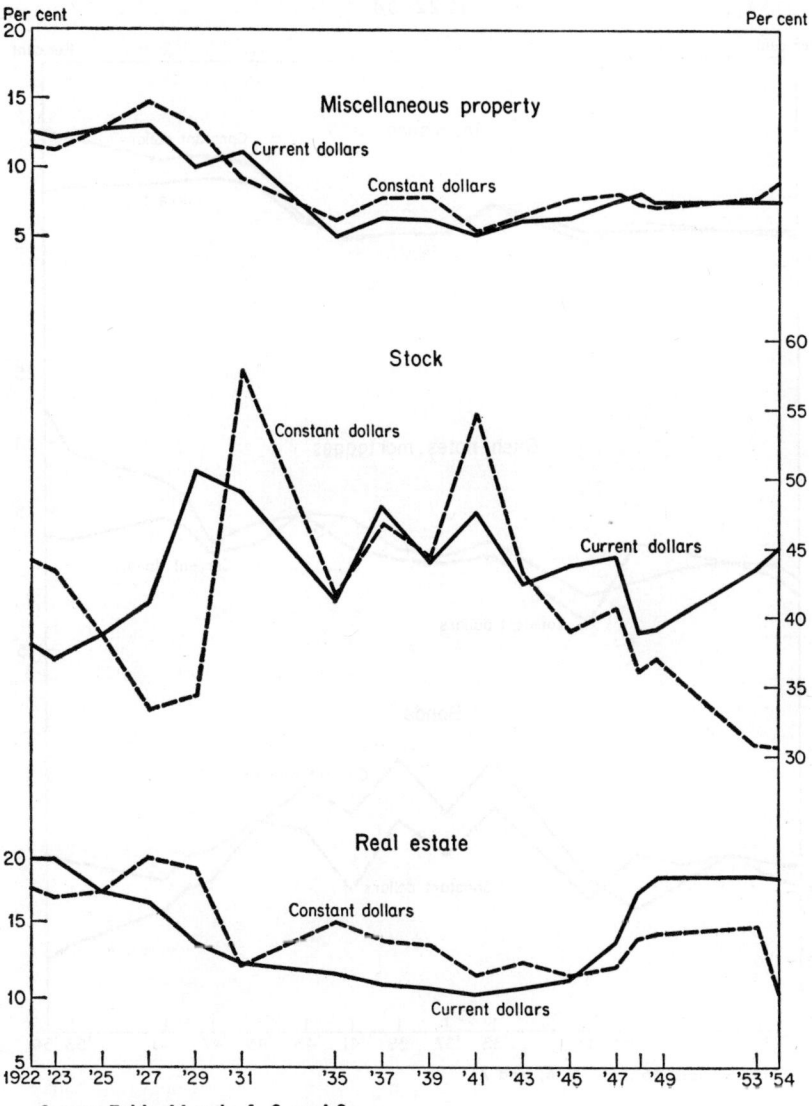

Source: Table 66, cols. 1, 2, and 3.

CHART 23
Nonequities Expressed as Percentage in Current and Constant Dollars of Total Assets of Decedents with Net Taxable Estates over $100,000, 1922–54

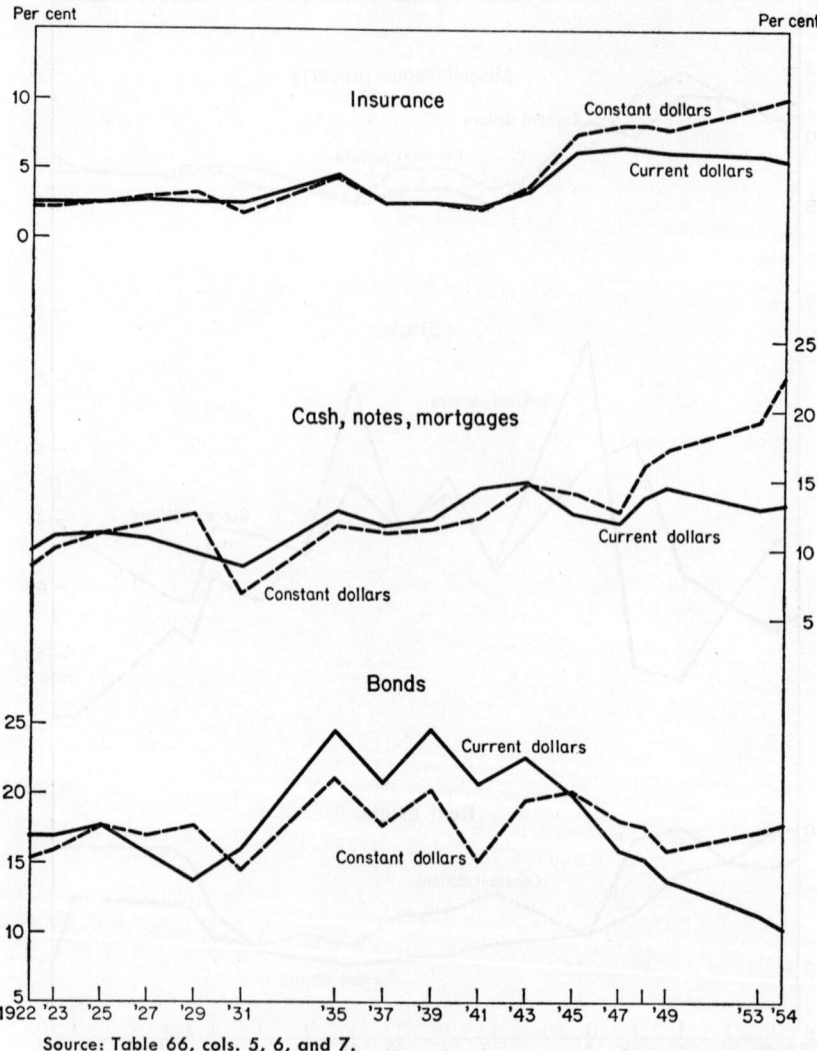

Source: Table 66, cols. 5, 6, and 7.

This line of thought leads us to ask how much of the observed change in the pattern of asset holding (measured in constant dollars) is consistent with changes in relative yields. If yield changes alone were sufficient to explain changes in investments, we would reach the tentative conclusion that investor preferences have not changed. We will not attempt to relate these changes in any precise way, but merely to note the direction of change, first over the long term and then in the cyclical period. It will be instructive to relate yield changes to changes in composition (measured both in terms of constant and current dollars).

We note in Charts 22 and 23 the remarkable rise in the share (measured in constant dollars) held in cash from 10–12 per cent in the 1920's to 17–24 per cent in 1947–54. This may be explained by a fall in the yields of noncash assets (Chart 24). Stock yields and more particularly bond and mortgage yields exhibit a long-term decline, which means that the price of holding cash was falling. Hence, a rational investor could hold more cash without changing his preferences, or without rearranging his investment motives. This is also consistent with the need for larger amounts of cash in the face of rising consumer prices.

A long-term stability of the share in bonds (again measured in constant dollars) can be observed in the face of changing yield. This would suggest a change in preference. Perhaps it indicates a rise in emphasis on security at the expense of yield. However, this should also be considered in the light of the relative yields of stocks and bonds. The ratio of stock yields to bond yields generally rose over the long period (Table 68). This would lead one to predict a rising share in stocks and a falling share in bonds. Since this did not happen, we tentatively conclude there was a shift in preference, in favor of certainty.

Similarly, we note a rising preference for insurance and a falling preference for real estate and miscellaneous property. All of this confirms the thought that investor decisions were not guided by yields alone and that, therefore, preferences may be said to have changed. All of this is based upon constant dollar composition.

Turning now to the long-term relationship between yields and composition measured in current rather than constant dollars, we find the following picture. As would be expected, cash rises. There is a predictable fall in bonds in current dollars. Moreover, there is a predictable shift in the stock-bond ratio in current dollars (from about 2.3 in the 1920's to about 3.0 in 1947–54). Similarly, the share in real estate is roughly predictable on the basis of comparative yields. However, yield changes cannot explain the long-term rise in the insurance share. Hence, in the present context this may be called evidence of a change in preference.

CHART 24
Relationship Between Stock-Bond Yields and Stock-Bond Holdings of Decedents with Net Taxable Estates over $100,000, 1926–56

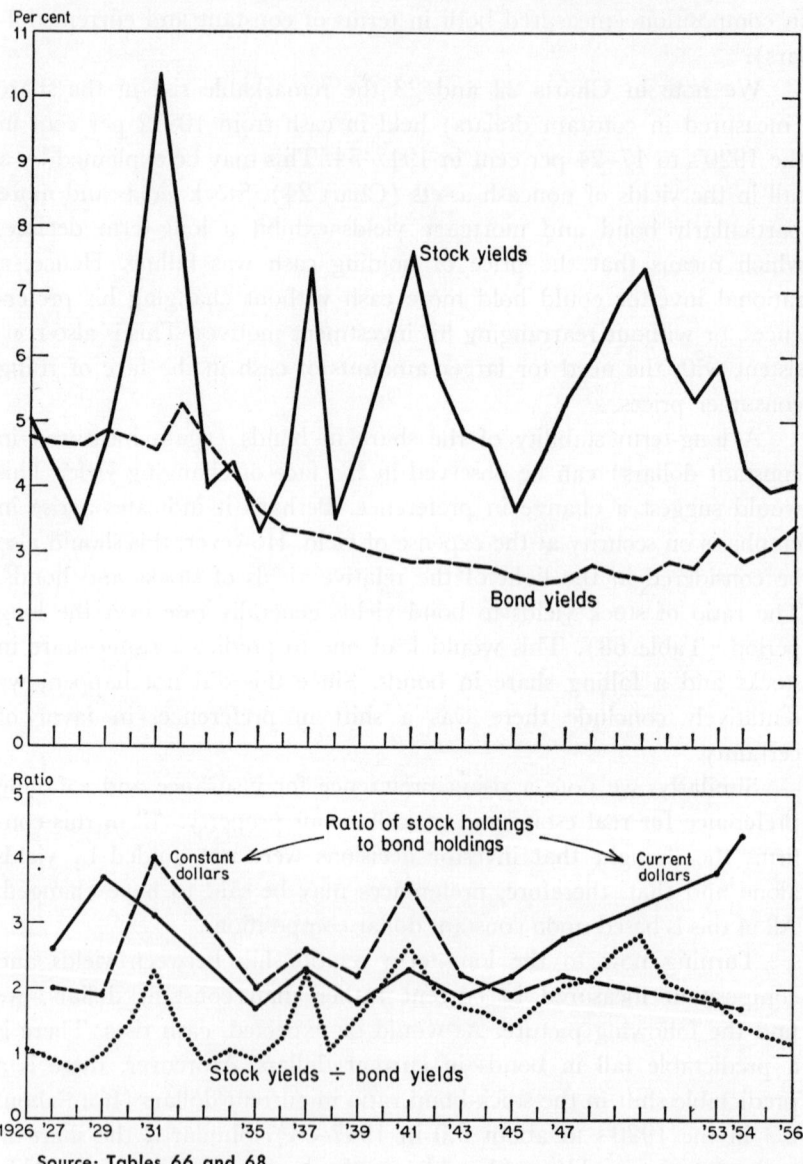

Source: Tables 66 and 68.

Thus, we find contradictory evidence on the possible change in investor preferences over the long term. If investors are thought to make decisions with reference to a portfolio valued in current dollars, we can safely say that differences in yields have guided composition changes in the recent period in the same way as in the 1920's. Hence, on this basis, we would deduce there had been no important change in preference, a rise in preference for insurance being the only exception. However, if investors are thought to make decisions with reference to a portfolio valued in constant dollars, then the evidence suggests that there have been changes in preferences, with less preference for equities and more for bonds and other debt claims.

Since there is some uncertainty about whether to use constant or current dollars to measure long-term change, it must remain uncertain whether or not there has "really" been a change in preference. This writer leans toward the view that in measuring long-term change it is more plausible to use composition in current dollars, and hence to the view that there has been no important change in preference.

In considering the problem of cyclical as contrasted to long-term change of preference, it seems quite plausible to use composition in constant dollars, simply because many investors do not respond quickly to price changes. Following this method, there is considerable basis for sticking to the theory that differences in yields guide decisions. Chart 24 relates changes in the balance of stocks and bonds to changes in the ratio of stock yields to bond yields. The general picture here is one of close correlation between changes in relative yields of stocks and rises in the percentage of wealth held in stock (see the constant dollar line).

Composition of Estate by Age and Sex of Top Wealth-Holders, 1953

The Survey of Consumer Finances finds that consumer capital goods as a percentage of net worth fall as age increases, that business and investment assets rise in importance, and that debt falls (Table 69). Partly as a result of the shifts over to business assets, and partly as a result of rise in total estate with increasing age, business assets are concentrated in the middle- and older-age groups (Table 70).

Somewhat similar differences by age are observable for the top wealth-holders (Tables 71, 72, and 73). The percentage of estate held in stock tends to rise with age, at least after age 40. This positive correlation is clearer for men than for women. Both real estate and life insurance equity[8] are "middle-age" assets, with the former reaching its peak share of gross estate in the 50 to 55 age bracket and the latter in the 60 to 65 age bracket. The most remarkable decline with increasing age is observed in the case of miscellaneous property. The effect of age within estate sizes is explored in the following section. There is, at least at first glance, a striking difference in the composition of estate by sex. The fact that women estate tax wealth-holders are older than the men (the median age for women is 56 compared to 52 for men) and that they have considerably larger estates on the average (average gross estate is $220,000 for females and $163,000 for males) should lead us to expect some differences in types of property held. Men have a relatively higher percentage in real estate (25 compared to 19 per cent for women), a lower percentage in stock (35 vs. 45 per cent), a higher percentage in insurance (4.6 vs. 0.5 per cent), and a lower percentage in state and local bonds (1.6 vs. 6.4 per cent). Men have debts and mortgages against their gross estates of 11 per cent while women have only a 5 per cent claim against their gross estates (Table 74).

Looking inside the age groups, the sex difference still obtains. It is notable that in the age groups under 50 the males have an extraordinary (compared to females) concentration upon real estate, while females have a particularly high concentration on stock. Remembering the remarkably large estate size of younger women leads us to suggest that this difference in composition is, to an important degree, a function of the difference in estate sizes between the sexes. Looking, then, at the composition of estates of men and women with the same estate size, the "pure" sex difference is reduced to men having less in bonds, less in stock, and less in mortgages and notes, but considerably more in insurance and miscellaneous property and much heavier claims against their gross estates. (See Table 74 for one example and Tables 76 and 77 for more detail.) These observed differences are compatible with the idea that women typically hold less assets associated with business operations (real estate and interest in unincorporated business) and family responsibilities (insurance).

Composition of Estate by Size

Estate size appears to be a more important variable in determining composition of estate than either age or sex (Tables 75, 76, and 77).

[8] Reducing life insurance amounts to estimated equity, as has been done in these estimates, shows smaller estates for younger persons, a more unequal estate

PROPERTY HELD BY TOP WEALTH-HOLDERS

Among the top wealth-holders, as gross estate increases in size, real estate declines in relative importance and corporate stock rises in importance; there is a particularly sharp rise in state and local bonds across the highest estate sizes. Large estates show less emphasis upon real estate, mortgages and notes, cash, and miscellaneous property than smaller estates. Insurance and indebtness both reach a peak percentage in the middle of the range at around $150,000 to $200,000 of gross estate. U.S. bonds and "other bonds" show no clear change in relative importance by estate size.

These differences in type of property held by the several estate size groups among the top wealth-holders are associated with different degrees of inequality for each type of asset. The most unequally distributed type of property is state and local bonds and the least concentrated is real estate (Table 78, 79, and 80, and Charts 25, 26, and 27). For the total population, the Survey of Consumer Finances reports a similar pattern of concentration. Most concentrated is corporate stock. In descending order of concentration, the types of property are stock, business, other real estate, farms, life insurance, livestock and crops, houses, and cars (Table 81).

Table 82, based on 1953 data, is designed to show the pure estate size effect on composition of estate after standardizing for age and sex. Reading down the columns, it is clear that the share that real estate is of gross estate tends to fall as gross estate rises in young-, middle-, and old-age groups of both men and women. U.S. bonds show a slight tendency to fall as estate size rises but state and local and "other" bonds rise. The share of stock is positively associated with estate size in each age-sex group, although the association is not very clear for younger women. Cash falls sharply as a share, although the same irregularity is noted for younger women. Mortgages and notes do not vary with estate size, except for the old-age group where there is a negative association. Life insurance shows little change through estate sizes under $500,000 and then falls off as a share of gross estate. Much the same pattern is found for miscellaneous property. Debts and mortgages exhibit a more complicated pattern. For middle-aged men there is a positive association with estate size, but no clear variation is apparent for any other age-sex group. Chart 28 shows some of these relationships for men.

---

size distribution, and a larger difference between the average estates of men and women than would have been the case had we entered the face value of life insurance.

Table 83 shows the pure age effect within estate sizes by sex. Age does not seem to play an important role for the share of real estate in gross estate. U.S. government bonds seem to be positively associated with age except for men in the highest estate size shown here. On the other hand, state and local bonds and "other" bonds seem unrelated

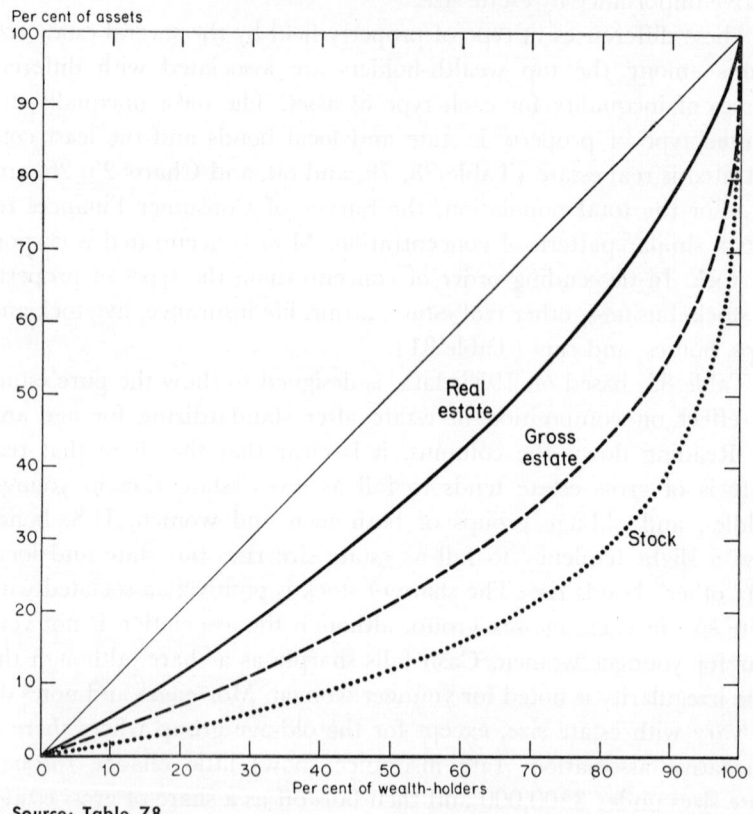

CHART 25

Lorenz Curves of Gross Estate, Real Estate, and Stock Among Top Wealth-Holders, 1953

Source: Table 78.

to age, except possibly for state and local bonds for men in the highest estate size. The share of stock in gross estate rises with age in every estate size and sex group although, curiously, there is an extraordinarily heavy concentration on stock in the age groups under 30.[9] There is a tendency to hold a higher percentage of gross estate in cash with increasing age up through age 65, after which the share is constant. Considerable irregularity is noted for the highest estate size. Mortgages

[9] Sample sizes are too small in these age groups to draw any firm conclusions.

148

and notes do not change with age, except for the lowest estate size for men where a positive association is observed. Life insurance appears to be a "middle-age asset." Among men, its peak share is in the 60 to 65 age bracket for each of the three estate sizes. For women, the peaks are between 40 and 60 years of age. Miscellaneous property is strongly affected by age for both men and women, with the share falling as

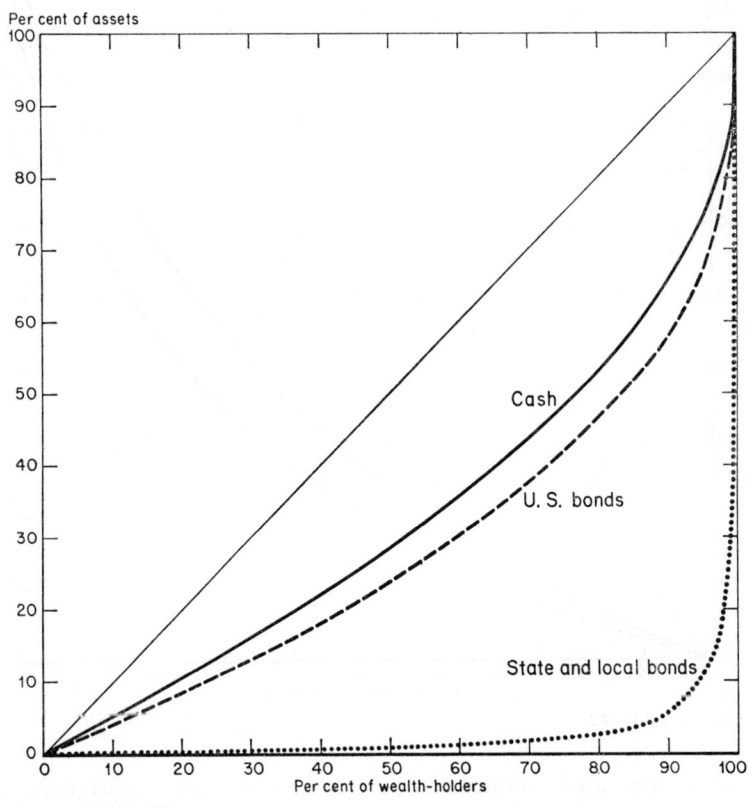

CHART 26
Lorenz Curves of Cash, U.S. Bonds, and State and Local Bonds Among Top Wealth-Holders, 1953

Source: Table 78.

age increases. Much the same pattern of negative association is found for debts and mortgages. Some of these relationships are shown in Chart 29.

Combining the findings of Tables 82 and 83, we note that real estate is predominantly a smaller-estate asset. U.S. bonds are a smaller-estate and older-age asset. State and local bonds and "other" bonds are a larger-estate asset. Stock is a larger-estate and older-age asset.

Cash is a smaller-estate and older-age asset. Mortgages and notes are smaller-estate and older-age assets. Life insurance is a lower- and middle-estate and middle-age asset. Miscellaneous property is a lower- and

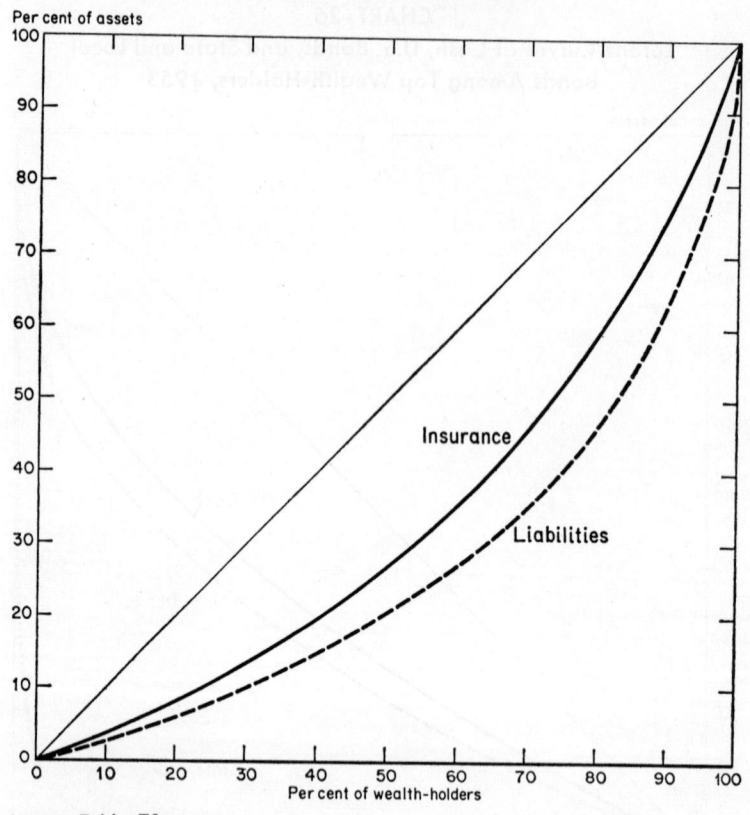

CHART 27
Lorenz Curves of Insurance and Liabilities Among Top Wealth-Holders, 1953

Source: Table 78.

middle-estate and younger-age asset. Debts and mortgages are younger-age liabilities.[10]

[10] In a study of the covariation of four asset types, gross estate size, and age, Mendershausen found that in 1944: (1) unincorporated business was a "lower wealth-younger age group" asset; (2) insurance was a "lower wealth-middle age group" asset; (3) state and municipal bonds appeared as a "higher wealth asset"; (4) federal bonds showed no systematic variation (Goldsmith, *Saving in U.S.*, III, pp. 364–366). He also observed that a multiple correlation with the same variables showed age had little explanatory value except for unincorporated business (p. 366).

PROPERTY HELD BY TOP WEALTH-HOLDERS

CHART 28
Distribution of Selected Assets by Gross Estate Size
Within Three Age Groups, Males, 1953

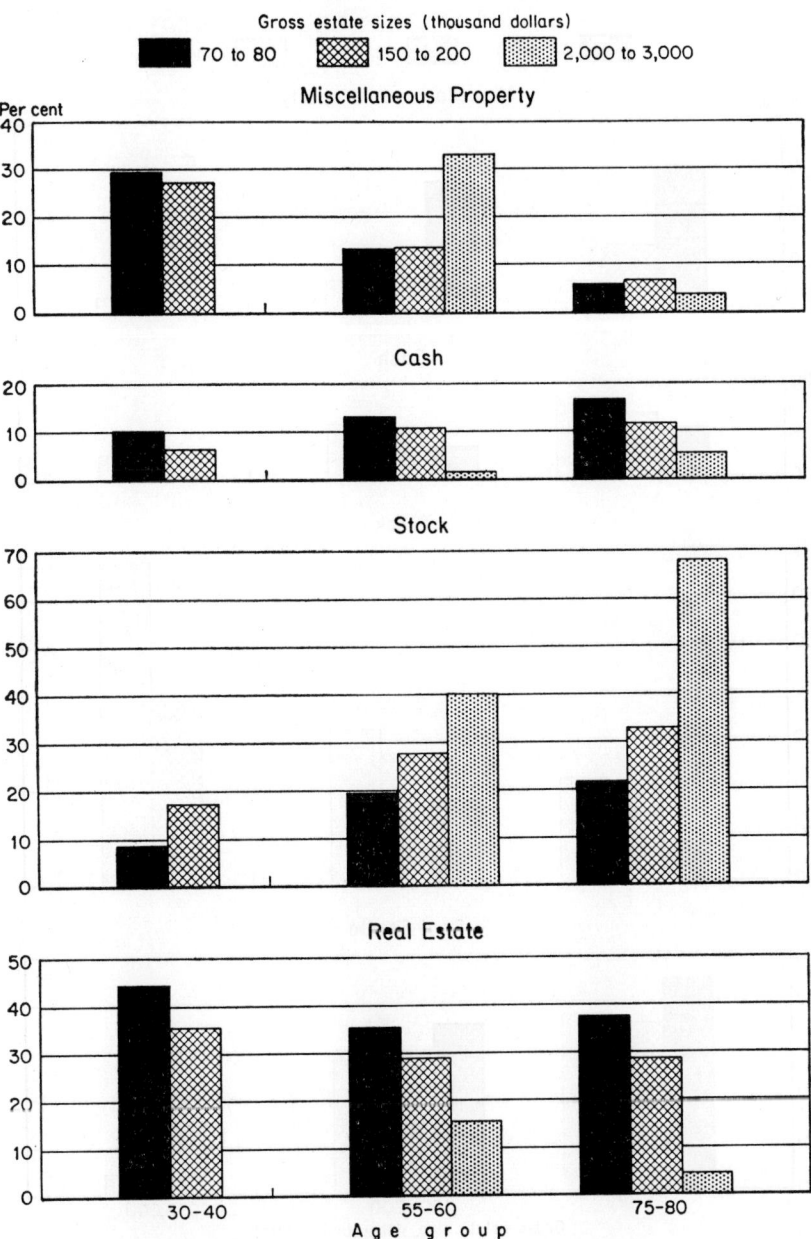

Source: Table 82.

PROPERTY HELD BY TOP WEALTH-HOLDERS

CHART 29
Distribution of Selected Assets by Age Group Within Three Estate Sizes, Males, 1953

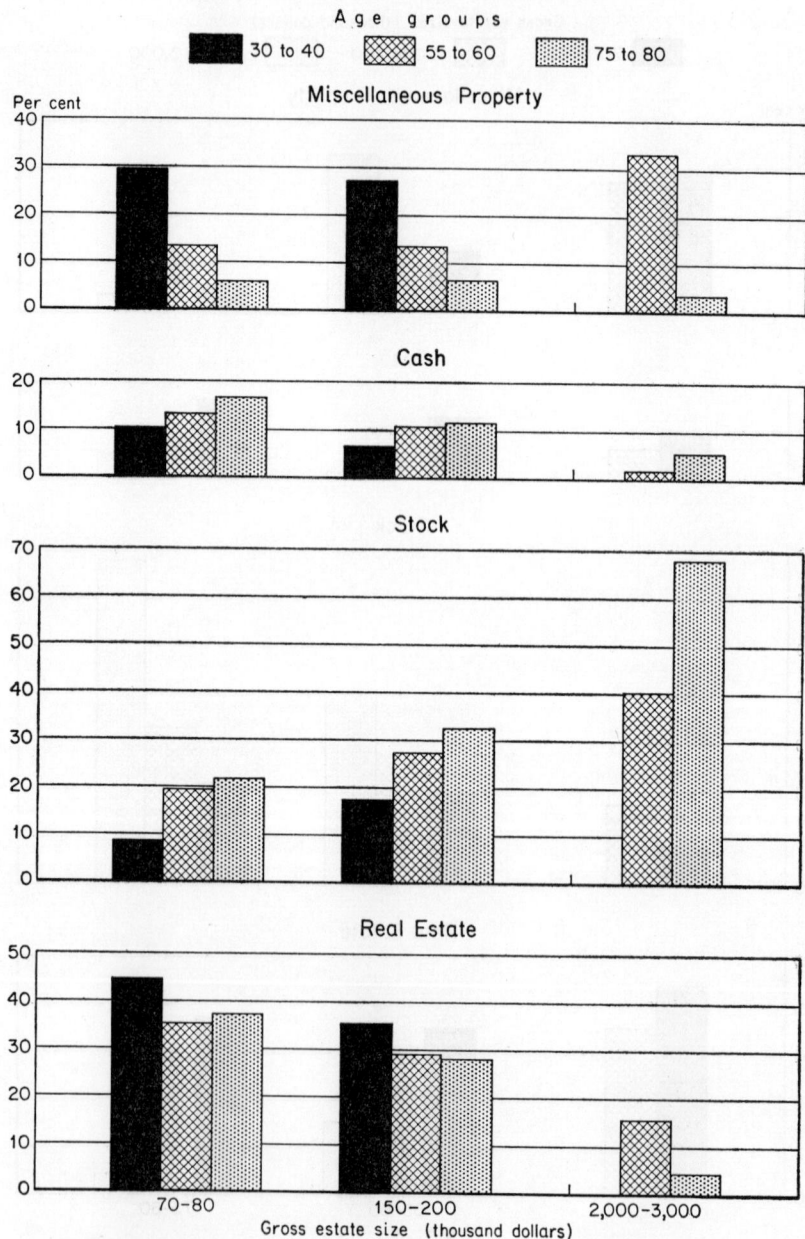

Source: Table 83.

Composition of Estate by Income Level

The Survey of Consumer Finance reports indicate that there is a sharp break in the pattern of estates by income level. This break occurs at some point above $7,500 of income (Table 84). The $7,500 and over income group had only 32 per cent of their net worth in consumer capital and 61 per cent in business and investment assets, while all spending units had 45 per cent in consumer capital and 51 per cent in business and investment assets. There is no clear difference in the percentage of net worth held in fixed value assets by income level. Debt, on the other hand, rises to a peak percentage of 22 in the $5,000 to $7,000 income bracket, and falls to 8 per cent in the $7,500 and over bracket. A full explanation of this pattern would require exploration of the ways in which age, estate size, and other variables are interrelated with income.

Considerable concentration of stock and business assets is to be found in the $7,500 and over income group, who hold 75 per cent of all stock and 65 per cent of all "business" property (Table 85). The lowest income groups have a disproportionate share (compared to their share of total assets or income) of the farm and livestock and crops assets. The middle income groups ($3,000 to $5,000) have disproportionate amounts of retirement funds, life insurance, houses, and cars.

Butters, Thompson, and Bollinger gathered income information from the 746 "active investors" in their sample, most of whom had incomes above the $7,500 lower limit of the Survey of Consumer Finance's open-end income bracket.[11] No direct comparison with the Survey findings in Table 84 is possible, however, since different assets are included and different methods of tabulation are followed. The only asset types which Butters *et al.* found to rise as a percentage of total assets over the whole income range are state and local bonds, and "own business," including closely held corporations and unincorporated business (Table 86). Trust property is most important for the $100,000 and over income group.[12] All other types of property reported either show no income effect or fall as income rises. These authors emphasize that a majority of those with $7,500 of income or over stress capital appreciation as an investment objective.[13]

---

[11] *Effects of Taxation.*
[12] The authors also point out that "more than two-thirds of the individuals with incomes of $50,000 and over either were beneficial owners of property in trust or had established trusts or planned to do so" (*ibid.*, p. 361).
[13] *Ibid.*, p. 35.

Table 86 also shows the findings of Butters and others on composition of estate by wealth level. While no extended comparison of these findings with ours for top wealth-holders seems called for, it is important to note that the study of "active investors" highlights the importance of several types of property on which estate tax data provide no detail. Particularly noteworthy is the importance for the higher wealth groups of the "own business" classifications, "other closely held corporations," and trust property.

Atkinson, by capitalizing Wisconsin State income tax returns, was able to establish even more detailed relationships between income and holdings of a limited range of financial assets. He found that composition of financial assets (those which the tax returns enabled him to identify were time deposits, savings and loan association shares, non-federal debt obligations, and corporate stocks) by income level was such that the higher income groups received much higher returns per dollar of such assets than the lower income groups. Atkinson estimated that the group with incomes under $5,000 had an actual yield of 3.71 per cent and successively higher income groups up to the $50,000 and over income group had yields of 4.60, 5.47, 5.98, and 6.79 per cent.[14] Perhaps Atkinson's most remarkable finding was that there is a definite shift within corporate equity assets from traded to untraded stocks for successively higher income groups (Table 87).

Atkinson also studied the proportionate holdings of each type of financial asset simultaneously by income and by a rough measure of wealth, namely, the amount of financial assets held. He states that:

> It appears that both income and wealth are important causative factors in determining the composition of an individual's financial assets. Within each income group, as individuals with larger financial asset holdings are considered, an increasing proportion of the amount held is found to consist of corporate equities. Furthermore, within each size class of financial asset holdings corporate equities become more important the higher the income group. In the lower income group, as individuals with more assets are considered, the proportion of funds held in the form of direct debt investment is found to increase. That this is not true in the higher income groups is probably because corporate bond yields compare unfavorably with stock yields and because there is less need in the high income groups for safety of investment.[15]

---

[14] Thomas R. Atkinson, *The Pattern of Financial Asset Ownership, Wisconsin Individuals, 1949,* Princeton for National Bureau of Economic Research, 1956, p. 79, Table 16.

[15] *Ibid.*, p. 80.

Atkinson goes on to observe that:

> In the lower ranges of income and asset size . . . the proportion of the value of financial assets consisting of corporate equities seems to vary more with income than with the size of asset holdings. . . . In the upper ranges of income and asset holdings the opposite appears to be the case. . . . One possible factor bearing on this problem [is that] . . . particularly in the case of closely held issues, stock owners are frequently major executives of the corporation.[16]

Atkinson also made an analysis of the character of traded stocks held by persons of different income groups. He found that preferred as opposed to common stock shares were considerably more important in the holdings of the lower than of higher income groups. Also, he found that: "In general, the lower income group holds a greater proportion of the amount of its traded stock in issues of industries which are commonly regarded as conservative investments than the upper income groups do of theirs."[17] The average riskiness of issues held increases with the income of the investors. However, the average number of issues held is greater for groups with progressively higher incomes.[18]

Composition of Estate by Occupation

Self-employed persons, farm operators, and retired persons stand out from the rest of the population in having a high proportion of net worth in business and investment assets[19] (Table 88). These three groups also have relatively small debt as a percentage of net worth. A descending order of emphasis upon business and investment assets is observable for the professional and semiprofessional, managerial, clerical and sales, unskilled and service, and skilled and semiskilled occupational groups.

Stock and "business" assets are heavily concentrated in the hands of the self-employed, managerial, and professional groups; 58 per cent of stock and 98 per cent of business assets are held by these three groups (Table 89). Farm operators, as would be expected, hold virtually all the unincorporated farm assets. Automobiles, houses, and retirement funds are more widely distributed among the occupational groups than are other assets.

[16] *Ibid.*, p. 83.
[17] *Ibid.*, p. 138.
[18] *Ibid.*, pp. 138–139.
[19] The extraordinarily high percentage of farm operators' net worth in business and investment assets is presumably due in part to the inclusion of farm houses in this category.

Atkinson found that investment was frequently guided by occupational attachments. "Active interest in business firms with which the investor is closely allied appears to be a major determinant of corporate stock ownership. About two-thirds of the value of untraded stock holdings, but only about one-tenth of the value of traded stocks, represent issues of corporations from which individuals also receive wage or salary income."[20] He also found that investors prefer to keep their capital near home. For example, he observed that about 30 per cent of the value of traded stock held by Wisconsin investors represented stocks of corporations carrying on major operations within the state.[21]

[20] Atkinson, *Financial Asset Ownership*, p. 106.
[21] *Ibid.*, p. 107.

PROPERTY HELD BY TOP WEALTH-HOLDERS

TABLE 63
PERCENTAGE DISTRIBUTION OF GROSS ESTATE[a] BY TYPE OF PROPERTY
FOR ALL PERSONS AND FOR TOP WEALTH-HOLDERS, 1953

Type of Property	All Persons[b]	Top Wealth-Holders
Real estate	39	22
U.S. govt. bonds	4	6
State and local bonds	1	4
Other bonds	1	1
Corporate stock	15	39
Cash	14	9
Mortgages and notes	3	3
Life insurance reserves[c]	6	2
Miscellaneous property	18	13
Gross estate	100	100
Debts and mortgages	12	9
Economic estate	88	91

[a] Prime wealth variant
[b] Table 90, col. 7.
[c] Based on estimated equity in life insurance. If it were based on face value, insurance would be about 12 per cent of gross estate of top wealth-holders and about 30 per cent of gross estate for all persons. Total life insurance in force in the U.S. in 1953 was $304 billion. The face value of policies held by the top wealth-holders was about $43 billion.

TABLE 64
ESTATE COMPOSITION, LIVING TOP WEALTH-HOLDERS, 1944 AND 1953
(per cent)

	1944[a]	1953
Real estate	16.5	22.4
U.S. govt. bonds	7.7	5.6
State and local bonds	4.6	3.5
Other bonds	3.3	0.9
Stock	38.8	39.2
Cash	9.4	9.2
Mortgages and notes	3.3	3.4
Life insurance	4.4	2.3
Unincorporated business	6.5 ⎫	⎫
Other intangible personal property	4.1 ⎬ 12.0	12.7 ⎬
Tangible personal property	1.4 ⎭	⎭
Gross estate	100.0	100.0
Debts and mortgages	9.1	8.8
Economic estate	90.9	91.2

[a] Mendershausen, in Raymond Goldsmith, *A Study of Saving in the United States*, III, Princeton, 1956, Table E-60.

TABLE 65
Composition of Gross Estate, by Type of Property, for All Estate Tax Returns, Current Values, 1922–54[a]

Per Cent of Gross Estate, Inferred Year of Death

Type of Property	1922 (1)	1923 (2)	1924 (3)	1925 (4)	1926 (5)	1927 (6)	1928 (7)	1929 (8)	1930 (9)	1931 (10)	1932 (11)	1933 (12)	1934 (13)	1935 (14)	1936 (15)
1. Real estate	24.7	23.5	22.0	19.1	18.2	17.4	14.8	13.7	13.4	15.5	19.0	16.9	15.8	15.4	15.6
2. U.S. govt. bonds	4.4	5.1	4.6	4.4	3.8	3.2	2.4	3.0	3.2	3.4	5.1	5.7	5.9	5.0	5.0
3. State and local bonds	3.3	3.1	3.1	4.3	3.7	3.9	3.9	4.4	5.7	6.9	7.8	8.7	7.3	6.1	5.9
4. Corporate bonds	7.2	6.6	7.9	7.5	7.3	6.8	6.8	6.8	6.3	6.9	8.4	8.0	8.2	8.0	6.9
5. Corporate stock	31.3	31.4	32.9	37.4	38.9	43.3	48.4	47.7	47.2	38.2	31.8	34.9	37.0	40.2	40.9
6. Cash	—	—	—	—	—	—	—	—	—	—	—	—	—	—	—
7. Mortgages, notes, and cash[b]	12.9	13.0	12.2	11.5	11.4	11.0	9.9	9.7	9.6	12.2	15.9	14.4	14.5	13.7	13.9
8. Insurance[c]	3.1	3.2	3.3	2.7	2.8	3.0	3.3	3.1	3.3	4.8	6.6	6.4	5.9	5.6	5.5
9. Interest in unincorp. business	—	—	—	—	—	—	—	—	—	—	—	—	—	—	—
10. Other intangible property	—	—	—	—	—	—	—	—	—	—	—	—	—	—	—
11. Unclassified by type[d]	13.1	14.1	14.0	13.1	13.9	11.4	10.5	11.6	11.3	12.1	5.4	5.0	5.4	6.0	6.3
12. Tangible personal property	—	—	—	—	—	—	—	—	—	—	—	—	—	—	—
13. Total gross estate	100.0	100.0	100.0	100.0	100.0	100.0	100.0	100.0	100.0	100.0	100.0	100.0	100.0	100.0	100.0
14. Debts	11.8	11.5	10.7	9.5	9.9	11.2	9.1	9.4	10.4	14.0	16.8	14.0	21.2	11.9	14.4
15. Economic estate	88.2	88.5	89.3	90.1	90.1	88.8	90.9	90.6	89.6	86.0	83.2	86.0	78.8	88.1	85.6

(continued)

PROPERTY HELD BY TOP WEALTH-HOLDERS

TABLE 65 (concluded)

Per Cent of Gross Estate, Inferred Year of Death

Type of Property	1937 (16)	1938 (17)	1939 (18)	1940 (19)	1941 (20)	1942 (21)	1943 (22)	1944 (23)	1946 (24)	1947 (25)	1948 (26)	1949 (27)	1953 (28)	1954 (29)
1. Real estate	14.3	15.3	15.5	15.2	16.5	15.8	15.1	15.2	18.1	18.7	19.3	20.5	20.9	20.9
2. U.S. govt. bonds	6.1	5.2	5.6	5.6	5.4	7.0	7.0	8.4	9.0	9.1	8.7	8.7	6.6	6.1
3. State and local bonds	7.0	8.6	6.1	6.6	6.4	6.3	5.5	5.7	3.9	3.2	3.9	2.8	3.2	1.1
4. Corporate bonds[e]	6.3	5.8	5.7	5.1	5.0	4.8	4.4	4.0	2.6	2.2	1.9	1.8	1.3	1.1
5. Corporate stock	40.6	38.0	39.6	39.9	37.6	36.4	39.2	39.5	38.4	37.1	36.5	36.0	40.2	41.1
6. Cash	—	—	—	}16.2	11.2	11.4	10.3	9.5	10.4	11.6	11.1	10.7	10.1	10.0
7. Mortgages, notes, and cash[b]	13.7	14.9	15.0		5.5	4.9	4.1	3.6	3.3	3.2	3.5	3.9	3.4	3.7
8. Insurance[c]	5.2	5.7	6.0	5.9	6.1	6.9	7.1	7.0	6.8	6.8	7.1	7.3	6.4	6.3
9. Interest in unincorp. business	—	—	—	—	—	2.1	3.2	3.2	3.5	4.0	4.5	4.4	—	—
10. Other intangible property	—	5.3	5.2	4.2	4.8	2.7	2.9	2.7	2.8	2.9	2.3	2.8	7.9	8.1
11. Unclassified by type[d]	6.3	—	—	—	—	—	—	—	—	—	—	—	—	—
12. Tangible personal property	—	1.2	1.3	1.3	1.5	1.7	1.2	1.2	1.2	1.2	1.2	1.1	—	—
13. Total gross estate	100.0	100.0	100.0	100.0	100.0	100.0	100.0	100.0	100.0	100.0	100.0	100.0	100.0	100.0
14. Debts	10.1	9.8	9.5	9.4	9.2	9.8	7.5	6.1	5.5	5.7	5.8	6.0	5.4	5.1
15. Economic estate	89.9	90.2	90.5	90.6	90.8	90.2	92.5	93.9	94.5	94.3	94.2	94.0	94.6	94.9

SOURCE: For 1922–46, Mendershausen in Goldsmith, *Saving in U.S.*, III, Table E-15.

[a] No data available for years excluded.
[b] Mortgages and notes only for 1941–54.
[c] Includes tax-exempt insurance for years before 1942.
[d] Includes, through 1927, jointly owned property, other miscellaneous property (intangible and tangible), as well as transfers, powers of appointment, estate previously taxed; from 1928–31, 1932–37, and 1953–54, miscellaneous property (tangible and intangible) including all other property in the gross estate not elsewhere tabulated, such as judgments, leaseholds, mineral and patent rights, pensions, royalties, tax sale certificates, debts due decedent, interest in unincorporated business, household goods and personal effects, farm products and growing crops, livestock, farm machinery, automobiles, shares in co-partnerships or trust funds, remainderman interest, and annuities unless reported as insurance.
[e] For 1947–54, tabulation heading is "other bonds."

PROPERTY HELD BY TOP WEALTH-HOLDERS

TABLE
PERCENTAGE COMPOSITION OF NET TAXABLE ESTATES OVER $100,000 FOR

	Stock		Real Estate		Miscellaneous		Total Equity	
	Current Dollars	Constant Dollars	Current Dollars	Constant Dollars	Current Dollars	Constant Dollars	Current Dollars	Constant Dollars
	(1)		(2)		(3)		(4)	
1922	38.0	44.1	20.0	17.9	12.5	11.5	70.5	73.5
1923	37.0	43.3	20.0	17.3	12.2	11.3	69.2	71.9
1925	38.7	38.7	17.6	17.6	12.7	12.7	69.0	69.0
1927	41.0	33.4	16.9	20.0	13.0	14.7	70.9	68.1
1929	50.5	34.3	14.0	19.3	10.0	13.1	74.5	66.7
1931	49.0	57.6	12.5	12.4	11.0	9.3	72.5	79.3
1935	41.3	41.6	11.8	15.3	5.0	6.1	58.1	63.0
1937	48.0	46.6	11.0	14.2	6.3	7.7	65.3	68.5
1939	44.0	44.4	10.7	13.9	6.2	7.8	60.9	66.1
1941	47.5	54.7	10.2	11.7	5.1	5.4	62.8	71.8
1943	42.5	43.3	10.6	12.5	6.1	6.5	59.2	62.3
1945	43.7	39.0	11.3	11.6	6.4	7.6	61.4	58.2
1947	44.3	40.6	14.0	12.3	7.5	8.0	65.8	60.9
1948	38.9	36.3	17.6	14.2	8.0	7.4	69.5	57.9
1949	39.1	37.0	18.7	14.6	7.5	7.1	65.3	58.7
1953	43.5	30.9	18.7	15.1	7.5	7.8	69.7	53.8
1954	45.0	30.6	18.6	10.4	7.5	8.9	71.1	49.9

Selected Years, 1922–54, in Current and Constant 1925 Dollars

| Bonds | | Cash, Mortgages | | Insurance | | Total Nonequity | |
| Current Dollars | Constant Dollars | Current Dollars | Constant Dollars | Current Dollars | Constant Dollars | Current Dollars | Constant Dollars |
(5)		(6)		(7)		(8)	
17.0	15.4	10.0	8.9	2.5	2.2	29.5	26.5
17.0	15.9	11.0	10.0	2.5	2.2	30.5	28.1
17.6	17.6	11.1	11.1	2.5	2.5	31.2	31.2
15.7	17.0	10.8	11.9	2.6	2.9	29.1	31.8
13.7	17.6	9.8	12.5	2.5	3.2	26.0	33.3
16.0	14.5	8.8	6.8	2.5	1.8	27.3	21.2
24.4	21.0	12.7	11.7	4.5	4.3	41.6	37.0
20.7	17.8	11.8	11.3	2.5	2.5	35.0	31.6
24.5	20.0	12.2	11.5	2.5	2.5	39.2	34.0
20.6	15.1	14.4	12.3	2.3	2.1	37.3	29.5
22.5	19.5	15.0	14.8	3.4	3.6	40.9	37.9
20.0	20.1	12.6	14.2	6.2	7.4	38.8	41.8
16.0	18.1	12.0	12.8	6.5	8.1	34.5	39.0
15.4	17.6	13.7	16.1	6.4	8.1	35.5	41.8
13.7	16.0	14.5	17.3	6.2	7.9	34.4	41.2
11.3	17.3	13.0	19.3	6.0	9.5	30.3	46.1
10.3	17.8	13.1	22.3	5.5	10.0	28.9	50.1

Source: For assets valued in current dollars, Chart 21. For assets valued in 1925 constant dollars, obtained by deflating each asset (in current dollars) by its own price index (Table 67). The federal bond index was chosen to represent price change for all bonds.

TABLE 67
INDEXES OF ASSET PRICES, 1919–57
(1925 = 100)

Year	(1) Res. Cost	(2) Farm Land	(3) Bond Price			(4) Consumer	(5) Stock
			Corp. High-Grade	Munic. Tax-Exempt	U.S. Govt.		
1919	95.74		92.75	95.14	90.36	85.73	78.74
1920	123.39		85.16	88.77	84.46	114.27	71.57
1921	99.17		86.75	87.55	86.73	101.87	61.52
1922	91.16	121.71	96.83	98.08	94.99	95.47	75.43
1923	102.18	114.29	96.26	97.87	94.30	97.20	76.86
1924	100.73	107.43	98.07	98.58	97.64	97.47	81.17
1925	100.00	100.00	100.00	100.00	100.00	100.00	100.00
1926	100.73	92.57	102.04	100.10	102.06	100.80	112.91
1927	99.38	89.71	103.74	101.52	106.29	98.93	137.58
1928	99.69	85.71	103.96	100.51	106.49	97.73	178.72
1929	103.95	74.29	100.91	97.67	103.05	97.73	233.36
1930	101.53	70.86	102.94	100.20	106.05	95.20	188.61
1931	93.45	67.43	105.16	101.21	91.25	86.67	122.51
1932	79.11	65.71	95.58	92.81	87.41	77.87	62.15
1933	79.21	64.00	103.28	92.11	91.54	73.73	80.36
1934	86.17	62.29	111.21	100.91	83.81	76.27	88.25
1935	83.68	60.57	119.48	109.92	97.84	78.27	95.07
1936	87.53	58.86	124.01	115.81	99.61	79.07	138.74
1937	97.40	57.14	124.80	114.68	99.21	81.87	138.21
1938	100.10	55.43	126.50	118.02	100.79	80.40	103.05
1939	101.87	53.71	129.90	120.45	103.44	79.20	108.16
1940	105.72	51.43	131.70	125.10	105.41	79.87	98.83
1941	113.93	57.14	133.30	132.49	109.14	83.87	88.07
1942	120.37	65.14	132.96	127.73	99.02	92.93	77.76
1943	125.99	72.00	133.98	133.40	98.82	98.67	103.14
1944	137.32	78.86	134.43	137.45	98.62	100.27	111.84
1945	146.47	85.71	137.71	141.30	100.29	102.53	135.46
1946	162.27	92.00	139.75	141.80	103.05	111.20	153.18
1947	196.67	98.29	138.25	134.41	102.06	127.33	136.08
1948	218.81	104.57	133.86	126.82	99.16	137.07	139.28
1949	212.37	110.86	137.03	130.47	100.98	135.73	136.57
1950	224.17	117.14	138.05	135.02	100.79	137.07	165.02
1951	241.16	122.86	133.30	134.62	97.25	148.00	200.36
1952	247.61	128.57	131.14	130.87	95.67	151.33	219.73
1953	251.77	134.29	126.95	121.15	92.33	152.53	221.79
1954		140.00	132.73	127.33	97.84	153.07	266.28
1955			129.56	124.60	94.40	152.67	363.14
1956	255.58	136.31	123.56	117.71	91.45	154.93	418.17
1957			114.72	107.09	89.09	158.53	398.03

SOURCE: Col. 1: Boeckh Residential Construction Cost Index, as given in Leo Grebler, David Blank, and Louis Winnick, *Capital Formation in Residential Real Estate*, Princeton for National Bureau of Economic Research, 1956, p. 342; col. 2: A. S. Tostlebe, *Capital in Agriculture*, Princeton for National Bureau of Economic Research, 1957, p. 60, Chart VII; col. 3: A: Standard and Poor's, *Statistics; Security Price Index Record*, New York, 1957, p. 150, converted to 1925 base; B: *ibid.*, p. 173; C: *Statistical Abstract*; col. 4: *Statistical Abstract*; col. 5: Standard and Poor's, *Statistics; Security Price Index Record*, p. 4.

TABLE 68
BOND AND STOCK YIELDS, 1926–56
(end of year)

	Common Stock Yields (1)	Corporate Bond Yields (2)	Stock Yields ÷ Bond Yields (3)
1926	5.04	4.77	1.06
1927	4.24	4.65	.91
1928	3.45	4.63	.75
1929	4.74	4.86	.98
1930	6.72	4.71	1.43
1931	10.35	4.55	2.27
1932	7.47	5.28	1.41
1933	3.98	4.69	.85
1934	4.38	4.14	1.06
1935	3.30	3.61	.91
1936	4.11	3.34	1.22
1937	7.34	3.30	2.22
1938	3.50	3.20	1.07
1939	4.71	3.02	1.56
1940	6.10	2.92	2.09
1941	7.62	2.84	2.68
1942	5.70	2.85	2.00
1943	4.82	2.80	1.72
1944	4.62	2.78	1.66
1945	3.66	2.61	1.40
1946	4.42	2.51	1.76
1947	5.34	2.58	2.07
1948	6.00	2.80	2.14
1949	6.88	2.65	2.60
1950	7.31	2.59	2.82
1951	5.95	2.84	2.10
1952	5.31	2.75	1.93
1953	5.87	3.18	1.85
1954	4.25	2.87	1.48
1955	3.94	3.04	1.30
1956	4.01	3.38	1.19

SOURCE: Col. 1: Standard and Poor's, *Statistics; Security Price Index Record*, New York, 1959, Supplement, p. 150; col. 2: *ibid.*, p. 24; col. 3: col. 1 ÷ col. 2.

TABLE 69
Composition of Net Worth Within Age Groups, 1953
(per cent)

Age Group of Head of Spending Unit	Net Worth	Variable Value Assets			Total Assets	Debt[d]
		Consumer Capital Goods[a]	Business and Investment Assets[b]	Fixed Value Assets[c]		
18 to 25	100	64	51	26	141	41
25 to 35	100	71	47	16	134	34
35 to 45	100	56	50	16	122	22
45 to 55	100	41	53	15	109	9
55 to 65	100	35	55	16	106	6
65 and over	100	35	49	20	104	4
All spending units	100	45	51	17	113	13

Source: Derived from 1953 Survey of Consumer Finances, published in *Federal Reserve Bulletin*, 1953, Supplementary Table 2, p. 2.

[a] Includes automobiles and owner-occupied nonfarm houses.

[b] Includes owner-occupied farms, farm machinery, livestock, crops, interest in unincorporated business, privately held corporations, real estate other than home or farm on which owner is living, and corporate stock.

[c] Includes liquid assets and loans made by spending units.

[d] Includes mortgages, other real estate debt, instalment, and other short-term debt.

TABLE 70
DISTRIBUTION OF SELECTED BALANCE SHEET ITEMS BY AGE GROUP, 1950
(per cent)

	Age Group							
Item	18 to 25 (1)	25 to 35 (2)	35 to 45 (3)	45 to 55 (4)	55 to 65 (5)	65 and over (6)	Not Ascertained (7)	All Cases (8)
Liquid assets	2	11	19	27	19	21	1	100
Car	7	25	26	22	13	6	1	100
House	1	14	24	24	20	16	1	100
Farm	1	9	22	25	23	20	b	100
Livestock and crops	5	14	29	27	18	7	b	100
Life insurance	1	7	19	30	25	17	1	100
Other real estate	1	8	18	20	31	21	1	100
Stock	b	2	16	26	26	29	1	100
Business[a]	1	12	21	28	34	4	b	100
Retirement fund	2	22	27	29	15	3	2	100
Total assets	2	11	21	25	24	16	1	100
Debt	3	29	29	22	10	6	1	100
Net worth	1	9	20	26	25	18	1	100
1949 income	7	23	26	22	15	7	b	100

SOURCE: Goldsmith, *Saving in U.S.*, III, Table W-52.
[a] Includes closely held corporations.
[b] No cases reported or less than 0.5 per cent.

TABLE 71

Percentage Distribution of Gross Estate by Type of Property and Age Group, Top Wealth-Holders of Both Sexes, 1953

Type of Property	Total	Under 21	21 to 30	30 to 40	40 to 50	50 to 55	55 to 60	60 to 65	65 to 70	70 to 75	75 to 80	80 to 85	85 and over
Real estate	22.4	11.1	10.2	19.4	23.4	26.5	25.7	24.8	21.7	20.4	20.1	19.2	19.0
U.S. govt. bonds	5.6	6.2	3.1	2.7	5.9	5.3	6.0	5.6	5.8	6.7	7.1	7.7	9.4
State and local bonds	3.5	4.2	2.6	3.7	5.8	1.1	1.6	2.5	1.8	4.6	3.0	4.4	5.1
Other bonds	0.9	1.4	1.5	0.9	0.6	0.6	0.9	1.0	1.0	1.4	1.3	1.7	1.8
Stock	39.2	20.6	51.1	48.9	34.5	33.3	35.2	36.2	40.7	43.0	45.3	46.5	46.8
Cash	9.2	2.7	8.6	8.3	7.2	9.5	9.7	10.6	10.8	10.4	11.2	10.6	10.2
Mortgages and notes	3.4	0	2.9	1.9	3.4	4.0	4.1	3.8	4.3	3.3	3.5	2.9	2.6
Life insurance equity	3.0	0	0.6	1.2	2.6	3.9	4.3	4.5	3.8	3.0	2.4	1.8	1.2
Misc. property	12.7	53.4	19.4	13.0	16.4	16.0	12.4	11.1	9.0	7.1	5.9	5.1	3.9
Gross estate	100.0	100.0	100.0	100.0	100.0	100.0	100.0	100.0	100.0	100.0	100.0	100.0	100.0
Debts and mortgages	8.8	1.0	5.7	12.7	11.3	11.2	9.7	8.0	5.6	4.3	3.3	2.5	3.2
Economic estate	91.2	99.9	94.3	87.3	88.7	88.8	90.3	92.0	94.4	95.7	96.7	97.5	96.8

TABLE 72

PERCENTAGE DISTRIBUTION OF GROSS ESTATE BY TYPE OF PROPERTY AND AGE GROUP, MALE TOP WEALTH-HOLDERS, 1953[a]

Type of Property	Total	Under 21	21 to 30	30 to 40	40 to 50	50 to 55	55 to 60	60 to 65	65 to 70	70 to 75	75 to 80	80 to 85	85 and over
							Age Group						
No. of wealth-holders	1,084,065	5,555	30,832	135,011	269,529	147,700	138,645	123,559	94,310	64,847	40,428	21,040	12,609
Aggregate gross estate ($ mill.)	176,022	761	6,276	14,163	38,453	22,929	23,003	22,372	18,542	13,412	8,472	4,620	3,019
Real estate	24.9%	20.6%	7.6%	32.9%	28.7%	25.8%	25.3%	24.5%	22.4%	21.0%	20.5%	22.0%	19.3%
U.S. govt. bonds	5.1	15.9	3.5	2.6	4.0	4.8	5.6	5.4	5.4	6.4	7.0	8.0	9.2
State and local bonds	1.6	—	3.2	0.7	0.8	0.7	1.6	2.0	2.2	2.8	2.2	3.4	4.2
Other bonds	0.9	4.2	1.7	0.9	0.6	0.5	0.7	1.1	0.8	1.3	1.2	1.5	1.7
Corporate stock	35.4	49.7	49.7	26.7	30.4	33.0	33.7	35.3	39.7	42.2	44.5	42.0	46.5
Cash	9.2	4.2	9.9	7.0	7.6	9.7	9.4	10.0	10.4	10.3	10.7	11.0	10.2
Mortgages and notes	3.7	0.1	2.3	3.4	3.3	4.2	4.2	3.8	4.4	3.9	4.0	3.5	3.0
Life insurance	4.6	0.7	0.7	2.9	4.3	5.2	5.7	6.1	5.4	4.6	3.9	3.1	1.9
Misc. property	14.5	4.2	21.5	22.8	20.3	16.1	13.8	12.0	9.3	7.6	6.0	5.4	4.0
Gross estate	100.0	100.0	100.0	100.0	100.0	100.0	100.0	100.0	100.0	100.0	100.0	100.0	100.0
Debts and mortgages	11.3	1.2	6.2	20.6	16.1	13.0	11.7	9.9	6.6	5.0	3.8	3.1	4.0
Economic estate	88.7	98.8	93.8	79.4	83.9	87.0	88.4	90.1	93.4	95.0	96.2	96.9	96.0

[a] Adjusted mortality rates have been used and insurance amounts have been reduced to estimated equities.

TABLE 73

PERCENTAGE DISTRIBUTION OF GROSS ESTATE BY TYPE OF PROPERTY AND AGE GROUP, FEMALE TOP WEALTH-HOLDERS, 1953[a]

Type of Property	Total	Age Group										
		Under 21	21 to 30	30 to 40	40 to 50	50 to 55	55 to 60	60 to 65	65 to 70	70 to 75	75 to 80	80 to 85	85 and over
No. of wealth-holders	525,472	6,667	16,000	51,819	100,400	65,767	61,003	58,958	53,594	45,522	33,295	19,776	12,671
Aggregate gross estate ($ mill.)	116,918	1,554	1,536	22,262	29,235	10,198	9,777	10,129	9,596	9,253	6,385	4,382	2,611
Real estate	19.5%	6.4%	20.6%	10.8%	16.6%	27.9%	26.8%	25.1%	20.3%	19.5%	19.6%	16.3%	18.7%
U.S. govt. bonds	6.4	1.5	1.8	2.8	8.5	6.2	7.1	6.2	6.7	7.1	7.3	7.4	9.6
State and local bonds	6.4	6.2	—	5.6	12.4	2.0	1.8	3.6	4.2	7.2	4.1	5.5	6.1
Other bonds	1.0	—	1.0	0.9	0.5	0.8	1.4	1.0	1.5	1.6	1.4	2.0	2.0
Corporate stock	44.8	6.4	56.8	62.9	40.0	34.0	38.7	38.2	42.6	44.3	46.4	51.2	47.1
Cash	9.2	1.9	3.4	9.0	6.8	9.0	10.4	12.0	11.6	10.7	11.9	10.1	10.2
Mortgages and notes	2.9	—	5.6	1.0	3.7	3.5	3.7	3.5	4.2	2.6	2.9	2.3	2.2
Life insurance	0.5	—	0.3	0.1	0.3	0.8	1.0	1.1	0.6	0.7	0.6	0.4	0.3
Misc. property	10.0	77.4	10.6	6.8	11.3	15.9	9.1	9.2	8.5	6.4	5.8	4.7	3.8
Gross estate	100.0	100.0	100.0	100.0	100.0	100.0	100.0	100.0	100.0	100.0	100.0	100.0	100.0
Debts and mortgages	5.0	0.8	3.9	7.8	5.0	7.3	5.0	4.1	3.7	3.3	2.6	1.9	2.3
Economic estate	95.0	99.2	96.1	92.3	95.0	92.7	95.0	96.0	96.3	96.7	97.4	98.1	97.7

[a] Adjusted mortality rates have been used and insurance amounts have been reduced to estimated equities.

TABLE 74
Percentage Distribution of Gross Estate by Type of Property and Sex, Top Wealth-Holders, Selected Estate Sizes, 1953

Type of Property	Males		Females	
	All Estate Sizes	$120,000 to $150,000 Estate Size	All Estate Sizes	$120,000 to $150,000 Estate Size
Real estate	24.9	30.8	18.7	29.3
U.S. govt. bonds	5.1	5.6	6.4	6.6
State and local bonds	1.6	0.2	6.4	0.4
Other bonds	0.9	0.9	1.1	1.3
Corporate stock	35.4	24.4	44.8	33.8
Cash	9.2	11.1	9.2	11.1
Mortgages and notes	3.8	4.1	3.0	5.2
Life insurance	4.6	5.6	0.5	0.7
Misc. property	14.5	17.3	9.9	11.6
Gross estate	100.0	100.0	100.0	100.0
Debts and mortgages	11.3	11.1	5.0	5.9
Economic estate	88.7	88.9	95.0	94.1

TABLE 75

PERCENTAGE DISTRIBUTION OF GROSS ESTATE BY TYPE OF PROPERTY AND GROSS ESTATE SIZE, TOP WEALTH-HOLDERS OF BOTH SEXES, 1953[a]

Type of Property	Total	Under 60	60 to 70	70 to 80	80 to 90	90 to 100	100 to 120	120 to 150	150 to 200	200 to 300	300 to 500	500 to 1,000	1,000 to 2,000	2,000 to 3,000	3,000 to 5,000	5,000 to 10,000	10,000 and over
Real estate	22.4	17.7	36.1	36.8	38.1	35.4	34.2	30.3	29.7	26.4	19.6	14.3	10.1	12.5	4.4	2.3	0.9
U.S. govt. bonds	5.6	3.8	6.9	6.7	6.0	6.2	6.1	5.9	6.0	4.8	5.2	6.3	2.9	3.4	6.0	0.9	12.2
State and local bonds	3.5	—	0.1	0.1	0.1	0.2	0.1	0.3	0.2	0.7	1.7	3.3	6.9	12.1	11.3	4.9	26.1
Other bonds	1.0	—	1.4	0.5	0.6	0.8	0.6	1.0	0.7	1.1	1.5	1.3	1.0	0.6	1.5	0.7	0.2
Corporate stock	39.2	62.0	20.0	20.3	22.2	23.4	25.7	27.3	30.1	34.6	42.1	49.9	58.9	43.9	56.3	82.2	51.7
Cash	9.2	8.9	14.8	13.8	11.1	11.9	11.3	11.1	9.6	9.1	7.8	7.3	6.9	12.9	7.7	5.9	3.7
Mortgages and notes	3.5	—	4.5	4.3	4.1	4.1	3.5	4.4	4.3	4.6	3.4	3.0	2.2	1.4	0.7	0.4	3.6
Life insurance	2.9	1.3	3.2	3.7	4.0	3.9	4.1	4.1	4.7	3.9	3.0	2.2	1.3	1.0	0.7	0.4	0.2
Misc. property	12.7	6.3	13.0	13.8	13.8	14.1	14.4	15.6	14.7	14.8	15.7	12.4	9.8	12.2	11.4	2.3	1.4
Gross estate	100.0	100.0	100.0	100.0	100.0	100.0	100.0	100.0	100.0	100.0	100.0	100.0	100.0	100.0	100.0	100.0	100.0
Debts and mortgages	8.8	3.8	7.1	7.2	10.0	9.0	9.3	9.6	10.6	12.5	10.7	8.0	5.8	12.1	7.9	2.5	0.7
Economic estate	91.2	96.2	92.9	92.8	90.0	91.0	90.7	90.4	89.4	87.5	89.3	92.0	94.2	87.9	92.1	97.5	99.3

[a] Adjusted mortality rates have been used and insurance amounts have been reduced to estimated equities.

TABLE 76

PERCENTAGE DISTRIBUTION OF GROSS ESTATE BY TYPE OF PROPERTY AND GROSS ESTATE SIZE, MALE TOP WEALTH-HOLDERS, 1953[a]

Type of Property	Total	Under 60	60 to 70	70 to 80	80 to 90	90 to 100	100 to 120	120 to 150	150 to 200	200 to 300	300 to 500	500 to 1,000	1,000 to 2,000	2,000 to 3,000	3,000 to 5,000	5,000 to 10,000	10,000 and over
Real estate	24.9	18.6	37.0	38.5	37.1	35.8	34.5	30.8	30.1	26.4	20.9	17.1	10.1	11.5	3.5	7.6	1.7
U.S. govt. bonds	5.1	4.7	6.5	5.9	6.2	5.5	5.8	5.6	5.8	4.6	5.2	4.7	3.0	5.7	4.3	2.4	3.6
State and local bonds	1.6	—	0.1	0.1	0.1	0.2	0.1	0.2	0.1	0.4	1.0	1.7	4.3	9.2	9.5	9.0	16.1
Other bonds	0.9	—	0.3	0.4	0.3	0.5	0.4	0.9	0.6	1.2	1.2	1.2	0.7	0.7	2.0	1.8	0.5
Stock	35.4	69.7	15.3	17.4	18.9	19.3	21.7	24.4	26.2	32.5	41.2	47.1	61.0	53.1	64.6	71.2	69.3
Cash	9.2	2.3	14.1	12.6	11.4	12.2	10.9	11.1	9.5	8.9	8.3	7.0	6.2	6.8	9.5	3.0	3.4
Mortgages and notes	3.8	—	3.4	3.8	3.6	4.3	3.6	4.1	4.6	5.0	3.9	3.7	2.6	3.1	0.6	0.5	1.1
Life insurance	4.6	—	5.1	5.4	5.9	5.8	5.9	5.6	6.5	5.3	4.3	3.0	2.0	2.3	0.9	1.6	0.9
Misc. property	14.5	4.7	18.2	15.9	16.5	16.4	17.1	17.3	16.6	15.7	14.0	14.5	10.1	7.6	5.1	2.9	3.4
Gross estate	100.0	100.0	100.0	100.0	100.0	100.0	100.0	100.0	100.0	100.0	100.0	100.0	100.0	100.0	100.0	100.0	100.0
Debts and mortgages	11.3	4.7	8.4	8.9	11.7	11.0	10.7	11.1	12.6	14.1	13.3	10.7	7.3	8.2	11.4	9.9	3.7
Economic estate	88.7	95.3	91.6	91.1	88.3	89.0	89.3	88.9	87.4	85.9	86.7	89.3	92.7	91.8	88.6	90.1	96.3

[a] Adjusted mortality rates have been used and insurance amounts have been reduced to estimated equities.

TABLE 77

PERCENTAGE DISTRIBUTION OF GROSS ESTATE, BY TYPE OF PROPERTY AND GROSS ESTATE SIZE, FEMALE TOP WEALTH-HOLDERS, 1953[a]

								Gross Estate Size (thousand dollars)								
Type of Property	Total	Under 60	60 to 70	70 to 80	80 to 90	90 to 100	100 to 120	120 to 150	150 to 200	200 to 300	300 to 500	500 to 1,000	1,000 to 2,000	2,000 to 3,000	3,000 to 5,000	5,000 to 10,000	10,000 and over
Real estate	18.7	16.7	35.1	34.1	39.7	34.7	33.5	29.3	28.7	26.5	17.1	9.4	10.1	13.2	6.0	0.8	0.8
U.S. govt. bonds	6.4	2.8	7.5	7.9	5.7	7.3	6.6	6.6	6.3	5.2	5.2	9.0	2.7	2.0	8.9	0.4	13.3
State and local bonds	6.4	—	0.3	0.1	0.1	0.2	0.2	0.4	0.5	1.2	3.0	6.0	11.3	13.9	14.2	3.7	27.3
Other bonds	1.1	—	2.7	0.7	1.1	1.4	0.9	1.3	0.9	1.1	1.9	1.4	1.5	0.6	0.7	0.3	0.2
Stock	44.8	52.7	25.5	25.2	27.3	30.5	33.1	33.8	38.6	39.8	44.0	54.9	55.3	38.1	42.5	85.5	49.4
Cash	9.2	16.7	15.6	15.7	10.7	11.4	12.1	11.1	10.0	9.6	6.9	7.6	8.0	16.7	4.8	6.7	3.7
Mortgages and notes	3.0	—	5.6	5.1	4.8	3.7	3.4	5.2	3.6	3.4	2.4	1.9	1.5	0.3	0.8	0.4	4.0
Life insurance	0.5	2.8	0.9	1.0	1.0	0.6	0.9	0.7	0.6	0.6	0.3	0.8	0.3	0.1	0.3	—	0.1
Misc. property	9.9	8.3	6.8	10.2	9.6	10.2	9.3	11.6	10.8	12.6	19.2	9.0	9.3	15.1	21.8	2.2	1.2
Gross estate	100.0	100.0	100.0	100.0	100.0	100.0	100.0	100.0	100.0	100.0	100.0	100.0	100.0	100.0	100.0	100.0	100.0
Debts and mortgages	5.0	2.8	5.6	4.4	7.3	5.6	6.7	5.9	6.2	8.7	5.6	3.4	3.4	14.6	2.0	0.3	0.3
Economic estate	95.0	97.2	94.4	95.6	92.7	94.4	93.3	94.1	93.8	91.3	94.4	96.6	96.6	85.4	98.0	99.7	99.7

[a] Adjusted mortality rates have been used and insurance amounts have been reduced to estimated equities.

TABLE 78

PERCENTAGE DISTRIBUTION OF TYPE OF PROPERTY BY GROSS ESTATE SIZE, TOP WEALTH-HOLDERS OF BOTH SEXES, 1953[a]

Type of Property	Total	Gross Estate Size (thousand dollars)																	
		Under 60	60 to 70	70 to 80	80 to 90	90 to 100	100 to 120	120 to 150	150 to 200	200 to 300	300 to 500	500 to 1,000	1,000 to 2,000	2,000 to 3,000	3,000 to 5,000	5,000 to 10,000	10,000 and over
No. of wealth-holders	100.0	0.1	10.8	10.6	10.5	9.1	13.5	13.0	11.2	10.1	6.1	3.1	1.2	0.2	0.1	0.1	0.0
Real estate	100.0	0.0	5.8	6.6	7.4	6.8	11.0	11.5	12.6	14.2	10.3	7.0	3.7	1.9	0.6	0.4	0.2
U.S. govt. bonds	100.0	0.0	4.5	4.7	4.7	4.7	7.9	9.0	10.1	10.3	11.0	12.4	4.3	2.0	3.0	0.7	10.7
State and local bonds	100.0	—	0.2	0.1	0.1	0.3	0.3	0.7	0.7	2.2	5.6	10.4	16.5	11.5	8.9	6.0	36.6
Other bonds	100.0	—	5.2	2.2	2.8	3.6	4.4	9.0	7.0	14.2	17.7	14.8	8.6	2.0	4.3	3.0	1.1
Stock	100.0	0.1	1.8	2.1	2.5	2.6	4.7	6.0	7.3	10.6	12.7	14.1	12.5	3.7	4.0	9.0	6.5
Cash	100.0	0.0	5.8	6.0	5.2	5.5	8.9	10.3	9.9	11.9	10.0	8.7	6.2	4.6	2.3	2.7	2.0
Mortgages and notes	100.0	—	4.7	5.0	5.2	5.1	7.4	11.0	11.8	16.0	11.6	9.7	5.2	1.3	0.6	0.5	5.2
Life insurance	100.0	0.0	3.9	5.1	5.8	5.7	10.2	11.9	15.0	16.1	11.9	8.1	3.8	1.1	0.6	0.6	0.2
Misc. property	100.0	0.0	3.7	4.3	4.7	4.8	8.2	10.4	11.0	14.0	14.6	10.8	6.4	3.2	2.5	0.8	0.6
Gross estate	100.0	0.0	3.5	4.0	4.4	4.3	7.2	8.5	9.5	12.0	11.8	11.0	8.3	3.3	2.8	4.3	4.9
Debts and mortgages	100.0	0.0	2.9	3.3	5.0	4.4	7.7	9.3	11.5	17.3	14.4	10.1	5.5	4.6	2.5	1.2	0.4
Economic estate	100.0	0.0	3.7	4.1	4.3	4.3	7.2	8.4	9.3	11.6	11.5	11.1	8.6	3.2	2.8	4.6	5.4

[a] Adjusted mortality rates have been used and insurance amounts have been reduced to estimated equities.

PROPERTY HELD BY TOP WEALTH-HOLDERS

TABLE

PERCENTAGE DISTRIBUTION OF TYPE OF PROPERTY BY GROSS

Type of Property	Total	Gross Estate Size (thousand dollars)					
		Under 60	60 to 70	70 to 80	80 to 90	90 to 100	100 to 120
No. of wealth-holders	1,084,073	828	99,714	111,574	108,711	97,825	148,925
Aggregate gross estate (million $)	175,900	43	5,719	7,315	7,783	7,923	13,862
No. of wealth-holders	100.0%	0.1%	9.2%	10.3%	10.0%	9.0%	13.7%
Real estate	100.0	0.0	4.8	6.4	6.6	6.5	10.9
U.S. govt. bonds	100.0	0.0	4.2	4.9	5.4	4.9	9.0
State and local bonds	100.0	—	0.1	0.2	0.2	0.6	0.5
Other bonds	100.0	—	1.0	1.9	1.5	2.4	3.6
Corporate stock	100.0	0.1	1.4	2.4	2.4	2.5	4.8
Cash	100.0	0.0	5.0	5.7	5.5	5.9	9.3
Mortgages and notes	100.0	—	3.0	4.2	4.3	5.2	7.5
Life insurance	100.0	—	3.6	4.9	5.7	5.8	10.1
Misc. property	100.0	0.0	4.1	4.6	5.0	5.1	9.3
Gross estate	100.0	0.0	3.2	4.2	4.4	4.5	7.9
Debts and mortgages	100.0	0.0	2.4	3.3	4.6	4.4	7.5
Economic estate	100.0	0.0	3.4	4.3	4.4	4.5	7.9

PROPERTY HELD BY TOP WEALTH-HOLDERS

79
Estate Size, Male Top Wealth-Holders, 1953[a]

			Gross Estate Size (thousand dollars)						
120 to 150	150 to 200	200 to 300	300 to 500	500 to 1,000	1,000 to 2,000	2,000 to 3,000	3,000 to 5,000	5,000 to 10,000	10,000 and over
152,768	129,527	120,501	66,976	31,512	11,644	1,608	1,365	472	123
17,394	19,020	25,060	22,802	20,383	15,177	3,764	5,067	2,895	1,693
14.1%	11.9%	11.1%	6.2%	2.9%	1.1%	0.2%	0.1%	0.0%	0.0%
12.2	13.1	15.1	10.9	8.0	3.5	1.0	0.4	0.5	0.1
11.0	12.4	12.8	13.3	10.8	5.0	2.4	2.4	0.8	0.7
1.6	0.8	3.8	8.1	12.3	23.2	12.3	17.2	9.4	9.7
10.2	7.5	18.7	18.0	16.2	6.8	1.6	6.6	3.3	0.6
6.8	8.0	13.0	15.1	15.4	14.9	3.2	5.3	3.3	1.9
11.9	11.1	13.8	11.7	8.9	5.8	1.6	3.0	0.5	0.3
10.6	13.1	19.0	13.4	11.2	5.9	1.7	0.5	0.2	0.3
12.1	15.4	16.4	12.3	7.6	3.7	1.1	0.6	0.6	0.2
11.7	12.3	15.4	12.4	11.5	6.0	1.1	1.0	0.3	0.2
9.9	10.8	14.2	13.0	11.6	8.6	2.1	2.9	1.7	1.0
9.8	12.1	17.8	15.3	11.0	5.6	1.6	2.9	1.4	0.3
9.9	10.7	13.8	12.7	11.7	9.0	2.2	2.9	1.7	1.1

[a] Adjusted mortality rates have been used and insurance amounts have been reduced to estimated equities.

PROPERTY HELD BY TOP WEALTH-HOLDERS

TABLE
PERCENTAGE DISTRIBUTION OF TYPE OF PROPERTY BY GROSS

Type of Property	Total	Gross Estate Size (thousand dollars)					
		Under 60	60 to 70	70 to 80	80 to 90	90 to 100	100 to 120
No. of wealth-holders	525,457	664	75,848	59,664	59,994	49,040	68,808
Aggregate gross estate (million $)	116,917	36	4,826	4,381	4,933	4,608	7,362
No. of wealth-holders	100.0%	0.1%	14.4%	11.3%	11.4%	9.3%	13.1%
Real estate	100.0	0.0	7.7	6.8	8.9	7.3	11.3
U.S. govt. bonds	100.0	0.0	4.8	4.6	3.8	4.5	6.5
State and local bonds	100.0	—	0.2	0.0	0.1	0.1	0.2
Other bonds	100.0	—	10.1	2.5	4.3	5.1	5.3
Corporate stock	100.0	0.0	2.4	2.1	2.6	2.7	4.6
Cash	100.0	0.1	7.0	6.4	4.9	4.9	8.2
Mortgages and notes	100.0	—	7.9	6.4	6.9	4.9	7.2
Life insurance	100.0	0.2	7.2	7.1	8.1	5.0	11.6
Misc. property	100.0	0.0	2.8	3.8	4.1	4.0	5.9
Gross estate	100.0	0.0	4.1	3.8	4.2	3.9	6.3
Debts and mortgages	100.0	0.0	4.6	3.3	6.2	4.4	8.5
Economic estate	100.0	0.0	4.1	3.8	4.1	3.9	6.2

PROPERTY HELD BY TOP WEALTH-HOLDERS

80
ESTATE SIZE, FEMALE TOP WEALTH-HOLDERS, 1953[a]

				Gross Estate Size (thousand dollars)					
120 to 150	150 to 200	200 to 300	300 to 500	500 to 1,000	1,000 to 2,000	2,000 to 3,000	3,000 to 5,000	5,000 to 10,000	10,000 and over
57,299	51,194	42,403	31,197	17,874	6,805	2,314	826	1,050	468
7,583	8,751	10,248	11,718	11,928	9,150	5,948	3,048	9,680	12,717
10.9%	9.7%	8.1%	5.9%	3.4%	1.3%	0.4%	0.2%	0.2%	0.1%
10.2	11.5	12.4	9.2	5.1	4.2	3.6	0.8	0.3	0.5
6.7	7.4	7.2	8.2	14.4	3.3	1.6	3.6	0.5	22.8
0.4	0.6	1.6	4.7	9.6	13.9	11.1	5.8	4.8	46.8
7.5	6.3	8.8	17.3	13.2	10.9	2.6	1.6	2.6	1.8
4.9	6.4	7.8	9.8	12.5	9.6	4.3	2.5	15.8	12.0
7.8	8.1	9.1	7.4	8.4	6.8	9.2	1.4	6.0	4.4
11.6	9.2	10.1	8.1	6.7	3.9	0.5	0.7	1.2	14.7
8.9	9.6	11.3	6.6	15.0	4.9	1.2	1.5	0.7	1.2
7.6	8.1	11.1	19.4	9.3	7.3	7.7	5.7	1.8	1.3
6.5	7.5	8.8	10.0	10.2	7.8	5.1	2.6	8.3	10.9
7.7	9.3	15.3	11.2	6.9	5.4	14.8	1.1	0.5	0.8
6.4	7.4	8.4	10.0	10.4	8.0	4.6	2.7	8.7	11.4

[a] Adjusted mortality rates have been used and insurance amounts have been reduced to estimated equities.

TABLE 81
Distribution of Selected Balance Sheet Items by Owners' Net Worth, 1950
(per cent)

Net Worth	Liquid Assets (1)	Car (2)	House (3)	Farm (4)	Live-stock and Crops (5)	Life Insur-ance (6)	Other Real Estate (7)	Stock (8)	Busi-ness[a] (9)	Retire-ment Fund (10)	Total Assets (11)	Debt (12)	Net Worth (13)
Negative	b	1	b	b	1	1	b	b	b	1	b	13	−1
Zero	b	b	b	b	b	b	b	b	b	b	b	b	0
Under $500	b	1	b	b	b	2	b	b	b	b	b	1	b
$500 to $1,000	1	4	b	b	1	3	b	b	b	2	1	2	1
$1,000 to $2,000	3	8	2	b	2	4	b	b	b	5	2	5	1
$2,000 to $5,000	7	16	8	4	5	10	2	1	1	20	6	14	5
$5,000 to $10,000	14	19	24	6	17	15	4	2	2	24	13	22	12
$10,000 to $25,000	27	27	38	20	25	25	25	8	17	31	26	22	27
$25,000 to $60,000	25	15	18	35	29	16	34	13	19	14	22	13	23
$60,000 and over	23	9	10	35	20	24	35	76	61	3	30	8	32
All cases	100	100	100	100	100	100	100	100	100	100	100	100	100

Source: Goldsmith, *Saving in U.S.*, III, Table W-53.
[a] Includes closely held corporations.
[b] No cases reported or less than 0.5 per cent.

TABLE 82
Percentage Composition of Gross Estate by Estate Size and Sex for Selected Age Groups, 1953

Gross Estate Size (thous. dollars)	Number of Wealth-Holders			Real Estate			U.S. Govt. Bonds			State and Local Bonds		
	Age Group 30–40	Age Group 55–60	Age Group 75–80	Age Group 30–40	Age Group 55–60	Age Group 75–80	Age Group 30–40	Age Group 55–60	Age Group 75–80	Age Group 30–40	Age Group 55–60	Age Group 75–80
MALE												
60 to 70	9,445	12,753	4,536	30.5%	38.6%	39.0%	1.1%	7.8%	8.3%	—	—	—
70 to 80	14,466	14,275	4,680	44.6	35.2	37.3	1.6	6.7	8.4	—	.2%	.4%
80 to 90	19,446	14,391	3,948	40.0	36.9	35.1	3.3	6.4	8.4	.1%	.1	.2
90 to 100	17,779	11,525	3,192	37.3	32.1	36.6	1.7	6.7	8.3	—	.3	.4
100 to 120	20,537	19,540	4,824	37.4	35.3	34.1	3.1	7.4	9.1	—	.1	.3
120 to 150	14,446	18,604	7,545	27.8	33.1	30.2	1.2	5.7	7.4	.4	.1	.2
150 to 200	12,779	17,902	4,524	35.5	29.0	28.3	5.6	5.7	7.8	—	.2	.5
200 to 300	16,668	13,924	4,200	38.5	25.9	22.9	3.7	4.8	7.3	.3	.5	.8
300 to 500	7,223	9,243	2,844	22.6	20.7	17.4	.7	6.5	7.2	3.5	.4	1.4
500 to 1,000	1,667	4,856	1,716	10.7	15.4	15.2	1.4	6.0	6.6	1.8	1.1	2.9
1,000 to 2,000	—	1,170	660	—	11.5	8.7	—	2.7	6.6	—	2.5	4.2
2,000 to 3,000	—	176	168	—	15.6	4.1	—	—	9.3	—	6.4	4.9
3,000 to 5,000	—	235	84	—	1.2	1.9	—	2.8	3.5	—	24.6	4.8
5,000 to 10,000	—	59	36	—	27.2	4.7	—	—	4.6	—	—	9.3
10,000 and over	—	—	24	—	—	2.0	—	—	.2	—	—	9.1
FEMALE												
60 to 70	4,547	8,861	4,878	31.1	37.4	35.2	4.7	8.3	8.2	—	.6	.4
70 to 80	1,818	9,769	4,380	13.0	38.5	29.9	—	5.1	9.1	—	—	.3
80 to 90	10,000	6,475	3,124	48.8	44.3	33.3	1.3	6.6	8.5	—	.2	.3
90 to 100	4,545	5,112	2,753	37.6	38.0	31.0	1.3	10.1	9.8	—	.1	—
100 to 120	3,636	6,702	3,928	44.5	39.5	28.2	2.2	5.3	10.0	—	—	.4
120 to 150	6,364	6,589	3,912	23.0	36.5	28.8	4.9	6.6	8.6	—	.6	.6
150 to 200	3,636	6,702	3,397	36.9	25.0	25.4	.3	7.9	8.3	—	.2	.4
200 to 300	6,363	5,112	3,107	32.1	30.5	22.4	3.4	6.2	7.0	.4	—	1.5
300 to 500	4,545	3,294	1,899	14.6	17.7	13.4	2.2	8.9	7.4	2.3	1.2	2.0
500 to 1,000	2,727	1,591	1,352	4.3	16.1	15.8	22.9	2.7	7.5	5.1	.3	5.4
1,000 to 2,000	1,818	568	354	5.9	6.8	5.6	.3	2.1	6.5	3.5	7.0	13.9
2,000 to 3,000	909	—	80	4.9	—	2.2	.2	—	3.0	13.1	7.4	9.8
3,000 to 5,000	—	114	48	.6	2.5	2.0	—	24.8	2.0	24.5	—	19.8
5,000 to 10,000	909	—	32	—	—	1.1	—	—	.6	1.6	—	1.4
10,000 and over	—	—	16	—	—	2.2	—	—	.6	—	—	21.6

(continued)

PROPERTY HELD BY TOP WEALTH-HOLDERS

TABLE 82 (continued)

Gross Estate Size (thous. dollars)	Other Bonds			Stock			Cash			Mortgages and Notes		
	Age Group 30-40	Age Group 55-60	Age Group 75-80	Age Group 30-40	Age Group 55-60	Age Group 75-80	Age Group 30-40	Age Group 55-60	Age Group 75-80	Age Group 30-40	Age Group 55-60	Age Group 75-80
MALE												
60 to 70	—	.6%	.5%	8.4%	13.9%	18.2%	11.6%	14.8%	18.3%	1.4%	3.0%	5.5%
70 to 80	.3%	.2	.6	8.5	19.5	21.7	10.1	13.1	16.8	1.9	4.5	4.6
80 to 90	.1	.3	.7	24.8	16.5	22.8	6.5	10.8	16.2	1.9	3.6	4.8
90 to 100	.1	.7	.9	18.9	19.6	20.6	10.0	14.0	15.4	3.6	5.6	6.0
100 to 120	.3	.6	.5	22.6	19.8	25.5	8.4	11.0	13.6	1.8	4.3	5.4
120 to 150	1.4	.7	.8	25.3	22.4	29.6	6.4	10.0	13.6	2.8	3.7	4.9
150 to 200	1.1	.4	1.3	17.3	27.7	33.0	6.6	10.9	11.8	2.7	4.9	5.5
200 to 300	1.8	.6	1.0	22.3	31.7	39.7	5.6	9.4	11.6	6.0	5.0	5.5
300 to 500	1.3	.6	1.4	38.9	28.2	44.7	7.7	8.4	11.7	1.1	5.6	5.0
500 to 1,000	—	—	1.9	73.6	46.9	53.2	1.3	7.9	8.1	10.3	6.3	2.7
1,000 to 2,000	—	2.0	2.0	—	57.4	59.0	—	5.5	8.1	—	4.4	2.2
2,000 to 3,000	—	.9	1.2	—	40.1	68.0	—	1.9	5.5	—	.5	.4
3,000 to 5,000	—	—	—	—	62.7	79.0	—	7.1	3.9	—	—	.4
5,000 to 10,000	—	—	2.4	—	68.4	69.2	—	.2	6.5	—	—	.4
10,000 and over	—	—	.9	—	—	84.1	—	—	1.8	—	—	.4
FEMALE												
60 to 70	—	.3	1.4	37.7	23.6	27.9	15.1	16.2	17.1	.9	4.0	4.0
70 to 80	.7	1.3	1.1	54.8	23.4	32.0	10.3	16.7	16.9	.7	4.8	5.4
80 to 90	1.2	.5	.9	25.8	24.1	28.7	6.6	11.7	18.1	3.7	3.8	3.2
90 to 100	.5	2.3	1.3	21.6	22.8	32.3	16.0	12.2	14.8	4.4	3.9	4.3
100 to 120	.2	1.1	1.5	28.9	28.2	35.9	12.4	11.8	14.4	—	3.9	4.2
120 to 150	4.9	1.0	1.4	49.8	33.3	36.0	7.3	9.7	14.4	1.6	4.3	3.5
150 to 200	.4	.3	1.4	43.8	33.9	42.7	8.6	13.7	12.8	3.8	7.1	3.5
200 to 300	1.2	2.3	1.9	35.2	42.5	45.3	8.3	8.4	10.9	3.1	2.8	4.1
300 to 500	4.3	—	1.9	53.2	51.3	58.5	4.0	7.6	10.8	2.2	3.3	2.9
500 to 1,000	—	—	2.3	56.3	50.5	51.8	3.1	11.0	9.6	—	3.9	1.9
1,000 to 2,000	1.5	3.0	1.1	75.3	51.7	61.8	1.7	3.7	9.1	.1	.1	1.9
2,000 to 3,000	—	—	.2	28.1	—	64.0	31.5	—	4.5	—	—	1.0
3,000 to 5,000	.3	—	.4	—	61.2	58.5	—	4.7	7.5	.5	.7	1.2
5,000 to 10,000	—	—	—	87.8	—	91.8	7.0	—	3.4	—	—	—
10,000 and over	—	—	—	—	—	31.5	—	—	40.1	—	—	—

(continued)

PROPERTY HELD BY TOP WEALTH-HOLDERS

TABLE 82 (concluded)

Gross Estate Size (thous. dollars)	Life Insurance			Miscellaneous Property			Debts and Mortgages			Economic Estate		
	Age Group 30–40	Age Group 55–60	Age Group 75–80	Age Group 30–40	Age Group 55–60	Age Group 75–80	Age Group 30–40	Age Group 55–60	Age Group 75–80	Age Group 30–40	Age Group 55–60	Age Group 75–80
MALE												
60 to 70	4.3%	7.6%	3.7%	41.6%	14.1%	6.5%	20.5%	7.7%	3.4%	79.6%	92.6%	96.6%
70 to 80	3.2	7.0	4.3	29.5	13.5	6.0	15.6	6.3	3.3	84.0	93.5	96.7
80 to 90	2.9	8.1	5.0	20.4	17.2	6.9	19.6	9.9	4.6	80.4	90.1	95.4
90 to 100	2.7	7.6	3.9	25.8	13.9	7.9	19.3	8.7	3.1	80.7	91.7	96.9
100 to 120	3.1	7.1	4.2	23.2	14.3	7.5	17.8	9.7	3.3	82.1	90.2	96.9
120 to 150	2.9	7.0	5.5	31.8	17.1	7.7	16.4	10.8	4.5	83.6	89.2	95.3
150 to 200	3.8	7.6	5.4	27.4	13.8	6.9	21.1	10.1	4.8	78.0	89.9	95.8
200 to 300	3.8	6.4	5.1	17.9	16.0	5.6	35.0	11.4	4.3	65.0	88.7	95.6
300 to 500	1.9	5.2	4.3	22.3	14.4	6.8	15.0	10.2	4.3	85.0	89.7	95.7
500 to 1,000	.1	3.7	3.9	1.0	10.7	6.2	8.7	12.2	4.3	91.6	87.8	95.7
1,000 to 2,000	—	3.1	2.5	—	12.1	6.3	—	10.9	4.6	—	89.2	95.2
2,000 to 3,000	—	2.3	2.5	—	33.3	3.9	—	27.5	2.5	—	72.5	97.4
3,000 to 5,000	—	1.0	1.8	—	.9	4.6	—	25.5	3.0	—	74.9	96.9
5,000 to 10,000	—	.3	1.0	—	4.0	1.9	—	28.5	.9	—	71.5	99.1
10,000 and over	—	—	.2	—	—	1.4	—	—	.5	—	—	99.5
FEMALE												
60 to 70	.2	1.0	.6	9.8	8.7	5.2	19.8	5.7	2.2	80.0	94.5	97.7
70 to 80	.6	.9	.7	19.9	9.6	4.5	2.7	5.3	2.2	97.2	94.9	97.8
80 to 90	.8	1.2	.7	11.8	7.6	6.2	10.7	6.4	2.8	89.4	93.8	97.2
90 to 100	.1	1.2	.6	18.5	9.2	6.8	20.6	5.6	2.9	79.2	94.3	97.2
100 to 120	.6	1.2	.8	11.2	9.0	4.4	15.1	8.2	3.1	85.0	91.9	97.0
120 to 150	.1	1.2	.6	8.3	7.3	7.1	9.8	4.9	3.2	90.0	95.2	96.8
150 to 200	.3	1.5	.7	5.4	10.1	6.8	5.3	7.2	3.2	94.7	92.8	96.8
200 to 300	.5	1.8	.7	14.1	6.2	6.1	18.4	6.6	2.4	81.6	93.3	97.3
300 to 500	.2	.1	.3	14.2	8.4	4.0	13.3	5.7	3.1	86.8	94.3	97.0
500 to 1,000	.1	.4	1.1	9.8	5.5	5.0	6.0	1.1	2.5	94.0	98.9	97.7
1,000 to 2,000	.2	.4	—	2.0	24.6	5.6	4.1	.9	2.5	96.0	98.9	97.5
2,000 to 3,000	—	—	.2	10.9	—	11.9	23.1	—	5.9	76.9	—	94.1
3,000 to 5,000	—	.6	.7	—	3.2	13.2	.2	.4	.6	99.6	99.6	99.4
5,000 to 10,000	—	—	.1	2.0	—	2.7	—	—	1.5	—	—	98.4
10,000 and over	—	—	—	—	—	4.0	—	—	.8	—	—	99.2

TABLE 83

Percentage Composition of Gross Estate by Age and Sex for Selected Estate Sizes, 1953

Age Group	Number of Wealth-Holders			Real Estate			U.S. Govt. Bonds			State and Local Bonds		
	Estate Size A	Estate Size B	Estate Size C	Estate Size A	Estate Size B	Estate Size C	Estate Size A	Estate Size B	Estate Size C	Estate Size A	Estate Size B	Estate Size C
MALE												
Under 21	3,333	—	—	—	—	—	—	—	—	—	—	—
21 to 30	14,446	833	—	19.7	18.4	—	10.4	—	—	—	—	—
30 to 40	24,220	12,779	—	44.6	35.5	—	1.6	5.6	—	—	—	—
40 to 50	16,000	37,551	444	39.0	30.4	9.8	4.7	4.5	9.0	.1	—	9.8
50 to 55	14,275	18,200	176	38.5	32.5	—	4.7	5.7	—	—	.1	—
55 to 60	13,548	17,902	232	35.2	29.0	15.6	6.7	5.6	6.1	.2	.2	6.4
60 to 65	9,753	14,977	332	38.7	28.7	17.7	6.2	6.4	4.0	.1	.2	17.4
65 to 70	7,680	11,340	145	39.3	27.5	10.1	8.2	7.2	2.0	.1	.1	2.9
70 to 75	4,680	7,590	168	40.2	29.1	16.7	8.0	6.8	9.3	.4	.5	11.1
75 to 80	2,240	4,524	64	37.3	28.1	4.1	8.4	7.8	3.6	.1	.6	4.9
80 to 85	1,399	2,384	47	39.7	30.1	10.5	8.0	9.0	7.3	.2	.5	16.8
85 and over		1,447		40.4	28.8	1.7	10.1	8.5				13.3
Total	111,574	129,527	1,608	38.6	30.1	11.5	5.9	5.8	5.7	.1	.1	9.2
FEMALE												
Under 21	2,000	—	—	—	—	—	—	—	—	—	—	—
21 to 30	1,818	2,000	—	41.6	—	—	3.0	1.7	—	—	—	—
30 to 40	10,000	3,636	909	13.0	36.9	4.9	—	.3	.2	—	.4	24.5
40 to 50	6,923	11,600	400	35.8	36.1	47.4	7.2	5.4	.7	—	.6	—
50 to 55	9,769	5,769	192	27.8	32.2	2.1	11.4	6.4	5.3	—	.5	—
55 to 60	7,837	6,702	—	38.5	25.0	—	5.1	7.8	—	—	.2	—
60 to 65	7,420	5,032	144	38.0	28.8	8.0	8.3	6.4	1.5	.1	1.0	15.2
65 to 70	5,508	4,664	212	33.8	26.5	4.3	8.6	7.3	6.8	.2	.4	11.3
70 to 75	4,380	4,995	243	34.1	25.3	3.0	9.7	8.6	3.0	—	.4	11.0
75 to 80	2,515	3,397	80	29.9	25.4	2.2	9.1	8.3	8.1	.3	.4	9.8
80 to 85	1,494	2,054	77	35.2	22.1	13.7	8.8	7.6	10.7	.3	.9	17.0
85 and over		1,345	57	32.2	26.1	7.3	11.3	9.1		.3	1.0	5.5
Total	59,664	51,194	2,314	34.1	28.6	13.1	7.9	6.3	2.0	.1	.5	13.9

(continued)

PROPERTY HELD BY TOP WEALTH-HOLDERS

TABLE 83 (continued)

Age Group	Other Bonds			Stock			Cash			Mortgages and Notes		
	Estate Size A	Estate Size B	Estate Size C	Estate Size A	Estate Size B	Estate Size C	Estate Size A	Estate Size B	Estate Size C	Estate Size A	Estate Size B	Estate Size C
MALE												
Under 21	—	—	—	—	—	—	—	—	—	—	—	—
21 to 30	.3	1.1	—	51.6	67.1	—	2.1	—	—	2.9	13.9	—
30 to 40	.6	.4	—	8.5	17.3	—	10.1	6.6	—	1.9	2.7	—
40 to 50	.3	.3	—	15.4	25.6	66.8	11.7	7.2	3.4	3.2	4.5	—
50 to 55	.2	.4	—	14.3	20.1	—	12.3	9.3	—	4.1	4.2	.5
55 to 60	.4	.7	—	19.5	27.7	40.1	13.1	10.9	1.9	4.5	4.9	1.8
60 to 65	.6	.6	1.3	17.5	26.9	37.8	12.8	10.5	6.5	3.6	4.9	11.9
65 to 70	.3	1.2	1.4	18.2	29.8	41.9	14.1	12.4	15.6	4.8	4.7	2.7
70 to 75	.6	1.3	1.2	18.2	31.2	53.2	15.6	11.9	6.0	4.5	5.2	.4
75 to 80	.6	.8	1.3	21.6	32.7	68.0	16.8	11.7	5.5	4.6	5.4	.4
80 to 85	.7	1.5	1.6	20.7	32.5	59.6	16.6	11.5	3.3	5.2	4.9	.2
85 and over	.7	1.5	1.6	19.7	35.4	63.8	16.2	13.2	8.2	4.8	4.4	.4
Total	.4	.6	.7	17.4	26.2	53.2	12.6	9.5	6.8	3.8	4.6	3.1
FEMALE												
Under 21	—	—	—	—	—	—	—	—	—	—	—	—
21 to 30	.7	.4	—	54.8	80.0	—	10.4	.6	—	.7	3.8	—
30 to 40	.3	.4	—	23.5	43.8	28.1	10.3	8.6	31.5	5.4	2.0	—
40 to 50	.4	.8	.3	22.4	31.5	15.0	15.2	6.8	4.0	6.6	2.8	—
50 to 55	1.3	1.0	—	23.4	37.8	87.0	15.3	7.0	.1	4.8	7.6	—
55 to 60	.2	.9	—	21.0	33.9	—	16.7	13.2	—	5.6	4.7	.2
60 to 65	1.1	1.6	1.7	27.0	37.2	35.3	15.8	12.1	24.3	5.3	3.3	1.3
65 to 70	.6	1.3	3.3	27.2	37.5	67.8	17.2	12.8	6.3	5.4	3.9	.9
70 to 75	1.1	1.4	.2	32.0	37.2	50.5	16.8	13.7	4.3	5.4	3.5	1.2
75 to 80	1.4	1.9	1.6	30.5	42.7	64.0	16.9	10.9	7.5	4.5	4.5	1.5
80 to 85	1.5	2.4	.3	32.1	44.4	44.3	14.7	13.1	11.8	3.1	2.6	1.7
85 and over					42.5	67.7	14.7	11.2	3.4			
Total	.7	.9	.6	25.2	38.5	38.7	15.7	9.9	16.7	5.1	3.6	.3

(continued)

TABLE 83 (concluded)

Age Group	Life Insurance			Miscellaneous Property			Debts and Mortgages			Economic Estate		
	Estate Size A	Estate Size B	Estate Size C	Estate Size A	Estate Size B	Estate Size C	Estate Size A	Estate Size B	Estate Size C	Estate Size A	Estate Size B	Estate Size C
MALE												
Under 21	—	—	—	—	—	—	—	—	—	—	—	—
21 to 30	.4	.5	—	12.9	—	—	2.6	21.5	—	97.5	78.4	—
30 to 40	3.2	3.8	—	29.5	27.4	—	15.6	21.1	—	84.0	78.9	—
40 to 50	4.6	6.0	.7	20.9	21.5	.3	13.2	17.7	1.1	86.9	82.5	98.9
50 to 55	7.1	6.8	—	18.8	21.0	—	11.3	16.1	—	88.7	83.9	—
55 to 60	7.0	7.6	2.3	13.5	13.8	33.3	6.3	10.2	27.5	93.5	89.9	72.5
60 to 65	7.4	8.5	3.9	12.8	13.4	9.0	8.0	9.3	15.9	91.6	90.7	84.3
65 to 70	5.1	6.7	3.5	9.4	11.1	8.7	4.8	5.2	7.1	95.1	94.8	92.9
70 to 75	5.3	7.2	3.1	7.9	7.2	4.0	3.5	4.5	7.5	96.6	95.5	92.6
75 to 80	4.3	5.4	2.5	6.0	6.8	3.9	3.3	4.8	2.5	96.7	95.0	97.4
80 to 85	4.1	5.4	.4	5.1	5.3	4.2	2.7	4.4	6.8	97.3	95.7	93.2
85 and over	2.8	2.7	1.5	5.1	4.9	2.2	3.3	2.8	1.0	96.7	97.1	98.9
Total	5.4	6.5	2.3	16.0	16.6	7.7	9.0	12.6	8.2	91.3	87.4	91.8
FEMALE												
Under 21	.4	.4	—	44.6	17.3	—	13.4	—	—	86.6	100.0	—
21 to 30	.6	.3	—	19.9	5.4	10.9	2.7	5.3	23.1	97.2	94.7	76.9
30 to 40	1.4	.2	.6	10.9	17.0	32.8	5.8	11.1	18.0	94.1	88.8	82.0
40 to 50	1.1	.5	—	14.8	12.1	4.5	3.3	8.4	3.5	96.6	91.7	96.5
50 to 55	.9	1.6	—	9.6	10.0	—	5.3	8.3	—	94.9	92.8	—
55 to 60	.9	1.0	.1	9.7	7.5	16.6	4.3	3.7	2.9	95.4	96.0	96.9
60 to 65	1.1	.7	—	6.0	9.7	5.9	3.8	3.7	4.6	96.4	96.1	95.4
65 to 70	.7	1.0	.4	5.2	8.1	19.6	3.5	3.3	6.1	96.3	96.5	93.8
70 to 75	.7	.7	.2	4.5	6.8	11.9	2.2	3.2	5.9	97.8	96.8	94.1
75 to 80	.5	.5	.2	4.0	5.0	2.9	2.5	2.8	.8	97.5	97.2	99.2
80 to 85	.2	.3	.1	4.7	4.7	3.1	2.6	3.4	1.2	97.4	96.5	98.7
85 and over	.9	.7	.1	10.2	10.7	15.1	4.4	6.2	14.6	95.5	93.5	85.4

Estate size A = $70,000 to $80,000.   Estate size B = $150,000 to $200,000.
Estate size C = $2,000,000 to $3,000,000.

TABLE 84
COMPOSITION OF NET WORTH WITHIN INCOME GROUPS, 1953
(per cent)

1952 Money Income Group (before taxes) of Spending Unit	Net Worth	Variable Value Assets			Total Assets	Debt[d]
		Consumer Capital Goods[a]	Business and Investment Assets[b]	Fixed Value Assets[c]		
Under $1,000	100	38	50	19	107	7
$1,000 to $2,000	100	45	47	15	107	7
$2,000 to $3,000	100	45	48	19	112	12
$3,000 to $4,000	100	55	40	20	115	15
$4,000 to $5,000	100	67	37	17	121	21
$5,000 to $7,000	100	63	39	20	122	22
$7,500 and over	100	32	61	15	108	8
All spending units	100	45	51	17	113	13

SOURCE: Derived from 1953 Survey of Consumer Finances, published in *Federal Reserve Bulletin*, 1953, Supplementary Table 2, p. 9.

[a,b,c,d] See Table 69 for definitions of these terms.

TABLE 85
DISTRIBUTION OF SELECTED BALANCE SHEET ITEMS BY INCOME GROUP, 1950
(per cent)

Money Income (1949) Before Taxes (dollars)	Liquid Assets (1)	Car (2)	House (3)	Farm (4)	Livestock and Crops (5)	Life Insurance (6)	Other Real Estate (7)	Stock (8)	Business[a] (9)	Retirement Fund (10)	Total Assets (11)	Debt (12)	Net Worth (13)	1949 Income (14)
Under 1,000	6	3	6	22	19	4	5	1	1	b	6	7	6	2
1,000 to 2,000	9	9	9	13	15	6	9	1	2	2	8	6	8	9
2,000 to 3,000	15	15	14	14	14	13	12	4	4	9	12	16	11	16
3,000 to 4,000	15	18	19	10	12	16	14	7	5	26	14	20	13	19
4,000 to 5,000	11	15	16	3	8	14	8	5	6	24	11	15	11	15
5,000 to 7,500	18	22	19	18	13	21	19	6	15	23	17	20	17	19
7,500 and over	26	16	16	19	18	25	30	75	65	16	31	14	33	20
Not ascertained	b	2	1	1	1	1	3	1	2	b	1	2	1	b
All cases														
Per cent	100	100	100	100	100	100	100	100	100	100	100	100	100	100
Billion	91	30	175	57	16	43	70	42	79	10	613	64	549	170

SOURCE: Goldsmith, *Saving in U.S.*, III, Table W-50.
[a] Includes closely held corporations.
[b] No cases reported or less than 0.5 per cent.

TABLE 86
PERCENTAGE DISTRIBUTION OF ASSET HOLDINGS OF INDIVIDUALS IN ACTIVE INVESTOR SAMPLE, BY INCOME AND WEALTH GROUPS

	Income Group (thousand dollars)						
	Under 7.5	7.5 to 12.5	12.5 to 25	25 to 50	50 to 100	100 and over	Not Ascertained
No. of cases	193	173	156	120	42	24	38
Cash deposits and U.S. govt. bonds	18%	21%	19%	13%	10%	14%	
State and local securities	b	1	2	2	4	7	
Senior corporate securities	8	6	3	4	3	5	
Marketable common stock	40	34	28	27	19	28	
Own business, unincorporated	2	3	10	16	34	12	
Own business, incorporated	7	7	7	6	9	10	
Other closely held corporations	1	2	6	6	7	6	
Cash surrender value of insurance	6	9	9	7	4	3	
Income-producing real estate	8	9	8	11	7	3	
Notes and mortgages	1	b	1	2	2	b	
Trusts[a]	6	5	6	6	1	12	
Other	3	3	1	b	b	b	
Total	100	100	100	100	100	100	

(continued)

TABLE 86 (concluded)

	Wealth Group (thousand dollars)						
	Under 25	25 to 50	50 to 100	100 to 250	250 to 500	500 to 1,000	1,000 and over	Not Ascertained
No. of cases	146	120	130	156	76	40	41	37
Cash deposits and U.S. govt. bonds	35%	23%	23%	17%	15%	15%	10%	
State and local securities	b	b	1	1	2	3	5	
Senior corporate securities	3	5	5	5	4	4	4	
Marketable common stock	36	39	35	31	27	30	21	
Own business, unincorporated	b	1	3	8	16	12	22	
Own business, incorporated	6	5	9	9	6	9	8	
Other closely held corporations	1	2	3	4	6	5	7	
Cash surrender value of insurance	15	13	11	9	6	6	2	
Income-producing real estate	3	10	7	8	11	6	6	
Notes and mortgages	1	b	b	b	1	b	1	
Trusts[a]	b	2	2	6	5	9	14	
Other	b	b	1	2	1	1	b	
Total	100	100	100	100	100	100	100	

Source: Butters, et al., *Effects of Taxation*, Table A-13, p. 468.

[a] Trusts in this table include only trust property not managed or controlled by the respondent or a member of his immediate family unit. The total beneficial interest of respondents in trust property is shown in Table 33.

[b] Less than 0.5 per cent.

TABLE 87

COMPOSITION OF CORPORATE EQUITY ASSET HOLDINGS FOR INCOME GROUPS OF WISCONSIN INDIVIDUALS, 1949
(per cent)

Income Group	Traded Stock	Untraded Stock	Total
$0 to $5,000	77.2	22.8	100.0
$5,000 to $10,000	67.0	33.0	100.0
$10,000 to $20,000	62.4	37.6	100.0
$20,000 to $50,000	54.3	45.7	100.0
$50,000 and over	43.1	56.9	100.0

Source: Atkinson, *Financial Asset Ownership*, p. 70, Table 11.

TABLE 88
COMPOSITION OF NET WORTH WITHIN OCCUPATIONAL GROUPS, 1953
(per cent)

Occupational Group	Net Worth	Variable Value Assets			Total Assets	Debt[d]
		Consumer Capital Goods[a]	Business and Investment Assets[b]	Fixed Value Assets[c]		
Professional and semi-professional	100	53	40	24	117	17
Self-employed	100	27	67	12	106	6
Managerial	100	54	38	22	114	14
Clerical and sales	100	72	25	25	122	22
Skilled and semiskilled	100	93	14	20	127	27
Unskilled and service	100	91	19	17	127	27
Farm operators	100	3	96	11	110	10
Retired	100	34	56	17	107	7
Other[e]	100	50	39	18	107	7
All spending units	100	45	51	17	113	13

SOURCE: Derived from 1953 Survey of Consumer Finances, published in *Federal Reserve Bulletin*, 1953, Supplementary, Table 2, p. 9.

[a] Includes automobiles and owner-occupied nonfarm houses.

[b] Includes owner-occupied farms, farm machinery, livestock, crops, interest in unincorporated business and privately held corporations, real estate other than home or farm on which owner is living, and corporate stock.

[c] Includes liquid assets and loans made by spending units.

[d] Includes mortgages and other real estate debt, instalment, and other short-term debt.

[e] Includes spending units headed by housewives, unemployed persons, students, protective service workers, and persons whose occupations were not ascertained.

TABLE 89

DISTRIBUTION OF SELECTED BALANCE SHEET ITEMS BY OCCUPATIONAL GROUP, 1950
(per cent)

Occupational Group	Liquid Assets (1)	Car (2)	House (3)	Farm (4)	Livestock and Crops (5)	Life Insurance (6)	Other Real Estate (7)	Stock (8)	Business[a] (9)	Retirement Fund (10)	Total Assets (11)	Debt (12)	Net Worth (13)	1949 Income (14)
Professional and semi-professional	12	11	10	b	b	13	12	18	5	27	10	9	10	11
Managerial	7	6	8	b	b	8	7	5	7	11	7	8	6 }	21
Self-employed	17	15	16	b	b	21	24	35	85	2	25	15	27 }	21
Clerical and sales	11	14	12	b	b	12	7	4	1	21	8	14	7	13
Skilled and semiskilled	15	26	27	b	b	19	10	2	1	23	14	24	13	28
Unskilled and service	4	5	6	b	b	5	4	1	b	6	4	5	4	10
Farm operator	10	13	b	100	100	6	10	2	b	b	16	17	15	7
Retired	15	3	9	b	b	8	16	24	b	1	9	2	10 }	10
All other	9	7	12	b	b	8	10	9	1	9	7	6	8 }	10
All cases	100	100	100	100	100	100	100	100	100	100	100	100	100	100

SOURCE: Goldsmith, *Saving in U.S.*, III, Table W-51.
[a] Includes closely held corporations.
[b] No cases reported or less than 0.5 per cent.

CHAPTER 6

The Share of Top Wealth-Holders in Personal Wealth, 1922–56

IN THIS chapter we seek to discover the relative importance of top wealth-holders whom estate tax data enable us to identify for most years after 1922. What part of the total population and of the adult population are they? What share of the wealth of all persons do they hold? What types of property are most highly concentrated in their hands? Have the number and the wealth of this top group changed over the years to indicate increasing or decreasing concentration of wealth over time?

We shall first present the picture for 1953, then compare our findings with those of the Survey of Consumer Finances for that year, and then discuss historical changes. Finally, the observed changes in the concentration of wealth-holding are compared with changes over a similar period in England and Wales.

The Share of Top Wealth-Holders in 1953

The 1,659,000 persons who are estimated to have had $60,000 or more of gross estate in 1953 comprised 1.04 per cent of the total population, and 1.6 per cent of the adult population. This group of top wealth-holders held over a quarter of the total personal wealth, on the basis of either the prime wealth or the total wealth variant of personal wealth (see Chart 2 in Chapter 1 and Table 90).

Table 90 needs some explanation. The data in columns 1–7 are derived from national balance sheet accounts as developed by Raymond W. Goldsmith.[1] These accounts record estimates of aggregate assets, liabilities, and equities for sectors of the economy. Several of these sectors have been combined and adjusted to form a "personal sector" which is conceptually adapted for comparison with the holdings of individual wealth-holders. As shown in Table 90, the definition of the personal sector includes the following subsectors: "household,"

[1] Tables for certain benchmark years were published in his book, *A Study of Saving in the United States*, III, Princeton, 1956.

TABLE 90

ROLE OF TOP WEALTH-HOLDERS IN NATIONAL BALANCE SHEET ACCOUNTS, 1953
(billion dollars)

	All Sectors	Personal Sector					Wealth Held by Top Wealth-Holders			Share of Wealth Held by Top Wealth-Holders		
	Total Wealth Variant[a] (1)	House-hold (2)	Personal Trust Funds (3)	Farm Business (4)	Nonfarm, Noncorporate Business (5)	Total Wealth Variant (6)	Prime Wealth Variant (7)	Basic Variant (8)	Prime Variant (9)	Total Variant[b] (10)	Col. 8 ÷ Col. 7 (11)	Col. 9 ÷ Col. 7 (12)	Col. 10 ÷ Col. 6 (13)
Real estate	$765.1	$317.9	$2.0	$78.8	$45.9	$444.6	$442.6	$70.1		$71.7	15.8%		16.1%
Structures, residential	294.9	270.6			14.5								
Structures, non-residential	260.3			14.7	17.3								
Land	209.9	49.3		64.1	14.1								
U.S. govt. bonds	260.6	47.3	7.3		5.8	60.4	53.1	17.4		23.2	32.8		38.2
State and local bonds	33.9	7.8	8.2			16.0	7.8	10.8		17.3			e
Other bonds							2.8	2.8		5.4	100.0		88.5
Corporate bonds	56.0	2.8	3.3			6.1	2.8						
Stock[d]	245.5	127.2	28.5		13.0	155.7	127.2	105.7		128.3	83.2		82.2
Cash[e]	306.5	138.8	2.6	6.6	0.2	160.0	158.4	44.6		46.7	28.2		29.1
Monetary metals	27.4			0.2	12.8								
Currency and deposits	258.1			6.4									
Deposits in other financial institutions	20.9												
Mortgages and notes	234.0	19.5	1.2		10.5	31.2	30.0	10.5		11.3	35.0		36.2
Receivables from business	106.7	0.6			6.3								
Receivables from households	31.1				4.2								
Loans on securities	4.9	1.1											
Mortgages, nonfarm	84.1	14.6											
Mortgages, farm	7.2	3.0											

Life insurance reserves	$69.8				$78.2	$78.2	$7.1	$10.4	9.0%	13.3%
Pension and retirement funds	56.7	$78.2								
Private	8.8	63.5			63.5			3.8		5.9
Government	47.9	11.0								
Miscellaneous property	611.0	52.5	$0.9	$39.2	$35.6					
Durables, producer	134.7	332.5		17.2	19.5	220.8	219.9	39.6	40.3	18.0	18.2
Durables, consumer	122.7	128.8								
Inventories	106.8			18.9	16.1					
Equities, farm and nonfarm	187.4	187.4ᶠ					20.0			
Equities, mutual financial institutions	16.1	16.1								10.9
Other intangibles	43.3	0.2	0.9	3.1						
Gross estate	2,639.3	1,135.5	54.1	124.6	110.8	1,237.6	1,120.0	309.2	327.5	381.1	27.6	29.2%	30.8
Total tangible		447.9	2.0	115.1	81.7						
Total intangible		687.4	52.1	9.5	29.1						
Debts and mortgages	299.8	85.0		13.8	34.1	132.8	132.8	27.7	28.8	28.8	21.3		22.1
Payables to banks	44.9	9.6		2.8	6.9						
Other payables to business	79.9	13.2		2.7	9.1						
Payables to households	3.2	3.2								
Borrowing on securities	91.2	58.8		7.8	15.1						
Mortgages	80.6			0.4	3.0						
Other liabilities											
Economic estate	2,339.3	1,050.5	54.1	110.8	76.6	1,104.8	987.2	281.5	298.8	352.4	28.5	30.2	32.0

(notes on page 194)

"farm business," "nonfarm, noncorporate business," and "personal trust funds." (We have excluded nonprofit organizations entirely.)

Since the household subsector consolidates balance sheets of all households, the debts owed by one household to another are canceled out. In other words, intrahousehold debt is excluded both as an asset and as a liability. Another difficulty arises in the treatment of households' equity in unincorporated business. Because the national balance sheets do not consolidate the household, farm business, and nonfarm business subsectors while the estate tax wealth data in effect do consolidate them,[2] the balance sheet totals for most types of property are relatively overstated. This means that we do not have strict comparability on a line-by-line basis, but this does not appear to be a serious difficulty for most types of property. Double-counting of the equity in unincorporated business is avoided by showing it in the household sector but not adding it into the personal sector totals. Hence, this does not lead to any errors in the total gross and economic estate figures. Following the concepts developed in Chapter 3, we refer to the prime

[2] That is, estate tax wealth is not uniformly classified to show all assets held by unincorporated enterprises as "equity in unincorporated business." In some cases they are separately listed as real estate, cash, etc. The equity item is listed under the heading of miscellaneous in Table 90.

NOTES TO TABLE 90

SOURCE: For cols. 2–7, preliminary national balance sheet estimates for 1953 by National Bureau of Economic Research.

[a] Preliminary estimates for 1952. All-sector totals are not yet prepared for 1953.

[b] 80 per cent of each type of asset in personal trust fund wealth is allocated to the top wealth-holder group because the tabulations of fiduciary income tax returns suggest that 80 per cent of fiduciary income distributable to beneficiaries went to persons with estates worth $60,000 or more since it was from parcels of wealth of at least $60,000 in value. Since available data do not enable us to identify the share of each type of property (e.g., real estate and stock) in the personal trust fund aggregate allocable to the top wealth-holders, we have applied the 80 per cent ratio to each type of property. For pensions and retirement funds, 10 per cent of private and 5 per cent of government funds are so allocated, and 20 per cent of annuities are estimated to belong to the top wealth-holders. This column does not add to gross estate as shown. The gross estate figure of $381.1 billion is our best estimate.

[c] In excess of 100 per cent.

[d] The original estate tax data for stock include shares in savings and loan associations. However, we have adjusted the top wealth-holder account in cols. 8 and 10 to exclude those shares from "stock" and to include them in "cash." The assumption used for 1953 was that the top wealth-holders held 70 per cent of the $22.5 billion worth of shares in savings and loan associations held by "individuals." This assumption is based on the belief that such shares are less concentrated than corporate stock and corporate bonds.

[e] Including shares in savings and loan associations. See footnote d.

[f] Excluded from cols. 6 and 7 but included in gross estate and economic estate in col. 2.

wealth and total wealth variants of personal wealth. Prime wealth differs from total wealth in excluding personal trust funds, annuities, and pension and retirement funds.

The top wealth-holders in 1953 held 30.2 per cent of the prime wealth in the personal sector, and 32.0 per cent of the total wealth (Table 90, cols. 12 and 13).[3] These columns also show estimates for the share of each of several types of property held by top wealth-holders. These range from over 100 per cent for state and local bonds down to 9 per cent for life insurance reserves. Particular interest attaches to the corporate stock figure. Our estimate for 1953 is that the top wealth group held 82 per cent of all the stock in the personal sector. This matter is discussed in more detail below in the section on type of property.

Comparison with Survey of Consumer Finances Findings for 1953

The broadest view obtainable of wealth-holdings in 1953 is that furnished by the Survey of Consumer Finances for that year. According to the Survey, the median net worth of the nation's 54 million spending units was $4,100; 4 per cent of the nation's spending units had a net worth of $50,000 or more; 11 per cent had a net worth of $25,000 or more. This upper 11 per cent held 56 per cent of the total assets and 60 per cent of the total net worth. While this group held only 30 per cent of consumer capital goods, they held 80 per cent of business and investment assets (Table 91).

Inspection of the 1950 and 1953 Surveys suggests that the spending units with $60,000 or more of net worth were 3 per cent of all spending units in 1953. These spending units held 30 per cent of total assets and 32 per cent of total net worth.[4] These particular figures on the top 3 per cent are the ones we would like to compare with our estimates of the holdings of the top wealth group made by the estate-multiplier method.

First, however, it should be noted that there are some limitations to the 1953 Survey data as a representation of wealth-holdings. Not all types of property were included in the count. Insurance, consumer

[3] Distributing the top wealth-holders' interest in personal trust funds by type of property (col. 10) is done largely in ignorance. We assumed that the top wealth-holders owned 80 per cent of the amount of each type of property in personal trust funds.

[4] It is of interest that the Survey conclusions about this top group are based upon interviews with 124 spending units.

durables other than automobiles, currency, personal trust funds, annuities, pension reserves, bonds of corporations and of state, local and foreign governments were all omitted. Further, there appears to be some understatement of those assets which were included, with perhaps the largest understatement for liquid assets.[5] These exclusions

TABLE 91
PROPORTION OF NET WORTH AND COMPONENTS HELD WITHIN NET WORTH GROUPS, 1953
(per cent)

Net Worth Group (dollars)	Spending Units	1952 Money Income Before Taxes	Consumer Capital Goods[a]	Business and Investment Assets[b]	Fixed Value Assets[c]	Total Assets	Debt[d]	Net Worth
Negative and 0 to			1	e	e	(1)	6	f
1,000	31	19	1	e	2	1	4	1
1,000 to 5,000	23	20	13	1	9	7	18	5
5,000 to 25,000	35	37	55	19	37	36	51	34
25,000 and over	11	24	30	80	52	56	21	60
All cases	100	100	100	100	100	100	100	100
Aggregation valuation ($ bill.)	—	219	288	328	109	725	84	641

SOURCE: 1953 Survey of Consumer Finances, reprinted from *Federal Reserve Bulletin*, 1953, Supplementary Table 5, p. 11.

[a] Includes automobiles and owner-occupied nonfarm houses.

[b] Includes owner-occupied farms, farm machinery, livestock, crops, interest in unincorporated business, and privately held corporations, real estate other than home or farm on which owner is living, and corporate stock.

[c] Includes liquid assets and loans made by spending units.

[d] Includes mortgages and other real estate debt, instalment and other short-term debt.

[e] Less than 0.5 per cent.

[f] Negative or less than 0.5 per cent.

and the difficulty of getting full representation of top wealth-holders and complete reporting of their holdings would lead one to suspect that the Survey has probably understated the degree of inequality of wealth distribution on a prime wealth basis and more certainly on a total wealth basis.

Since all our estate tax data are for individuals, it is awkward to

---

[5] Approximately 80 to 85 per cent of the full value of the items included is accounted for by the Survey. Among the excluded items, personal trust funds, annuities, and pension reserves (which together totaled about $100 billion) fall outside our definition of prime wealth. For a comparison of Survey and national balance sheet aggregates, see Goldsmith's *Saving in U.S.*, III, p. 107, Table W-44. Further difficulties with Survey data are discussed in the *Federal Reserve Bulletin*, September 1958, p. 1047.

check them against the spending unit estimates of the Survey. While the top wealth-holder group in 1953 made up 1.6 per cent of all adults, they represented a minimum of 2.3 per cent of the families (see Chapter 4). More precisely, in 2.3 per cent of the families there were one or more persons with $60,000 or more of gross estate. In some unknown number of other families the combined holdings of two or more persons equaled $60,000 or more. In the light of this, the Survey's estimate that 3 per cent of the spending units have $60,000 or more of net worth seems altogether reasonable. Similarly, their estimate that this group had 30 per cent of the total assets and 32 per cent of the total net worth seems compatible with our findings that the top 1.6 per cent of adults held 30.2 per cent of total economic estate. To add another 0.7 per cent of all families would mean adding another 400,000 persons to the top wealth-holder group. If we impute $60,000 to each one of them, this would add $24 billion or an extra two percentage points to the top group's share of total economic estate: 30.2 plus 2 equals 32.2, which is close to the Survey's finding of 32 per cent of net worth. In spite of the fact that the Survey figures tend to minimize the degree of inequality by excluding certain kinds of property, we find only slightly more inequality than found by the Survey. However, the principal conclusion is that the Survey gives some confirmation of our estimates at one end of the historical series.

Historical Changes in Inequality[6]

Table 90 and the companion Appendix Tables A-17 through A-21 enable us to compare top wealth-holders and the personal sector for 1953, 1949, 1945, 1939, 1929, and 1922. In looking for trends over the decades, the reader should remember that varying numbers of

---

[6] As far as is known, this is the first attempt to relate estate tax data to national balance sheet aggregates. Several other students of wealth distribution have examined changes in concentration *within* the group of decedent estate tax wealth-holders. W. L. Crum studied the returns for 1916–33 and concluded that "with respect to curvature, as with respect to the coefficients of average inequality, a rough lagging correlation with the economic cycle is evident. Prosperity is followed by a much greater stretching into high total valuations of the few largest estates than is depression" (*The Distribution of Wealth*, Boston, 1935, p. 10).

Working from a distribution of estate tax returns by net classes, Mendershausen was able to make some comparisons of inequality among living top wealth-holders for the 1920's and the 1940's. He concludes that ". . . we find less inequality in the 1944 and 1946 distributions than in those for 1922 and 1924. This pertains of course to all returns for each of the several years, which, as has been noted before, extended over a changing range of wealth classes owing to changes in exemptions" (Goldsmith, *Saving in U.S.*, III, p. 344). These exemptions were $50,000 in 1922 and 1924, and $60,000 in the 1940's.

The introduction of the marital deduction in 1948 makes the net estate data

CHART 30
Top Wealth-Holders and Adult Population, Selected Years, 1922–56

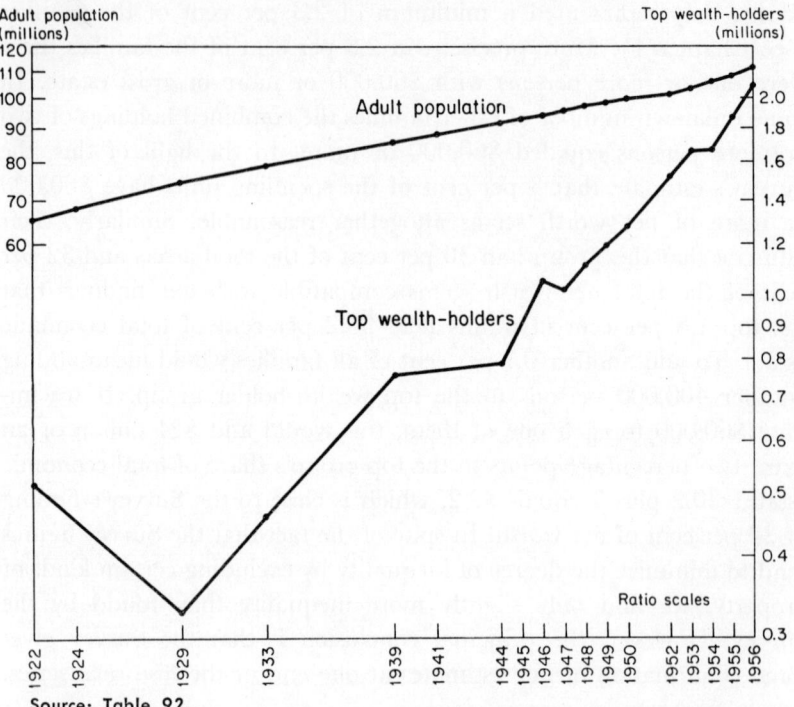

Source: Table 92.

Note: As defined in the text, a "top wealth-holder" is a living person with more wealth than the estate tax exemption level. The sharp drop in the number of top wealth-holders in 1929 was due to the extraordinarily high estate tax exemption of $100,000 effective in that year.

wealth-holders are involved in each year. These changes are due to changing exemption limits, changing prices and incomes, and changing population numbers. Chart 30 records the changing number of top wealth-holders and the changing population between 1922 and 1953.

---

after that year not comparable with those for earlier years. Hence, we cannot compare the inequality among top wealth-holders in the 1920's and 1940's with that in the 1950's. It is possible to compare the distribution of gross estate among the top wealth-holders in 1944 and 1953. We find virtually no difference in inequality in the two years. The great difficulty of presenting a meaningful comparison of the degree of inequality among estate tax wealth-holders over the years should be emphasized. Because of the dollar exemption (which itself changes), the changing level of asset prices, and the general growth in the economy, the top wealth-holders constitute a varying proportion of the total population. To compare the inequality within a group whose limits are so arbitrary and whose relative importance is so variable is apt to raise more questions than it answers.

IN PERSONAL WEALTH, 1922–56

Comparison over the years, at least of aggregate economic estate, is facilitated by Table 92. Here we have shown as much information as could be assembled for 1922–56. In some cases the results are the product of interpolation. The estimates shown for 1929, 1933, 1939, 1954, and 1956 are particularly contrived, since the estate tax data for those years are not broken down by age and estate size and it has been necessary to use judgment in selecting devolution rates[7] for those years. The 1945 results are adjusted on the basis of 1944 findings, for which considerable basic data were available.

Columns 14 and 15 of Table 92 show the proportion that estate tax wealth-holders are of the total population and columns 16 through 18 show their share of total wealth. Thus, in 1922 0.47 per cent of the population held 29.2 per cent of the total equity of the personal sector. In 1949, 0.80 per cent of the population held 22.7 per cent of the total equity. In 1953, 1.04 per cent of the population held 28.5 per cent of the total equity. The whole set of figures suggests a downward drift in the degree of concentration of wealth, particularly from 1929 to 1945. The peak year for inequality in this series is 1929, with 0.27 per cent of the population holding 29.0 per cent of the wealth. There is considerable variability in these relationships over short periods. The variability may be due to sampling or other errors in the estate tax wealth estimates, to difficulties in the national balance sheet estimates, or to a combination of such errors. On the other hand, it is not altogether implausible that the degree of inequality should have increased during the 1920's, returned to below the pre-1929 level in the 1930's, fallen still more during the war, and then increased from 1949 to 1956.

Table 93 summarizes, perhaps in a clearer way, what changes in inequality are estimated.[8] It shows the shares of wealth for 1953 for the top percentiles of the population that estate tax wealth-holders were in some earlier years. This is shown graphically in Chart 31 which shows the upper right-hand section of a Lorenz curve.[9] The easiest

---

[7] A devolution rate is an average estate-multiplier for numbers of persons or amount of estate.

[8] This section has been much improved by the suggestions of Thor Hultgren.

[9] This chart should be read downward from the upper right-hand corner to the bottom left-hand corner. The line of equality shows the relationship that would obtain if the top 1 per cent of the population held 1 per cent of the wealth. It will be noted that the farther a line is from the line of equality, the greater is the inequality represented. According to this chart, the share of wealth held by the top 0.5 per cent moved, from 1929 to 1953, about one-third of the distance toward absolute equality.

TABLE 92
Selected Data Relating Top Wealth-Holders to Population and Estate Tax Wealth to National Balance Sheet Aggregates, for Selected Years, 1922–56

Year	Total Assets, Total Wealth Variant (billion dollars)		Total Equity, Personal Sector (billion dollars)		Total Population (millions)	Population Aged 20 and over (millions)	Number of Top Wealth-Holders (Basic Variant) (thousands)	
	All Sectors (1)	Personal Sector (2)	Total Wealth Variant (3)	Prime Wealth Variant (4)	(5)	(6)	White Mortality (7)	Adjusted Mortality (8)
1922	653.0	347.8	296.6	278.3	110.1	65.1	454[a]	517[a]
1924					114.1	68.0	495[a]	
1929	981.7	521.5	441.8	409.8	121.8	74.4	290[b]	330[b]
1933	733.1	387.9	329.1	300.7	125.7	78.8	402[b]	461[b]
1939	877.4	426.6	368.7	326.5	131.0	85.5	641[b]	758[b]
1941					133.4	87.8	529[a]	
1944					138.4	91.7	660[a]	782[a]
1945	1,626.2	722.5	671.8	598.4	139.9	92.9	759[a,c]	914[a,c]
1946					141.4	93.9	859[a]	1,045[a]
1947					144.1	95.5	967[a]	1,014[a]
1948					146.6	97.0	938	1,107
1949	2,063.5	942.7	855.0	760.6	149.2	98.0	1,003	1,187
1950					151.7	99.2	1,079	1,269
1952	2,639.3				157.0	101.4		
1953		1,237.6	1,104.8	987.2	159.6	103.4	1,417	1,659
1954		1,340.9	1,190.7	1,060.2	161.2	105.4		1,661
1955		1,465.4	1,292.0	1,142.4	164.3	107.8		
1956			1,400.0[d]	1,230.0[d]	167.2	111.0		2,109

200

IN PERSONAL WEALTH, 1922–56

	AGGREGATE ECONOMIC ESTATE OF TOP WEALTH-HOLDERS					TOP WEALTH-HOLDERS AS PERCENTAGE OF		SHARE OF PERSONAL WEALTH HELD BY TOP WEALTH-HOLDERS		
	Basic Variant		Prime Wealth Variant Adjusted Mortality[e]	Total Wealth Variant Adjusted Mortality[f]	Aggregate Gross Estate of Top Wealth-Holders, Basic Variant Adjusted Mortality	Total Popu- lation Col. 8 ÷ Col. 5	Adult Popu- lation Col. 8 ÷ Col. 6	Basic Variant Col. 10 ÷ Col. 4	Prime Variant Col. 11 ÷ Col. 4	Total Variant Col. 12 ÷ Col. 3
YEAR	White Mortality	Adjusted Mortality								
	(9)	(10)	(11)	(12)	(13)	(14)	(15)	(16)	(17)	(18)
	(billion dollars)							(per cent)		
1922	70.0[a,g]	81.3[a,g]	86.2[h]	98.1	92.2[g]	0.47	0.79	29.2	30.7	32.7
1924	75.9[a,g]	86.6[a,g]								
1929	104.2[b]	119.1[b,g]	126.1[h]	146.2	138.4[b,g]	0.27	0.44	29.0	30.7	33.2
1933	60.6[b]	70.1[b]	72.1[h]	89.9		0.37	0.44	23.3	24.0	27.3
1939	81.0[b]	95.1[b,g]	100.8	126.3	109.3[b,g]	0.58	0.89	29.1	30.6	34.1
1941	65.1[a,i]									
1944	105.0[a]	124.7[a]				0.56	0.86			
1945	117.8[a,c]	139.6[a,c]	1,480.0[h]	183.6	153.6	0.65	0.98	23.2	24.7	27.4
1946	130.5[a]	152.2[a,g]				0.74	1.11			
1947						0.70	1.06			
1948	133.9[g]	159.4[g]		223.9	177.0[g]	0.75	1.14	22.7	24.6	26.0
1949	144.0[g]	171.4[g]	181.7[h]	215.9	190.2[g]	0.80	1.26			
1950	162.9[g]	193.9[g]			216.2[g]	0.81	1.23			
1952										
1953	235.2	281.5	298.8	352.4	309.2	1.04	1.60	28.5	30.2	32.0
1954		297.0[b,g]	314.8[h]	375.8	315.0	1.04	1.57	28.0	29.7	31.5
1955										
1956		406.6[b,g]	431.0[h]	510.0	432.6	1.26	1.90	33.0	35.0	36.3

(notes on page 202)

TABLE 93
Share of Top Groups of Wealth-Holders in Total Population and in Total Equity,[a] Personal Sector, Selected Years, 1922–56
(per cent of wealth)

Per Cent of Population	1922	1929	1933	1939	1945	1949	1953	1954	1956
Top 0.27		29.0			16.9		18.0		
0.37			23.3		18.6		20.2		
0.47	29.2				20.4		22.0		
0.58				29.1	22.1		23.8		
0.65					23.2		24.8		
0.80						22.7	26.6		
1.04							28.5	28.0	
1.26									33.0
Top 0.50	29.8	32.4	25.2	28.0	20.9	19.3	22.7	22.5	25.0

Source: Table 92, cols. 14 and 16. Percentages for top 0.5 per cent of population, shown in last row, are derived from Chart 31 by extension of lines from known points. The extensions were made by drawing lines parallel to that for 1953, except for 1945, for which detail is available for the top 0.65 per cent. The 1953 data are derived from adjusted data from Table 24.

[a] Basic variant.

way to see what changes are involved is to hold the percentage of the population constant, which can be done with minimum guessing only for the top 0.5 per cent of the population for the series of years (bottom row in Table 93). This shows quite clearly that there were three periods when inequality declined in jumps from the 1920's to the 1930's and then to the war and postwar periods.

Notes to Table 92

[a] Multiplier process carried out for both sexes combined, hence these estimates are slightly high compared to those of 1948–53.

[b] Estimates of wealth-holders and aggregate economic estate made by multiplying number of returns and economic estate on returns by selected devolution rates. The rates were selected by inspection of devolution rates in surrounding years and with reference to changing exemption limits.

[c] Estimated from 1944 and 1946 findings.

[d] Estimated from 1953, 1954, and 1955 balance sheets.

[e] Relationship between basic variant and prime wealth variant estimated on basis of 1953 findings.

[f] Personal trust funds allocated to estate tax wealth-holders on the following basis: 1953, 85 per cent of the total; 1949, 80 per cent; 1939, 75 per cent; 1933, 1929, and 1922, 66 per cent.

[g] Includes a reduction of life insurance to equity value. For 1950 this correction was estimated to be $20 billion; for 1949 and 1948, $19 billion; for 1946, $15 billion; for 1939 and 1929, $7 billion; for 1922 and 1924, $5 billion.

[h] Basic variant adjusted to prime wealth variant on basis of 1953 relationship of basic to prime wealth.

[i] Apparently there was an abnormally old group of decedent wealth-holders in 1941.

The change in inequality over time is modified somewhat by considering the percentage that estate tax wealth-holders are of adults rather than of the total population. In 1920, persons over 20 made up 57.9 per cent of the total population; in 1930, 61.1; in 1940, 65.9; in 1950, 65.7 per cent; and in 1955, 63.8. In view of this striking change, and also because adulthood is relevant to wealth-holding status, we have shown the percentage that estate tax wealth-holders

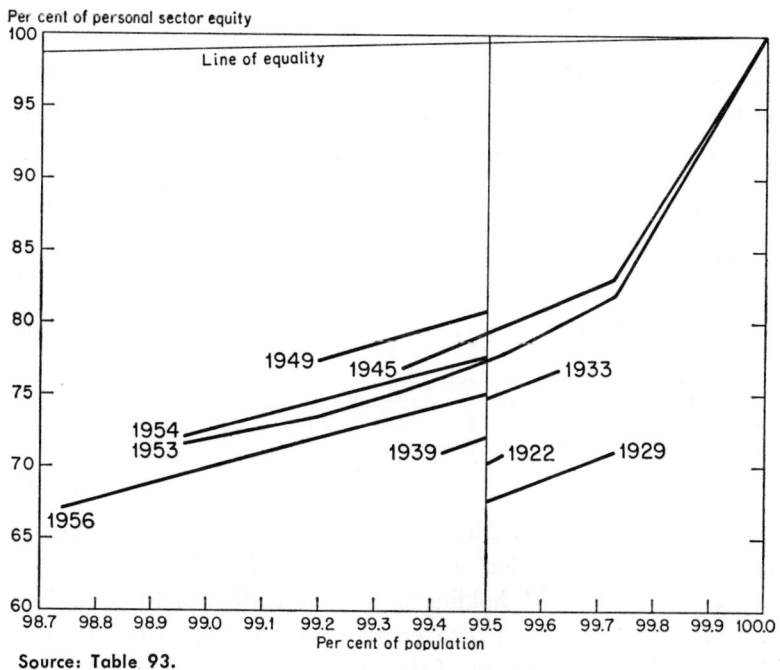

CHART 31

Upper Sections of Lorenz Curves of Personal Sector Equity (Basic Variant) Held by Upper Percentiles of Total Population, Selected Years, 1922–56

Source: Table 93.

were of the adult population in column 15 of Table 92. While the share of wealth held by the top 0.5 per cent of all persons fell from 32.4 in 1929 to 22.7 per cent in 1953 (Table 93), the share held by the top 0.44 per cent of adults had a slightly larger percentage fall, from 29.0 to 18.3 per cent (Table 94). The fact that there were more children (most of whom held no wealth) per hundred of the population in the 1920's than in the 1950's means that the top 1 per cent of adults were a larger part of the total population in 1956 than in 1922.

Further, it means that to include the top 1 per cent of adults in 1956 one has to count down to smaller estate sizes than in 1922. Presumably it is because of this that we find a greater loss of share on an adult than on an all-person basis. The share of the top 1 per cent of adults shows a greater fall over the years than does the share of wealth of the top 0.5 per cent of all persons.[10] The top 1 per cent of adults held 31.6 per cent of wealth in 1922, 24.2 per cent in 1953, and 26 per cent in 1956 (Table 94, bottom row, and Chart 32).

TABLE 94
SHARE OF TOP GROUPS OF WEALTH-HOLDERS IN TOTAL ADULT POPULATION AND IN TOTAL EQUITY,[a] PERSONAL SECTOR, SELECTED YEARS, 1922–56
(per cent of wealth)

Per Cent of Population Aged 20 and over	1922	1929	1933	1939	1945	1949	1953	1954	1956
Top 0.44		29.0	23.3				18.3		
0.79	29.2						22.3		
0.89				29.1			23.3		
0.98					23.2		24.1		
1.26						22.7	26.4		
1.57							28.4	28.0	
1.60							28.5		
1.90									33.0
Top 1.00	31.6	36.3	28.3	30.6	23.3	20.8	24.3	24.0	26.0

SOURCE: Table 92, cols. 15 and 16. Percentages for top 1 per cent of adults, shown in last row, are derived from Chart 32 by extension of lines from known points. The 1953 data are derived from adjusted data from Table 24.
[a] Basic variant.

Evaluation of the finding that inequality among all persons and among all adults has fallen over the period 1922–53 is aided by using the family as the wealth-holding unit. As was discussed in Chapter 4, the nearest that estate tax data enable us to come to a family wealth distribution is a rough count of the number of families having at least one member with at least $60,000. This was established by subtracting the number of married women from the total of top wealth-holders. Thus, for 1953 the total of 1.6 million top wealth-holders less the 0.3

[10] A comment by P. F. Brundage to the author makes it clear that one may make a further step here to say that a statistical determinant of the degree of inequality of wealth-holding is the age composition of the population. Increasing the percentage that adults are of the total population tends to decrease the degree of inequality, or to offset a rise in inequality. However, increasing the percentage that older-aged adults are of the total adult population tends to increase inequality (Chapter 7).

million married women yields the minimum estimate of 1.3 million families. The identical calculation for 1922 is 517,000 top wealth-holders less 45,000 married women, which yields the minimum estimate of 472,000 families.[11]

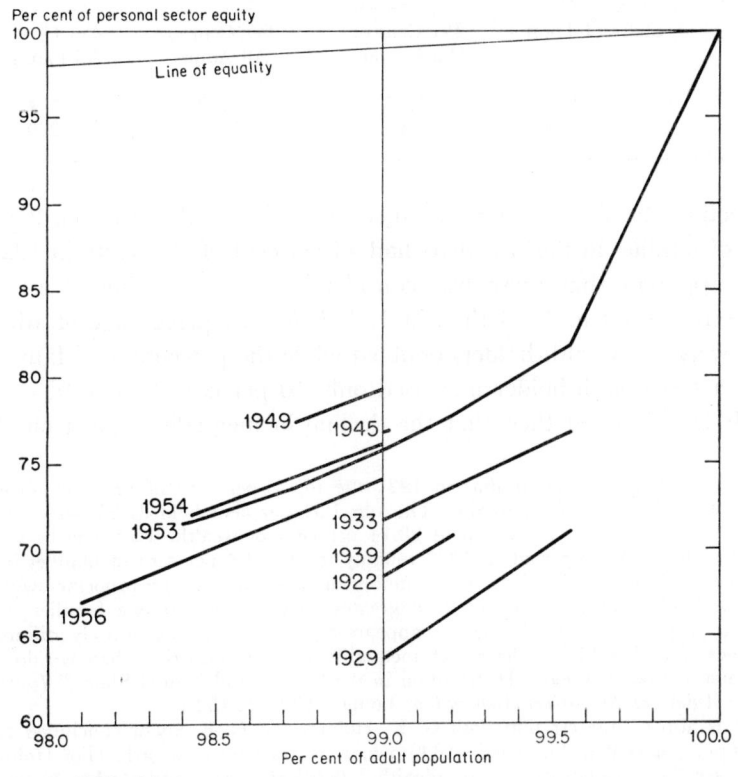

CHART 32

Upper Sections of Lorenz Curves of Personal Sector Equity (Basic Variant) Held by Upper Percentiles of Adult Population, Selected Years, 1922–56

Source: Table 94.

Setting these numbers of families among top wealth-holders against the numbers of total adults less married women in the total population, we find that families among the top wealth-holder group were

[11] Married women were 9.7 per cent of decedent estate tax wealth-holders in 1953, but only 5.5 per cent in 1922. (They were 5.3 and 6.0 per cent in 1923 and 1924 and 8.1 per cent in 1948.) In the estimate of living top wealth-holders, married women were 18 per cent in 1953 and 8.5 per cent in 1922. Unfortunately, estate tax data do not make possible a continuous series on this relationship.

1.4 per cent of all families in 1922[12] and 2.0 per cent in 1953. Since the top wealth-holder groups in the two years held almost the same share of total equity (29.2 and 28.5 per cent, respectively), it follows that the reduction in inequality is shown by the increase in the percentage of families.[13] By plotting these points on a Lorenz curve and

TABLE 95
SELECTED DATA ON TOP WEALTH-HOLDERS, 1922 AND 1953

Year	Top Wealth-Holders			
	Share of Total Personal Equity	Per Cent of All Persons	Per Cent of All Adults	Per Cent of All Families
1922	29.2	0.47	0.79	1.4
1953	28.5	1.04	1.60	2.0

projecting the lines a short distance, we estimate that the top 2 per cent of families in the two years had 33 per cent of all wealth in 1922. It is apparent that there was considerably more splitting of estates between spouses in 1953 than in 1922 since the percentage of adults who were top wealth-holders doubled while the percentage of families with a top wealth-holder increased only 40 per cent (Table 95).

It is concluded then that the decline in inequality shown on the

---

[12] W. I. King estimated that in 1921 the top 2 per cent of property owners held 40.19 per cent of all wealth. The top 1.54 per cent held 37.25 per cent of wealth; the top 0.63 per cent held 28.14 per cent of wealth. This may be compared with our finding that in 1922 roughly the top 1.4 per cent of families held 29.2 per cent of wealth. Since some families include two or more property owners, it is probable that there would be a greater concentration among families than among property owners. Hence, it appears that King, by his entirely different methods, found a higher degree of inequality in wealth-holding than we do for the same period. ("Wealth Distribution in the Continental United States," *Journal of the American Statistical Association,* January 1927, p. 152.)

It is also of interest that both G. K. Holmes and C. B. Spahr concluded that the top 1 per cent of families in 1890 owned 51 per cent of wealth. (For Holmes' work, see "The Concentration of Wealth," *Political Science Quarterly,* December 1893, pp. 589–600. Spahr's estimates are reported in his book, *The Present Distribution of Wealth in the United States,* New York, 1896.) It is difficult to believe that wealth was actually that highly concentrated in 1890 in view of the 1921 and 1922 measures.

[13] Using the Census definition of "households" yields the even smaller change of from 1.9 per cent in 1922 to 2.3 per cent in 1953. However, this overlooks an important change in household size over the years. In the 1920's households included many more subfamilies than was the case in any period since. (In 1910, 23 per cent of persons were heads of households; in 1950, 29 per cent were heads of households. Paul Glick, *American Families,* New York, 1957, p. 11.) To get around this difficulty it seemed best to adopt the "adults less married females" concept referred to above as the family measure.

basis of individuals tends to overstate the decline which would be found on a family basis (see Chart 3 in Chapter 1).

Another way to test whether we have really found a decline in inequality is to find out how much error there would have to be in the balance sheet estimates upon which all the percentage estimates of wealth-holdings are based in order to invalidate our finding of a decline. Suppose the balance sheet estimates of total personal equity are 10 per cent too high in 1953 and 10 per cent too low in 1922. This error (assumed in the direction unfavorable to a decline in inequality) would mean that instead of having 29.2 per cent of total equity in 1922 and 29.5 per cent in 1953, the top wealth-holders would have 26 per cent in 1922 and 32 per cent in 1953. Plotting these points on Chart 32 would indicate that both points could very well lie on the same Lorenz curve and hence that no decline in inequality actually

TABLE 96

Share of Total Equity, Personal Sector, Held by Top 0.47 Per Cent of Persons, 1922 and 1953
(per cent)

Year	Adjusted Mortality Rates	White Mortality Rates
1922	29.2	—
1953	22.0	19.0

took place. In this writer's judgment, however, there is little likelihood of an error of this size.

Interestingly, the conclusions about changes over the years are not affected by the selection of the wealth variant. The gap between prime wealth and total wealth as here defined changed very little in the thirty-year period (Table 92, cols. 16, 17, and 18). A more significant difference may be involved in the choice of mortality rates. The findings shown in Table 95 are based on our adjusted mortality rates, calculated as constant percentages of white rates for the respective years. However, it is generally believed that social and economic differentials in mortality have narrowed over time and, to the extent that such narrowing has taken place, we have understated the decline in inequality between 1922 and 1953. This means the multipliers used for 1922 are too low because the mortality rates are too high. The maximum possible error here is suggested by a comparison of the results for 1922 using the adjusted mortality rates with those for 1953 using white mortality rates. Estimates of numbers of top wealth-holders using white mortality rates are shown in Table 92, column 7. The 1922 result of the top 0.47 per cent of the population holding 29.2 per cent of the wealth then compares with the top 0.88 per cent of the population in 1953 (1.4 million top wealth-holders) holding 24.6 per cent of the wealth. This means that the top 0.47 per cent in 1953 held 19.0 per cent of the wealth, according to white mortality rate estimates. It is possible then that the fall in the share of the top 0.47 per cent of the population was on the order of 29.2 per cent in 1922 to 19.0 per cent in 1953[14] (Table 96). It is difficult to imagine any combination of errors that would yield a result of increasing concentration over time.

Changes in Share of Wealth Held by Top One Per Cent of Adults, by Type of Property

Between 1922 and 1953 the top 1 per cent of the adult population experienced a decline in the share of total equity in the personal sector and a decline in the share of most types of property (Table 97). Notable exceptions are "stock" and "other bonds," which appear to have changed little in degree of concentration. All studies of stock ownership indicate that this asset is highly concentrated.[15]

However, the unreasonable variation of some of these series plus the greater than 100 per cent figures for state and local bonds yield a less than convincing picture. It would seem appropriate to review the possible sources of error in the whole process of estimating wealth distribution. The irregularities referred to above could have arisen out of

---

[14] The relative fall of 10 percentage points is meant to be indicated here. The percentage for 1953 is believed to be substantially too low.

[15] Butters, Thompson, and Bollinger give the following as their best estimate for 1949 (based on SRC data, tax return data, and their own field surveys): The upper 3 per cent of spending units as ranked by income owned 75 per cent of marketable stock; the top 1 per cent, 65 per cent; the top 0.5 per cent, slightly over one-half; and the top 0.1 per cent, about 35 per cent of all the marketable stock owned by private investors. They indicate that these percentages would be higher if the stock held by personal trust funds were allocated to individuals. (*Effects of Taxation: Investments by Individuals*, Boston, 1953, p. 25, and also Chapters XVI and XVII.) As to a ranking by size of stock holdings, the 1 per cent of all spending units that owned $10,000 or more of stock accounted for at least two-thirds of the total value of stock reported to the 1952 Survey of Consumer Finances (*Federal Reserve Bulletin*, September 1952, p. 985). For one measure of concentration of stock ownership by use of a total wealth ranking, see Goldsmith, *Saving in U.S.*, III, Table W-53. He estimated that in 1950 those spending units with $60,000 or more of net worth held 76 per cent of corporate stock. The reader is cautioned that rankings by income and wealth are not interchangeable.

random errors in the sampling process.[16] For example, the stock figure in one year could be too high because of an unrepresentative age distribution of decedents with large stock holdings. Another possible cause is the selection of mortality rates; we could have the wrong measure of the differential mortality enjoyed by the rich, or there could be errors in the way property is valued or classified on the estate

TABLE 97

SHARE OF PERSONAL SECTOR ASSETS AND LIABILITIES[a] HELD BY TOP ONE PER CENT OF ADULTS, 1922, 1929, 1939, 1945, 1949, AND 1953
(per cent)

Type of Property	1922	1929	1939	1945	1949	1953
Real estate	18.0	17.3	13.7	11.1	10.5	12.5
U.S. govt. bonds	45.0	100.0	91.0	32.5	35.8	31.8
State and local bonds	88.0	b	b	b	77.0	b
Other bonds	69.2	82.0	75.5	78.5	78.0	77.5
Corporate stock	61.5	65.6	69.0	61.7	64.9	76.0
Cash	—	—	—	17.0	18.9	24.5
Mortgages and notes	—	—	—	34.7	32.0	30.5
Cash, mortgages, and notes	31.0	34.0	31.5	19.3	20.5	25.8
Pension and retirement funds	8.0	8.0	6.0	5.9	5.5	5.5
Insurance	35.3	27.0	17.4	17.3	15.0	11.5
Miscellaneous property	23.2	29.0	19.0	21.4	15.0	15.5
Gross estate	32.3	37.7	32.7	25.8	22.4	25.3
Liabilities	23.8	29.0	26.5	27.0	19.0	20.0
Economic estate	33.9	38.8	33.8	25.7	22.8	27.4

SOURCE: Table 90 and Appendix Tables A-17 through A-21, col. 13. National balance sheet data used for 1922, 1929, and 1939 are from Goldsmith, *Saving in U.S.*, III; for 1945, 1949, and 1953, from preliminary unpublished tables prepared by the National Bureau of Economic Research.
[a] Total wealth variant.
[b] In excess of 100 per cent. See text.

tax returns. On the other hand, we could be confronted with difficulties in the national balance sheet aggregates for the several types of property.[17] It also is possible that we have double-counted some of the assets in personal trust funds in making adjustments to move from the basic to the prime to the total wealth variant for top wealth-holders.

All of these considerations urge that the whole of Table 97 be used

---

[16] The top wealth-holder group held substantially more market value in stocks in 1953 than 1949. The aggregate gross estate of decedent top weath-holders was 36.5 per cent in stock in 1949, but 40.5 per cent in stock in 1953.

[17] It seems probable, for example, that balance sheet difficulties are responsible for the high percentages for state and local bonds in 1929 and 1939.

THE SHARE OF TOP WEALTH-HOLDERS

in evaluating any single figure in it, and that each individual item be treated with caution.

Comparison with Wealth Distribution in England and Wales

In appraising a given degree of inequality in wealth distribution, it is useful to have not only a historical perspective, but also a comparison with other national economies. The only other nation for which similar studies have been made is Great Britain. British study of wealth distribution by the estate-multiplier method goes back to the work of

CHART 33

Persons with Gross Estates Greater Than Stated Amounts, England and Wales, 1946–47, and United States, 1953

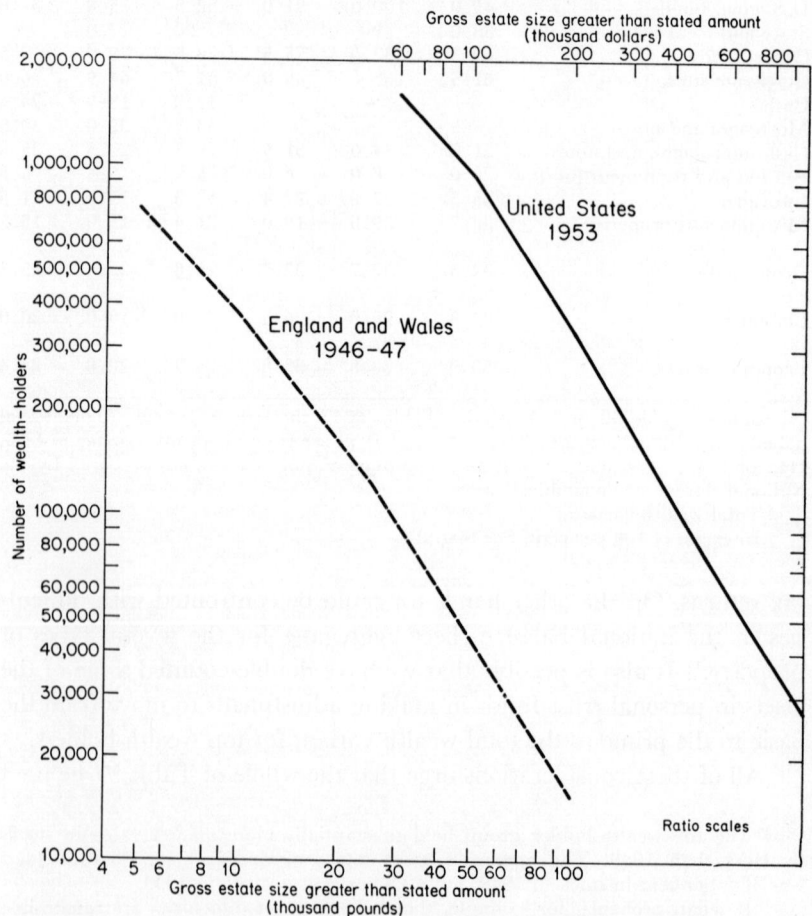

Source: Table 24 for the United States; Table 98 for England and Wales.

Bernard Mallet in 1908 and includes the later work of G. H. Daniels, H. Campion, and T. Barna. More recently Allan M. Cartter, an American, and Kathleen M. Langley have used this method with British tax data. The British estate tax has had a low filing requirement of £100 and hence the estate-multiplier method can give a much more nearly complete picture of wealth distribution for Britain than for this country.

Comparison of inequality in the United States and in England and Wales is made possible by our findings set forth above and those

TABLE 98

NUMBER OF PERSONS AGED 25 AND OVER IN EACH CAPITAL GROUP, ENGLAND AND WALES, 1946 AND 1947

Capital Group (pounds)	All Persons		Males		Females	
	Thousands	Per Cent	Thousands	Per Cent	Thousands	Per Cent
100 or less	16,856	60.62	7,027	53.72	9,829	66.76
100 to 1,000	7,727	27.79	4,272	32.66	3,455	23.47
1,000 to 5,000	2,465	8.87	1,352	10.33	1,113	7.56
5,000 to 10,000	383	1.38	221	1.69	162	1.10
10,000 to 25,000	251	0.90	139	1.06	112	0.76
25,000 to 100,000	106	0.38	60	0.46	46	0.31
Over 100,000	15.5	0.06	11	0.08	4.5	0.03
Total	27,804	100.00	13,082	100.00	14,722	100.00

SOURCE: Kathleen M. Langley, "The Distribution of Capital in Private Hands in 1936–38 and 1946–47 (Part I)," *Bulletin of the Oxford University Institute of Statistics*, December 1950, Table XIII, p. 353.

of Langley,[18] who related her own study of postwar wealth distribution to studies by others of earlier periods. Except for the exclusion of life insurance, the British data seem to be quite comparable to our own. Property in trust is treated in the same way in the two countries. This comparison shows a much greater inequality in England and Wales than in the United States.

In 1946–47 the top 1.5 per cent of adults owned 53 per cent of the total wealth in England and Wales, while in 1953 the top 1.5 per cent of adults in the United States owned only 27 per cent of the wealth.[19] Chart 33 shows, by use of a Pareto curve, how the upper tails in the two countries compare.

[18] Kathleen M. Langley, "The Distribution of Capital in Private Hands in 1936–38 and in 1946–47," *Bulletin of the Oxford University Institute of Statistics*, December 1950, pp. 339–359, and February 1951, pp. 34–54.

[19] The findings for the two countries are not strictly comparable for several reasons. First, the percentage of population column refers to persons over 25 in England and Wales and persons over 20 in the United States. Since the wealth-

CHART 34
Lorenz Curves of Gross Estates Among Adults, England and Wales, 1946–47, and United States, 1953

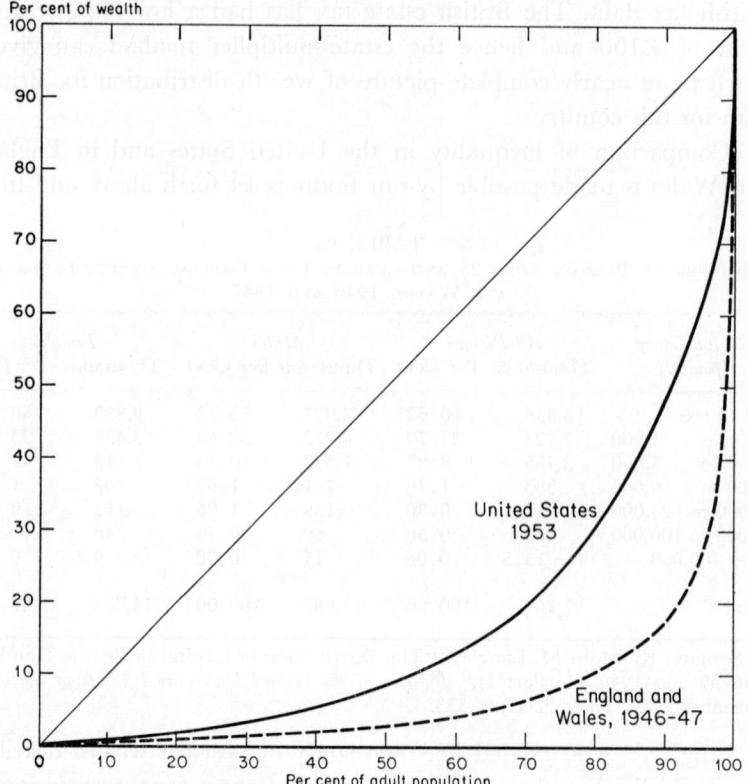

Source: Table 100 for England and Wales; Table 99 for the United States.

A rough estimate of the way the two distributions compare through the whole range of wealth-holders is offered in Tables 98 and 99 and Chart 34. The comparison is particularly rough because the estimated American distribution is built up from very few clues, as can be seen from the following description of our procedure. Our primary finding that 1.7 million individuals have "estate tax wealth" of over $60,000

---

holders would be a larger part of the population over 25 than of the population over 20, this means we have overstated inequality in the United States compared to that in England and Wales. Secondly, the British data are estimated using general mortality rates while we have used adjusted mortality rates, which again tends to overstate the inequality in the United States. Finally, the British data exclude Scotland, which understates the inequality in Britain. To some extent these differences offset each other, but we have undoubtedly understated the difference between the two countries in Chart 34.

and that they hold an aggregate of $309.2 billion of basic variant gross estate is complemented by the deduction that there were another 101.7 million individuals over age 20 who held the remaining part of the aggregate gross estate in the hands of all individuals. These 101.7 million persons are undoubtedly spread over the estate sizes below $60,000 in a very skewed distribution, with more than half of them under $4,000. The median net worth of a spending unit in 1953 was $4,100, so the individual median may be presumed to lie below that

TABLE 99
Estimated Distribution of Total Adult Population by Gross Estate Size, United States, 1953

Gross Estate Size (dollars)	Number of Persons Aged 20 and over (millions)	Per Cent	Average Estate Size (dollars)	Total Gross Estate (Basic Variant) Billion Dollars	Per Cent
0 to 3,500	51.70	50.0	1,800	93.1	8.3
3,500 to 10,000	19.00	18.4	6,000	114.0	10.2
10,000 to 20,000	21.89	21.2	15,000	328.4	29.3
20,000 to 30,000	6.00	5.8	25,000	150.0	13.4
30,000 to 40,000	2.00	1.9	35,000	70.0	6.3
40,000 to 50,000	0.80	0.8	45,000	36.0	3.2
50,000 to 60,000	0.35	0.3	55,000	19.3	1.7
Total under 60,000[a]	101.74	98.4	7,900	810.8	72.4
60,000 to 70,000[b]	0.18	0.1	61,000	10.5	0.9
60,000 and over[a]	1.66	1.6	186,265	309.2	27.6
All estate sizes	103.40	100.0	10,800	1,120.0	100.0
Median estate size[c]			3,500		

[a] Derived from Table 92.
[b] Table 24.
[c] Estimated from fact that median net worth of a spending unit in 1953 was $4,000.

at, say, $3,500. The rate of increase in the number of wealth-holders in the $10,000 estate classes above $60,000 is variable, but is generally smaller at the lower end of the range (Table 24). There is a flattening of the frequency curve between $90,000 and $60,000, with almost the same numbers in each bracket in that range. However, ignoring this peculiarity and extending the long swing of the line back to the $0 to $10,000 class, we come up with the distribution shown in Table 99.

A similar finding of greater inequality in England appears when the distribution of net worth among English income units in 1953 is compared (with certain cautions noted below) with the American

CHART 35
Upper Section of Lorenz Curves of Gross Estate Held by Top Percentiles of Adults, England and Wales and United States, Selected Years, 1911–53

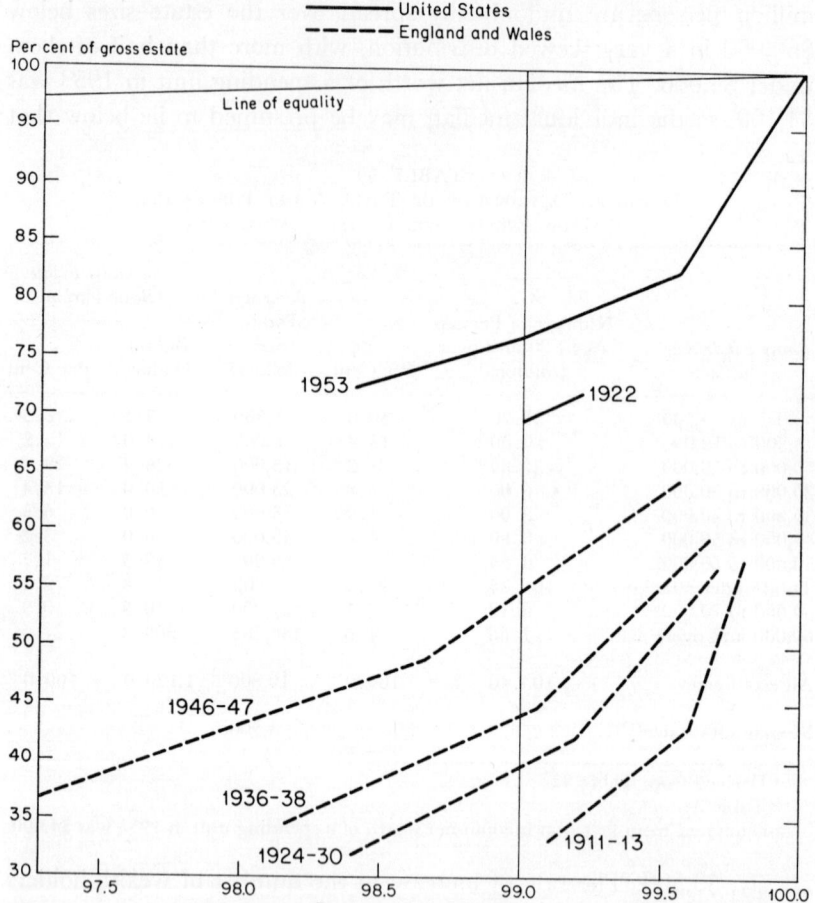

Source: For England and Wales, Kathleen M. Langley, "The Distribution of Capital in Private Hands in 1936–38 and 1946–47 (Part II)," *Bulletin of the Oxford University Institute of Statistics*, February 1951, Table XVB, p. 46. For the United States, the 1953 point for the top 1.6 per cent of adults and the 1922 point for the top 0.79 per cent of adults were estimated from Table 92. The slope of the two lines was estimated from Table 94.

Survey of Consumer Finances finding in Table 91. In Britain the top 2.9 per cent of income units held 48.9 per cent of the total net worth; the top 9.9 per cent held 75.7 per cent of the total net worth. In the United States, on the other hand, the top 3 per cent of spending units held about 33 per cent of net worth; the top 10 per cent about 56 per cent of net worth. Apparently the leading difference in the two surveys was the use of the income unit in Britain as opposed to the spending unit in the United States. Since there are more income than spending units (particularly single-person units) as the two are defined, it is probable that inequality is relatively overstated for Britain in a straight comparison.[20]

It would appear that the historical picture of decline in the degree of inequality of wealth distribution is similar in the two countries, at least for the period 1922–46 (Chart 35). However, throughout the whole period the inequality has been considerably greater in England and Wales than in the United States (Table 100). Langley explains this table as follows: "The distribution of capital had gradually become more equal during these years. One per cent of the persons aged 25 and over in England and Wales owned 50 per cent of the total capital in 1946–47; in 1936–38 the percentage was 55; in 1924–30 one per cent of the persons owned 60 per cent of the total capital; while in 1911–13, one per cent of the persons owned 70 per cent of the total capital."[21]

Comparison with Changes in Income Inequality

It helps to place the findings on changes in wealth inequality in perspective to compare them with Simon Kuznets' findings on income in-

---

[20] In discussing the two surveys, K. H. Straw ("Consumers' Net Worth, the 1953 Savings Survey," *Bulletin of the Oxford University Institute of Statistics*, February 1956, Table II, p. 4) supplies us with some clues to the reasons for the difference in inequality. In Great Britain 16 per cent of the population is over 60 years of age, while the comparable figure for the United States is 12 per cent. In the United States 9 per cent of the spending units are headed by farm operators, while only 1 per cent of the British income units are so headed. In the United States half the spending units own their own homes, while in Britain only 27 per cent of the primary income units own their homes.

Straw declares that "probably the most interesting feature of the comparison is the generally higher ratio of net worth to income found in the United States. Over all the spending units in America net worth amounted to almost three years' gross income, compared with a little less than two years' in Great Britain" (*ibid.*, p. 55). Also see Harold Lydall and J. B. Lansing, "A Comparison of Distribution of Personal Income and Wealth in the United States and Great Britain," *American Economic Review*, March 1959, pp. 43–67.

[21] *Bulletin of the Oxford University Institute of Statistics*, February 1951, p. 47.

THE SHARE OF TOP WEALTH-HOLDERS

TABLE 100
DISTRIBUTION OF CAPITAL IN ENGLAND AND WALES, 1911–13, 1924–30, 1936–38, AND 1946–47
(cumulative percentages)

Capital Group (pounds)	1946–47		1936–38		1924–30		1911–13	
	Persons	Capital	Persons	Capital	Persons	Capital	Persons	Capital
Total	27,804,000	£24.3 bill.	25,502,000	£17.2 bill.	22,336,000	£13.7 bill.	18,745,000	£6.0 bill.
Total	100.00%	100.00%	100.00%	100.00%	100.00%	100.00%	100.00%	100.00%
More than 100	39.38	95.85	24.75	94.71	21.4	96.4	11.7	93.3
More than 1,000	11.58	84.26	6.92	82.84	5.8	85.6	3.0	83.0
More than 5,000	2.72	63.27	1.84	65.45	1.6	68.1	0.9	66.9
More than 10,000	1.34	51.92	0.94	55.26	0.8	57.9	0.4	57.0
More than 25,000	0.44	35.49	0.33	40.46	0.3	43.1	0.2	42.4
More than 100,000	0.06	16.31	0.05	21.07	0.04	23.9	0.03	22.9

SOURCE: Kathleen M. Langley, "The Distribution of Capital in Private Hands in 1936–38 and 1946–47 (Part II)," *Bulletin of the Oxford University Institute of Statistics*, February 1951, Table XVB, p. 46. Based on general mortality rates.

NOTE: Figures are for persons aged 25 and over.

equality presented in *Shares of Upper Income Groups in Income and Savings.*[22] He traced changes in the shares of the upper 1 and 5 per cent of persons in a per capita distribution from 1913 to 1948 and found that the top 5 per cent's share of basic variant income had a rather narrow range of movement during the period 1919–38, with no perceptible and sustained change. However, he found that "from 1939 to 1944 it dropped from 23.7 to 16.8 per cent—almost 7 percentage points in five years; and in 1947 and 1948 its level was only slightly higher—17.6 and 17.8 per cent respectively. During the last decade, then, the share of the top 5 per cent declined about a quarter."[23] The fall for the top 1 per cent was from 12 per cent in 1939 and 1940 to about 8.5 per cent in 1947 and 1948. In the disposable income variant the top 5 per cent's share fell by well over three-tenths, from 27.1 to 17.9 per cent.

Our finding that the share of wealth held by the top 2 per cent of families fell from about 33 to 29 per cent from 1922 to 1953, or about one-eighth, would seem compatible with Kuznets' findings[24] and with the general belief that there has been some lessening of economic inequality in the United States in recent decades. Wealth distribution appears to have changed less than income distribution during this period.

[22] New York, National Bureau of Economic Research, 1953.
[23] *Ibid.*, p. xxxvii.
[24] Kuznets' per capita distribution of income should not be confused with a per earner distribution. In the former, family income is divided by number of family members to obtain an array of families (or individuals) by per capita income. Since our wealth-holder data are not calculated on a per capita basis, we cannot make a direct comparison with Kuznets' findings on income. Our estimates of the distribution of wealth by families seem to be conceptually closest to Kuznets' per capita procedure. It is worth mentioning here that our method of ranking cannot reach all the change in economic inequality which occurred. Kuznets ranked persons by income but ignored changes on capital account. We have ranked persons by wealth and ignore changes in their income account. The ideal study would catch both kinds of change for both rankings.

CHAPTER 7

Determinants of Inequality of Wealth-Holding

IN THIS chapter an attempt is made to find the causes of changes in wealth distribution reported in Chapter 6.

List of Determining Factors

The many factors that determine the degree of inequality of wealth-holding at any one time may be grouped under the following headings: (1) inequality in the previous generation; (2) the transfer of wealth between and within generations; (3) differential rates of accumulation from income; and (4) differential changes in the prices of assets.

TABLE 101
PERSONAL SECTOR WEALTH IN 1922 PRICES AND IN CURRENT PRICES, 1922–53
(billion dollars)

End of Year	Gross Estate, Total Wealth Variant	
	1922 Prices	Current Prices
1922	347.8	347.8
1929	460.7	521.5
1939	461.3	426.6
1949	695.5	942.7
1953	821.3	1,237.6

SOURCE: Table 106, gross estate in cols. 1 and 3.

Estimates of personal wealth do not in themselves indicate how inequality is determined but they do give some rough clues to the general size of the last three of these factors. If we consider thirty years as a generation, then the difference in total personal wealth after a thirty-year span would represent the accumulation of a generation. In the period 1922-53, this total rose from $348 billion to $821 billion in 1922 prices (Table 101). Roughly two-fifths (that is, 348 divided by 821) of the property owned in 1953 may thus be said to have come into the hands of its current owners by transfer between generations in the form of bequest, gift, insurance proceeds, etc. The remaining three-fifths represents accumulation by the current generation.

By shifting over to current prices, the importance of price change can be seen. In 1922 prices total personal sector wealth changed by $473 billion (from $348 billion in 1922 to $821 billion in 1953), but in current prices it changed by $890 billion (from $348 billion to $1,238 billion). Therefore, $417 billion of the latter rise was due to price change. Of the $1,238 billion of personal wealth in 1953, $348 billion (or 28 per cent) was accumulated by previous generations, $473 billion (or 38 per cent) was accumulated by the current generation, and $417 billion (or 34 per cent) arose out of price change during the lifetime of the current generation. This method of estimating overstates the relative importance of accumulation, as opposed to price change, since it does not isolate the effect of price change on the assets acquired out of money saved between 1922 and 1953. As noted before, these data do not give any indication of how the several factors influenced the degree of inequality of wealth-holding.

Relating these data to estate tax wealth estimates provides more insight into the inequality question. National balance sheet estimates and estate tax data are not fully adequate to determine the importance of the factors that contribute to changes in inequality. They do, however, furnish us with the basis for some rough estimates of the general direction of the effect of these factors. Such rough estimates may point up the needs and perhaps offer bases for further research by other methods into the causes of inequality.[1]

We begin with the observed finding of a general decline in inequality of wealth-holding from 1922 to 1953. The share of personal sector wealth of the top 1 per cent of adults fell from 32 to 25 per cent in this period (Table 102). The share of the top 2 per cent of families fell from 32 to 29 per cent in the same period. In order to discover what caused this fall in share, we shall study the effect of the following factors: (1) price change, (2) saving, and (3) changes in transfer of wealth.

[1] Further insight into the determinants of inequality requires a more sophisticated analysis than is employed here. Such an analysis might include representation of the population by a model in which the various types of families and individuals in the real world could be given an explicit role. The assumed behavior and interaction of these units over time could then be studied by simulation techniques. Before such a study can be carried out more data and more knowledge of the interrelationships among the many variables need to be developed. For instance, how does saving differ by age within estate size? How does receipt of a large inheritance alter patterns of saving and investment? What connection is there between wealth-ranking and extraordinary capital gains? What personal characteristics are associated with significant loss of rank in wealth-holding? Are the people who enjoy capital gains also the ones who save most? How much stability is there in the population of the top 1 per cent of wealth-holders?

INEQUALITY OF WEALTH-HOLDING

TABLE 102
SELECTED DATA ON TOP ONE PER CENT OF ADULTS, 1922–53

Year	Numbers of Persons in Top 1 Per Cent (thousands) (1)	Percentage Share of Aggregate Gross Estate[a] Held by Top 1 Per Cent (2)	Average Gross Estate[a]	
			All Adults (3)	Top 1 Per Cent of Adults (dollars) (4)
1922	651	32	5,342	172,700
1929	744	38	7,009	264,200
1939	855	33	4,989	163,100
1945	929	26	7,777	200,600
1949	980	22	9,619	215,500
1953	1,030	25	11,968	303,900

[a] Total wealth variant.

Price Change as a Determinant of Inequality[2]

Let us think of change in the value of assets owned as a source of wealth distinct from either inheritance or accumulation out of current money income. (It should carefully be noted that we are assigning corporate saving to the "price change" effect rather than to the "saving" effect by this distinction.) Two kinds of change in value may be noted. One is particular or relative change and the other is general price change. Even in the absence of a general inflationary or deflationary movement in which most prices and incomes move in the same direction, there are, of course, many changes in the relative prices of individual pieces of property. Indeed, individual wealth items, other than liquid assets and insurance, are constantly fluctuating in money value. Land, a capital good, a security, a patent right, or other right to income has value only insofar as it has a prospective net yield, and its current value is the result of dividing that prospective net yield by the going rate of interest. Hence, when either the prospective net yield or the going rate of interest is altered, the market value of the wealth item is altered. Yields of property are affected either favorably or unfavorably by new discoveries of natural resources, changes in technique, in consumer preferences, in accessibility to markets, and other changes. Corporate stock may change in price because of corporate saving. Because of these changes, individual owners of property are likely to rise or fall in wealth-holder rank over the years.

[2] In this section, only the effects of price change upon inequality are considered. Some other effects of price change are discussed in Chapter 5 and in Appendix B.

Change in the general price level as it affects broad types of property (e.g., all stocks) will also affect inequality of wealth-holding. In general, the major drift of price change in the years since the depression has been such as to favor investment in equities and to disadvantage investment in assets of constant dollar value or of fixed yield. If two persons in 1939 had gross estates of $30,000, and one of them held all equities, such as real estate, stock, and interest in unincorporated business, while the other held liquid assets or debt claims, the one with equities would have been quite likely to rise into the $60,000 and over class by 1953, while the one with no equities most assuredly would not.

Since the depression stock prices have more than tripled and real estate prices (as indicated by the composite construction cost index)[3] have risen almost as much (Table 67). Over the period since, 1935, the most dramatic short-period change occurred in stock prices from 1949 to 1956, with the greater part of this rise from 1954 to 1956. The real estate index shows a much more gradual rise over the whole period. Bonds show relatively little change. Cash and life insurance do not, of course, change in money value. Mortgages and notes, it may be assumed, move in the same way as bonds. (Lack of an organized market for such assets makes this assumption somewhat unreal.) Miscellaneous property includes a mixture of equity and debt ownership and is here assumed to move with the level of consumer prices.

Looking at the period before 1940, it appears that one of the most important changes among the price-sensitive assets was the long slide in real estate values from the early 1920's to the end of the 1930's. The radical rise and fall of stock prices around 1929 means that the selection of a set of beginning and terminal dates is critical to the result. However, in the period 1922–35 real estate values fell (particularly because of farm land prices) while stock prices rose, which suggests that the price change increased inequality. Also, in the long period of 1922–53 stock prices rose more than real estate prices.

Tables 103 and 104 show, in terms of the 1953 composition of estates, that price changes over most but not all of the period here considered have, in conjunction with typical difference of estate com-

---

[3] Apparently residential construction costs have risen somewhat more than costs of other types of construction (indexes of S. H. Boeckh and associates in *Construction Review*). Farm land prices show a movement generally parallel to that of construction costs (Alvin S. Tostlebe, *Capital in Agriculture: Its Formation and Financing since 1870,* Princeton for National Bureau of Economic Research, 1957, p. 60).

position among estate sizes, increased inequality of wealth-holding. That is, the large estates have tended to appreciate more in size than the smaller estates. The same general set of relationships is illustrated in Table 105, which is based upon the 1922 composition of estates.

There is one respect in which the lower estate sizes have tended to gain through inflation at the expense of the higher estate sizes—and that is debt position. By having a larger debt-to-asset ratio—in other words, doing more "trading on the equity"—the former group tends to be better armed against inflation with debts which could be paid off in depreciated dollars. Within the top wealth-holder group there is no important difference in liabilities as a percentage of gross estate (Table 74). However, top wealth-holders have smaller debts, as a

TABLE 103
PERCENTAGE CHANGES IN MONEY VALUE OF TYPICAL 1953 ESTATES OF SELECTED SIZES, 1922–56

1953 Estate Size (dollars)	1922–56	1922–29	1929–35	1922–35	1935–56	1935–46	1946–53	1953–56
7,960	+53.5	− 1.9	−12.4	−14.1	+78.7	+33.8	+28.0	+ 3.4
65,000	+73.9	+12.1	−30.4	−22.0	+123.0	+43.3	+30.0	+20.5
250,000	+130.3	+39.1	−33.8	− 7.9	+150.1	+45.7	+29.3	+32.7
1,500,000	+206.7	+82.6	−41.5	+ 6.8	+187.2	+49.5	+25.7	+52.7
Aggregate gross estate of top wealth-holders $292.8 billion	+146.7	+49.4	−34.6	− 2.3	+152.4	+45.7	+27.0	+36.4

SOURCE: Table 104.

proportion of their gross estate, than the rest of the population. For both groups there is a strong association of younger age and high ratios of debt to net worth. While the top wealth-holders' debt-to-asset ratio is 9 per cent, that of the rest of the population is 12 per cent (Table 63). This means that differential gain through decline in value of debts would offset very little the general trend of greater gain for the higher estate sizes.

It is clear from the above discussion that prices moved from 1922 to 1953 in such a way as to increase inequality. One way to quantify the importance of that effect is to deflate, using 1922 as the base year, the holdings of the top 1 per cent of wealth-holders and of the whole personal sector in each succeeding year for which we have share estimates. In this way, we find that the share on a deflated basis is less than on a current dollar basis in each benchmark year after 1922 (Chart 36 and Table 106). At the end of the series in 1953, the share

INEQUALITY OF WEALTH-HOLDING

TABLE 104
Changes in Money Value of Typical 1953 Estates of Selected Sizes from Application of Asset Prices of Selected Years
(dollars)

	\multicolumn{8}{c}{Asset Prices of Years Shown}
	1922	1925	1929	1935	1940	1946	1953	1956
\multicolumn{9}{c}{$65,000 ESTATE, 1953 COMPOSITION}
Real estate	12,861	12,091	10,837	8,635	9,784	15,205	23,465	25,222
U.S. bonds	4,614	4,859	5,006	4,210	4,790	4,893	4,485	4,405
State and local bonds	45	54	52	59	67	76	65	63
Other bonds	694	717	723	856	944	1,002	910	886
Stock	4,422	5,861	13,684	5,701	6,059	9,623	13,000	24,500
Other assets	20,402	20,782	20,174	15,665	15,881	19,473	23,075	23,261
Total	45,038	44,364	50,476	35,126	37,525	50,272	65,000	78,337
\multicolumn{9}{c}{$250,000 ESTATE, 1953 COMPOSITION}
Real estate	36,160	33,984	30,397	24,288	27,522	42,768	66,000	70,943
U.S. bonds	12,345	13,001	13,393	11,264	12,817	13,091	12,000	11,786
State and local bonds	1,223	1,444	1,411	1,588	1,806	2,049	1,750	1,700
Other bonds	2,098	2,167	2,186	2,587	2,853	3,028	2,750	2,677
Stock	29,422	38,999	91,053	37,939	40,318	64,027	86,500	163,018
Other assets	62,832	64,311	61,944	54,990	55,747	68,354	81,000	81,653
Total	144,080	153,906	200,384	132,656	141,063	193,317	250,000	331,777
\multicolumn{9}{c}{$1,500,000 ESTATE, 1953 COMPOSITION}
Real estate	83,150	78,299	70,021	55,752	63,176	98,172	151,500	162,847
U.S. bonds	44,753	47,129	48,549	40,833	45,462	47,454	43,500	42,726
State and local bonds	72,327	85,396	83,468	93,916	106,812	121,198	103,500	100,530
Other bonds	11,442	11,820	11,924	14,114	15,561	16,520	15,000	14,601
Stock	300,510	398,332	930,000	387,503	411,799	653,967	883,500	1,665,044
Other assets	234,963	240,501	231,638	205,703	208,534	255,696	303,000	305,443
Total	747,145	861,477	1,364,600	797,821	852,344	1,193,007	1,500,000	2,291,191
\multicolumn{9}{c}{AGGREGATE GROSS ESTATE OF TOP WEALTH-HOLDERS, 1953 COMPOSITION (BILLION DOLLARS)}
Real estate	32,693	31,762	29,395	24,149	27,365	42,524	65,623	70,538
U.S. bonds	16,830	17,724	18,258	15,356	17,473	17,846	16,359	16,068
State and local bonds	7,157	8,450	8,260	9,294	10,570	11,993	10,242	9,948
Other bonds	2,172	2,244	2,264	2,680	2,954	3,136	2,848	2,772
Stock	39,031	51,736	120,789	50,329	53,485	84,938	114,750	216,258
Other assets	63,937	65,813	62,776	56,341	57,116	70,034	82,990	83,659
Total	161,820	177,729	241,742	158,149	168,963	230,471	292,803[a]	399,243
\multicolumn{9}{c}{AVERAGE OF NON-TOP-WEALTH-HOLDERS (ESTATE SIZE, $7,960, 1953 COMPOSITION)}
Real estate	1,900	1,771	1,639	1,325	1,502	2,397	3,660	3,716
U.S. bonds	360	379	391	371	400	391	350	347
State and local bonds								
Other bonds								
Stock	71	95	232	90	94	145	210	396
Other assets	3,033	3,091	2,999	2,821	2,841	3,229	3,740	3,773
Total	5,364	5,336	5,261	4,607	4,837	6,162	7,960	8,232

[a] Not adjusted to account for those returns with no age specified.

INEQUALITY OF WEALTH-HOLDING

TABLE 105
EFFECTS OF PRICE CHANGE UPON 1922 ESTATES OF TWO SIZES, 1922–53

Year	Average Estate for All Adults in 1922		Average Estate for Top 1 Per Cent of Adults in 1922	
	Dollars	Index	Dollars	Index
1922	5,342	100	172,700	100
1929	6,784	127	284,955	165
1933	4,594	86	160,511	93
1939	5,182	97	224,510	130
1945	6,464	121	267,685	155
1949	7,746	145	295,317	171
1953	8,501	161	376,486	218
PERCENTAGE CHANGE IN MONEY VALUE OF ESTATE				
1922–53		+61		+118
1929–53		+25		+ 32
1933–53		+84		+133
1939–53		+63		+ 67
1945–53		+31		+ 41
1949–53		+10		+ 27
1922–33		−14		− 8
1929–33		−33		− 44
1929–49		+14		+ 3
1933–49		+68		+ 83

SOURCE: Derived from Table 106.

CHART 36
Share of Wealth Held by Top One Per Cent of Adults, in Current Dollars and in 1922 Dollars, 1922–56

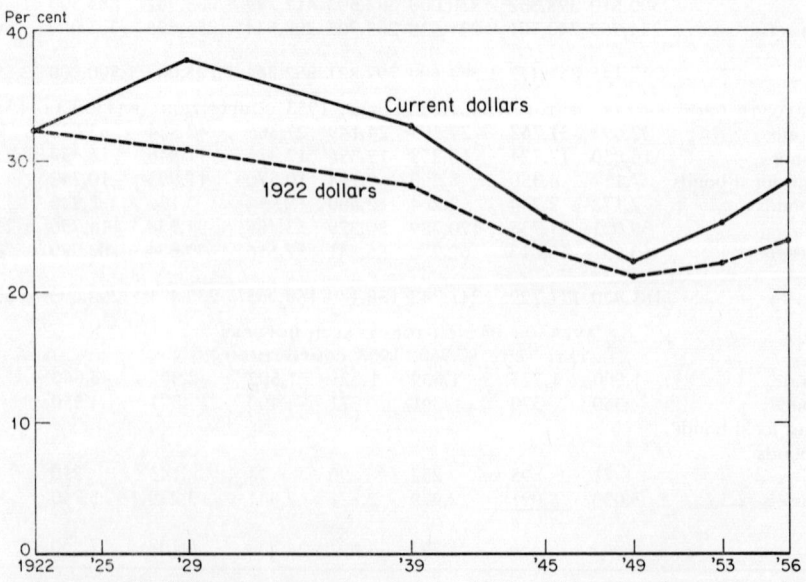

Source: Table 106, cols. 4 and 6, except for 1956, which was estimated from incomplete data.

INEQUALITY OF WEALTH-HOLDING

TABLE 106

CALCULATION OF SHARE OF WEALTH[a] HELD BY TOP ONE PER CENT OF ADULTS WITH EACH ASSET TYPE REDUCED TO 1922 PRICES

	Personal Sector Wealth (bill. dollars) (1)	Asset Price Indexes (2)	Personal Sector Wealth in 1922 Prices (bill. dollars) (3)	Share of Personal Wealth Held by Top 1% (per cent) (4)	Wealth of Top 1% in 1922 Dollars (bill. dollars) (5)	Share of Personal Wealth Held by Top 1% in 1922 Dollars (per cent) (6)
\multicolumn{7}{c}{1922}
Real estate	143.0	100.0				
Structures	76.5	100.0				
Land[b]	66.5	100.0				
U.S. govt. bonds	11.0	100.0				
State and local bonds	4.8	100.0				
Corporate bonds	14.5	100.0				
Corporate stock	54.5	100.0				
Cash and mortgages	53.4	100.0				
Cash	41.0					
Mortgages	12.4					
Pension funds	.3	100.0				
Insurance	8.7	100.0				
Misc. property	57.7	100.0				
Gross estate	347.8	100.0	347.8	32.3	112.3	32.3
Liabilities	51.2	100.0		23.8		
Economic estate	296.6	100.0		33.9		
\multicolumn{7}{c}{1929}
Real estate	184.4					
Structure	108.4	114.03	95.1	17.3	16.45	
Land[b]	76.0	61.04	124.6	17.3	21.56	
U.S. govt. bonds	5.0	108.48	4.6	100.0	4.6	
State and local bonds	7.4	99.58	7.4	100.0	7.4	
Corporate bonds	22.1	104.21	21.2	82.0	13.38	
Corporate stock	136.6	309.37	44.15	65.6	28.96	
Cash and mortgages	67.9			34.0		
Cash	50.1		50.1		17.03	
Mortgages	17.8	104.21	17.1		5.81	
Pension funds	2.0		2.0	.08	.16	
Insurance	17.6		17.6	.27	4.75	
Misc. property	78.6	102.37	76.8	29.0	22.27	
Gross estate	521.5		460.65	37.7	142.37	30.9
Liabilities	79.7			29.0		
Economic estate	441.8			38.8		

(continued)

TABLE 106 (continued)

	Personal Sector Wealth (bill. dollars) (1)	Asset Price Indexes (2)	Personal Sector Wealth in 1922 Prices (bill. dollars) (3)	Share of Personal Wealth Held by Top 1% (per cent) (4)	Wealth of Top 1% in 1922 Dollars (bill. dollars) (5)	Share of Personal Wealth Held by Top 1% in 1922 Dollars (per cent) (6)
1939						
Real estate	156.2					
Structures	102.6	111.75	91.84	13.7	12.58	
Land	53.6	45.54	117.7	13.7	16.12	
U.S. govt. bonds	8.9	108.9	8.2	91.0	7.5	
State and local bonds	7.9	122.81	6.4	100.0	6.4	
Corporate bonds	14.5	134.15	10.8	75.5	8.15	
Corporate stock	71.4	143.39	49.8	69.0	34.36	
Cash and mortgages	70.5			31.5		
Cash	57.1		57.1		17.99	
Mortgages	13.4	134.15	9.9		3.12	
Pension funds	7.2		7.2	6.0	4.32	
Insurance	29.2		29.2	17.4	5.08	
Misc. property	60.7	82.96	73.2	19.0	13.91	
Gross estate	426.6		461.31	32.7	129.53	28.1
Liabilities	57.9			26.5		
Economic estate	368.7			33.8		
1945						
Real estate	232.5					
Structures	148.8	160.67	92.6	11.1	10.28	
Land	83.7	70.42	118.9	11.1	13.20	
U.S. govt. bonds	62.4	144.22	43.9	32.5	14.27	
State and local bonds	9.5	144.06	6.6	100.0	6.60	
Corporate bonds	9.5	105.58	9.0	78.5	7.07	
Corporate stock	109.0	180.17	60.5	61.7	37.33	
Cash and mortgages						
Cash	116.8		16.8	17.0	19.86	
Mortgages	17.3	105.58	16.39	34.7	6.34	
Pension funds	28.3		28.3	5.9	1.67	
Insurance	44.8		44.8	17.3	7.75	
Misc. property	92.4	107.39	86.04	21.4	21.24	
Gross estate	722.5		623.83	25.8	145.61	23.3
Liabilities	50.7			27.0		
Economic estate	671.8			25.7		

(continued)

INEQUALITY OF WEALTH-HOLDING

TABLE 106 (concluded)

	Personal Sector Wealth (bill. dollars) (1)	Asset Price Indexes (2)	Personal Sector Wealth in 1922 Prices (bill. dollars) (3)	Share of Personal Wealth Held by Top 1% (per cent) (4)	Wealth of Top 1% in 1922 Dollars (bill. dollars) (5)	Share of Personal Wealth Held by Top 1% in 1922 Dollars (per cent) (6)
1949						
Real estate	336.3					
Structures	241.7	232.46	103.75	10.5	10.89	
Land	94.6	91.08	103.87	10.5	10.91	
U.S. govt. bonds	64.4	141.52	45.51	35.8	16.29	
State and local bonds	11.5	133.02	8.65	77.0	6.66	
Corporate bonds	6.6	106.31	6.20	78.0	4.84	
Corporate stock	106.4	181.08	58.76	64.9	38.4	
Cash and mortgages						
Cash	130.6		130.60	18.9	24.68	
Mortgages	22.9	106.31	21.54	32.0	6.89	
Pension funds	44.4		44.40	5.5	2.44	
Insurance	60.0		60.00	15.0	9.00	
Misc. property	159.6	142.17	112.26	15.0	16.84	
Gross estate	942.7		695.54	22.4	147.58	21.2
Liabilities	87.7			19.0		
Economic estate	855.0			22.8		
1953						
Real estate	444.6					
Structure	324.6	276.18	124.05	17.5	15.51	
Land	120.0	110.34	108.75	12.5	13.59	
U.S. govt. bonds	60.4	131.11	46.07	31.8	14.65	
State and local bonds	16.0	143.10	11.18	100.0	11.18	
Corporate bonds	6.1	97.2	6.28	77.5	4.87	
Corporate stock	155.7	294.03	52.95	76.0	40.24	
Cash and mortgages						
Cash	160.0		160.00	24.5	39.20	
Mortgages	31.2	97.2	32.10	30.5	9.79	
Pension funds	63.5		63.50	5.5	3.49	
Insurance	78.2		78.20	11.5	8.99	
Misc. property	220.8	159.77	138.20	15.5	21.42	
Gross estate	1,237.6		821.28	25.3	182.93	22.3
Liabilities	132.8			20.0		
Economic estate	1,104.8			27.4		

Source: Col. 1: Table 90 and accompanying appendix tables; col. 2: Table 67; col. 3: col. 1 ÷ col. 2; col. 4: Table 97; col. 5: col. 4 times col. 3; col. 6: col. 5 ÷ col. 3.

a Total wealth variant.

b The index used for all land is that for farm land. This yields an improbable change in the value of land in the personal sector in the period 1922–29. 1922 was a near-peak year in the price of farm land and it is probable that nonfarm land had a different history. Slightly different results in the share of gross estate shown in col. 5 would follow from use of a different price index for land.

of the top 1 per cent of adults was 22 per cent on a deflated basis and 25 per cent on a current basis. This would suggest that the price effect was operating over the period to increase the share of the top group by 3 percentage points. The converging of the current and constant dollar lines in Chart 36 indicates, however, that for 1929–49 price change was working to moderate inequality.

We gain more insight into the importance of price change by disregarding all other change. We take the actual holdings of all persons

TABLE 107
ACTUAL AND HYPOTHETICAL SHARES OF TOP WEALTH-HOLDER GROUPS IN PERSONAL SECTOR GROSS ESTATE,[a] 1922–53
(per cent)

	Actual Shares of		Hypothetical Shares of Top 1% of Adults			
	Top 1% of Adults (1)	Top 2% of Families (2)	Adding Only Price Change to 1922 Holdings (3)	Varying Price and Composition (4)	Varying Price, Composition, and Share of Saving[b] (5)	Changes Listed in Col. 5 plus Changes in Transfer of Wealth[c] (6)
1922	32	33	32	32	32	32
1929	38	—	40	37	38	—
1933	30	—	35	—	—	—
1939	33	—	37	36	36	—
1945	26	—	36	35	30	—
1949	22	—	33	33	27	—
1953	25	29	38	37	28	25

[a] Total wealth variant.

[b] Assuming top group accounted for 44 per cent of all personal saving in 1922–29, 10 per cent in 1930–49, and 15 per cent in 1950–53. These estimates are explained later (see pp. 234 ff).

[c] Derivation is explained later (see pp. 237 ff).

and of the top 1 per cent in 1922 and adjust each type of asset for price change. This method assumes no saving and no change in composition.[4] The results of this calculation are shown in column 3 of Table 107. They indicate that, on the basis of price change alone, it is not possible to explain fully the actual loss of the top wealth-holders.

[4] The reader should be alerted to the gross crudity of this method, which takes the 1922 population forward through time, assuming that nothing changes but the price of their assets. In fact, of course, some people die, others are born, some rise into the top 1 per cent ranking, and others fall out of it over time. This method makes no allowance for the great variations within either the top 1 per cent or the lower 99 per cent in type of assets held. Also the simple assumption is made that a single price index for one asset, e.g., corporate stock, can be applied to that asset for wealth-holders at all wealth levels without regard for any other characteristics. Some alternatives to this general method are mentioned in footnote 1.

INEQUALITY OF WEALTH-HOLDING

However, it is interesting that price change is sufficient to mark out the turning points in the share. That is, the hypothetical share in column 3 shows the prolonged fall from 1929 to 1949 and the rise in share from 1922 to 1929 and again from 1949 to 1953. Applying the price change to the estate composition for each benchmark year (instead of holding to the 1922 composition as in column 3) indicates that the shifts in composition made by the top wealth-holders contributed to a slight fall in share.[5] Comparison of columns 4 and 1 of Table 107 indicates, however, that there is still a considerable fall in the actual share which is not explained by the price and composition changes.

Changes in Share of Savings of Top Wealth-Holders

Could the actual fall in share of wealth be explained by a fall in the top wealth-holders' share of all current saving? On the basis of price and composition change, the share of wealth should have fallen over the 1929–49 period from 37 to 33 per cent. In actual fact, however, the share fell from 38 to 22 per cent. On the family basis, the share fell from 33 to 29 per cent over the longer 1922–53 period (Table 107, col. 2). The importance of the family measure is discussed in the section on transfer of wealth below.

Change in the price of assets, as discussed above, takes account of realized and unrealized capital gains. Some of these gains in turn arise out of corporate saving. Personal saving out of income, as discussed below, excludes the effects of change in the price of assets, but ideally should include saving in the form of consumer durables, since the latter are included in national balance sheets and estate tax wealth.

Aside from price change, the top group can maintain its share of wealth only if its saving is the same percentage of total personal saving as its original wealth was of total wealth. Thus, to maintain the 1922 share of 32 per cent, the top group had to account for at least 32 per cent of the saving. (The reader may wish to refer to Chart 36 in this connection. This is a purely mathematical relationship. There is no reason why this group should account for 32 per cent of the saving.) The particular question here is whether the top 1 per cent of wealth-holders has a smaller share of saving than the shares of wealth indi-

---

[5] In discussing composition change, it is relevant to note that the top group reduced its debt-to-asset ratio in 1945–53. In doing so, it reduced its share of personal sector liabilities (Table 97). Hence, one reason for the top group's loss of share was its decision to get out of debt, relatively speaking, while the rest of the population was adding to its assets by going into debt.

cated in column 4 of Table 107. If they do have a smaller share, is it small enough to explain the complete drop in share of wealth over the full period?

Digression on Relationships Between Wealth Inequality and Income Inequality

Before estimating the shares of saving of top wealth-holders, let us digress to consider some of the relationships among saving, income inequality, and wealth inequality.

One determinant of inequality in wealth-holding is differential rates of accumulation out of income. If those who inherit no

TABLE 108
Hypothetical Distribution of Wealth Among Adult Males[a]

Age Group	Adult Male Population, 1953		Average Estate Size (dollars)	Total Aggregate Estate	
	Millions	Per Cent		Billion Dollars	Per Cent
85 and over	.3	0.6	65,000	19.5	1.7
80 to 85	.6	1.2	60,000	36.0	3.1
70 to 80	1.9	3.8	55,000	104.5	8.9
60 to 70	5.6	11.3	45,000	252.0	21.4
50 to 60	8.0	16.1	35,000	280.0	23.7
40 to 50	10.2	20.5	25,000	255.0	21.6
30 to 40	11.6	23.3	15,000	174.0	14.8
20 to 30	11.5	23.1	5,000	57.5	4.9
Total 20 and over	49.7	100.0	23,712	1,178.5	100.0

[a] Assuming that they all accumulate wealth at identical rate of $1,000 per year (including interest) and that they all start with no estate at age 20.

wealth or small amounts of wealth accumulate wealth at a faster rate than those with large inheritances, accumulation may moderate the degree of inequality over time. The reverse would be the case, of course, if the rate of accumulation is higher for those who inherit relatively large amounts.

If there were no inheritance and the rate of accumulation among all adults were uniform, a moderate degree of inequality would obtain. Suppose that all males aged 0 to 19 had no wealth, but starting at age 20 each one accumulated property at the rate of $1,000 (including interest) per year. Those reaching the age of 85 would have estates of $65,000 and so on. Under these assumptions, the top estate owners, who would all be in the older age groups, would have a disproportionate share of the wealth. The top 1.8 per cent of adult males would have 4.8 per cent of the wealth (Table 108).

However, people accumulate wealth at very different rates, some saving large amounts each year and some dissaving, or decumulating wealth. The causes for these differences are manifold and include such incalculables as individual attitudes toward saving, and motivation and ability to systematically control household and business accounts

TABLE 109
COMPARISON OF DISTRIBUTION OF MONEY INCOME AND NET WORTH AMONG SPENDING UNITS, 1952–53

Per Cent of Spending Units Ranked by Income	Per Cent of Money Income in 1952 Before Taxes
Lowest 11	1
14	5
16	10
18	15
15	16
17	25
Highest 9	28
100	100

Per Cent of Spending Units Ranked by Net Worth	Per Cent of Net Worth in 1953
Lowest 31	1
23	5
35	34
11	60
100	100

SOURCE: 1953 Survey of Consumer Finances, reprinted from *Federal Reserve Bulletin*, 1953, Supplementary Table 5, p. 11.

toward the end of estate building. Aside from these individual differences, there are broad socio-economic characteristics which are useful in marking off the groups which have relatively high rates of saving. One such characteristic is income, which is a major determinant of saving rates. In all postwar years the top decile of spending units, ranked by income, has accounted for about three-fourths of the saving and the top four deciles for 100 per cent of the positive saving. (If we assume in Table 108 that throughout their lifetime one-half the males save at the rate of $2,000 per year and the other half do not save at all, then the degree of inequality would be considerably higher than in the previous example, with the top 0.9 per cent of adult males having 4.8 per cent of the wealth and the top 2.8 per cent having 13.7 per cent.)

Hence, it seems that the degree of income inequality is an important factor in differential rates of accumulation and hence in the degree of wealth inequality. All other things remaining the same, one

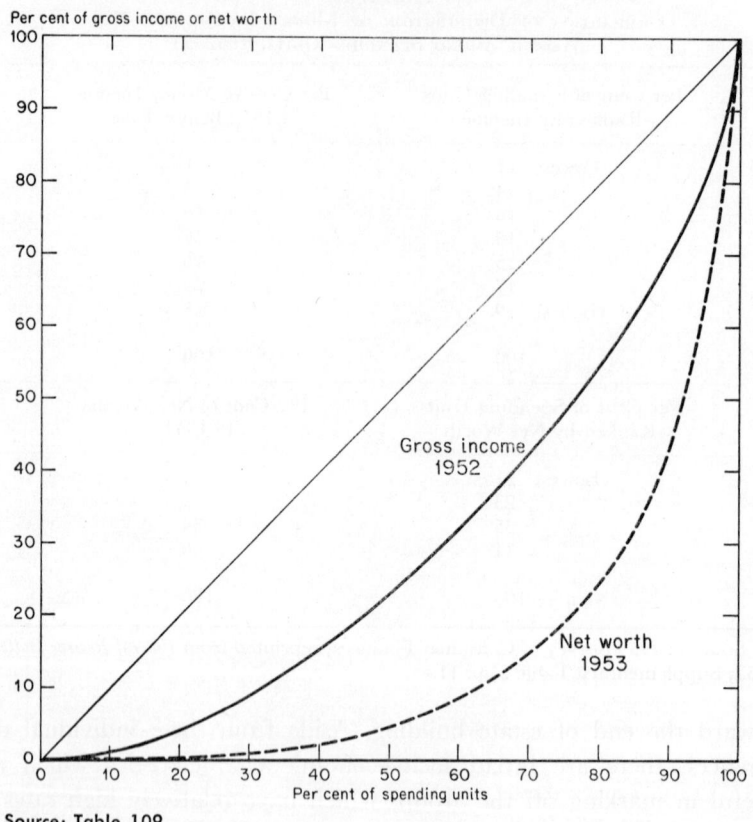

CHART 37

Lorenz Curves of Total Money Income and Net Worth Among Spending Units Ranked by Income and Net Worth

Source: Table 109.

would expect a lesser inequality of income to lead to a lesser inequality of wealth.

In this connection, it is of interest to compare inequality of wealth-holding with inequality of income. Perhaps the most sensible way to compare the two is to consider wealth distribution by itself and income distribution by itself. When this is done, as in Table 109, it is quite clear that wealth is more unequally distributed than income (Chart 37).

INEQUALITY OF WEALTH-HOLDING

The selection of the basis for ranking makes a difference. When spending units are ranked by net worth, wealth is more unequally distributed than income. (This particular finding is most relevant to the problem at hand.) The top 11 per cent of spending units ranked by net worth had only 24 per cent of the total income in 1953, but they had 60 per cent of total net worth. When spending units are ranked by income, however, the top 9 per cent are found to receive 28 per

TABLE 110
DISTRIBUTION OF INCOME AMONG ALL PERSONS, 1951

Total Money Income in 1951	Population Thousands (1)	Per Cent (2)	Aggregate Income Million Dollars (3)	Per Cent (4)
Loss	287	0.2	—	0.0
No income	79,786	52.7	—	0.0
$1 to $500	11,553	7.6	2,888	1.8
$500 to $1,000	8,968	5.9	6,726	3.7
$1,000 to $1,500	5,955	3.9	7,444	4.1
$1,500 to $2,000	6,314	4.2	11,050	6.0
$2,000 to $2,500	7,246	4.8	16,304	8.9
$2,500 to $3,000	6,385	4.2	17,559	9.6
$3,000 to $3,500	6,959	4.6	22,617	12.3
$3,500 to $4,000	5,309	3.5	19,909	10.8
$4,000 to $4,500	3,946	2.6	16,771	9.1
$4,500 to $5,000	2,296	1.5	10,906	5.9
$5,000 to $6,000	3,013	2.0	16,572	9.0
$6,000 to $7,000	1,363	0.9	8,860	4.8
$7,000 to $10,000	1,220	0.8	9,150	5.0
$10,000 to $15,000	502	0.3	6,275	3.4
$15,000 and over	430	0.3	10,750	5.8
Total	151,532	100.0	183,781	100.0

SOURCE: Cols. 1 and 2 from Herman P. Miller, *Income of the American People*, New York, 1955; col. 3 computed by multiplying midpoints of income range times col. 1, $25,000 assumed to be the average for the top income group.

cent of total money income and to hold 39 per cent of total net worth. It is also interesting to note that on this ranking by income the lowest 25 per cent have only 6 per cent of the income, but hold 14 per cent of the net worth.[6] This means that the Lorenz curves of wealth and income would cross above the middle decile when the two distributions are made with a ranking of spending units by income.

[6] 1953 Survey of Consumer Finances, reprinted from *Federal Reserve Bulletin*, 1953, Supplementary Table 5, p. 11. The cross rankings of income by net worth are not reproduced in the text but may be found in the 1953 Survey of Consumer Finances.

In the study of top wealth-holders, the unit for ranking is necessarily the individual and, hence, to have a direct basis for comparing our fragmentary data on wealth distribution with the distribution of income, we should have a distribution of income among all the individuals in the population. We have fashioned such a distribution in Table 110, which shows that over half the people in 1951 received no income and the lower three-fourths of the population received only 15.6 per cent of all income, while the top 1.4 per cent received 14.2 per cent of all income. The latter figures may be compared with the finding that the top 1.04 per cent of all persons in 1953 held 28.5 per cent of basic variant wealth. It is apparent, then, that on this basis wealth is more unequally distributed than income.

Estimate of Share of Saving of Top Wealth-Holders[7]

In 1950 the Survey of Consumer Finances indicated that the top 3 per cent of spending units (those with $60,000 and over of total assets), ranked by total assets, were responsible for about 15 per cent of all saving.[8] The top 3 per cent of spending units is a somewhat larger group than the top 1 per cent of adults referred to in Table 107, but

---

[7] A review of the literature reveals that understanding of who saves is widely recognized as a major gap in our knowledge. Thus Kuznets writes in *Shares of Upper Income Groups in Income and Savings* (New York, NBER, 1953, p. 173): "The data do not yield adequate annual estimates of even total savings of individuals, let alone savings of upper separately from those of lower income groups." Instead of giving share of savings by top groups, he merely ranked the years, saying, "we used ranks instead of the actual ratios because lack of confidence in the series on individuals' total savings made the ratios suspect" (*ibid.*, p. 178, footnote 1).

Similarly, Goldsmith observes that "one of the most serious gaps in our knowledge of the structural changes in the savings of households is the absence of information extending over long periods about the distribution of saving among saver groups of different income and wealth levels, different occupations, different ages, and other characteristics" (*A Study of Saving in the United States*, I, Princeton, 1956, p. 161). He does suggest that "the time series point to a decline in the share of upper income groups in savings due largely to an increase in the share of saving through consumer durables and through pension and retirement funds, most of which is attributable to the lower income groups, and part of which is voluntary" (*ibid.*, p. 162).

Irwin Friend and Stanley Schor conclude that "given the margin of error in the historical data on saving obtained from consumer surveys, little can be said with any certainty about the trends in the proportion of saving accounted for by the upper income groups. There is some reason to believe that this proportion has declined secularly in view of the evidence of a long-term decline in the income share of upper income groups" ("Who Saves?" in *The Review of Economics and Statistics*, May 1959, pp. 238–239).

[8] Appendix Table A-15.

INEQUALITY OF WEALTH-HOLDING

it would seem to be a fair estimate that the latter group accounted for about 15 per cent of all saving. Unfortunately, there are no similar data available on what this share was for earlier years.

There are some historical data on the share of savings of the top percentiles of income recipients. We have referred in Chapter 6 to the findings of Kuznets that income inequality declined over the period here under study. Kuznets does not make firm estimates of the share of saving of the top 1 per cent of income recipients. He does, however, provide the basis for a rough estimate assuming a constant savings-income ratio. Our estimates derived from this (Table 111) show a countercyclical change in the share of saving of the top income recipients and a long secular decline in that share. It is thus estimated that the share was 44 per cent in 1922–29, 115 per cent in 1930–39, 11 per cent in 1941–45, and 19 per cent in 1946–49.

But what is the connection between the top 1 per cent of income recipients and the top 1 per cent of wealth-holders? It would appear from inspection of Survey of Consumer Finances data that more than one-half of the top 1 per cent of income-receiving units have $60,000 or more in assets and that about one-half of those units with $60,000 in assets would have enough income to place them in the top 1 per cent of the income distribution in recent years. Thus we might deduce that the top wealth-holders would account for more than one-half of the saving of the top 1 per cent of income recipients. This assumes not merely a random association but a positive association between income and wealth in the top ranges. The share of saving of the top 3 per cent of spending units (roughly the same as the top 1 per cent of adults) was, we have already noted, 15 per cent in 1950. This checks closely with the estimate for 1946–48, which we get from Table 111. This gives us some basis for switching over to using the whole series of savings estimates in the latter table. However, it is doubtful that the overlap between the top wealth-holders and the top income recipients has always been the same as it was in 1950. This doubt arises from a series that shows what share of all property income has been received by upper income groups. Property income is, of course, a reflection of wealth-holding and hence deserves our interest. In 1948 the top 1 per cent of income recipients got about one-fourth of all property income, and property income was about one-third of the income of this group. The overlap indicated by these data would appear to have declined over the years, with a fall from one-half to one-third in the

235

TABLE 111
Calculation of Share of Saving of Top One Per Cent of Income Recipients, 1922–48

Year	Personal Disposable Income (mill. doll.) (1)	Share of Income Going to Top 1% (per cent) (2)	Income of Top 1% of Income Recipients (mill. doll.) (3)	Savings of Top 1% of Income Recipients (mill. doll.) (4)	Total Personal Saving (mill. doll.) (5)	Total Personal Saving Less Consumer Durables Saving (mill. doll.) (6)	Share of Col. 5 Saving of Top 1% of Income Recipients (per cent) (7)	Share of Col. 6 Saving of Top 1% of Income Recipients (per cent) (8)
1922	58,719	12.3	7,220	3,090	6,300	5,400	49	57
1923	68,138	11.6	7,900	3,330	9,880	7,300	34	45
1924	72,737	12.1	8,800	3,740	8,620	6,820	43	55
1925	75,510	12.9	9,700	4,160	10,740	8,110	39	51
1926	75,736	13.1	9,920	4,260	10,100	7,400	42	57
1927	77,474	13.5	10,450	4,510	10,070	8,390	45	53
1928	81,311	13.7	11,140	4,820	6,010	4,350	80	109
1929	81,156	13.6	11,040	4,780	11,490	9,540	42	50
1930	72,275	13.6	9,830	4,210	5,620	6,280	75	66
1931	61,249	13.0	7,960	3,410	+2,470	3,570		94
1932	45,982	12.7	5,840	2,490	−3,270	−1,170		
1933	44,330	11.8	5,230	2,210	−3,800	−2,310		
1934	54,272	11.6	6,290	2,640	− 950	− 290		
1935	56,807	11.1	6,310	2,640	2,350	1,790		
1936	64,709	11.6	7,510	3,190	5,280	3,510	60	91
1937	70,267	11.5	8,080	3,410	7,320	5,360	46	63
1938	64,905	10.5	6,820	2,820	3,720	3,580	76	78
1939	69,345	10.8	7,490	3,120	6,850	5,500	46	56
1940	74,392	10.4	7,740	3,210	8,540	6,310	38	51
1941	89,408	9.0	8,050	3,320	13,970	10,890	24	30
1942	110,676	7.1	7,860	3,130	33,240	31,930	9	10
1943	128,513	5.5	7,070	2,760	36,170	34,660	8	8
1944	142,878	5.7	8,140	3,090	39,300	37,640	8	8
1945	146,778	5.7	8,360	3,210	34,410	33,660	9	9
1946	158,055	6.0	9,480	3,790	22,530	16,130	17	24
1947	172,623	5.9	10,180	4,070	20,190	11,110	20	37
1948	189,617	6.3	11,950	4,780	26,720	16,190	18	29

Source: Col. 1: Total income receipts (Kuznets, *Shares of Upper Income Groups*, p. 571, Table 114, col. 11) plus imputed rent (*ibid.*, p. 578, Table 115, col. 6) minus federal income taxes (*ibid.*, p. 578, Table 115, col. 7); col. 2: *ibid.*, p. 596, Table 118, col. 4; col. 3: col. 1 times col. 2; col. 4: col. 3 times savings-income ratio (*ibid.*, p. 176, Table 47, col. 2); col. 5: Goldsmith, *Saving in U.S.*, I, p. 353; col. 6: Goldsmith, *Saving in U.S.*, I; col. 7: col. 4 divided by col. 5; col. 8: col. 4 divided by col. 6.

NOTE: There are several difficulties in this table involving the concept of saving. As mentioned in the text, the ideal concept for our purposes is the one that includes consumer durables. However, the estimate of savings done by the top income recipients in col. 4 excludes consumer durables, as does the estimate of total personal savings in col. 6. Hence the percentages in col. 8 exclude consumer durable saving and are doubtless

latter ratio from the 1920's to the 1950's.[9] One might suspect that the break in the relationship occurred with the depression.

Working from this fragmentary information, we suggest that plausible estimates (and here we are leaning toward the greatest possible drop in share) for the share of saving of the top 1 per cent of wealth-holders would be 44 per cent in the 1920's, 10 per cent in the depression and war periods, and 15 per cent in 1949–53. Applying these estimates to the share of wealth which would be held by the top group on the basis of price and composition changes[10] yields the interesting finding that such a drastic change in assumed savings patterns would not be enough to explain the drop in share of wealth which we found on an individual basis (Table 107, cols. 5 and 1). However, it is enough to explain the fall indicated on the basis of families (Table 107, col. 2). The fact that we do not find a sharp fall in share from 1929 to 1939, even with the most extreme assumption about fall in relative saving, is the principal reason for suspecting that some other factor was at work in that depression decade which must have caused a greater fall to appear in the individual wealth-holder series than in the family series. That factor, we suspect, was changing practice in transfer of wealth. If we can thus account for this divergence between the individual and the family series, it would seem fair to say that the observed fall in the family series is fully explained by price and savings changes.

The Process of Transfer of Wealth

The practices of transfer of wealth and the institutional arrangements restraining and encouraging certain kinds of transfer may increase or moderate the degree of inequality of wealth in the following generation. If those persons with large estates divide them among a larger number of heirs, donees, and beneficiaries than is generally the case for those with smaller estates, the effect will be to moderate in-

[9] See Tables 59 and 60, which show these relationships for 1919–38, and Kuznets, *Shares of Upper Income Groups*, p. 649.

[10] The method used here is the one described on p. 228. Footnote 4 is also relevant here.

---

too high on that account, since consumer durable saving is less concentrated among higher income groups than other types of saving. On the other hand, the percentages in col. 7 are probably too low since the estimate of top group saving (col. 4) excludes consumer durables, while the estimate of total saving (col. 5) includes consumer durables. However, it is the direction of change in share of saving that we are interested in here, and both col. 7 and col. 8 indicate similar changes.

equality.[11] The rate schedules of estate, inheritance, and gift taxes are designed to have that effect. These progressive tax rate schedules also tend to divert a larger share of larger estates than of smaller estates to the public sector in the form of taxes.[12] This system of rates also encourages philanthropic gifts, which remove wealth from the personal sector. A principal route of escape from the designed effect of transfer taxes—namely, the splitting up of large estates—is the use of personal trust funds, but this route occasions the loss of a considerable part of the bundle of property rights.

Taxes have two kinds of effect upon inequality: they discourage the accumulation and encourage the splitting up of large estates. The equalizing effect of the whole battery of transfer taxes, including estate, inheritance, and gift taxes, is doubtless quite substantial, although it is beyond the scope of this study to measure this effect quantitatively. Neither is it possible here to appraise in detail the direction of change in equalizing effect over recent decades. However, from examination of tax law changes, it would seem plausible to conclude that the greatest degree of equalizing occurred in the decade of the 1930's and early war years.[13] The postwar period has seen some

[11] In a study of the Wisconsin inheritance tax, Wallace I. Edwards found that estates valued at $100,000 and over had an average of more than nine beneficiaries per estate. He also found that movement of property is "what might be described as downward by somewhat less than one generation, 63 per cent of the transferees were down one generation, 11 per cent down two or more generations, 24 per cent same generation, 1 per cent up one or two generations ("Wisconsin Inheritance Taxation," unpublished Ph.D. dissertation, University of Wisconsin, 1953, pp. 139 and 313). *Statistics of Income* for 1946 and 1947 (Part I, Tables 7 and 9) show the number of estate tax returns by heirs, devisees, and legatees and also the number of returns by number of children. Of 20,899 returns in 1946, 6,774 report no children; 5,899 report that the recipients of bequests are children only. The data suggest that larger estates tend to have more heirs than smaller estates.

[12] G. Z. Fijalkowski-Bereday, in his paper on "The Equalizing Effects of the Death Duties" (*Oxford Economic Papers,* June 1950, pp. 176–196), concludes that a higher death tax has its main effect on the main bequest. On the other hand, William McKinstry comes to exactly the opposite conclusion in his study of Connecticut inheritance tax data. (See his unpublished Ph.D. dissertation, "An Estimate of the Impact of Increasing Death Tax Rates on Beneficiaries of Federally Taxable Estates," Yale University, 1959.)

[13] In 1932 the exemption was dropped from $100,000 to $50,000 and in 1935 to $40,000. At the same time the maximum rate of tax went from 20 per cent on that portion of the estate over $10 million to 70 per cent on that portion over $50 million. Maximum rates on the gift tax were doubled. For a brief summary of tax changes from 1913 to 1940, see Sidney Ratner, *American Taxation,* New York, 1942, Appendix Table 3. A more recent and detailed account is that of Louis Eisenstein, "The Rise and Decline of the Estate Tax," *Federal Tax Policy for Economic Growth and Stability,* U.S. Congress, Joint Committee on the Economic Report, Washington, 1955, pp. 819–847. Also see the special issue of the *California Law Review* (March 1950), which offers a critique of estate and gift taxation.

relaxing of this effect due to the rise in number of persons with estates subject to tax and to legislative changes designed to reduce the severity of the taxes. Most noteworthy among the latter changes was the introduction of the marital deduction on the estate tax, and the extension to residents of all states of community property rights for both federal income and gift tax purposes in 1948.[14]

The timing of transfers is also an important determinant of inequality. If estates are customarily held in the name of the patriarch or matriarch until his or her death, the effect will be greater inequality than if estates are divided well in advance of the year of death. Gifts and bequests to grandchildren rather than to children also tend to moderate inequality. Laws which permit women and minors to hold property influence this pattern. Community property law is also relevant here. As an increasing percentage of the population is found in states with this law, the degree of inequality among persons should be lessened. Widespread ownership of life insurance would alter the age at which persons appear in the higher estate sizes, to the extent that life insurance beneficiaries include more relatively young people than are found among all heirs.

On the other hand, rising longevity would tend to delay the division of estates and to increase the average age of heirs, thereby increasing inequality. In the period 1922–53 the adult population became markedly older (Table 112). This, in itself, was clearly a factor which increased inequality. In 1922, 54 per cent of the adult population were in the 20 to 40 age bracket and 5 per cent were over 70. In 1953, only 45 per cent were aged 20 to 40 and 7 per cent were 70 or older. By setting the number of top wealth-holders per 100 in the age groups (as found for 1953 in Table 113) and the

---

[14] For a discussion of this and related matters, see C. Lowell Harriss, "Erosion of the Federal Estate and Gift Tax Bases," *Proceedings of 48th Annual Conference of National Tax Association*, 1955, pp. 350–358. Also of interest is G. S. A. Wheatcroft, "The Anti-Avoidance Provisions of the Law of Estate Duty in the United Kingdom," *National Tax Journal*, March 1957, pp. 46–56. A most ingenious effort to measure the combined effect of personal income, gift, and estate taxes upon the distribution of wealth is that of Charles Stewart, published in 1938. He related income and property classes to each other, projected the accumulation of estate by classes by assuming a consumption function. He then compared the distribution of wealth at the beginning and end of a thirty-year period. He concluded that the top 11 per cent of income recipients (considering only the groups with more than $5,000 income), who owned 57 per cent of property in 1930, would increase their share of property to 61 per cent in thirty years if no personal taxes upon income or wealth were imposed. However, he concluded, 1936 tax rates would reduce their share of property to 51 per cent. (Gerhard Colm and Fritz Lehmann, *Economic Consequences of Recent American Tax Policy*, Supplement I, New York, 1938, Appendix A.)

average estate size by age (as found for 1953 in Table 45) against the changing age and sex[15] composition (Table 112), we are able to quantify the effect of aging upon inequality. The hypothetical share of the top 1 per cent of adults rises, due to aging, by 2 percentage points on a base of 20. The rise is slightly higher if we use 1922 estate size by age and number of top wealth-holders per 100 in 1922 relationships; in that case the share of the top 1 per cent rises from 30 to 35 due to aging. It should seem fair to conclude, then, that if there had been no other changes but the aging of the adult population, the share of the top 1 per cent would have risen from 32 per cent in 1922 to about 35 per cent in 1953. That is to say, in order to obtain the observed fall in share of wealth, there had to be factors at work to

TABLE 112
Composition of Total Adult Population, by Sex and Age Group, 1922 and 1953
(millions)

Age Group	1922		1953	
	Male	Female	Male	Female
20 to 40	17.2	16.8	23.1	23.7
40 to 60	10.8	9.6	18.2	18.6
60 to 70	2.7	2.4	5.7	6.0
70 and over	1.4	1.5	3.6	4.4
Total	32.1	30.3	50.6	52.7

more than offset the increasing-inequality effect of aging. (Aging is not here considered to have an effect separate from the saving and price change effects.)

That there were such factors is apparent from the age data on top wealth-holders. While the total adult population was getting older, the top wealth-holders were getting younger. Adjusting the percentage of the population for comparability, it appears that the median age of the top 1 per cent of the population fell from 57 in 1922 to 55 in 1953 (despite the fact that for women the median age rose from 53 to 56). The percentage of each age-sex group who were top wealth-holders in the two years is shown in Table 113. (Top wealth-holders were a smaller part of the total population in 1922 than in 1953.)

It would appear, then, that top wealth has been shifted to younger

[15] The higher percentage of women, in itself, would lead to a prediction of a lower frequency of top wealth-holders.

INEQUALITY OF WEALTH-HOLDING

TABLE 113
Top Wealth-Holders as a Percentage of Total Adult Population, by Sex and Age Group, 1922 and 1953

Age Group	1922		1953	
	Male	Female	Male	Female
20 to 40	0.3	0.1	0.8	0.3
40 to 60	1.7	0.6	3.2	1.2
60 to 70	2.7	1.0	3.9	1.7
70 and over	3.5	1.4	4.0	2.6

Source: For 1922, Appendix Table A-5; for 1953, Table 35.

TABLE 114
Actual and Hypothetical (Assuming 1922 Frequency Rates) Number of Top Wealth-Holders, by Sex and Age Group, 1953

Age Group	Number of Top Wealth Holders		Col. 1 Minus Col. 2 (3)	Col. 3 ÷ Col. 1 (4)	Average Gross Estate 1953 (dollars) (5)	Col. 3 Times Col. 5 (billion dollars) (6)
	Actual 1953 (1)	1953, Assuming 1922 Frequency Rates (2)				
			MALES			
20 to 40	184,800	69,300	115,500	.63	120,000	13.9
40 to 60	582,400	309,400	273,300	.47	170,000	45.9
60 to 70	222,300	153,900	68,400	.31	180,000	12.6
70 and over	144,000	126,000	18,000	.12	210,000	4.0
Total	1,133,500	658,600	474,900	.42	162,000	76.4
			FEMALES			
20 to 40	71,100	23,700	47,700	.66	350,000	17.5
40 to 60	223,200	111,600	111,600	.50	190,000	20.9
60 to 70	102,000	60,000	42,000	.58	180,000	7.6
70 and over	114,400	61,600	42,800	.37	210,000	8.4
Total	510,700	256,900	253,800	.50	220,000	54.4
			TOTAL			
Total	1,644,200	915,500	728,700	.45	182,000	130.8

Source: Col. 1, Table 35; Col. 2, Table 113; Col. 5, Table 38.

people and to women. It is possible to measure this effect for 1922–53 by comparing the actual number of top wealth-holders in 1953 with the number there would have been had the frequencies of top wealth-holders which obtained in 1922 held for 1953 (Table 114). This assumes that the total population and age-sex composition of 1953 are constant. Instead of the actual number of 1.6 million, there would have been 0.9 million top wealth-holders, or 0.7 million fewer.

Columns 3 and 4 of Table 114 make it quite clear that it was women and young people who added relatively great numbers of top wealth-holders to their ranks. Of the 728,700 "additional" wealth-holders, 253,800 are women and 115,500 are men under 40. Only 86,400 of them are men over 60. It would seem hard to explain this differential growth in numbers on any ground other than a change in the method and timing of transfer of wealth. Thus, it would seem unlikely that either price change or savings practices could have been responsible. We would, of course, expect the percentage of the total population with over $60,000 of wealth to rise over this period because the average wealth of all adults rose from $5,342 in 1922 to $11,968 in 1953. However, we would expect the frequencies of top wealth-holders to rise more evenly for all age and sex groups. Increased employment of women and increased frequency of widowhood would lead one to predict a differential rise in the percentage of women top wealth-holders, but it seems doubtful that such a dramatic rise would have occurred on this account alone.

Suppose we assume that the whole difference in number of top wealth-holders is due to changes in transfer practice, that is, more gifts to wives and children, more families living in community property states, and so forth. Following this assumption, what shift in inequality of wealth-holding could be explained by the change in transfer practice? In 1953 1.6 million people actually held $298 billion of basic variant gross estate (calculated from Table 114). This is compatible with 1 per cent of the adult population holding 19 per cent of the aggregate gross estate. If the $298 billion had been held by only the 915,500 people shown in column 2 of Table 114, there would be a much more unequal distribution of wealth, with the top 1 per cent holding 24 per cent.

In one respect, this tends to overstate the effect of splitting and earlier transfers, since, as suggested above, there are other factors which have contributed to the higher frequency of top wealth-holders in all age and sex groups. This is offset to some extent by the fact that we do not take account of the splitting which drops people below $60,000 in 1953. All things considered, it would seem plausible that changes in transfer practices could account for a fall of several percentage points in the share of wealth of the top 1 per cent. It will be recalled that by relating price change and changes in savings to the 1922 share, we were able to explain all but three points of the fall from 32 per cent of total wealth in 1922 to 25 per cent in 1953.

INEQUALITY OF WEALTH-HOLDING

An alternative way to rationalize the effect of splitting is as follows. Note first that the top 1 per cent of adults held 25 per cent of all wealth (gross estate, total wealth variant), or about $310 billion. To have held 28 per cent, they would have needed $347 billion, or $36 billion more than they actually held. Does it seem reasonable that $36 billion could be accounted for by attributing family holdings to one person? By 1922 standards, in which year 8.5 per cent of the top wealth-holders were wives, there should have been 85,000 wives in the 1953 top wealth-holder group, but in fact there were 18 per cent, or 180,000.[16] This difference of about 95,000 we can throw out of the top 1 per cent, leaving their wealth with their husbands, and in their place bring in another 95,000 persons from below the cut-off. For the top 1 per cent this cut-off is at about the $100,000 range. Multiplying 95,000 times $100,000 gives us $9.5 billion out of the $36 billion. In addition to this, it may be assumed that some of the 600,000 married men in the top 1 per cent had wives with less wealth than the $100,000 and hence who were not in the top 1 per cent. Suppose we say that this number was about 300,000 and that each of them had $50,000. This would yield a total of $15 billion. Hence splitting wealth with wives might account for about $24.5 billion, leaving about $11 billion to be explained by splits with other family members. Table 114 suggests that a good deal of increase in splitting with younger men may have occurred between 1922 and 1953, so that it would seem reasonable to account for the $11 billion in this way.

We conclude that there are two alternative ways to account for the discrepancy between the individual and the family series. The fact that the share of wealth held by the top 1 per cent of individuals fell by three percentage points more than the share held by the top 2 per cent of "families" (as defined in Chapter 6) is due, we submit, to changing practices in the transfer of wealth.

---

[16] It was noted in Chapter 6 that married women form an increasingly important part of the top wealth-holding group. This is presumably due largely to the increasing importance of community property states and to the increasing frequency of overt gifts from husbands to wives and from parents to daughters. One independent check upon the data given in Chapter 6 is the percentage of individual income tax returns filed by married women, i.e., wives filing separate returns. This was 1.9 per cent in 1922 and 3.2 per cent in 1938. These are the best years for such a comparison since the total number of returns were about the same in those two years and legal provisions about filing separate returns were not notably different. A good continuous series on this relationship cannot be developed, unfortunately. Ideally, we would like to have the number of returns by marital status for property income only, by size of income. This series is not available to us.

Summary Statement on Causes of Changes in Wealth Inequality, 1922–53

Four separate factors are seen to have contributed to the fall in the share of wealth held by the top 1 per cent of adults. This share was 32 per cent in 1922, rose to 38 per cent in 1929, fell to 22 per cent in 1949, and rose to 25 per cent in 1953 (see Table 107, col. 1). Relative change in the price of assets explains the turning points in this share, but does not explain the secular drop. Indeed, if only price changes had occurred, there would have been much greater inequality in 1953 than in 1922 (see Table 107, col. 3). A second change we have noted is the shift in composition of estate. In the boom periods of 1922–29 and 1949–53, the top group reduced its concentration upon price-sensitive assets and this tended to cut its share somewhat (see Table 107, col. 4). A third change—one which cut its share substantially between 1939 and 1949—was a reduction in the share of all saving of the top group (see Table 107, col. 5). Varying price, composition, and share of saving leads to a prediction of a fall in share from 32 per cent in 1922 to 28 per cent in 1953 (Table 107). However, the actual fall was to 25 per cent. This three-point discrepancy is explained by changing practices in the transfer of wealth. These changing practices, which have led to a sharp increase over the thirty-year period in the number of women and younger persons among top wealth-holders, include a larger population in community property states, more gifts by living persons to wives and other family members, and more use of life insurance. The discrepancy between column 5 and column 1 in Table 107 is thus found to be reconcilable with the fact that the share of wealth held by the top 2 per cent of families fell less than the share of the top 1 per cent of adults (see col. 6).

In making predictions of the future share of wealth which will be held by the top group, attention should be given to these four changes. In the future the two most important changes to watch are differential price changes (which have been very important in 1953–60) and changes in the share of saving of the top 1 per cent. As long as the top 1 per cent accounts for as little as 15 per cent of all saving, this will be a heavy drag on their share of all wealth. Recent experience suggests that changes in composition of estate and in transfer practice can be expected to have relatively little influence in determining the share of wealth to be found in the hands of the next generation of top wealth-holders.

Appendix A: Underlying Data and Estimates

TABLE A-1

Estate Tax Returns Filed in 1954 for Male Decedents with Gross Estate Sizes of $60,000 to $70,000 in Non-Community Property States, by Age Group and Type of Property

Type of Property (thousand dollars)

Age Group	No. of Returns	Real Estate	U.S. Govt. Bonds	State and Local Bonds	Other Bonds	Stock	Cash	Mortgages and Notes	Life Insurance	Misc. Property	Gross Estate	Debt and Mortgages
Under 21	1	16	8	—	—	16	—	—	—	20	60	—
21 to 30	3	46	—	—	—	45	6	4	65	28	195	47
30 to 40	15	208	7	—	—	31	78	9	343	313	990	142
40 to 50	80	1,559	354	1	4	630	571	127	990	1,014	5,249	439
50 to 55	119	2,623	414	—	11	973	882	167	1,404	1,285	7,760	585
55 to 60	180	3,971	843	3	69	1,275	1,482	318	2,362	1,482	11,805	821
60 to 65	205	4,199	1,086	—	23	2,159	1,977	523	2,019	1,510	13,495	695
65 to 70	282	6,449	1,453	3	84	2,802	2,892	805	2,058	1,954	18,501	921
70 to 75	301	7,257	1,415	35	110	3,160	3,546	890	1,626	1,608	19,648	690
75 to 80	312	7,447	1,671	11	128	3,688	3,823	1,081	1,186	1,369	20,404	564
80 to 85	253	6,380	1,463	26	185	3,019	3,152	739	578	880	16,422	393
85 and over	246	6,778	1,706	49	218	3,115	2,504	630	442	658	16,099	364
Age unknown	92	2,504	460	12	67	875	935	183	306	613	5,956	297

UNDERLYING DATA AND ESTIMATES

TABLE A-2
ESTATE TAX RETURNS FILED IN 1954 FOR FEMALE DECEDENTS IN COMMUNITY PROPERTY STATES, BY AGE GROUP AND TYPE OF PROPERTY

Type of Property (thousand dollars)

Age Group	No. of Returns	Real Estate	U.S. Govt. Bonds	State and Local Bonds	Other Bonds	Stock	Cash	Mortgages and Notes	Life Insurance	Misc. Property	Gross Estate	Debts and Mortgages	Economic Estate
Under 21	1	7	—	29	—	4	—	—	5	359	404	4	400
21 to 30	2	46	2	—	—	70	15	—	6	35	174	10	164
30 to 40	19	896	493	84	47	2,669	221	108	177	469	5,164	656	4,508
40 to 50	77	5,082	551	21	75	4,067	1,331	630	252	4,102	16,114	1,789	14,325
50 to 55	87	5,324	717	294	66	2,104	1,102	692	214	4,637	15,149	1,413	13,736
55 to 60	130	6,318	2,048	168	34	6,635	2,001	1,433	374	2,604	21,615	1,133	20,482
60 to 65	190	10,917	1,705	1,539	120	10,298	4,558	1,651	445	4,819	36,051	1,629	34,422
65 to 70	292	13,926	3,081	844	318	15,104	6,086	3,374	451	5,331	48,516	2,048	46,468
70 to 75	348	17,476	4,964	3,077	332	24,844	7,213	2,503	589	2,968	63,965	2,474	61,491
75 to 80	409	21,251	4,740	1,984	760	26,819	8,790	2,484	643	6,353	73,824	2,989	70,835
80 to 85	407	20,157	4,862	783	830	27,014	9,236	3,292	470	4,767	71,412	1,523	69,889
85 and over	437	26,151	5,846	1,600	938	33,935	8,815	1,959	363	4,113	83,720	2,410	81,310
Age unknown	88	4,599	657	86	231	2,492	1,395	581	103	706	10,849	1,046	9,803

UNDERLYING DATA AND ESTIMATES

TABLE A-3
WHITE AND ADJUSTED MORTALITY RATES AND MULTIPLIERS, FOR BOTH SEXES, BY AGE GROUP, 1922, 1924, 1944, 1946, AND 1947

Age Group	1922				1924			
	White Mortality Rates	Adjusted Mortality Rates	White Multipliers	Adjusted Multipliers	White Mortality Rates	Adjusted Mortality Rates	White Multipliers	Adjusted Multipliers
20 to 30	3.9	2.6	256.4	384.6	3.6	2.4	277.8	416.7
30 to 40	5.4	4.2	185.1	238.1	5.2	4.1	192.3	243.9
40 to 50	8.5	6.5	117.6	153.8	8.5	6.5	117.6	153.8
50 to 60	16.0	14.1	62.5	70.9	15.9	14.0	62.9	71.4
60 to 70	35.1	32.6	28.5	30.7	34.2	31.8	29.2	31.4
70 to 80	69.0	64.4	14.4	15.5	67.5	63.0	14.8	15.9
80 and over	140.3	130.5	7.1	7.7	139.7	129.9	7.2	7.7

Age Group	1944			1946		
	White Mortality Rates	White Multipliers	Adjusted Multipliers	White Mortality Rates	White Multipliers	Adjusted Multipliers
20 to 30	2.1	485.4	714.3	1.6	611.0	937.0
30 to 40	3.1	321.5	416.7	2.5	396.4	510.9
40 to 55	6.7	149.3	263.2	6.9	144.5	178.9
55 to 65	19.7	50.9	55.2	18.7	53.6	58.1
65 to 75	44.9	22.3	23.5	42.9	23.3	24.6
75 to 85	107.0	9.3	10.1	98.8	10.1	11.0
85 and over	221.4	4.5	4.8	234.8	4.2	4.6

Age Group	1947			
	White Mortality Rates	Adjusted Mortality Rates	White Multipliers	Adjusted Multipliers
Under 20	1.1	0.8	909.1	1,250.0
20 to 30	1.5	1.0	666.7	1,000.0
30 to 40	2.4	1.9	416.7	526.3
40 to 50	5.4	4.1	185.1	243.9
50 to 55	10.3	8.7	97.1	114.9
55 to 60	15.2	14.0	65.8	71.4
60 to 65	23.4	21.5	42.7	46.5
65 to 70	36.1	34.0	27.7	29.4
70 to 75	54.7	52.0	18.3	19.2
75 and over	120.2	111.7	8.3	9.0

TABLE A-4

White Mortality Rates and White and Adjusted Multipliers, by Sex and Age Group, 1922 and 1947–50

	1922				1947			1948			1949			1950		
Age Group	White Mortality Rates	White Multipliers	Adjusted Multipliers	Age Group	White Mortality Rates	White Multipliers	Adjusted Multipliers	White Mortality Rates	White Multipliers	Adjusted Multipliers	White Mortality Rates	White Multipliers	Adjusted Multipliers	White Mortality Rates	White Multipliers	Adjusted Multipliers
							MALES									
20 to 30	3.9	256.4	384.6	Under 20	1.4	714.3	1,000.0	1.4	714.3	1,000.0	1.3	769.2	1,111.1	1.3	769.2	1,111.1
30 to 40	5.6	178.6	227.3	20 to 30	1.9	526.3	762.2	1.8	555.6	833.3	1.7	588.2	909.1	1.7	588.2	909.1
40 to 50	9.0	111.1	144.9	30 to 40	2.9	344.8	434.8	2.7	370.4	476.2	2.6	384.6	500.0	2.5	400.0	500.0
50 to 60	17.2	58.1	66.2	40 to 50	6.7	149.3	196.1	6.5	153.8	200.0	6.3	158.7	208.3	6.2	161.3	212.8
60 to 70	37.4	26.7	28.7	50 to 55	13.2	75.8	90.1	13.0	76.9	91.7	12.4	80.6	96.2	12.1	82.6	98.0
70 to 80	72.2	13.9	14.9	55 to 60	19.4	51.5	55.9	19.0	52.6	56.8	18.7	53.5	57.8	18.8	53.2	57.5
80 and over	143.2	7.0	7.5	60 to 65	29.2	34.2	37.3	28.5	35.1	38.2	28.2	35.5	38.6	28.1	35.6	38.8
				65 to 70	43.7	22.9	24.3	43.4	23.0	24.4	43.0	23.3	24.7	40.7	24.6	26.1
				70 to 75	63.7	15.7	16.5	63.1	15.8	16.7	62.6	16.0	16.8	60.4	16.6	17.4
				75 to 85	128.6	7.8	8.4	127.6	7.8	8.5	126.0	7.9	8.6	105.3	9.5	10.3
				85 and over										221.1	4.5	4.9
							FEMALES									
20 to 30	3.9	256.4	384.6	Under 20	.8	125.0	1,666.7	.7	1,428.6	2,000.0	.6	1,428.6	2,000.0	.6	1,666.7	2,500.0
30 to 40	5.3	188.7	243.9	20 to 30	1.1	909.1	1,428.6	1.1	909.1	1,428.6	.9	1,111.1	1,666.7	.9	1,111.1	1,666.7
40 to 50	7.9	126.6	166.7	30 to 40	1.9	426.3	666.7	1.8	555.6	714.3	1.7	588.2	769.2	1.6	625.0	769.2
50 to 60	14.7	68.1	77.5	40 to 50	4.1	243.9	322.6	3.8	263.2	344.8	3.7	270.3	357.1	3.6	277.8	370.4
60 to 70	32.7	30.6	32.9	50 to 55	7.1	135.1	161.3	7.1	140.8	166.7	6.8	147.1	175.4	6.6	151.5	181.8
70 to 80	65.7	15.2	16.4	55 to 60	11.0	90.9	98.0	10.6	94.3	102.0	10.2	98.0	106.4	10.2	98.0	106.4
80 and over	137.6	7.3	7.8	60 to 65	17.5	57.1	62.1	16.8	59.5	64.9	16.1	62.1	67.6	16.2	61.7	67.1
				65 to 70	28.9	34.6	36.8	28.1	35.6	37.7	27.5	36.4	38.6	25.2	39.7	42.2
				70 to 75	46.6	21.5	22.6	45.3	22.1	23.3	44.4	22.5	23.7	42.6	23.5	24.7
				75 to 85	113.2	8.8	9.6	111.2	9.0	9.7	108.1	9.3	10.0	84.8	11.8	12.8
				85 and over										196.8	5.1	5.5

UNDERLYING DATA AND ESTIMATES

TABLE A-5
Distribution of Economic Estate[a] by Age Group, Based on Adjusted Mortality Rates, 1922, 1944, and 1946

Age Group	Number of Wealth-Holders			Economic Estate	
	Male	Female	Total	Total (million dollars)	Average (dollars)
1922[b]					
Under 30	11,538	3,077	14,615	1,269	86,842
30 to 40	37,732	12,439	50,171	7,307	145,636
40 to 50	82,883	26,505	109,388	15,673	143,279
50 to 60	97,115	26,815	123,930	22,951	185,185
60 to 70	72,668	22,964	95,632	18,837	196,977
70 to 80	38,725	15,006	53,731	11,900	221,468
80 and over	10,448	5,632	16,080	3,394	211,088
Total	389,645	127,725	517,370	81,331	157,201
1944[b]					
Under 30			72,144	9,572	132,674
30 to 40			82,090	10,626	129,441
40 to 50			183,450		
40 to 55				41,632	147,634
50 to 55			98,294		
55 to 65			152,738	27,434	179,617
65 to 75			105,468	23,230	220,254
75 to 85			45,218	10,375	229,437
85 and over			7,747	1,791	231,238
Total			782,173	104,972	134,206
1946[c]					
Under 30			66,527	10,963	164,789
30 to 40			97,582	14,969	153,403
40 to 55			386,424	54,260	140,417
55 to 65			232,636	36,905	158,639
65 to 75			140,843	23,414	166,244
75 to 85			61,564	10,656	173,083
85 and over			10,138	2,000	197,287
Total			995,843	153,168	153,807

SOURCE: Derived from findings based on white mortality rates in Mendershausen's study in Raymond Goldsmith, *A Study of Saving in the United States*, III, Princeton, 1956, Tables E-41, E-38, and E-44.

[a] After insurance correction.
[b] Including age unknown.
[c] Excluding age unknown.

TABLE A-6
DISTRIBUTION OF GROSS ESTATE[a] BY AGE GROUP, BASED ON ADJUSTED MORTALITY RATES, 1947–50

Age Group	Number of Wealth-Holders			Gross Estate Male Female Total (million dollars)			Average Gross Estate Male Female (dollars)	
	Male	Female	Total	Male	Female	Total	Male	Female
				1947				
Under 21			5,000					
21 to 30			36,000					
30 to 40			94,208					
40 to 50			269,997					
50 to 55			145,923					
55 to 60			141,443					
60 to 65			116,622					
65 to 70			87,465					
70 to 75			66,509					
75 and over			79,578					
Total			1,042,745					
				1948				
Under 21	3,000	2,000	5,000	318	244	562	106,000	122,000
21 to 30	24,999	18,572	43,571	3,054	3,324	6,378	122,165	178,979
30 to 40	90,002	41,429	131,431	14,316	6,337	20,653	159,063	152,960
40 to 50	193,200	66,891	260,091	34,462	12,296	46,731	178,375	183,821
50 to 55	101,970	37,508	139,478	16,778	5,399	22,177	164,539	143,943
55 to 60	93,095	38,964	132,059	16,737	7,496	24,233	179,784	192,382
60 to 65	82,474	32,385	114,859	14,360	7,135	21,495	174,115	220,318
65 to 70	53,924	29,858	83,782	12,067	5,383	17,450	223,778	180,287
70 to 75	42,919	26,469	69,388	8,583	4,780	13,373	199,981	180,589
75 and over	47,524	36,850	84,374	11,634	7,237	18,971	244,803	196,391
Total	733,107	330,926	1,064,033	132,309	59,614	191,923	180,477	180,143
				1949				
Under 21	6,667	2,000	8,667	667	286	953	100,045	143,000
21 to 30	27,273	21,667	48,940	5,020	2,480	7,500	184,065	114,460
30 to 40	88,000	31,537	119,537	14,037	6,216	20,253	159,511	197,102
40 to 50	201,843	78,205	280,048	35,273	11,956	47,229	174,755	152,880
50 to 55	116,979	41,921	158,900	20,612	9,466	30,078	176,202	225,806
55 to 60	101,439	41,602	143,041	17,835	7,894	25,729	175,820	189,750
60 to 65	84,688	40,222	124,910	16,128	7,777	23,905	190,440	193,352
65 to 70	59,922	31,999	91,921	11,271	5,638	16,909	188,095	176,193
70 to 75	42,722	28,724	71,446	8,508	5,386	13,894	199,148	187,509
75 and over	50,258	41,290	91,548	10,659	7,699	18,358	212,086	186,462
Total	779,791	359,167	1,138,958	140,010	64,798	204,808	179,664	180,412
				1950				
Under 21	5,556	5,000	10,556	677	665	1,342	121,850	133,000
21 to 30	37,273	11,666	48,939	5,782	1,798	7,580	155,126	154,123
30 to 40	90,000	27,690	117,690	12,885	5,219	18,104	143,167	188,480
40 to 50	210,034	78,895	288,929	36,950	14,294	51,244	175,924	181,178
50 to 55	120,932	53,996	174,928	21,458	8,305	29,763	177,439	153,808
55 to 60	109,940	43,412	153,352	20,657	8,732	29,389	187,893	201,143
60 to 65	92,111	45,158	137,269	17,410	7,221	24,631	189,011	159,905
65 to 70	70,679	38,106	108,785	13,724	6,674	20,398	194,174	175,143
70 to 75	49,033	31,913	80,946	10,580	15,626	26,206	215,773	489,644
75 and over	56,201	47,221	103,422	12,547	9,231	21,778	223,252	195,485
Total	841,759	383,057	1,224,816	152,670	77,767	230,435	181,370	203,017

[a] No insurance adjustment has been made and no correction has been made for returns with age unspecified.

TABLE A-7
Distribution of Gross Estate[a] by Estate Size, Based on Adjusted Mortality Rates, 1948–50

Gross Estate Size (thous. dollars)	Number of Wealth-Holders			Gross Estate (million dollars)		
	Male	Female	Total	Male	Female	Total
1948						
Under 60	861	86	947	47	4	51
60 to 70	78,624	52,556	131,180	5,142	3,424	8,567
70 to 80	82,510	41,221	123,731	6,187	3,081	9,268
80 to 90	75,828	36,681	112,509	6,444	3,097	9,541
90 to 100	63,572	27,309	90,881	6,013	2,585	8,598
100 to 120	104,946	40,644	145,590	11,454	4,475	15,929
120 to 150	95,607	39,987	135,594	12,799	5,388	18,187
150 to 200	83,222	30,069	113,291	14,319	5,185	19,504
200 to 300	75,321	28,568	103,889	18,256	6,893	25,149
300 to 500	40,044	16,217	56,261	15,199	5,916	21,115
500 to 1,000	23,805	13,230	37,035	16,547	8,766	24,313
1,000 to 2,000	6,897	3,237	10,134	9,547	4,301	13,848
2,000 to 3,000	748	287	1,035	1,719	684	2,403
3,000 to 5,000	613	247	860	2,350	1,026	3,376
5,000 to 10,000	156	529	685	1,063	3,706	4,769
10,000 and over	358	65	423	5,222	1,085	6,307
Total	733,107	330,926	1,064,033	132,310	59,618	191,928
1949						
Under 60	197	241	438	10	12	22
60 to 70	84,551	47,239	131,790	5,508	3,077	8,585
70 to 80	87,134	54,722	141,856	6,530	4,105	10,635
80 to 90	76,946	39,228	116,174	6,519	3,328	9,847
90 to 100	70,957	30,668	101,625	6,729	2,913	9,642
100 to 120	108,985	40,966	149,951	11,927	4,491	16,418
120 to 150	106,364	48,377	154,741	14,105	6,480	20,585
150 to 200	88,227	39,639	127,866	15,155	6,938	22,093
200 to 300	80,254	22,807	103,061	19,276	5,546	24,822
300 to 500	42,115	18,940	61,055	15,962	7,145	23,107
500 to 1,000	24,946	10,524	35,470	17,000	7,253	24,253
1,000 to 2,000	5,965	3,093	9,058	7,781	4,260	12,041
2,000 to 3,000	1,211	1,658	2,869	2,901	4,273	7,174
3,000 to 5,000	1,555	751	2,306	6,601	2,650	9,251
5,000 to 10,000	144	314	458	916	2,327	3,243
10,000 and over	242	—	242	3,090	—	3,090
Total	779,791	359,167	1,138,958	140,010	64,798	204,810

(continued)

UNDERLYING DATA AND ESTIMATES

TABLE A-7 (concluded)

Gross Estate Size (thous. dollars)	Number of Wealth-Holders			Gross Estate (million dollars)		
	Male	Female	Total	Male	Female	Total
1950						
Under 60	709	67	776	40	4	44
60 to 70	89,219	53,394	142,613	5,826	3,474	9,301
70 to 80	100,392	49,776	150,168	7,529	3,733	11,262
80 to 90	84,625	45,375	130,000	7,198	3,851	11,049
90 to 100	72,172	34,396	106,568	6,840	3,246	10,086
100 to 120	114,066	45,478	159,544	12,498	4,963	17,461
120 to 150	119,715	43,365	163,080	15,986	5,757	21,743
150 to 200	96,063	36,784	132,847	16,576	6,441	23,016
200 to 300	78,810	32,948	111,758	19,091	8,153	27,244
300 to 500	49,003	23,953	72,956	18,390	9,175	27,565
500 to 1,000	25,393	11,753	37,146	16,851	8,910	25,761
1,000 to 2,000	8,529	4,441	12,970	11,757	7,413	19,171
2,000 to 3,000	1,758	332	2,090	4,389	3,060	7,449
3,000 to 5,000	433	778	1,211	1,686	5,259	6,945
5,000 to 10,000	687	179	866	5,147	1,079	6,226
10,000 and over	194	38	232	2,864	3,248	6,112
Total	841,759	383,057	1,224,816	152,670	77,767	230,435

a No insurance adjustment has been made and no correction has been made for returns with age unspecified.

UNDERLYING DATA AND ESTIMATES

TABLE A-8
DISTRIBUTION OF ECONOMIC ESTATE BY AGE GROUP, BASED ON WHITE RATES, BEFORE AND AFTER CORRECTIONS FOR INSURANCE AND FOR AGE UNSPECIFIED, 1922, 1944, AND 1946

Age Group	Number of Wealth-Holders		Total Economic Estate	
	Before Age Correction	After Age Correction	Before Insurance Correction	After Insurance Correction
1922				
Under 30	9,700		1.8%	1.2%
30 to 40	40,200		8.4	8.2
40 to 50	86,000		18.2	16.9
50 to 60	113,300		28.6	28.5
60 to 70	92,100		23.9	24.9
70 and over	66,000		19.1	20.3
70 to 80			14.9	15.8
80 and over			4.2	4.5
Total	407,200	454,154	$74.4 bill.	$70.0 bill.
1944				
Under 30	49,000		6.5%	6.2%
30 to 40	63,300		8.4	7.8
40 to 55	228,000		33.4	30.2
55 to 65	140,900		23.3	24.1
65 to 75	100,200		18.9	21.0
75 and over	48,900		9.5	10.7
75 to 85			8.1	9.1
85 and over			1.4	1.6
Total	630,400	659,767	$117.8 bill.	$105.0 bill.
1946				
Under 30	43,400		5.7%	5.5%
30 to 40	75,700		7.7	8.9
40 to 55	293,300		31.8	33.6
55 to 65	212,900		26.9	26.1
65 to 75	132,900		18.1	17.0
75 and over	65,700		9.8	8.9
75 to 85			8.2	7.5
85 and over			1.6	1.4
Total	823,800	858,949	$145.6 bill.	$130.5 bill.

SOURCE: Mendershausen in Goldsmith, *Saving in U.S.*, III, Tables E-37, E-38, E-43, and E-44.

UNDERLYING DATA AND ESTIMATES

TABLE A-9
Distribution of Gross Estate[a] by Age Group, Based on White Mortality Rates, 1947–50 and 1953

Age Group	Number of Wealth-Holders			Gross Estate		
	Male	Female	Total	Male	Female	Total
			1947			
Under 21			3,636			
21 to 30			24,001			
30 to 40			74,589			
40 to 50			204,906			
50 to 55			123,317			
55 to 60			130,350			
60 to 65			107,092			
65 to 70			82,407			
70 to 75			63,391			
75 and over			73,389			
Total			887,078			
			1948			
Under 21	2,143	1,429	3,572	227	174	401
21 to 30	16,668	11,818	28,486	2,036	2,115	4,151
30 to 40	70,006	32,225	102,231	11,135	4,929	16,064
40 to 50	148,571	51,061	199,632	26,502	9,366	35,868
50 to 55	85,513	31,680	117,193	14,070	4,561	18,631
55 to 60	86,211	36,023	122,234	15,500	6,930	22,430
60 to 65	75,781	29,691	105,472	13,194	6,542	19,736
65 to 70	50,830	28,195	79,025	11,375	5,083	16,458
70 to 75	40,606	25,106	65,712	8,121	4,543	12,664
75 and over	43,610	34,191	77,801	10,676	6,714	17,390
Total	619,939	281,430	901,369	112,837	50,959	163,796
			1949			
Under 21	4,615	1,429	6,044	462	204	666
21 to 30	17,646	14,444	32,090	3,248	1,653	4,901
30 to 40	67,690	24,116	91,806	10,797	4,753	15,550
40 to 50	153,780	59,196	212,976	26,874	9,050	35,924
50 to 55	98,010	35,157	133,167	17,270	7,939	25,209
55 to 60	93,892	38,318	132,210	16,508	7,271	23,779
60 to 65	77,887	36,950	114,837	14,833	7,144	21,977
65 to 70	56,526	30,176	86,702	10,632	5,317	15,949
70 to 75	40,688	27,270	67,958	8,103	5,113	13,216
75 and over	46,168	38,400	84,568	9,791	7,160	16,951
Total	656,903	305,450	962,353	118,519	55,603	174,122
			1950			
Under 21	3,846	3,333	7,179	468	443	911
21 to 30	24,116	7,778	31,894	3,741	1,199	4,940
30 to 40	72,000	22,500	94,500	10,308	4,240	14,548
40 to 50	159,203	59,171	218,374	28,007	10,721	38,728
50 to 55	101,928	44,996	146,924	18,086	6,921	25,007
55 to 60	101,718	39,984	141,702	19,112	8,043	27,155
60 to 65	84,514	41,524	126,038	15,977	6,640	22,617
65 to 70	66,617	35,849	102,466	12,935	6,279	19,214
70 to 75	46,779	30,362	77,141	10,093	5,844	15,937
75 and over	51,805	43,577	95,382	11,565	8,519	20,084
Total	712,526	329,087	1,041,613	130,292	58,849	189,141

(continued)

UNDERLYING DATA AND ESTIMATES

TABLE A-9 (concluded)

				GROSS ESTATE (MILLION DOLLARS)					
				Male		Female		Total	
				Before Insurance Correction	After Insurance Correction	Before Insurance Correction	After Insurance Correction	Before Insurance Correction	After Insurance Correction
AGE GROUP	Number of Wealth-Holders Male	Female	Total						
				1953					
Under 21	3,846	4,000	7,846	597	527	940	930	1,537	1,458
21 to 30	20,557	10,000	30,557	4,779	4,183	1,009	961	5,788	5,143
30 to 40	105,656	40,715	146,371	14,699	11,084	17,773	17,494	32,422	28,575
40 to 50	205,604	76,053	281,657	35,067	28,333	22,418	22,146	57,485	51,479
50 to 55	124,068	55,165	179,233	21,578	19,260	8,703	8,554	30,281	27,814
55 to 60	128,217	56,546	184,763	23,266	21,273	9,204	9,062	32,470	30,333
60 to 65	113,636	54,284	167,920	22,079	20,576	9,449	1,326	31,528	29,901
65 to 70	88,784	50,560	139,344	18,321	17,455	9,106	9,053	27,427	26,519
70 to 75	61,640	43,162	104,802	13,177	12,748	8,816	8,773	21,993	21,521
75 and over	68,178	60,516	128,694	15,067	14,831	12,349	12,312	27,416	27,151
Total	920,186	451,001	1,371,187	168,630	150,270	99,767	98,619	268,397	249,884

[a] No insurance adjustment has been made except where indicated and no correction has been made for age unspecified.

TABLE A-10
DISTRIBUTION OF NET OR ECONOMIC ESTATE[a] BY ESTATE SIZE, BASED ON
WHITE MORTALITY RATES, 1922, 1944, AND 1946

Net Estate Size (thous. dollars)	Number of Wealth-Holders			Net or Economic Estate		
	Male	Female	Total	Male	Female	Total
				(billion dollars)		
1922[b]						
Under 100	207,325	67,038	274,363	14.3	4.6	18.9
100 to 200	52,431	15,824	68,255	7.2	2.2	9.4
200 to 300	15,579	5,275	20,854	3.8	1.3	5.1
300 to 500	11,385	3,644	15,029	4.4	1.4	5.8
500 to 1,000	8,988	2,589	11,577	6.1	1.7	7.8
1,000 to 2,000	2,696	1,151	3,847	3.8	1.6	5.4
2,000 to 5,000	899	384	1,283	2.6	1.1	3.7
5,000 and over	300	—	300	1.8	.4	2.2
Total	299,603	95,905	395,508	44.0	14.3	58.3
1922[c]						
Under 100			315,183			23.6
100 to 200			78,569			11.3
200 to 300			24,070			6.2
300 to 500			17,258			6.8
500 to 1,000			13,170			9.2
1,000 to 2,000			4,087			6.3
2,000 to 5,000			1,362			4.1
5,000 and over			455			2.5
Total			454,154			70.0
1944[c]						
Under 60			86,429			5.7
60 to 80			178,797			12.2
80 to 100			106,222			9.2
Under 100			371,448			27.1
100 to 150			135,252			16.3
150 to 200			57,340			10.1
100 to 200			192,592			26.4
200 to 300			42,225			10.5
300 to 500			28,370			10.5
500 to 1,000			17,154			11.1
1,000 to 2,000			5,278			7.3
2,000 to 5,000			1,979			6.0
5,000 and over			721			6.1
Total			659,767			105.0
1946[c]						
Under 60			126,265			8.1
60 to 80			240,506			16.4
80 to 100			137,432			12.3
Under 100			504,203			36.8
100 to 150			159,765			18.8
150 to 200			69,575			12.3
100 to 200			229,340			31.1
200 to 300			60,985			14.6
300 to 500			35,217			13.4
500 to 1,000			18,038			14.0
1,000 to 2,000			7,731			9.9
2,000 to 3,000			2,577			8.1
5,000 and over			858			2.6
Total			858,949			130.5

SOURCE: Mendershausen in Goldsmith, *Saving in U.S.*, III, Tables E-47, E-37, E-38, and E-40.

[a] After adjustment for age unspecified.
[b] No adjustment for insurance has been made.
[c] Adjustment for insurance has been made.

TABLE A-11
Distribution of Gross Estate[a] by Estate Size, Based on White Mortality Rates, 1948–50

Gross Estate Size (thous. dollars)	Number of Wealth-Holders			Gross Estate (million dollars)		
	Male	Female	Total	Male	Female	Total
1948						
Under 60	729	80	809	40	4	44
60 to 70	66,863	44,394	111,257	4,373	2,893	7,266
70 to 80	69,441	35,352	104,793	5,209	2,642	7,851
80 to 90	63,662	31,307	94,969	5,410	2,646	8,056
90 to 100	53,500	23,446	76,946	5,060	2,219	7,278
100 to 120	88,003	34,428	122,431	9,606	3,787	13,393
120 to 150	81,039	33,304	114,343	10,847	4,485	15,332
150 to 200	70,206	25,814	96,020	12,081	4,454	16,535
200 to 300	63,961	24,527	88,488	15,501	5,920	21,421
300 to 500	34,351	13,889	48,240	13,020	5,100	18,120
500 to 1,000	20,563	10,974	31,537	14,264	7,264	21,528
1,000 to 2,000	5,919	2,926	8,845	8,174	3,901	12,075
2,000 to 3,000	688	266	954	1,585	635	2,220
3,000 to 5,000	567	229	796	2,180	952	3,132
5,000 to 10,000	144	434	578	983	3,061	4,044
10,000 and over	301	60	361	4,507	995	5,502
Total	619,939	281,430	901,369	112,837	50,959	163,796
1949						
Under 60	182	224	406	10	11	21
60 to 70	71,293	40,942	112,235	4,646	2,666	7,312
70 to 80	73,492	46,031	119,523	5,509	3,452	8,961
80 to 90	64,785	33,284	98,069	5,489	2,824	8,313
90 to 100	59,140	25,946	85,086	5,607	2,464	8,071
100 to 120	91,347	35,218	126,565	9,999	3,858	13,857
120 to 150	88,807	39,777	128,584	11,784	5,321	17,105
150 to 200	74,750	33,219	107,969	12,840	5,800	18,640
200 to 300	67,879	20,199	88,078	16,311	4,910	21,221
300 to 500	36,059	16,380	52,439	13,662	6,190	19,852
500 to 1,000	21,330	9,129	30,459	14,546	6,303	20,849
1,000 to 2,000	5,154	2,780	7,934	6,792	3,820	10,612
2,000 to 3,000	1,064	1,380	2,444	2,553	3,524	6,077
3,000 to 5,000	1,297	649	1,946	5,469	2,296	7,765
5,000 to 10,000	133	292	425	848	2,164	3,012
10,000 and over	191	—	191	2,454	—	2,454
Total	656,903	305,450	962,353	118,519	55,603	174,122
1950						
Under 60	569	62	631	32	3	35
60 to 70	74,746	46,776	121,522	4,880	3,045	7,925
70 to 80	84,680	43,015	127,695	6,350	3,225	9,575
80 to 90	72,296	38,512	110,808	6,148	3,269	9,417
90 to 100	60,829	29,197	90,026	5,766	2,756	8,522
100 to 120	96,453	39,365	135,818	10,568	4,295	14,863
120 to 150	100,524	36,837	137,361	13,426	4,893	18,319
150 to 200	81,779	31,526	113,305	14,112	5,509	19,621
200 to 300	66,766	28,008	94,774	16,151	6,914	23,065
300 to 500	42,086	20,492	62,578	15,810	7,846	23,656
500 to 1,000	21,738	10,292	32,030	14,452	7,207	21,659
1,000 to 2,000	7,370	3,829	11,199	10,159	5,089	15,248
2,000 to 3,000	1,519	314	1,833	3,789	778	4,567
3,000 to 5,000	397	660	1,057	1,547	2,482	4,029
5,000 to 10,000	597	166	763	4,459	995	5,454
10,000 and over	180	36	216	2,645	545	3,190
Total	712,529	1,573,712	2,286,241	130,292	58,849	189,141

[a] No insurance adjustment has been made and no correction has been made for age unspecified.

TABLE A-12

NUMBER OF DECEDENT ESTATE TAX WEALTH-HOLDERS BY SEX, AGE GROUP, AND MARITAL STATUS, 1953

Age Group	Married Number	Married Per Cent of Total	Widowed	Divorced or Separated	Unmarried	Total	In Community Property States Number	In Community Property States Per Cent of Total
MALES								
Under 21		0.0			5	5	2	40.0
21 to 30	18	48.7	1		18	37	7	18.9
30 to 40	201	82.7	3	13	26	243	35	14.8
40 to 50	1,086	89.5	25	34	68	1,213	194	16.0
50 to 55	1,305	88.4	40	37	95	1,477	233	15.8
55 to 60	2,035	85.9	89	75	171	2,370	316	13.3
60 to 65	2,692	84.1	188	91	229	3,201	466	14.6
65 to 70	2,853	77.4	370	105	356	3,684	540	14.6
70 to 75	2,486	69.8	580	106	391	3,563	568	15.9
75 to 80	1,978	58.7	849	64	478	3,369	497	14.8
80 to 85	1,199	45.6	962	66	403	2,630	374	14.2
85 and over	678	28.5	1,257	47	397	2,379	332	14.0
Age unknown	428	57.0	166	36	121	751	113	15.1
Total	16,949	68.0	4,530	674	2,758	24,922	3,677	14.8
FEMALES								
Under 21		0.0	1		1	2	1	50.0
21 to 30	3	37.5	1	1	3	8	2	25.0
30 to 40	41	71.9	6	5	5	57	19	33.3
40 to 50	188	74.9	42	7	14	251	77	30.7
50 to 55	228	66.7	82	8	24	342	87	25.4
55 to 60	335	62.4	172	10	20	537	130	24.2
60 to 65	417	50.9	350	14	38	819	190	23.2
65 to 70	525	41.5	652	18	69	1,264	292	23.1
70 to 75	560	33.1	1,011	26	90	1,687	348	20.6
75 to 80	521	25.2	1,407	19	120	2,067	409	19.8
80 to 85	368	17.9	1,547	16	129	2,060	407	19.8
85 and over	277	12.5	1,762	23	162	2,224	437	19.6
Age unknown	112	24.4	305	11	31	459	88	19.2
Total	3,575	30.3	7,338	158	705	11,777	2,487	21.1

UNDERLYING DATA AND ESTIMATES

NOTES TO TABLE A-12

Statistics of Income for 1953 (Washington, 1954, Table 5, pp. 76–79) gives marital status by age and by the following procedure we were able to construct this table showing marital status by age and sex. The totals for males and females by age group were first written into the table. Then in the table for females the numbers of widows were written in and the numbers of nonwidows were allocated to the married, divorced or separated, and unmarried categories on the basis of the proportions each of these categories bore to the total in the age group. The number of males in each cell aside from widowers (for whom actual figures were available) were obtained by subtracting the females from the total in each cell. (Multiplying through by the adjusted mortality rates yields an estimate of the marital status of living estate tax wealth-holders by age and sex as presented in Table 50.)

It is worth mentioning that the estimates of marital status are biased by the fact that married persons have a more favorable mortality than the nonmarried. Dublin, Lotka, and Spiegelman observe that "among white males at age 20 and over in the United States in 1940, the single had a death rate just $1\frac{2}{5}$ times that of the married; for the widowers, the ratio was $1\frac{3}{4}$, while that for the divorced was more than 2. The corresponding ratios for white women at ages 20 and over were $1\frac{1}{6}$ for the single, $1\frac{1}{8}$ for the widowed, and $1\frac{3}{4}$ for the divorced" (*Length of Life*, rev. ed., New York, 1949, p. 140). By applying the same inverse mortality rates for the married and the nonmarried, we have tended to understate the total number of living wealth-holders and to overstate the proportion of nonmarried persons in the wealth-holder group.

UNDERLYING DATA AND ESTIMATES

TABLE A-13
ESTATE TAX RETURNS AND TAXABLE GROSS ESTATE FOR 1949, 1950, 1953, AND 1954 COMBINED RELATED TO POPULATION AND INCOME PAYMENTS IN NON-COMMUNITY PROPERTY STATES AND AVERAGE OF COMMUNITY PROPERTY STATES, 1953

	1953 Per Capita Income (dollars) (1)	Share of Returns ÷ Share of Population (2)	Share of Gross Estate on Taxable Returns ÷ Share of Income Payments (3)
1. Delaware	2,482	1.50	2.00
2. Connecticut	2,418	1.36	1.61
3. New Jersey	2,224	1.28	1.11
4. Illinois	2,185	1.40	1.08
5. New York	2,150	1.41	1.35
6. Michigan	2,120	0.60	0.62
7. Ohio	2,032	0.94	0.77
8. Maryland	1,986	0.93	1.06
9. Massachusetts	1,963	1.09	1.24
10. Indiana	1,920	0.96	0.64
11. Rhode Island	1,893	1.20	1.80
12. Pennsylvania	1,892	0.95	1.02
13. Wyoming	1,861	1.00	1.00
14. Oregon	1,811	1.00	0.90
15. Montana	1,786	1.25	0.75
16. Wisconsin	1,770	1.13	0.86
17. Colorado	1,735	1.22	0.88
18. Average of community property states	1,733	0.95	0.94
19. Missouri	1,720	0.84	0.92
20. Minnesota	1,646	1.05	0.88
21. Kansas	1,641	1.53	1.16
22. Nebraska	1,578	1.77	1.43
23. New Hampshire	1,576	1.33	1.33
24. Florida	1,556	1.23	1.53
25. Iowa	1,546	2.17	1.13
26. Utah	1,528	0.40	0.25
27. Virginia	1,481	0.72	1.00
28. Oklahoma	1,459	0.86	1.00
29. Maine	1,455	1.00	1.20
30. Vermont	1,441	1.00	1.00
31. South Dakota	1,331	1.00	0.66
32. West Virginia	1,278	0.41	0.44
33. Georgia	1,246	0.43	0.62
34. North Dakota	1,228	0.75	0.66
35. Kentucky	1,224	0.68	0.77
36. Tennessee	1,219	0.47	0.73
37. North Carolina	1,165	0.50	0.82
38. South Carolina	1,132	0.36	0.66
39. Alabama	1,081	0.40	0.58
40. Arkansas	988	0.50	0.83
41. Mississippi	874	0.36	0.57

SOURCE: Col. 1: *Statistical Abstract of the United States: 1957*, Washington, 1957, p. 303; cols. 2 and 3: Table 57, cols. 9 and 10.

TABLE A-14
Distribution of Spending Units by Total Assets Within Income Groups, 1950
(per cent)

Money Income Group Before Taxes, 1949	All Cases (1)	Zero (2)	Total Assets (dollars)							
			100 to 400 (3)	500 to 1,000 (4)	1,000 to 2,000 (5)	2,000 to 5,000 (6)	5,000 to 10,000 (7)	10,000 to 25,000 (8)	25,000 to 60,000 (9)	60,000 and over (10)
Under $1,000	100	23	15	8	9	12	17	11	4	1
$1,000 to $2,000	100	15	22	11	10	13	13	14	2	a
$2,000 to $3,000	100	3	12	12	15	19	18	16	4	1
$3,000 to $4,000	100	1	5	7	12	21	22	26	5	1
$4,000 to $5,000	100	1	2	4	8	18	20	37	8	2
$5,000 to $7,500	100	a	1	2	3	11	19	42	18	4
$7,500 and over	100	a	a	a	a	3	5	22	37	33
All spending units	100	7	10	8	10	15	17	22	8	3

Source: Goldsmith, *Saving in U.S.*, III, Table W-58.
a No cases reported or less than 0.5 per cent.

TABLE A-15
Distribution of Spending Units by Saving Within Asset Groups, 1950
(per cent)

Saving Group, 1949	Total Assets (dollars)							
	Under 400a (1)	500 to 1,000 (2)	1,000 to 2,000 (3)	2,000 to 5,000 (4)	5,000 to 10,000 (5)	10,000 to 25,000 (6)	25,000 to 60,000 (7)	60,000 and over (8)
Positive savers								
$2,000 and over	b	b	b	2	2	5	22	50
$1,000 to $2,000	b	b	3	4	7	16	16	16
$500 to $1,000	1	5	8	12	15	23	11	7
$200 to $500	5	11	14	20	19	16	13	1
$100 to $200	9	10	11	10	7	5	5	2
Under $100	28	25	15	12	11	8	4	4
Zero savers	21	7	3	3	4	1	1	b
Negative savers								
Under $100	16	10	10	7	6	2	1	b
$100 to $500	15	19	20	13	15	7	8	4
$500 and over	5	13	16	17	14	17	19	16
All cases	100	100	100	100	100	100	100	100

Source: Goldsmith, *Saving in U.S.*, III, Table W-55.
a Includes zero assets.
b No cases reported or less than 0.5 per cent.

UNDERLYING DATA AND ESTIMATES

TABLE A-16
DISTRIBUTION OF SPENDING UNITS BY TOTAL ASSETS WITHIN SAVING GROUPS, 1950
(per cent)

		Total Assets (dollars)								
Saving Group, 1949	All Cases (1)	Zero (2)	100 to 500 (3)	500 to 1,000 (4)	1,000 to 2,000 (5)	2,000 to 5,000 (6)	5,000 to 10,000 (7)	10,000 to 25,000 (8)	25,000 to 60,000 (9)	60,000 and over (10)
Positive savers										
$2,000 and over	100	a	a	a	1	5	5	22	38	29
$1,000 to $2,000	100	a	a	a	3	9	18	47	17	6
$500 to $1,000	100	a	1	3	7	16	22	42	7	2
$200 to $500	100	a	5	6	10	22	24	26	7	a
$100 to $200	100	3	18	9	13	20	15	16	5	1
Under $100	100	11	24	13	11	13	13	12	2	1
Zero savers	100	51	10	9	4	8	12	5	1	a
Negative savers										
Under $100	100	14	24	10	13	15	14	8	2	a
$100 to $500	100	7	13	11	15	16	19	13	5	1
$500 and over	100	2	3	7	11	19	18	26	11	3
All spending units	100	7	10	8	10	15	17	22	8	3

SOURCE: Goldsmith, *Saving in U.S.*, III, Table W-59.
a No cases reported or less than 0.5 per cent.

TABLE A-17

ROLE OF TOP WEALTH-HOLDERS IN NATIONAL BALANCE SHEET ACCOUNTS, 1949

(billion dollars)

	All Sectors Total Wealth Variant (1)	Personal Sector					Prime Wealth Variant (7)	Wealth Held by Top Wealth-Holders			Share of Wealth Held by Top Wealth-Holders		
		House-hold (2)	Personal Trust Funds (3)	Farm Business (4)	Nonfarm Business (5)	Total Wealth Variant (6)		Basic Variant (8)	Prime Variant (9)	Total Variant (10)	Col. 8 ÷ Col. 7 (11)	Col. 9 ÷ Col. 7 (12)	Col. 10 ÷ Col. 6 (13)
Real estate	$597.4	$234.7	$ 1.0	$62.1	$38.5	$336.3	$335.3	$41.7		$42.3	12.4%		12.6%
Structures, residential	227.4	199.6		11.4	12.5								
Structures, nonresidential	201.7			50.7	13.7								
Land	168.3	36.1			12.3								
U.S. govt. bonds	252.7	43.2	15.0		6.2	64.4	49.4	15.2		25.2	30.7		39.3
State and local bonds	24.9	6.5	5.0			11.5	6.5	5.7		9.0	87.6		78.2
Other bonds	46.0	2.6	4.0			6.6	2.6	2.7		5.3	103.8		80.3
Stock	148.4	86.4	20.0			106.4	86.4	66.3		79.5	76.7		75.0
Cash	268.4	110.1	2.0	6.7	11.8	130.6	128.6	18.4		19.7	14.2		15.0
Monetary metals	28.5	1.0		0.2	0.2								
Currency and deposits	226.5	41.7		6.5	11.6								
Deposits in other financial institutions	13.4	69.4											
Mortgages and notes	156.0	14.5	1.0		7.4	22.9	21.9	7.4		8.0	33.6		34.8
Receivables from business	69.3	0.3			4.6								
Receivables from households	20.3				2.8								
Loans or securities	3.7	1.0											
Mortgages, nonfarm	57.1	12.7											
Mortgages, farm	5.6	2.3											
Life insurance reserves	56.9	6.0				60.0	60.0	7.6		9.6	12.6		16.0

Pension and retirement funds	43.7	44.4	—		44.4	—		—		2.3	—	5.2
Private	4.6	0.5										
Government	39.1	39.4										
Miscellaneous property	469.0	256.5	2.0	33.8	24.7	159.6	157.6	24.6		26.6	15.6	16.6
Durables, producer	97.8	—		12.6	13.1							
Durables, consumer	90.1	90.1		—	—							
Inventories	79.2	—		18.9	11.6							
Equities, farm and nonfarm	157.4	(157.4)						(8.3)				
Equities, mutual financial institutions	10.0	10.0										
Other intangibles	34.5	0.1	2.0	2.3	—							
Gross estate	2063.5	858.9	50.0	102.6	88.6	942.7	848.3	189.4	199.7	243.0	22.3	25.8
Debts and Mortgages	190.2	53.9		10.0	23.8	87.7	87.7	18.0	19.1	19.1	20.4	20.4
Payables to banks	28.6	6.0		2.0	5.4							
Payables to other business	51.8	13.8		2.0	5.3							
Payables to household	0.9	—		—	—							
Borrowing on securities	3.8	1.9		—	—							
Mortgage	62.7	32.1		5.6	11.3							
Other liabilities	42.4	0.1		0.3	1.8							
Total liabilities	871.5			—								
Economic estate	1873.3	805.0	50.0	92.6	64.8	855.0	760.6	171.4	181.7	223.9	22.5	26.0

TABLE A-18
ROLE OF TOP WEALTH-HOLDERS IN NATIONAL BALANCE SHEET ACCOUNTS, 1945
(billion dollars)

	All Sectors Total Wealth Variant (1)	Personal Sector						Wealth Held by Top Wealth-Holders			Share of Wealth Held by Top Wealth-Holders		
		House-hold (2)	Personal Trust Funds (3)	Farm Business (4)	Nonfarm Business (5)	Total Wealth Variant (6)	Prime Wealth Variant (7)	Basic Variant (8)	Prime Variant (9)	Total Variant (10)	Col. 8 ÷ Col. 7 (11)	Col. 9 ÷ Col. 7 (12)	Col. 10 ÷ Col. 6 (13)
Real estate	$393.1	$154.7	$1.4	$50.8	$25.6	$232.5	$231.1	$25.3		$26.2	10.9%		11.2%
Structures, residential	133.6												
Structures, nonresidential	131.5												
Land	128.0												
U.S. govt. bonds	274.4	41.5	12.4	—	8.5	62.4	50.0	11.8		20.0	23.6		32.5
State and local bonds	15.9	5.0	4.5	—	—	9.5	5.0	7.1		10.1	142.0		106.0
Other bonds	25.9	5.9	3.6	—	—	9.5	5.9	5.1		7.5	86.4		78.5
Stock	150.8	91.0	18.0	—	—	109.0	91.0	59.6		71.6	65.5		65.7
Cash	259.6	95.9	1.8	7.1	12.0	116.8	115.0	14.4		15.6	12.5		13.3
Monetary metals	23.7												
Currency and deposits	191.9												
Deposits in other financial institutions	44.0												
Mortgages and notes	98.6	10.8	1.4	—	5.1	17.3	15.9	5.1		6.0	31.4		34.6
Receivables from business	41.0												
Receivables from households	11.7												
Loans on securities	8.1												
Mortgages, nonfarm	33.1												
Mortgages, farm	4.7												
Life insurance reserves	44.3	44.8	—	—	—	44.8	44.8	6.8		7.8	15.1		17.3

Pension and retirement funds	28.4	28.3				28.3				1.6	—	5.9
Private	2.9											
Government	25.5											
Miscellaneous property	344.1	175.0	0.2	23.1	—	12.7	92.4	90.4	18.4	—	19.7	20.4	21.4
Durables, producer	50.3											
Durables, consumer	51.0	46.3										
Inventories and livestock	52.2	—										
Equities, nonfarm	120.4	(120.4)							(10.0)			
Equities, mutual financial institutions	3.3	7.5										
Equities, govt. corporations	17.2											
Accruals	19.0											
Other intangibles	30.7	0.8										
Gross estate	1,626.2	532.5	45.1	81.0	63.9	722.5	649.1	153.6	162.8	199.4	23.7	27.5
Debts and mortgages	473.6	26.2	—	7.1	17.4	50.7	50.7	14.0	14.8	14.8	23.3	27.4
Payables to banks	18.6											
Payables to other business	31.7											
Payables to households	.8											
Borrowing on securities	8.1											
Mortgages	37.8											
Bonds and notes	320.3											
Accruals	19.0											
Other liabilities	37.3											
Economic estate	1,152.6	506.3	45.1	73.9	46.5	671.8	598.4	139.6	148.0	183.6	23.2	24.7	27.4

TABLE A-19

ROLE OF TOP WEALTH-HOLDERS IN NATIONAL BALANCE SHEET ACCOUNTS, 1939
(billion dollars)

	All Sectors Total Wealth Variant (1)	Personal Sector				Total Wealth Variant (6)	Prime Wealth Variant (7)	Wealth Held by Top Wealth-Holders			Share of Wealth Held by Top Wealth-Holders		
		Non-farm House-holds (2)	Personal Trust Funds (3)	Farm House-holds and Farm Business (4)	Unincor-porated Business (5)			Basic Variant (8)	Prime Variant (9)	Total Variant (10)	Col. 8 ÷ Col. 7 (11)	Col. 9 ÷ Col. 7 (12)	Col. 10 ÷ Col. 6 (13)
Real estate	$277.1	$106.5	$1.8	$32.2	$15.7	$156.2	$154.4	$18.7		$19.9	12.1%		12.7%
Structures, residential	91.2	81.5		4.9		87.0	86.4						
Structures, nonresidential	97.3	19.5	1.8	4.1	11.5	15.6	15.6						
Land, residential	22.9	5.5		11.6	2.1	33.8	33.2						
Land, nonresidential	65.7	5.5		11.6	2.1	19.8	19.2						
U.S. govt. bonds	47.0	4.3	3.5	0.2	0.9	8.9	5.4	5.5		7.9	101.8		88.8
State and local bonds	19.8	3.7	4.2			7.9	3.7	6.1		8.9	164.9		112.7
Corporate bonds	32.5	7.5	7.0			14.5	7.5	5.8		10.4	77.3		71.7
Corporate stock	100.1	58.4	13.0			71.4	58.4	42.3		50.9	72.4		71.3
Cash, mortgages, and notes	133.4	50.4	3.8	3.9	12.4	70.5	66.7	16.5		19.1	24.7		27.1
Monetary metals	20.8	0.4		0.1		0.5	0.5						
Commercial bank deposits	54.1	20.4		2.8	5.6	29.3	28.8						
Deposits in other financial institutions	28.8	15.4	1.4			15.9	15.4						
Currency	22.4	3.2		0.9		4.5	4.1						
Receivables from business	26.3	0.4			5.3	5.7	5.7						
Receivables from households	14.6				1.2	1.2	1.2						
Loans on securities	2.7												
Mortgages, nonfarm	32.0	9.5	2.0			11.5	9.5						
Mortgages, farm	6.6	1.1	0.4	0.1	0.3	1.9	1.5						
Pension funds	7.2	7.1		0.1		7.2				.4			5.6
Private	1.0	1.0											
Government	6.2	6.1		0.1		0.1	0.1						
Insurance	29.2	26.6		2.6		29.2	29.2	4.5		5.0	15.4		17.1

Miscellaneous property	155.8	61.8	1.8	15.3	7.9	60.7	58.9	9.9	11.1	16.8		18.3
Durables, producer	34.2	—	—	3.5	3.8	7.3	7.3					
Durables, consumer	32.5	30.0	—	2.6	—	32.6	32.6					
Inventories	25.3	—	—	2.2	4.1	6.3	6.3					
Livestock	5.1	—	—	5.1	—	5.1	5.1					
Other intangible property	18.0	4.0	1.8	1.1	—	6.9	5.1					
Equity, financial nonprofit institutions	2.3	1.7	—	0.6	—	2.3	2.3					
Equity, govt. corporations	4.5	—	—	0.2	—	0.2	0.2					
Accruals	7.8	—	—	—	—	—	—					
Interest in nonfarm business unincorporated	26.1	26.1	—	—	—	26.1	26.1					
Gross estate	877.4	326.4	35.0	54.4	36.9	426.6	384.4	109.3	141.4	28.4		32.9
Total tangible property	395.0	136.7	1.8	45.7	23.6	207.8	206.0					
Total intangible property	482.4	189.7	33.2	8.7	13.3	218.8	178.5					
Debts and mortgages	356.5	36.5	—	10.6	10.8	57.9	57.9	14.2	15.1	24.5		—
Payables to financial intermediaries	17.4	5.9	—	2.2	1.7	9.8	9.8					
Payables to other business	24.6	4.7	—	1.0	6.0	11.7	11.7					
Payables to households	0.4	—	—	—	—	—	—					
Borrowing on securities	2.7	1.9	—	—	—	1.9	1.9					
Mortgages	38.6	18.6	—	6.6	2.4	27.6	27.6					
Bonds and notes	107.3	0.5	—	—	0.7	1.2	1.2					
Accruals	7.8	4.3	—	0.5	—	4.8	4.8					
Other liabilities	15.9	0.6	—	0.2	—	0.8	0.8					
Economic estate	520.9	289.9	35.0	43.8	26.1	368.7	326.5	95.1	100.8	126.3	29.1	30.6	34.1

TABLE A-20
ROLE OF TOP WEALTH-HOLDERS IN NATIONAL BALANCE SHEET ACCOUNTS, 1929
(billion dollars)

	All Sectors Total Wealth Variant (1)	Personal Sector						Wealth Held by Top Wealth-Holders			Share of Wealth Held by Top Wealth-Holders		
		Non-farm Households (2)	Personal Trust Funds (3)	Farm Households and Farm Business (4)	Unincorporated Business (5)	Total Wealth Variant (6)	Prime Wealth Variant (7)	Basic Variant (8)	Prime Variant (9)	Total Variant (10)	Col. 8 ÷ Col. 7 (11)	Col. 9 ÷ Col. 7 (12)	Col. 10 ÷ Col. 6 (13)
Real estate	$303.4	$117.2	$1.5	$47.2	$18.5	$184.4	$182.9	$20.9		$21.9	11.4%		11.9%
Structures, residential	95.9	84.4		6.4		91.3	90.8						
Structures, nonresidential	93.9	—	1.5	5.9	11.2	17.1	17.1						
Land, residential	24.1	20.8		}34.9	}7.3	42.5	42.0						
Land, nonresidential	89.5	12.0				33.5	33.0						
U.S. govt. bonds	16.2	3.1	0.9	0	1.0	5.0	4.1	4.2		4.8	102.4		96.0
State and local bonds	16.9	4.4	3.0	—	—	7.4	4.4	5.5		7.5	125.0		101.4
Corporate bonds	38.1	15.3	6.8	—	—	22.1	15.3	9.0		13.6	58.8		61.5
Corporate stock	186.7	124.0	12.6	—	—	136.6	124.0	63.7		72.1	51.4		52.8
Cash, mortgages, and notes	192.9	49.1	3.9	3.3	11.6	67.9	64.0	13.5		16.1	21.1		23.7
Monetary metals	5.0	0.4		0.1		0.5	0.5						
Commercial bank deposits	44.8	18.2	0.9	2.9	4.9	26.9	26.0						
Deposits in other financial institutions	17.9	15.5		—	—	15.5	15.5						
Currency													
Receivables from business	46.7	1.2	—	—	6.0	1.2	1.2						
Receivables from households	15.3	—	—	—	—	—	—						
Loans on securities	16.3	11.0	2.4	—	—	13.4	11.0						
Mortgages, nonfarm	37.3	2.8	0.6	0.3	0.7	4.4	3.8						
Mortgages, farm	9.6					2.0	—						
Pension funds													
Private	0.5	0.5	—	—	—	0.5	—						
Government	1.5	1.5	—	—	—	1.5	—				.2	—	10.0
Insurance	17.5	15.9	—	1.7	—	17.6	17.6	3.5		4.0	19.9		22.7

Miscellaneous property	201.5	75.2	1.4	18.5	11.0	78.6	77.2	18.0		19.0	23.3	24.2
Durables, producer	38.4	—	—	3.9	4.6	8.5	8.5					
Durables, consumer	42.2	38.4	—	3.8	—	42.2	42.2					
Inventories	31.5	—	—	3.0	6.4	9.4	9.4					
Livestock	6.5	—	—	6.5	—	6.5	6.5					
Other intangible property	45.3	7.7	1.4	0.7	—	9.8	8.4					
Equity, financial nonprofit institutions	2.1	1.6	—	0.5	—	2.1	2.1					
Equity, govt. corporations	0.4	—	—	0.1	—	0.1	0.1					
Accruals	7.6	—	—	—	—	—	—					
Interest in nonfarm business unincorporated	27.5	27.5	—	—	—	27.5	27.5					
Gross estate	981.7	406.2	30.0	70.7	42.1	521.5	489.5	138.4	146.6	166.8	28.3	32.1
Total tangible property	426.9	156.0	1.5	64.4	29.6	251.5	250.0					
Total intangible property	554.8	252.1	28.5	6.8	13.9	273.8	243.3					
Debts and mortgages	324.3	48.3	—	15.5	15.9	79.7	79.7	19.4	20.6	20.6	24.3	—
Payables to financial intermediaries	25.4	6.9	—	3.0	4.7	14.6	14.6					
Payables to other business	28.6	4.5	—	2.0	6.1	12.6	12.6					
Payables to households	1.2	—	—	—	—	—	—					
Borrowing on securities	16.3	11.6	—	—	—	11.6	11.6					
Mortgages	46.9	21.9	—	9.6	3.4	34.9	34.9					
Bonds and notes	76.1	1.4	—	—	1.7	3.1	3.1					
Accruals	7.6	3.6	—	0.6	—	4.2	4.2					
Other liabilities	33.5	0.3	—	0.2	—	0.5	0.5					
Economic estate	657.4	359.8	30.0	55.7	27.6	441.8	409.8	119.0	126.0	146.2	29.0	33.2

TABLE A-21

ROLE OF TOP WEALTH-HOLDERS IN NATIONAL BALANCE SHEET ACCOUNTS, 1922

(billion dollars)

	All Sectors Total Wealth Variant (1)	Personal Sector						Wealth Held by Top Wealth-Holders			Share of Wealth Held by Top Wealth-Holders		
		Non-farm House-holds (2)	Personal Trust Funds (3)	Farm House-holds and Farm Business (4)	Unincor-porated Business (5)	Total Wealth Variant (6)	Prime Wealth Variant (7)	Basic Variant (8)	Prime Variant (9)	Total Variant (10)	Col. 8 ÷ Col. 7 (11)	Col. 9 ÷ Col. 7 (12)	Col. 10 ÷ Col. 6 (13)
Real estate	$227.3	$75.8	$1.4	$53.9	$11.7	$143.0	$140.1	$22.8		$23.7	16.3%		16.7%
Structures, residential	63.2	54.8		6.6									
Structures, nonresidential	71.3	—	1.4	5.8	8.2								
Land, residential	15.4	14.0		—	3.5								
Land, nonresidential	77.4	7.0		41.5									
U.S. govt. bonds	23.0	8.8	0.9	0.4	0.9	11.0	10.1	4.0		4.6	39.6		41.8
State and local bonds	10.4	3.0	1.8			4.8	3.0	3.0		4.2	100.0		87.5
Corporate bonds	23.7	10.9	3.6			14.5	10.9	6.6		9.0	60.6		62.1
Corporate stock	76.1	48.2	6.3			54.5	48.2	28.8		33.0	59.8		60.6
Cash, mortgages, and notes	133.8	33.9	3.2	4.3	12.0	53.4	50.2	11.9		13.9	23.7		26.0
Monetary metals	4.6	0.4		0.1		0.5	0.5						
Commercial bank deposits	34.2	15.1	0.5	2.7	4.5	22.8	22.3	—			—		
Deposits in other financial institutions	10.5	8.6				8.6	8.6						
Currency	6.9	2.1		0.6		2.7	2.7						
Receivables from business	32.7	0.5			5.9	6.4	6.4						
Receivables from households	11.1	—			0.7	0.7	0.7						
Loans on securities	6.7					—	—						
Mortgages, nonfarm	16.3	4.4	1.6			6.0	4.4						
Mortgages, farm	10.8	3.5	1.1	0.9	0.9	6.4	5.3						
Pension funds	0.4	0.3				0.3	—						
Private	0.1	0.1				0.1							
Government	0.3	0.2				0.2							
Insurance	8.7	7.8		0.9		8.7	8.7	2.8		3.0	32.2		34.5

Miscellaneous property	149.7	53.4	0.8	16.4	10.1	58.5	57.7	12.1	12.6	21.5
Durables, producer	30.8	—	—	3.3	3.4	6.7	6.7			
Durables, consumer	30.9	27.2	—	3.7	—	30.9	30.9			
Inventories	27.2	—	—	3.1	6.7	9.8	9.8			
Livestock	5.4	—	—	5.4	—	5.4	5.4			
Other intangible property	26.6	3.2	0.8	0.5	—	4.5	3.7			
Equity, financial nonprofit institutions	1.2	0.8	—	0.4	—	1.2	1.2			
Equity, govt. corporations	0.7	—	—	—	—	—	—			
Accruals	4.7	—	—	—	—	—	—			
Interest in nonfarm business unincorporated	22.2	22.2	—	—	—	—	—			
Gross estate	653.0	241.1	18.0	75.9	34.7	347.8	329.5	92.2	107.7	30.8
Total tangible property	326.2	102.3	1.4	69.5	21.8	195.0	193.6	22.8	11.8	
Total intangible property	326.8	138.8	16.6	6.4	12.9	152.5	135.9	69.4	51.1	
Debts and mortgages	161.1	20.8	—	17.7	12.7	51.2	51.2	10.9	11.5	21.3
Payables to financial intermediaries	20.4	2.2	—	3.3	4.7	10.2	10.2			
Payables to other business	23.0	2.1	—	2.9	5.6	10.6	10.6			
Payables to households	0.5	—	—	—	—	—	—			
Borrowing on securities	6.7	4.5	—	—	—	4.5	4.5			
Mortgages	27.1	9.2	—	10.8	2.2	22.2	22.2			
Bonds and notes	59.5	0.3	—	—	0.2	0.5	0.5			
Accruals	4.7	2.4	—	0.5	—	2.9	2.9			
Other liabilities	19.9	0.1	—	0.2	—	0.3	0.3			
Total liabilities	222.4	20.6	—	17.7	12.6	50.9	50.9			
Economic estate	430.6	220.4	18.0	58.2	22.2	296.6	278.3	81.3	98.1	32.7
								86.1	29.2	30.7

UNDERLYING DATA AND ESTIMATES

TABLE A-22
Percentage Distribution of Estate Tax Wealth by Gross Estate Size, 1944 and 1953

Gross Estate Size (thous. dollars)	1944 Wealth-Holders	1944 Gross Estate	1953 Wealth-Holders	1953 Gross Estate	1953[a] Wealth-Holders	1953[a] Gross Estate
Total	867,442	$149,591 mill.	1,609,530	$292,803 mill.	969,561	$247,566 mill.
Under 60	0.6%	0.2%	0.09%	0.03%	—	—
60 to 70	⎫		10.8	3.6	—	—
	⎬ 24.9	8.7	21.4	7.6	—	—
70 to 80	⎭		10.6	4.0	—	—
80 to 90	⎫		10.5	4.4	—	—
	⎬ 18.3	8.1	19.6	8.7		
90 to 100	⎭		9.1	4.3	2.47%	0.94%
100 to 120	⎫		13.5	7.3	22.46	8.57
	⎬ 25.4	15.2	26.5	15.8		
120 to 150	⎭		13.0	8.5	21.67	10.09
150 to 200	11.1	9.6	11.2	9.5	18.64	11.22
200 to 300	8.6	11.0	10.1	12.1	16.80	14.26
300 to 500	6.1	12.2	6.1	11.8	10.13	13.94
500 to 1,000	3.3	12.6	3.1	11.03	5.09	13.05
1,000 to 2,000	1.2	9.1	1.2	8.3	1.90	9.83
2,000 to 3,000	⎫		0.2	3.3	0.40	3.92
	⎬ 0.4	6.0	0.3	6.1	0.63	7.20
3,000 to 5,000	⎭		0.1	2.8	0.23	3.28
5,000 to 10,000	⎫		0.1	4.3	0.16	5.08
	⎬ 0.1	7.3	0.1	9.2	0.22	10.90
10,000 and over	⎭		0.04	4.9	0.06	5.82

Source: For 1944, Mendershausen in Goldsmith, *Saving in U.S.*, III, Table E-55.
[a] Recomputed to compare with 1944 (0.95 per cent of population 20 years and over).

Appendix B: Some Considerations of Price Change

In evaluating the "real wealth" of wealth-holders, it is of course important to consider price change. Suppose a person with a $100,000 estate were to have liquidated his holdings in 1953 and thus held $100,000 in cash. What amount of purchasing power in terms of construction and consumer goods and services would that $100,000 represent? When set against the construction cost index and the consumer price index, we find that $100,000 in 1953 would have bought only as much new construction as $36,851 would have in 1935 and as many consumer goods as $51,311 would have in 1935 (see Table B-1).

TABLE B-1
AMOUNT OF MONEY NEEDED IN 1929–52 TO HAVE CONSTRUCTION PURCHASING POWER AND CONSUMER PURCHASING POWER COMPARABLE TO $100,000 IN 1953
(dollars)

Year	Cost of $100,000 Construction	Cost of $100,000 Basket of Consumer Goods and Services
1929		64,073
1930		62,413
1931		56,818
1932		51,049
1933		48,339
1934		50,000
1935	36,851	51,311
1936	37,662	51,836
1937	40,950	53,671
1938	40,463	52,710
1939	40,584	51,923
1940	41,680	52,360
1941	45,576	54,983
1942	52,394	60,927
1943	55,073	64,685
1944	54,099	65,734
1945	55,763	67,220
1946	64,773	72,902
1947	77,232	83,479
1948	84,943	89,860
1949	83,807	88,986
1950	88,839	89,860
1951	94,683	97,028
1952	97,727	99,213
1953	100,000	100,000

SOME CONSIDERATIONS OF PRICE CHANGE

In other words, an estate valued at $100,000 would have been "worth" considerably more in a period when costs and prices were lower than in 1953.

Another view of the importance of price change is provided by applying the change in consumer prices to the estate sizes and comparing the number of wealth-holders in the base year with the number in another year. This is done for 1944 and 1953 in Table B-2. Through this process the estate size $60,000 to $70,000 becomes $91,260 to $106,470 and the number of people with estates of the latter actual size in 1953 can be compared with the number who actually had estates of $60,000 to $70,000 in 1944. The number of persons with gross estates of $60,000 and over in 1953 dollars was 1.66 million; but in 1944 dollars it was 1.1 million (see Table B-2, Part A, bottom line, col. 3). This was still a substantial rise over the number in 1944 who had gross estates of $60,000 and over in 1944 dollars. Part B of the same table shows the reverse of this process, namely, the adjusting of the 1944 distribution for price change to compare it with the actual 1953 distribution. Columns 6 through 9 in the two parts of the table make it possible to compare the inequality which would have obtained within the top wealth-holder groups between the two years in the absence of the change in the price level. There is no notable change in the degree of inequality.

There is some interest in seeing how many millionaires, that is, persons with gross estates of $1 million and over, there would have been in the two years if consumer prices had remained stable from 1944 to 1953. In 1944 there were 13,297 millionaires; in 1953 there were 27,502 millionaires in 1953 prices, but only 17,611 in 1944 prices (see Table B-2 and Chart 6).

TABLE B-2
COMPARISON OF ESTATE TAX WEALTH[a] DISTRIBUTION IN 1944 AND 1953, TAKING CONSUMER PRICE CHANGES INTO ACCOUNT

PART A

Actual 1944 Estate Size (thous. dollars)	Actual No. of Wealth-Holders in 1944 (1)	1944 Estate Size in 1953 Dollars (thous. dollars) (2)	No. of Wealth-Holders in 1953 in Adjusted Estate Sizes (3)	Actual 1944 Gross Estate (million dollars) (4)	1953 Gross Estate in Adjusted Estate Sizes (million dollars) (5)	Percentage Distribution of				
						Col. 1 (6)	Col. 3 (7)	Col. 4 (8)	Col. 5 (9)	
Under 60	4,693	Under 91.26	557,251	274	38,665	—	—	—	6.8	
60 to 70		91.26 to 160.47	216,992		18,288		19.7		6.5	
70 to 80		106.47 to 121.68	149,128		17,442		13.5		6.5	
60 to 80	194,761	91.26 to 121.68	366,120	11,936	35,730	25.0	33.2	8.7	13.3	
80 to 90		121.68 to 136.89	101,070		13,185		9.2		4.9	
90 to 100		136.89 to 152.1	108,523		12,600		9.8		4.7	
80 to 100	143,138	121.68 to 152.1	209,593	11,113	25,785	18.4	19.0	8.1	9.6	
100 to 120		152.10 to 182.52	111,794		17,596		10.1		6.5	
120 to 150		182.52 to 228.15	114,103		20,997		10.3		7.8	
100 to 150	198,672	152.10 to 228.15	225,897	20,854	38,593	25.5	20.4	15.2	14.3	
150 to 200	86,821	228.15 to 304.2	122,951	13,171	27,574	11.2	11.2	9.6	10.2	
200 to 300	67,267	304.2 to 456.3	76,924	15,092	27,704	8.7	7.0	11.0	10.2	
300 to 500	47,712	456.3 to 760.5	48,745	16,738	25,762	6.2	4.4	12.2	9.5	
500 to 1,000	25,812	760.5 to 1,521	34,331	17,287	29,735	3.3	3.1	12.6	11.0	
1,000 to 2,000	9,386	1,521 to 3,042	13,174	12,485	22,585	1.2	1.2	9.1	8.4	
2,000 to 3,000		3,042 to 4,563	1,762		4,542		0.2		1.7	
3,000 to 5,000		4,563 to 7,605	1,313		10,932		0.2		4.0	
2,000 to 5,000	3,129	3,042 to 7,605	3,075	8,232	15,474	0.4	0.4	6.0	5.7	
5,000 and over		7,605 and over	1,362		21,591		0.2		8.0	
5,000 to 10,000		7,605 to 15,210								
10,000 and over	782	15,210 and over		10,016		0.1	0.2	7.3		
Total	782,173		1,659,423	137,198	309,198	100	100	100	100	
Total over £0,000 (91,260)	777,480		1,102,172	136,924	270,533					

(continued)

TABLE B-2 (concluded)

PART B

Actual 1953 Estate Size (thous. dollars)	Actual No. of Wealth-Holders in 1953 (1)	1953 Estate Size in 1944 Dollars (thous. dollars) (2)	No. of Wealth-Holders in 1944 in Adjusted Estate Sizes (3)	Actual 1953 Gross Estate (million dollars) (4)	1944 Gross Estate[b] in Adjusted Estate Sizes (million dollars) (5)	Percentage Distribution of				
						Col. 1 (6)	Col. 3 (7)	Col. 4 (8)	Col. 5 (9)	
Under 60	1,538	Under 39.42		83						
60 to 70	181,004	39.42 to 45.99		11,136						
70 to 80	176,546	45.99 to 52.56		12,351						
60 to 80	357,550	39.42 to 52.56		23,487						
80 to 90	173,935	52.56 to 59.13		13,428						
90 to 100	151,427	59.13 to 65.70		13,233						
80 to 100	325,362	Under 65.70	63,121	26,661	3,855	23.1		8.6		
100 to 120	224,482	65.70 to 78.84		22,406		22.3		10.2		
120 to 150	216,579	78.84 to 98.55		26,370						
100 to 150	441,061	65.7 to 98.55	265,157	48,776	18,357	45.4	36.9	18.8	13.8	
150 to 200	186,323	98.55 to 131.4	137,491	29,326	14,040	19.2	19.1	11.3	10.5	
200 to 300	167,954	131.4 to 197.1	157,107	37,285	20,306	17.3	21.8	14.4	15.2	
300 to 500	101,216	197.1 to 328.5	79,156	36,453	18,225	10.4	11.0	14.1	13.7	
500 to 1,000	50,917	328.5 to 657	49,292	34,120	19,927	5.2	6.9	13.2	14.9	
1,000 to 2,000	19,021	657 to 1,314	20,499	25,686	15,750	2.0	2.8	9.9	11.8	
2,000 to 3,000	4,044	1,314 to 1,971		10,256		0.4		4.0		
3,000 to 5,000	2,259	1,971 to 3,285		8,569		0.2		3.3		
2,000 to 5,000	6,303	1,314 to 3,285	7,784	18,825	12,441	0.6	1.1	7.3	9.3	
5,000 and over		3,285 and over	2,566		14,297	0.2	0.4		10.7	
5,000 to 10,000	1,569	3,285 to 6,570		13,279		0.2		5.1		
10,000 and over	609	6,570 and over		15,217		0.1		5.9		
Total	1,659,423		782,173	309,198	137,198	100	100	100	100	
Total over 100,000	974,973		719,052	258,967	133,343					

[a] Basic variant.   [b] Amounts unadjusted for price change.

Appendix C: Predicting Estate Tax Returns

Since price changes are an important determinant of wealth-holder status, it is interesting to see how well one can predict the number of estate tax returns on the basis of price and population changes. The period from 1939 to 1953 is a good one to select for this purpose. We know that estate building is only indirectly related to income and price movements and hence would not expect the aggregate data on estates of decedents to move closely with any other single series, quite apart from any changes in law and practice.

In Chapter 2 we pointed out the extraordinary rise in the number of estate tax returns after 1944, from about 15,000 in the war period to over 36,000 in 1953 and 1954. What factors are responsible for this remarkable rise? The only important changes in the law (that is, important for our purposes) in the period after World War II were the 1948 repeal of the 1942 law as it affected community property states and the introduction of the marital deduction in 1948. The former, which restored the full effect of community property law in the eight states under such law, had mixed effects. By allowing more complete splitting of property, it encouraged smaller returns in those states. To the extent that the split reduced individual holdings below $60,000, it reduced the number of returns. To the extent, however, that there was a tax saving at the death of the first spouse to die, the number of reported estates of surviving spouses might have been expected to rise. On balance, however, the repeal of the 1942 amendment probably decreased the number of returns and certainly decreased the size of the average return.

The introduction of the martial deduction did not change the method of reporting gross estate but it did set up new incentives for property disposition both before and at the time of death. This deduction allows the taxpayer to reduce his taxable estate by an outright transfer at the time of death to his spouse of up to 50 per cent of his gross estate. While this provision reduces tax liability, it probably does not reduce the number of returns filed. To the extent that there is a tax saving, it would seem to encourage more returns by surviving spouses. It would reduce the incentive to make gifts to spouses before death and would thus encourage more estate tax returns. Finally, it reduces somewhat the incentive to place the bequest to a spouse in a life estate (such a disposition would not have qualified for the marital deduction until 1954) and hence encourages returns from surviving spouses. On balance, then, the marital deduction would seem to encourage more returns while not having any very important effect on the size of the average return.

Taken altogether, the 1948 changes in the law tend to cancel out each other's effects on number of returns and amount of gross estate reported during 1948–54. But it may be guessed that the net effect of these changes would be to raise the number of returns and the amount of reported gross estate.

How much of the rise in number of returns and total gross estate can be predicted on the basis of price and population changes? By applying such changes to both 1939 and 1944 data, we obtain a prediction of a smaller number of returns, a smaller total of gross estate, and a larger average size of return than was actually the case in 1953. The method used was as follows: First, the number of returns filed in the base year was raised by the percentage rise in population over age 20 from the base year to 1953. Second, the number of returns in the relevant (on the basis of price change) estate sizes below $60,000 in the base year was estimated by extending the frequency curve backward. Adding the number of returns in the two steps gives the predicted number of returns. Third, the number of returns in the first step was multiplied by the base year's average returns inflated by the rise in consumer prices. Fourth, the number of returns raised from below $60,000 (in step 2) was multiplied by $65,000. Finally, the amounts determined in steps 3 and 4 were added together to get the predicted total gross estate for 1953.

PREDICTING ESTATE TAX RETURNS

Using this method, the following results were obtained.

Base Year	Number of Returns	Total Gross Estate (billion dollars)	Average Return (dollars)
PREDICTED FOR 1953			
1939	24,000	6.4	266,000
1944	22,800	5.7	250,000
ACTUAL 1953			
	36,699	7.4	202,000

It would seem that some growth factor in addition to price and population is necessary in predicting estate tax returns. From 1944 to 1953 the number of returns rose 224 per cent and the amount of gross estate rose 217 per cent. Using 1939 as a base year, the number of returns rose 310 per cent and the amount of gross estate 274 per cent (only returns over $60,000 considered for 1939, insurance of first $40,000 excluded). Substituting asset prices for consumer prices would yield a somewhat better prediction.

Presumably the relevant growth factors in addition to price and population change are rises in income and savings. From 1944 to 1953 total personal disposable income rose 170 per cent and the number of families and unattached individuals with $5,000 or more total money income rose 285 per cent. Applying the latter factor to the 1944 returns yields the very high prediction of 50,455 returns for 1953. The *best result* is obtained by applying the personal disposable income percentage rise. The predicted number of returns for 1953 in this case is 32,192. The method followed here is to multiply the number of returns in 1944 by 170 and then add 5,200 for the number raised out of the $40,000 to $60,000 gross estate size into the $60,000 and over size. Aggregate gross estate was multiplied by the price rise.

INDEX

(Page numbers in *italic type* refer to tables and charts.)

Agassiz, Louis, 14
Annuities, 6, 17, 60–62, 82–83
   See also Property, by classes, miscellaneous
Ascoli, Max, 10 n.
Assets:
   defined, 2
   income from, 91
   preferences for, 139–140, 143–145, 149–152
   prices of, 140, *160–162*
   by types, *see* Property, by classes
   of wealth-holders, 21–22, 145–152, *165, 262–263*
   yield of, 143
Atkinson, Thomas R., 12, 154–156, 188
Australia, 13

Barna, T., 211
Bendix, R., 43
Beneficiaries, *see* Trusts, beneficiaries of
Bequests, *see* Gifts
Blank, David, 162
Boeckh Residential Construction Cost Index, 162, 221 n.
Bollinger, L. L., 11 n., 78, 80, 153, 208 n.
Bonds, *see* Property, by classes, bonds
Bowe, William J., 76 n.
Browne, Sir Thomas, 9
Brundage, P. F., 204 n.
Butters, J. K., 11 n., 12 n., 78, 80–81, 139 n., 153–154, 184, 188, 208 n.

Campion, H., 211
Capital, defined, 1, 2
Capital goods, consumer and durable, 2, 5
Capitalization of income, 12
Cartter, Allan M., 211
Cash, *see* Property, by classes, cash
Coale, Ansley, 46 n.
Colm, Gerhard, 239 n.
Committee on Ways and Means, 74 n.
Common law states, 101–104
   See also Non-community property states

Community property states, 20, 40, 60, 64, 92, 101–105, *118, 124–127, 261*
Corey, Lewis, 9
Crum, W. L., 10 n., 57 n., 68 n., 197 n.
Current Population Reports:
   Consumer Income, 109 n.
   Population Characteristics, 123 n.

Daniel, Mrs. Eleanor, 46 n.
Daniels, G. H., 211
Daric, J., 43 n.
Deaths, *see* Mortality rates
Debts, 22, 37–39, 50–56, 61, 138, 142–143, 146–150, *157–161, 166–188,* 221
   See also Property, by classes, mortgages and notes
Decedents, *see* Top wealth-holders, decedent
Derksen, J. B., 13 n.
Devolution rate, 53–56, 199
Dickinson, Frank, 44 n.
Doane, R. R., 9, 10 n.
Dorfman, Robert, 91 n, 116, 117
Dorn, Harold F., 43 n.
Dublin, Louis I., 43 n., 44 n., 91 n.

Edwards, Wallace I., 58, 238 n.
Eisenstein, Louis, 238 n.
England, wealth distribution in, 210–216
Equity, 2, 6
   See also Net worth
Estate:
   composition of, 21–23, 135–145, *157–161*
   by age, 145–152, *164–168, 182–184, 254–255*
   by income level, 153–155, *185–188*
   by occupation, 155–156, *188–190*
   by sex, 145–152, *169–177, 182–184*
   by size, 146–152, *170–177*
   economic, 30–31, 37–39, 50–56, 61–62, *156–159, 166–177, 179–184, 250, 254, 257*
   gross, 30–31, 37–39, 50–56, 64–65, 84–100, 109–110, *112–113,*

283

INDEX

Estate (cont.):
 gross, *117–121, 124–126, 251–253, 255–256, 258, 261, 274, 277–278*
Estate-multiplier, 10, 13, 31, 41–42, 48–56, 68, 82, 84, 195, 210–211, 248–249
Estate tax:
 data, 10–14, 57–58
 evasion of, 65–67
 exemptions, 28–30
 law, 57–60
Estate tax returns, 28–39, 78–79, *124, 128–131*, 238–240, *246–247, 261*
 prediction of, 279–281

Federal Reserve Bulletin, 196
Fiduciaries, *see* Income from fiduciaries
Fijalkowski-Bereday, G. Z., 238 n.
Foundations, *see* Trust funds
Friend, Irwin, 234 n.

Gifts, 67–71
 See also Transfers
Gift tax, 57, 59, 74, 238–239, 242
Gini, Corrado, 13
Glick, Paul C., 114, 206 n.
Goldsmith, Raymond W., 10, 77 n., 113–114, 132–134, 165, 178, 186, 190–191, 196, 197 n., 208 n., 209, 234 n., 236, 250, 257, 262–263
Government:
 ownership of wealth, 8
 regulation of wealth, 8
Great Britain:
 mortality rates, 43
 wealth distribution, 25–26, 210–216
 wealth estimates, 13
Grebler, Leo, 162
Groves, Harold M., 58
Guralnick, L., 44, 46 n.

Hamilton, C. Horace, 43 n.
Harriss, C. Lowell, 58 n., 66–67, 239 n.
Hauser, Philip M., 43
Holmes, G. K., 9, 206 n.
Homestead Act, 8
Hultgren, Thor, 199 n.

Income:
 effect on estate size, 107–108, *262*
 from fiduciaries, 76–79
 inequality of, 6–7, 26, 215–217, 230–234
 payments, *124, 128–131*
 property, 108, *132–133*, 235

Income (cont.):
 and savings, 107–108
 from trusts, 78–79
Ingalls, W. R., 9
Inheritance tax, 57, 58, 238
 See also Transfers
Insurance, 55–56
 See also Property, by classes, life insurance
Internal Revenue Code, 59
Internal Revenue Service, 12, 13
Italy, 13

King, W. I., 1 n., 9, 206
Klein, L. R., 12 n.
Knibbs, G. H., 13
Kuznets, Simon, 108, 132–133, 215, 219, 234 n., 235–237

Langley, Kathleen M., 13, 211, 214–216
Lansing, J. B., 115, 215 n.
Lehmann, Fritz, 9, 10 n., 239 n.
Lent, George E., 137–138
Lewis, James B., 59 n., 60 n.
Liabilities, 21, 22
 See also Debts; Property, by classes, mortgages and notes
Life insurance, *see* Property, by classes, life insurance
Lipset, S., 43
Logan, W. P. D., 43 n.
Lorenz curves, 95–97, 104–105, 148–150, 203, 205, 212, 214, 232–233
Lotka, Alfred J., 43 n., 91 n.
Lydall, Harold, 215 n.

Macaulay, Frederick R., 9
McKinstry, William, 238 n.
Mallett, Bernard, 13, 211
Martin, L. W., 44 n.
Marx, Karl, 1
Mayer, Albert J., 43
Medical expenses, 72
Mendershausen, Horst, 10, 13, 32–33, 43, 47 n., 54–56, 70, 89 n., 112, 150, 157 n., 159, 197 n., 250, 274
Merwin, C. L., Jr., 1 n.
Metropolitan Life Insurance Company, 45
Miller, Herman P., 109 n., 233
Millionaires, 276
Mincer, Jacob, 7 n., 109 n.
Morgan, J. N., 115
Moriyama, I. M., 44
Mortality rates, 14, 16, 24, 29, 42–49, 54–55, 89, 207–208, *248–253, 255–258*

284

INDEX

Mortgages, *see* Property, by classes, mortgages and notes

National balance sheet, 191–195, 209, *264–273*
 See also Wealth, distribution
Net worth, 153, *165, 178, 185–186, 189,* 195–197, 231–233
Netherlands, 13
New Zealand, 13
Non-community property states, 40, 63–64, 92, 101–104, *118–120, 124–127, 261*

Old Age, Survivors, and Disability Insurance, 8, 60 n.

Painter, Mary S., 9, 10 n.
Pareto curve, 211
Pension funds, 17, 61–62, 82–83
 See also Property, by classes, miscellaneous
Peterson, Ray M., 46 n.
Pitler, Morris, 46 n.
Population, 29, 32–33, *124, 128–131,* 240
Price changes:
 effect on wealth-holding, 26, 143, 219, 275–278
 effect on wealth inequality, 219–229, 244
Property:
 by classes:
  bonds, 23, 25, *37–39, 50–52,* 61, 135–138, 142–149, *157–163, 166–188,* 208–209, 221
  cash, 22–23, *37–39, 50–52,* 61, 135, 140–143, 145–152, 157–161, *165–190,* 209, 221
  corporate stock, 20, 22–23, 25, *37–39, 50–52,* 61, 135–152, *157–190,* 208–209, 220–221
  life insurance, 16–17, 22–23, *37–39, 50–52,* 55–56, 60–61, 63–65, 71–72, 135–136, 138, 142–143, 145–147, 149–150, 209, 220–221
  miscellaneous, *37–39, 50–52,* 61–62, 72–83, 146–152, *156–161, 166–188,* 209, 221
  mortgages and notes, 22–23, *37–39, 50–52,* 61, 138, 142–143, 146–150, *157–161, 166–188,* 209, 221
  real estate, 22–23, *37–39, 50–52,* 61, 135–137, 140–143, 147–148, *157–161, 170–184, 186, 190,* 209, 220–221

Property (cont.):
 defined, 2
 transfer of, 60
 See also Transfers

Ratner, Sidney, 238 n.
Real estate, *see* Property, by classes, real estate
Redei, Jena, 43 n.
Registrar-General, 43
Retirement funds, *see* Pension funds
Revenue Revision of 1950, 74 n.
Rosenthal, Irving, 46 n.

Savings, effect on wealth inequality, 219, 229–230, 234–237, 244
Schor, Stanley, 234 n.
Shapiro, Eli, 77 n.
Social insurance, 8
Spahr, C. B., 9, 206 n.
Spiegelman, Mortimer, 43 n., 46 n., 91 n.
Standard and Poor's, 137 n., 162, 163
Statistical Abstract of the United States, 131, 162, 261
Statistics of Income, 29, 58 n., 60, 61 n., 79, 131, 260
Stein, Emmanuel, 46 n.
Steiner, Peter O., 91 n., 116–117
Stewart, Charles, 9, 10 n., 239 n.
Stock, corporate, *see* Property, by classes, corporate stock
Stock, Sir Percy, 43
Straw, K. H., 12 n., 215 n.
Survey of Consumer Finances, 10–11, 18, 24, 89, 95, 101, 107, 109, 145, 147, 153, 164, 185, 189, 191, 195–197, 231, 233–235
Survey of Current Business, 131
Survey Research Center of University of Michigan, 10, 11
Sutherland, Ian, 43 n.

Tabah, Leon, 43 n.
Taxation, *see* Estate tax; Gift tax; Inheritance tax
Thompson, L. E., 11 n. 78, 80, 153, 208 n.
Top wealth-holders:
 by characteristics:
  age, 17–19, 21–22, 87–98, *110–115, 117–123, 125–126,* 240–242
  families, 18, 20, 24, 100–101, *114,* 205–206, 243
  female, 18–20, 22–24, 84–92, 96–100, 102, 104, *110–111, 117–118, 125–127,* 205, 240–243

285

INDEX

Top wealth-holders (cont.):
  by characteristics:
    male, 18–20, 22–23, 84–100, 102, *110–111, 117–123,* 125–127, 240–241
    marital status, 18, 20, 24, 99–104, *122–123,* 242–243
    occupation, 108, 109, *134*
    residence by region, 106–107, *128–131*
    spending units, 101, *114–117, 262–263*
  decedents, 11–14
    by age, 31–35, 38, 40, *50–52,* 54, 63, *259–260*
    female, 34–35, 38–40, *51–52,* 63–65, *259–260*
    male, 34–35, 37–40, *50–53,* 63–65, *259–260*
    by marital status, *259–260*
    defined, 16
Tostlebe, A. S., 162, 221 n.
Transfers, effect on wealth inequality, 68–73, 76, 218–219, 237–244
  See also, Annuities; Gifts; Insurance; Pension funds; Trust funds
Trust funds, 4, 15, 72, 208 n.
  revocable, 75–76
  See also Property, by classes, miscellaneous
Trusts, beneficiaries of, 72–73, 76–77, 80

Vandome, Peter, 12 n.
Veblen, Thorstein, 7 n.

Wales, wealth distribution in, 210–216
Wealth:
  accumulation, 5–6, 26, 218, 230–231
  concentration, 24–25, 86, 96–97, 103, 148
  defined, 1, 2, 5, 6
  distribution:
    intersectoral, 3–5
    personal sector, 24–25, 191–195, 200–205, 208–209, 219, *264–273*
    by states, 20–21
  inequality of, 6–7, 23–24, 26, 197–208, 218–244
    See also Price changes; Savings; Transfers
  personal, 3–4
  prime, 15, 57–58, 62–63, 76, 195
  variants:
    basic, 16–17, 20, 27, 192–195
    prime, 16–17, 62, 73, 191–195, *200–201,* 207, 209
    total, 16–17, 20, 62, 191–195, 200–201, 207, 209
Wealth-income ratio, 108
Wheatcroft, G. S. A., 239 n.
White, William K., 46 n.
Whitney, Jessamine, 42
Winnick, Louis, 162
Wisconsin, state income tax returns, 154

Yaple, Maxine, 9, 10 n.
Yeracaris, Constantine A., 42

Soc
HC
110
W4
L2

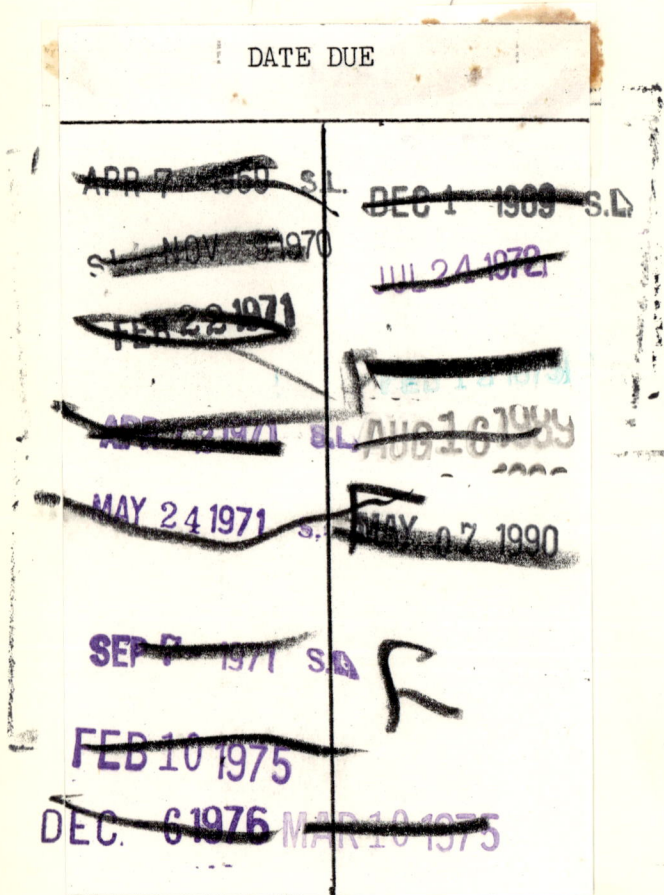